Rethinking
Development

David E. Apter

Rethinking Development

Modernization, Dependency, and Postmodern Politics

SAGE PUBLICATIONS
The International Professional Publishers
Newbury Park   London   New Delhi

For information address:

SAGE Publications, Inc.
2455 Teller Road
Newbury Park, California 91320

SAGE Publications Ltd
1 Oliver's Yard
55 City Road
London EC1Y 1SP

SAGE Publications India Pvt Ltd
B-42, Panchsheel Enclave
Post Box 4109
New Delhi 110 017

Printed in the United States of America
Originally published in French by ECONOMICA, 49, rue Hericart, 75015 Paris, France

Library of Congress Cataloging-in-Publication Data

Apter, David Ernest, 1924–
    Rethinking development.

    Includes bibliographies.
    1. Economic development. 2. Dependency.
3. Developing countries—Politics and government.
I. Title.
HD82.A657   1987   338.9   86-29642
ISBN   0-8039-2971-4
ISBN   0-8039-2972-2   (pbk.)

94 10 9 8 7 6 5 4

Contents

Preface

Development is the underlying theme of this book. It is a term that means many different things to many different people. It is loaded with ideological assumptions. These assumptions can be expressed as faith, science, or both. The term is so imprecise and vulgar that no doubt it should be stricken from any proper lexicon of technical terms. With it should go concepts like modernization and modernism. Despite its (and their) shortcomings, however, this will not happen. They and their assorted intellectual baggage will remain key concepts of social analysis. Whether one is for or against, believer or cynic, they are here to stay. The best thing about them is that their content changes and their meanings alter. That being the case, development is a continuous intellectual project as well as an ongoing material process.

There are various reasons why ideas of development and its related terms continue as an intellectual project. They embody the rationality of growth. Most ideas of purpose, function, and practical meaning derive from them. Take them away and we lose directionality. Process disappears. Organized life depends on how its location is fixed somewhere between history and prediction. Lose that frame and even the idea of the state changes, reverting perhaps to ideas that predate developmental growth. But that would be unacceptable, for the modern state is, above all, a state of distributive justice. In its democratic form, especially, legitimacy requires development.

The rationality of developmental theories enables democracy to substantiate its claim to moral uniqueness, and to maintain itself as a self-evidently superior form of politics. Of course, the concept of development represents a great variety of specific theories and approaches. But most of all, it is a hosting metaphor containing crucial connecting assumptions between growth and democracy.

One such connection follows an organismic, or organic, metaphor. Parallels between the lives of human beings and the life of society and the state are emphasized in evolutionary terms. Each is inseparable from the other. Describing how they intertwine under developmental circumstances by identifying key properties of their connection becomes the natural subject matter of developmental politics.

But within developmental politics there also remains an earlier aspect of the metaphor, one which replaces evolution with historicity. It lurks behind the "science" of development as something prescientific, primordial, a "noble lie" on which the state claims certain privileges and immortality, and uses the past as the present and validated patrimony of a people. This, the romantic side of developmental politics is, from the more scientific aspect, considered dangerous and perhaps primitive. When this primitivism is embedded deeply in current thinking it becomes integrated into the science of development. Sovereignty, nationalism, cultural uniqueness are all "principles" of right, loaded with premodern symbolic freight. Foundation stones for symbolic capital, they are intrinsic to the political discourse of the state. They endow the state itself with responsibilities that it may not be able to discharge effectively. So the tension between economic and symbolic capital, and between developmental science and primordial politics, contains a good deal of the good and evil of modern political life.

It is the science side that disguises the conflict between them. By emphasizing choice, the rules of allocation, notions of balance, equilibrium, cost and benefit, feedback and decision making, what begins in the organic can be linked to mechanical science, social engineering, cybernetical and information modeling, not to speak of formal choice theories and large structural explanations of change.

One can go from myths of the past to projections of the future: from Locke to Arrow, from Marx to Althusser, from Parsons to game theory, from methodological individualism to collectivism, and all in a good mood. For the developmental metaphor is a lively one. It couples easily with more conventional forms of optimism—the rationality of science, process as progress, and, more gratuitously perhaps, a certain long-term political exuberance. Developmental science, then, is the large glass through which one can see history converted to evolution and evolution to politics, and most of all the politics of intelligence, learning, and continuous material improvement as well as what Habermas calls the steering capacity of the state.

No wonder that terms such as *development, modernization, and modernism* remain fundamental to contemporary thinking. Moreover, they benefit from the vigor of a serious opposition. From the start all these assumptions have been challenged by a counterdiscourse in the form of a reasoned opposition. There have always been what some refer to as "gothic" formulations of development to attack this general hubris. Rousseau, Schiller, Ruskin, Morris, and many others criticize the science of development precisely because it is too romantic. The drama of innovation prevents us from seeing its negative consequences. The off side of development is not simply a conflict over aesthetics, although aesthetics may count for a great deal. It is rather that as a science of outcomes it is flawed. Instead, they argue, development, modernization, and modernism erode rather than enhance more humane considerations. Developmental rationality—far from legitimizing democracy—presides over the latter's conversion into the bureaucratization and instrumentalization of social life. For the more anarchically inclined, or those of a radical individualist persuasion, "developmental politics" is an evolution toward the mutual estrangement of society and the state.

Developmental "discourse" continues to create its own opposition. Moreover, today's debates are carried out by people of many different political views. Opposition to the conventional discourse of development creates strange bedfellows, right and left, conservative and radical. No wonder, then, that a brilliant and developmental theorist like Marx remains powerful. His was one of the most successful efforts to integrate both the science of development and the teleology of growth into a critique of what is a transforming political methodology. It may not work, but it is not a bad measure of what we need. One reason for the continuing attractiveness of Marx is that he offered a way out. He rooted a positive view of development in a transformational telos containing a romanticism of its own, with capitalism representing the negative moral pole, the starting point for the "overcoming" project. The evolutionary aspect of this overcoming is material and historical process. Marx expands the organic metaphor. More contemporary versions of his original position include those "dependency" theories that are locked in a "struggle" with "modernization" theories.

These comments are designed to call attention to some of the underlying reasons why developmental theory remains intrinsically important despite its confusions. One reason is that its ideas are so embedded in our thinking that they have a life of their own, a life quite divorced one might add from developmental practice. For in practice, with a few exceptions, few of the main premises of the science of development, liberal or Marxist, have been realized. Today even the most privileged nations, those with a high level of development and democracy and where the basic problems of society and state were believed to have been resolved in the social welfare or the social democratic state, changes in the structure of development are beginning to have unforeseen and negative consequences that pose new questions of democratic viability. The problem of political overload is one aspect of the problem. The spread of political violence is another.

This suggests that it is time for a fresh look at development, its science, romanticism, teleology, its gothic as well as its promising sides. We now have a remarkably diverse set of examples, cases that need to be sifted for the lessons they contain. If, for the reasons indicated, we continue to rely on conventional concepts of developmental change, we also need to become more aware of the ways in which these concepts deny negative possibilities, filtering out inconvenient variables that might pollute the models and the teleologies they represent.

By the same token, no single forthcoming theoretical approach is likely to be satisfactory. This is a time for tentativeness rather than conclusions. The ideas presented in this book do not pretend to be tightly integrated into a single system. They are linked together in terms of problems studied in the field as well as interpreted in comparative terms. There are certain underlying themes, the relation between development to democracy, the problem of innovation and marginality, questions of violence and governability.

Included too are concepts derived from the analysis of countries trying to control the consequences of growth and development. This includes sociological factors such as class, role, stratification, and the formation of "steering" elites, as well as political systems types, specifically, mobilization, reconciliation, bureaucratic, theocratic, and the way in which each country handles the problem of how best to direct social institutions toward greater development.

It should also be pointed out that the approach favored here avoids the emphasis on "appropriate values," or the "right" political or civic culture. It uses instead a notion of "predemocratic" on the practical grounds that if one waits for the right norms to be in place in order to become democratic, one will wait a long time. The question is not which norms are necessary but how development can be made to create certain democratic objects, needs that will lead to both growth and democracy. One emphasis here is on the growing need for information that development induces. Another, the connection between democratization and information access by those in power, assumes an inverse relationship at the top between information and coercion, that is, the more of one the less of the other. In short, the underlying theme of this book is that "systematically" development will generate democracy, but it will not do it easily, and there are snares along the way—snares that result in violence and affect the future of the state itself.

This book is divided into two parts, with the first being called "for the state." That is, it deals with the relationship between development (including the social consequences of political economy) and the state. It emphasizes different political systems and the advantages and disadvantages they possess in trying to promote innovative change and mediate its consequences.

The second part is "against the state." That is it recognizes certain structural problems which arise in the course of development that generate violence and protest, circumstances in which the state may become a target. Between these two perspectives one can locate a good many of today's political problems.

With the exception of Chapter 1, which was written expressly for this volume, the materials in this book have appeared elsewhere. Permission to reprint the others is gratefully acknowledged as follows. Chapters 2 and 3 first appeared in *The Politics of Modernization* (Chicago: University of Chicago Press, 1965, 1967, 1973), Chapter 3 in *Some Conceptual Approaches to the Study of Modernization* (Englewood Cliffs, New Jersey: Prentice-Hall, Inc., 1968), and Chapters 5 and 6 in *Choice and the Politics of Allocation* (New Haven: Yale University Press, 1971). A slightly altered version of Chapter 7 has appeared in Peter Merkl and Kay Lawson, editors, *When Parties Fail* (Princeton: Princeton University Press, 1987). Chapter 9 first appeared in the fall 1979 issue of *Daedalus* and subsequently in Stephen R. Graubard, *The State* (New York: W. W. Norton, 1979). "Thinking About Violence" appeared in French in *France Forum*, January-March 1986 and "The New Mytho-Logics and the Specter of Superfluous Man" was published in *Social Research* (Volume 52, no. 2, 1985).

I would particularly like to thank Professors Gerard Conac of the University of Paris I (Sorbonne) and Bertrand Badie of the University of Clement Ferrand for suggesting this book in the first place and for shepherding it through its French edition. I am also grateful to Professors Robert Dahl, Joseph LaPalombara, and members of the Political Theory Seminar at Yale University for their critical comments on Chapter 1.

—*David E. Apter*
Corpoyer-la-Chapelle

—1—

RETHINKING DEVELOPMENT

Modern societies are and must be futurist: they claim to know in advance what they will be like, and technicians are inclined to be even more irritated by the resistance of men than by that of things.

Raymond Aron
Marxism and the Existentialists

I. FROM "SCIENCE" TO "DISCOURSE"

Thinking about development is as old as theories of industrialization. The pedigree, traceable to the classical English political economists, to the French Physiocrats, and, as well, to Marx, remains embedded in contemporary thinking about developmental growth. Despite all the changes in theoretical styles, not to speak of the many varieties of capitalism and socialism, the early and original logics of industrialism remain in place in modern developmental doctrines.[1]

Venues have shifted. The original theoretical strands have branched out and become more variegated. The most important change has centered on the role of the state. Before World War II, public policy dealt mainly with problems of depression and economic recovery. Main lines of inquiry derived from Keynesianism and the evolution of the social welfare state, socialism, and social democracy. The principal concerns included corporatism, fascism, Stalinism, and the threat of totalitarianism.[2] After the war when preoccupations with the reconstruction of Europe receded, interest focused on development including colonial and so-called backward areas.[3] These latter required a rethinking of conventional ideas about political economy and the state, and incorporation of new kinds of knowledge about exotic cultures, customs, social practices, values, and beliefs. The following question was central: Which combinations of norms and institutions would impede, and which facilitate, development?[4] Which type of political system might best induce growth became a matter of the creation of new societies, social organizations, and political economy.[5] Development studies were inclined in an interdisciplinary direction, anthropological as well as economic, sociological as well as political. Such knowledge took on considerable political urgency as nationalism intensified and pressures for independence mounted in colonial territories.[6] How to promote development on terms favorable to the metropolitan powers was the first question. How to do it in terms favorable to developing countries became the enduring one.[7]

These concerns obviously went far beyond academia. Policy needs far outstripped academic thinking. One needed to know a great deal about development concretely, as it was particularized in terms of places, circumstances, and events. Required too were a diversity of experts and area specialists. In the United States and elsewhere, programs of research on developing countries were established in virtually every major university. Area experts were trained in considerable numbers. Theory was derived from comparative analysis. The latter incorporated two important general tendencies in the social sciences: "behavioral," introducing psychological variables into the study of development (motivation, perception, ideology, attitudes, socialization, and so on), and "operationalism," which emphasized empirical and quantitative methods. Applied to problems of growth and combined as "systems theory" (the core of which was one version or other of the "functional paradigm"), the combination stood for a more developmental science and political development with democracy as its outcome.[8]

If we accept developmental science and political development as criteria, then, in retrospect, the record of genuine accomplishment seems a good deal more meager than the outpouring of books on both subjects might attest. Perhaps it is the gratuitousness that accompanied both assumptions that accounts for why so little out of that huge corpus (which came to cover every field, discipline, and region of the world) has stood the test of time. The residue of worthwhile work is small. Too much of what passed for developmental "science" was confusing. Too much that passed for political development was ideological; theories were overkill, obvious, or wrong.[9]

Developmental hopes entertained by scholars, experts—not to speak of political leaders—went unrealized. Good results eluded the best laid plans. Discrepancies between policies and concrete results have been so great and experiences so often disastrous that another round of thinking is called for, this time in transdisciplinary rather than interdisciplinary terms.

Let us begin with a comparison of the two main theoretical rubrics: "modernization" and "dependency." The intellectual power of both lies in their origins, their original liberal and Marxist assumptions. Each has modified and amended these greatly.[10] Regrettably, the further they stray from liberal or Marxist designs, the less intelligent they become. Let us also hold on to the original political object of development— democracy, treating it as both valid in its own right and also as the subject of widespread practical concern.

Also useful in this regard are a number of ethnographically inclined field studies, the best of which have probed deeply into the particulars of a case while maintaining connections to broader theoretical questions. Their lessons can be applied more generally to current concerns such as the return to democratic politics in countries as diverse as Argentina, Brazil, and the Philippines. For in these countries and elsewhere, hopes have been raised that, after many grim years of corporatist, bureaucratic, authoritarian, and military regimes, people are rediscovering the virtues of democracy. Today's generation may be more willing than the last to favor democratic values even when it is sorely tested under difficult circumstances. But if we are to understand what this might really mean, we need to think through the "contradictions" of development. We also need to avoid the "pernicious postulates," as Tilly calls them, of modernization theory, and the overkill categories of dependency theory.

I want to examine these two main lines of developmental theory as modes of interpretation. My criticism is designed to provide first for their recombination and, second, to define a "space" that can be filled with theoretical elements that have played little part in the developmental discourse so far.

The emphasis is less on "science" than interpretation. This does not mean, however, that "science" is the problem. It is that conventional designs have produced misleading results. Positive scientific knowledge (especially quantitative) has relied on conceptual schemes that are unable to incorporate the range, scope, and number of variables required to understand development problems. It obliterates the tentativeness of more nuanced and internal knowledge. Quantitative or formalized styles of thinking in social analysis have led to poor predictions, stated with more pretentiousness than authority. The "science" of development remains privileged. But it is only one among several "languages."[11] Each is a mode of signifying and establishing meaning. No single one is powerful enough to monopolize so complex a subject. Each opens up different possibilities of meaning, using its own signs and referents. Beliefs in the efficacy of a cumulative and singular science no longer prevail in development studies. Today the conceptual opportunities provided by crosscutting or intersecting "languages" are wide open. It is then a good time to rethink development. Required is a strategy that, integrating system and process, will prevent the subject from becoming excessively fragmented and divided into hostile points of view. If right now the most tenable "discourse" is political economy, left or right (most of which is bad politics and worse economics), then a common developmental discourse must begin by "deprivileging" political economy.

This said, one must hasten to add that, of course, there will always be some underlying and common political economy framework, an understanding of which is essential in the analysis of any political problems. But it needs to be incorporated into other discourses. The theoretical criterion is to enable observers to transcend the immediacy of events and see alternatives and possibilities not visible on the ground or to the naked eye. Such a goal is itself a political matter. It assumes that by "rethinking" development, we can treat it as a fund of knowledge, a form of intellectual capital, which, more than common sense, can be "invested" in the kinds of problems for which solutions are currently wanting. In this sense, rethinking development ought to be more than an exercise. Its potential value as a constituted perceptual universe is a reordering of experience, the reevaluation of case materials, and the derivation of new comparative hypotheses. In the last analysis, we are talking about the power to appreciate the larger picture, to understand what lies behind events, and to think our way beyond present circumstances.

So rethinking development is the goal. What then are the ingredients? For the purposes there is, already available, a large number of ready-made and available concepts, a sort of *bricolage*, as Levi-Strauss has described it, garden variety for the most part. Some of these can certainly be applied to the changing developmental *problématique*.[12]

II. INGREDIENTS FOR ANALYSIS:
TERMS, CONCEPTS, AND THEORIES

Items of bricolage: as indicated in the preface, many key concepts—growth, development, and modernization—are used indiscriminately. Here, *development* will refer to expanding choice. *Choice* refers to the range of articulated alternatives available to individuals and collectivities. Increasing choice was and remains the central developmental "project." Distributive in character, choice can be operationalized in terms of access through networks of roles, classes, and institutions. When organized and ranked functionally according to contributions to industrialization access, these networks connect choice to hierarchy. Organized in terms of functionally germane reciprocities of wealth and power, the degree of symmetry or asymmetry represents power in terms of distributive equity. How to control access to choice and promote the sharing of it according to approved rules and conditions of equity has been the special political concern of development.

Industrialization, the dynamic factor, results from a process of augmentation of manufacturing outputs. In turn, these derive from the application of (increasingly rapid) innovation (scientific and technological) to the productive infrastructure. Although the term *modernization* is closely identified with industrialization, it has evolved separately and along two quite different lines. The first line (let us call it "modernization I") represents the recapitulation in nonindustrial settings of the functional roles, classes, and reciprocities that appeared first in the old "metropoles." So regarded, the development project is "modernization" of "traditional societies" through the establishment of networks and institutions similar to those of advanced industrial societies, including strategic norms of work, values of social discipline and beliefs about equity and motivations representing the internalization of these norms, values and beliefs in a manner ensuring role performance through appropriate behavior. Integrating these three dimensions in so-called developing areas is the classic "modernization I" problématique. Political development adds ideology to the mix to secure a "fit" between structural, normative, and behavioral components, enabling them to become mutually reinforcing and so achieve the same "steady state" in the "periphery" as obtains in the "metropole."

Other general theoretical questions built into "modernization I" are how best to convert growing complexity into social integration, how to create the nation by means of the state, and how to incorporate within the state social networks that generate development. In this view, state legitimization depends on the expansion of choice, with the state mediating the negative effects of developmental processes.[13] These assumptions have been severely criticized on a number of grounds, the most serious of which is that they fail to account for negative consequences systematically—that is, theoretically.

"Modernization II" describes the contradictions of growth. Among these are negative impacts of innovation on the labor force, the changing social composition of classes in terms of increasing asymmetrical reciprocities, growing inequality, and compensatory political controls. Modernization II has stimulated a perspective opposite to the more "integrative" assumptions of modernization theory. It is a form of conflict theory. It emphasizes the way innovation and efficiency lead to retrenchment, and how elimination of unprofitable enterprises and investment in capital-intensive rather than labor-intensive industry may result in the "marginalization" of industrial labor. Economic efficiency can thus lead to rising social overhead costs. These and other concerns of modernization II are central to "dependency" theory. It deals with the negative social consequences of increasing productivity, especially where technological innovations reduce the labor component without opening up new equivalent employment opportunities.[14]

Confidence that the first modernization will be successful has declined everywhere except perhaps in China, Japan, or Taiwan (where it is still accepted that innovation, increasing productivity, and growth will result in integrative change, more and better jobs, and greater choice despite temporary setbacks and the need for adjustments). In these countries as well, modernization I still represents the premise of collective mobility, democracy, hierarchy, and integration. Modernization II, on the other hand, suggests that enlarging choice—the ultimate goal—will require restricted access to it in the short run in order to generate surpluses, authoritarian controls, discipline, planning, and mobilization. It also poses the question of how to control new forms of class cleavage, especially those challenging the future prospects of the democratic state, a concern made explicit in certain dependency theories.

Parenthetically, it might be added that problems of modernization II made their appearance in highly modernized but not fully industrialized countries, which were precisely countries proceeding rapidly under developmental assumptions of modernization I such as Argentina,

Mexico, Chile, or Brazil. In all these countries, there has been both integrative growth and class cleavage—and all at the same time. An expanded middle class evolves simultaneously with marginalization, polarization, and political instability. Indeed, a bimodal class pattern with a large middle class has emerged. Marginality is at one end of the spectrum. Expertise is at the opposite end, as seen in Figure 1.1.

Marginal here does not only mean unemployed. It refers to a "pariah" subculture whose members are regarded as basically "unemployable," which can include a very diverse population: urban squatters, "lumpens," and many others living at the fringes of the productive system. Forming distinctive subcultures, "functionally superfluous" in terms of their contributions to a developmental output, they live under conditions of high uncertainty, great personal risk, and with few prospects for regular work. One of their chief characteristics is lack of mutual trust. Difficult to organize, prone to random violence, they can be mobilized by revivalist and populist appeals. *Marginality*, in this sense, means functional superfluousness. Marginals are those who contribute zero to the productive product or take out more than they put in. The emergence of authoritarian regimes is frequently related to their real or imagined potential for violence.[15]

Although a familiar feature of developing countries, marginality today is also beginning to appear in certain highly industrialized countries. Efforts to overhaul and restructure the economies of industrial societies by reducing social overhead costs for social services, withdrawing state subsidies from ailing enterprises, and shifting investment to innovative and more productive units help to compound the problem.

More will be said about all this later on in the discussion. For the moment, however, certain political implications of this bimodal class pattern need to be clarified. Modernization I assumes the growth of a generalized middle, the absorption of marginality, and the circulation of functional elites. *Political* development denotes regimes, state systems, and political systems whose institutional functions, evolving along with developmental equity, will require greater participation and elite accountability. The more appropriate structures, norms, and behavior become "embedded" in social networks, the more institutionalization, regime legitimization, stable authority. So, too, with political parties, legislatures, courts, and executive bodies, presidential or parliamentary.[16]

Modernization II casts doubt on these consequences. The more "development," the more "contradiction." "Democratic" institu-

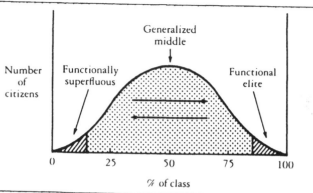

Figure 1.1 Class Composition

tionalization serves as a facade behind which *compradore* classes, external hegemonies, multinational corporations, and other instrumentalities work for their own interests. Internal efforts to realize internal growth in developing countries result in the partial expropriation of the surplus by external metropoles. Governments and citizens of such countries are less in control of their own resources over time and relatively worse off in terms of real choices. Political development under such circumstances leads to praetorian, bureaucratic, authoritarian, or corporatist regimes. The solution to this condition is the internal mobilization of resources, the assertion of autonomous political control, and the creation of internal productive rather than external exchange infrastructures by political means.[17]

The dynamic of modernization II arises out of a peculiar and unforeseen connection between innovation and retrenchment. The first is a "medicine" for curing the disease of declining productivity by means of improved work discipline and reduced social overhead costs. The political result is to increase the responsibility of the state for the victims of such policies. The question is what happens if the state needs to renege, at least in part, on the "social contract" of the welfare state.[18]

Modernization I and II represent alternative patterns of developmental change. Each is a discourse containing self-validating legitimacy formulas. Each assumes quite different normative teleologies. Each projects different logical outcomes in the name of science. The first is liberal in origin and mixes an organismic metaphor with a mechanics of "moving equilibrium." The second, Marxist in origin, emphasizes metaphors of crisis and contradiction. As applied to modernizations I and II, they can be summarized as seen in Figure 1.2.

Two other discourses should be briefly noted because they will play a part later on in the discussion. These are "modernism" and "post-modernism." The first specifies strategically significant normative patterns of culture associated with the aesthetics of modernization. "Modernism" in this sense is at times celebrated and at times severely criticized. It places the "machine" at the center of the modern age. On one hand, the machine can represent man's protean qualities, his creativity, his mastery of nature. On the other, it is demonic, sterile, representing technology as it reduces man to the status of victim.[19] The "ideology" of the "machine" serves both as an expression of liberation from want and oppression and as an attack on the bourgeois ethos (as in Dadaism and surrealism). It has been employed as a Nietzschean "signifier" for power, will, violence, the need for war, the superman or the super race, as in Italian futurism where the machine becomes anthropomorphic, even sexual—all speed, energy, and climax. It has been used as the symbol of rationality, a transformed future, as in Russian constructivism and supremacism, which, rejecting the capitalist mode of development as a negative pole to be transcended, celebrates modernism as socialist revolution.

Although modernism is outside the scope of this analysis, I mention it in part because it incorporates a discourse different from that of social science but crucial to an understanding of some of the ambiguities of modernization and developmentalism described above. I intend to use it as part of a discussion of violence, with violence as one expression of the negative side of development, a "postmodern" condition.

Any bricolage in the terms of the concepts and themes of the developmental literature would be incomplete without some reference to methodological considerations. Modernization I has relied on some version of *functionalism*. The latter is a general theoretical term based on the concept of social needs derived from what can be loosely called the organismic metaphor. Applied generally to developmental processes, it emphasizes equilibrium maintenance, the capacity of systems to survive under conditions of change by means of internal adaptation and differentiation. Applicable to concrete units at any level, the most general of which is society, it uses an extended notion of power shared among states, governments, regimes, parties, interest groups, families, and so on.[20]

Developmental
discourses

		Liberal	Marxist
Developmental tendencies	Mod I	Integrative pluralism	Contradiction and polarization
	Mod II	Innovative efficiency	Disjunctive transformation

Figure 1.2 Discourses and Development

The term *structure* is also used in several ways. The first denotes patterns of action by means of which requisite functions are carried out. This is "structural-functional" theory or "requisite analysis." Applied to modernization, it refers to crucial normative, structural, and behavioral requirements of a system differentiated in terms of abstracted binary sets. Various normative, structural, and behavioral combinations are integrative, functional, and/or malintegrative (dysfunctional) for order (system maintenance).[21] The term *requisite* implies that in the transformation from one "steady state" to another, certain minimal functions must be satisfied if a unit is to survive in its setting. "Functionalism" in its various forms accords with liberal ideas of development, although renewed interest in it has been manifested by certain new Marxist analysts.

The term *structure* has other meanings as well. At one level, of course, it simply denotes any set of ordering patterns. At another, it refers to *deep structures*, fundamental and embedded patterns of norms, speech, culture, and personality that impose boundaries over "surface" structures, the latter representing more epiphenomenal patterns of action.[22]

In classical Marxist usage, "structure" emphasizes crucial or deep structure modes of material production. It also divides into a set of binary exchange relations: "superstructural," including ensembles of beliefs, ideologies, states, classes, political parties, and so on, which can be transposed into "infrastructures," as these relate to and derive from productive processes.[23] In neo-Marxist and post-Marxian analysis, superstructures have been elevated to a more central analytical place than in classical Marxism, most importantly with regard to theories of the state.[24] It is this aspect of Marxism that has become crucial in radical dependency theory.

In turn, "infrastructures" have evolved into systems, that is, linguistic, semiotic, and symbolic orderings. The recent analytical turn in structuralism centers indeed on the "explosion of the superstructures" in terms of speech and language; signals and signs, signifiers and signifieds, tropes; syntagmatic and paradigmatic, narrative, text, writing, and so on.[25] The concept has come to mean the grids, frames, and linguistic binaries, by means of which one can see order as an expression of thought. It is only relatively recently that such "structural" concerns have become applicable to problems of politics and development.[26]

Finally and opposite to structure is another term rapidly gaining currency in the developmental discourse, *phenomenology*. Its emphasis is on the individual as acting subject. The starting point is intentionality. Understanding intentionality, and the life space and life worlds of the individual, depends on re-creating hermeneutical strategies with interpretive action a function of linguistic performatives, the consequences of which will affect the social space and determine the life worlds of those involved. In this sense, discourse represents a form of action. Language sets (games) give words their meanings.[27]

Phenomenological and hermeneutical emphases are best applied to concrete situations that reveal structural "breaks"—moral and disjunctive moments, particularly those where there is violence, revolution, and similar transforming events.[28] They combine easily with certain "post-Marxist" theories. Defined boundaries, limitations, horizons, all represent barriers, the transcending of which represent the overcoming project.[29] Hence, the way actions are interpreted, described to other people, used to think past current predicaments, to project solutions, is itself "action." The theoretical focus is on communication as interpretive understanding. Between the structural frame indicated above and the phenomenological is the difference between objectivist and subjectivist perspectives. Both focus on "breaks" and epistemic transformations.

This brings me to the emergent role of critical theory. Originally a critique of both classical Marxism and liberalism and an alternative to the sociology of knowledge in its original Frankfurt school tradition, it is today increasingly important as a generalized framework integrating development, modernization, political development, and political modernization within a larger philosophical synthesis.[30] It projects discourse as a "political" solution, albeit a special form of discourse, rational communication.[31] As a framework it incorporates linguistic, symbolic, and semiotic theories, and integrates them with structural and functional principles. Two very different intellectual practitioners of this kind of theory are Jürgen Habermas and Pierre Bourdieu. The first seeks a kind of closure in terms of rules for a rationally oriented choice universe based on discourse criteria within the communication process. The second is less concerned with closure than with the open-ended quality of symbolic formation as capital.[32]

III. SOME PRINCIPLES OF
MODERNIZATION THEORY

Keeping these terms, concepts, and theories in mind, let me now go from bricolage to system. I want to show how modernization I represented the analytical framework for liberal policymaking because of the logical and systematic principles contained within liberalism. With sociological and political variables added to liberal ideas of economic growth, various programmatic formulas could be applied as policy. Technical assistance, aid from the more developed to the less developed countries, and "institution building" would lead to democracy. The independent variable, indeed a perennial search, was for the functional equivalent of the Protestant ethic, that Holy Grail of many modernization I theorists.[33]

If the central problemmatique of liberal expressions of modernization I is the realization of developmental growth by means of cultural, social, and behavioral adaptation of prevailing institutions, functionalism emphasized their concrete variability. One did not need to replicate exactly the institutions found in industrial societies although some, such as bureaucracies and political parties, were more essential than others. If necessary, family, kinship, and voluntary associations had to be appropriately altered. Functionalism thus became a method for defining needs as critical elements in societal change, meeting the requirements of which became a process of institutional and infrastructural development.

Among the ingredients of functionalism are the following: an assumption of voluntarism, based on the principle of rational self-interest as a positive or social individualism; separation between private and public property; the idea of pluralism as economic, social, and political competition, formal and informal elite accountability; and, above all, freedom of choice.[34] The framework that would enable these principles to work systemically can be described as a double market. Composed of intersecting and mutually compensatory systems, each market represents different preference sets, economic and political. Each makes a different kind of information available.[35] The first, the economic marketplace, consists of priorities of need and preference pertaining to the goods and services available to individuals as producers and consumers and collectively as classes. The second consists of a political market made up of citizens as voters, officeholders, and candidates. The latter, representing various principles and policy principles, gives individuals and groups the opportunity to express their reactions to governmental priorities, policies, and programs by balloting and the periodic selection of officials. This double market provides information about choices. It renders time into electoral sequence. It registers changes in public attitudes according to principles of methodological individualism and consumer and citizen sovereignty. It converts attitudinal fluctuations into a process of continuous reconciliation.[36]

Imbalances in the economic marketplace that might result in—let us say—economic inequality can be compensated for by corrective policies in the political, say, redistributive taxes.[37] Because political parties require mass electoral support, the power of numbers will offset the power of money. The private sector will inhibit the concentration of public power while the public sector will ensure that the autonomony of the private will remain responsible. The result is a systematic as well as a principled conception of democracy, a moving equilibrium (ideally a polyarchry), and approximated in social welfare and social democratic states.[38]

The mixture of principle and system is itself a general political model that can be applied prescriptively to less developed politics. Sufficiently flexible to permit adaptations of culture, circumstances, and tradition, it represents a "permanent" political solution. However, as a political solution, it has had a very uneven record. As indicated, it is difficult for the double market to perform well under conditions of high scarcity. The latter requires the restriction of economic and social demands and a level of social discipline that would allow that withholding from current consumption whereby savings for investment can be induced and applied to public infrastructure development before consumer products. An attendant problem is the "dysfunction" of a "consumption"- rather than a "production"-oriented middle class, one that tends to dominate both the economic and the political markets and combine private with public power.[39]

Preferred solutions to such problems such as the building of institutional networks able to relieve pressure points, enhancing regime legitimacy, and preserving order and stability necessary for promoting a climate favorable to growth are all more difficult to realize in practice than in theory. Education, particularly strategic not only in terms of training or an increase in knowledge and proficiency but also as an instrument of socialization, is quite often a system of elite recruitment for some, and an elimination process for others. Civic virtue may be one aim of education.[40] Motivation may be another given that those who join the modern labor force must be equipped with the right attitudes about work and efficiency. But in practice, this works better at the top than at the bottom. But even at the top, "credentials" often substitute for performance.

Education in practice may contribute to rather than resolve what is one of the most common deficiencies of Western "models" as applied to developing countries: an inability to prevent wholesale social inequalities. Politically, and in case after case, private economic power has coalesced with public power. Parliamentary and other institutional structures have been dominated by economically privileged elites well beyond public accountability. Critics argue that the response to greater development and modernization is such a far cry from a moving equilibrium that the more development and modernization, the more disequilibrating are the consequences, that is, protest, violence, and insurrection, coups, military regimes, and petty despotism.[41]

IV. THE DEPENDENCY ALTERNATIVES TO MODERNIZATION

Not surprisingly, the alternative to the logic of modernization I— radical dependency theory—has as its objective not merely exposing some of the deficiencies in this or that principle or practice, but showing systematically why modernization theory fails. Radical dependency theory, like the Marxist critique of capitalism from which it derives, focuses on relations between center and periphery. It shifts the focus away from endogenous to exogenous causes of class polarization, a process universalized by such instrumentalities as multinational corporations and compradore classes. Dependency theory thus attacks liberal modernization theory at the point of discrepancies between its theory and practice, and, systemically, as a discourse. Most dependency theorists not only reject the double market as a system, they see in it a form of political thinking that in the guise of "rational self-interest" converts the commercialization of social life into "false consciousness" and "commoditization" with the labor market reducing labor to a commodity, a form of exchange value.[42]

To be sure, dependency theorists, like Marx before them, want development and want it desperately. Their criticisms have little in common with the more sentimental and nostalgic longing for bucolic or romanticized virtues of preindustrial society. While sympathetic to those victimized and misplaced by innovative practices and machine technologies resulting in new production methods, they do not, on the whole, share a pedigree with the long line of naysayers who opposed industrialization and development on aesthetic grounds (Schiller, Ruskin, Matthew, Arnold, William Morris, and so on).[43]

Nor are dependency theorists *Marxists* in the strict sense of the term. Most have also been influenced by such ancestral figures as Weber, Durkheim, and the Pareto. In this sense, some represent an opposition to, while others represent a variant of, modernization theory. As a variant, they tend to cover the same ground but with different emphases and conclusions. For those opposed, modernization theorists are not only considered wrong but wrongheaded. Refusing to see that development and democracy are, if anything, inversely related, the latter have no good general explanation for why it is that so many countries that managed to get off to a good start economically now confront overwhelming problems: runaway population growth, expanding marginalized sectors, indebtedness, the flight of capital, the unanticipated domestic costs of import substitutions with authoritarian and corporatist regimes the widespread consequence of "modernization."[44]

Even when they deal with "crises"—identity, legitimacy, participation, distribution, penetration—the political modernization theorists fail to deal with them "systemically."[45] As for Parsons, Shils, Levy, Smelser, Moore, Eisenstadt, Pye, Binder, Almond, Lerner, Coleman, and all the others inclined to worry more about institutionalization, legitimacy, public opinion, and democracy than the causes of external hegemony, they all conspire to ignore the destructive side of capitalism. As for the less analytically inclined scholars who scoop up, collect, store, and correlate large quantities of indicator data—cross-cultural, national, and regional (mostly of poor quality to begin with)—they are worse. They generalize complex questions with little or no substantive understanding. Stochastic, simulation, and other studies using hard data are pretty much worthless.

The critique does not end there. Comparative analytical schemes so solemnly worked out by the modernization theorists are also failures. Those that were analytically the best proved to be too clumsy for empirical use. Those easier to use were too superficial to have much intellectual value. In any case, most were little more than plundered versions of those combinatorial binaries used by an earlier generation of historical sociologists: preindustrial-industrial, *Gemeinschaft-Gesellschaft,* status-contract, folk-urban, and so on. So sweeping is the attack that some dependency theorists have declared modernization theory dead. Wallerstein performed its last rites. "Requiescat in Pace," he said, being in a charitable mood.[46]

If modernization theory is dead, however, a good many of its original concerns may be popping up again. So too is functionalism. One reason is that many of the "disjunction"-producing modernization "tendencies" that dependency theorists regarded as inevitable have not occurred. Liberal thinking about modernization, ideas of the system, function, norms, and beliefs, is becoming fashionable in socialist countries such as China as well as in capitalist ones such as Japan. Wherever some *modus operandi* is sought between promoting development and holding on to particular values (classic Maoism, Japaneseness), or where people wrestle with how to sustain nonmaterialist or spiritual values while avidly pursuing material goods and services, aspects of the original modernization calculus become appropriate.[47]

What seems to be gone is the kind of modernization thinking (to which political scientists were especially prone) that elevated simple heuristic categories to the status of "theory" by attaching to them pseudosystemic properties (inputs and outputs) or labels drawn from another discipline (political "culture," political "function").[48] Most of these enterprises did little more than convert Parsons's pattern variables into "strain" theories based on ideas of "cultural incompatibility," relying on criteria existing more in the eye of the observer than in daily life on the ground.[49]

A few of the liberal modernization I theorists are coming back, this time on the left. Parsons himself is the best example. If we were to ask "who now reads Parsons?," one answer is that Habermas does. So do other radical theorists, and for the right reasons, that is, less for the pattern variables or multidimensional space figures than the connection between analytic levels, systems theory, and symbolic discourse.[50]

Significant differences, however, between liberal modernization and dependency theorists remain. They use different concepts of power. They project different solutions. In functionalist versions of modernization theory, power is a highly generalized *social* concept. Deriving from multiple sources, it is *necessarily* pluralistic in character despite conceded coercive monopolies by states and governments. In radical dependency theory, power is a more focused and decisive political concept the primary units of which have to do not with society but the state.

Although these two discourses may seem at first glance mutually exclusive, and certain protagonists of each insist that they are, each can be applied to the same process to show different systemic tendencies simultaneously at work. It has been suggested that liberal modernization theorists emphasize the growth of a generalized middle class as a result of development, whereas dependency theorists stress polarization. Yet both processes can be correct simultaneously. Combining both approaches to a next stage of development analysis has certain advantages. Emphasis on modernization I styles of analysis draws attention to complex, differentiated, and component differentiated relationships and networks. The focus is less on *polarized* class reciprocities (symmetrical or asymmetrical, positive or negative), than generalized middle classes differentiated in terms of multiple networks of role, "stratification" and pluralization. Conflict—structural, normative, and behavioral—will be seen as largely internally induced and suppressed in mediating coalitional behavior.

From this point of view to consider development in terms of the agents of capitalism, compradore classes, multinational corporations, and other instruments of domination through which the workings of imperialism (whether as world system or some regional or territorial variant) will produce dependency as a kind of negative inevitability seems at best simple-minded. The absence of such instruments would not necessarily help countries develop.

What remains important about radical dependency theory is less its critique of liberal modernization theory than its emphasis on opposite tendencies. Dependency theory thus "reveals" that which liberal modernization theory ignores. But, like Marxism, it has been too dire in its critiques of capitalism and neocolonialism. It needs to be rescued from its protagonists, even the best of them—Frank, Cardozo, O'Donnell, Bettelheim, Saul, Leys, Evans, Wallerstein, Moore, and others.[51]

Modernization II in a context of radical dependency theory emphasizes "contradiction," polarization, and social and political cleavages. If our analysis is correct, both tendencies can exist simultaneously, and in highly industrial as well as developing countries. Just as there are tendencies to integration, so there are tendencies toward fragmentation and polarization. Omnipresent dynamic factors in a political process of conflict and its mediation is like "centralization" and "decentralization," they are both simply there. Separately, the key substantive arguments of modernization or radical dependency theory are most simply outdated. Taken together, they give us quite another story.

V. TOWARD A
MODIFIED DEPENDENCY THEORY

This suggests that at present there is the opportunity for a new project, that is, a renovated version of modernization theory to compensate for a radical dependency theory that itself produces too many crucial absences, omissions, and blindnesses. The former, offering a more diffuse notion of power and a distributional concept of equity, enabled us to enlarge the political scope of liberal doctrine beyond its original constitutional and institutional boundaries, going well beyond the market itself by using a societal instead of a state frame to incorporate multiple networks of role and function. It used concepts of socialization, internalization, and institutionalization, all of which more condensed notions of power downgrade or omit. On the other hand, radical dependency theory corrected the bland and benign liberal tendencies of modernization theory. It could tell us what went wrong in Argentina, Brazil, and elsewhere. But it doesn't help much in describing societal impulses toward "redemocratization."

Generally speaking, dependency narrows the much wider social interactive scope even of Marxism, reducing analysis to specific political economy factors. It lacks the breadth of Marx's brilliant and total view of the socially interactive properties of collective life. The result is that it loses the ability to see transforming strategies available to those inside a society. Too often, radical dependency theory is an outsider's view even when practiced by insiders. Its virtues—a condensed notion of power that treats the connections between economic and political power in a relatively unmediated and direct way—are pragmatic and operational. Its defects are its overkill conclusions. It is far less concerned than Marxism with having history on its side. It is more political than theoretical as a result. The reasons for this narrow focus are several but perhaps the crucial one is that dependency theorists want to be emancipated from the view that capitalism is the necessary transforming agent in the elimination of scarcity. They do not share Marx's admiration for the innovative, adaptive, and universalizing tendencies of capitalism. They question whether it really is necessary to go through all those class contradictions and confrontations that Marx believed necessary in order to bring about transition to socialism.[52]

Marx, for all his hatred of the bourgeoisie, was much more appreciative of its powers than the dependency theorists. Indeed, few have waxed more rhapsodic than he over its role in destroying the feudal system, allowing in the "fresh air" of naked self-interest, stripping away the heavenly ecstasies of religious fervor, and destroying reverence for tradition and established authority. Vigor, expansion of the market, universalization of exchange, creation of new wants, formation of vast urban centers, elimination of the "idiocy of rural life," the centralization of the power of the state—all these Marx considered to be the historical accomplishments of capitalism and the bourgeoisie.[53] *Dependistas* consider such views outmoded. Capitalism is by no means a necessary precondition for socialism. Nor is it the sole means of exploding man's previous material modes and conceptual limitations. At best, a state needs only a limited capitalistic phase in order to generate sufficient socialization of labor. One certainly does not need to wait until the end of a demonic cycle (as Marx would have it), like the sorcerer conjuring up all the explosive contradictory powers of the nether world, until at last the power of capitalism escapes control and comes to an end.

This narrower notion of political economy focuses on the way in which the forces of contradiction work, intensify, and take a political form. It enables one to see socialism as a doctrine for poor countries rather than rich capitalistic ones. It pays attention to the state, "bringing the state back in" as the crucial relevant actor. It accepts the idea of socialism under conditions of scarcity.

Radical dependency theory, then, not only attacks liberal modern-ization theory but, in modifying the original Marxist problemmatique, rejects capitalism as a stage so fundamental that socialism cannot be realized without it. Nor does it accept capitalism as the right medicine for curing the ills of the Asiatic mode of production. In this respect, radical dependency theory also goes beyond the inspiration of Hobson, Lenin, and other late Marxist theorists who argued in favor of stage-jumping, and in which the neocolonial or imperial "chain" is necessarily a late capitalistic one. For radical dependency theorists, socialism will work not only in the weaker links of the capitalist imperialist chain, but in any of these links. Political contradiction and polarization are always present developmentally. Politics takes command. It no longer matters whether socialism is the solution to the problems in highly industrialized capitalist countries because depriving capitalism of the receipts it obtains from colonial domination will in any case contribute to crises of capitalism, in the long run if not in the short.[54]

The trouble is that while dependency theorists do not agree on such matters, they are often simply wrong. Not only are fewer and fewer of today's practitioners of radical dependency theory Marxist, even dependency theorists now prefer liberal political solutions to any other. The real question is the appropriate role of the state. How can it generate development from above? How can one "privilege" the state without becoming the victim of its power, its bureaucracy as a class for itself?

And it is precisely on these and similar political questions that radical dependency theory is shot through with wishful thinking. Even if a dependent country could develop a strong state, escape from dependency, and put an end to domination from abroad, it is a good question whether or not it would be able to deprive the metropole for very long of lopsided enjoyment of benefits at the expense of the periphery. Nor, at the opposite end of the spectrum, has socialism in developing countries contributed much to contradictions in advanced capitalist countries.

On the whole, dependency theorists have remained remarkably distant from the consequences of arbitrary power, the negative effects of the politicization of social life, careerism, endemic conflicts, and party factionalism under "progressive" or socialist regimes. Like Marxists who prefer to ignore failed predictions (e.g., expansion rather than decline of the middle class, and decline rather than increasing significance of a proletariat), dependency theorists have also ignored radicalization for embourgeoisement (a rather awkward propensity of marginals in particular), problems of low productivity, alienated producers, corrupt and badly organized management, and political cynicism. Perhaps the weakest version of radical dependency theory is the world system variety with its overkill assumptions.[55] Not surprisingly, some dependency theorists who do real fieldwork, such as Colin Leys, have become more critical of it in recent years because it glosses over problems of state capitalism in the guise of socialism, ignores problems of bureaucratization, and favors the mobilizing of power of the radical single-party regime.[56]

VI. THE NEW MODERNIZATION AND THE PREDISPOSITION TO VIOLENCE

If both liberal modernization and radical dependency theory have their limitations, the question is whether it is possible in more than an eclectic way to take selected ingredients from both and form a better framework for contemporary analysis. Can one apply notions of functionally differentiated roles and networks to the social cleavages emphasized in dependency? Is there an appropriate problematic focus and a new and systemic developmental dynamic? Perhaps what we have called modernization II can provide such a focus because it enables us to see how integrative tendencies and a moving equilibrium can go together with polarization, and each as a function of growth.

Let us take the concept of polarization and apply it "developmentally" to two "classes," differentiated in terms of their relative contributions to development. One, a functional elite, constitutes itself in relation to innovation, technology, and science, that is, the information needs of industrial societies. The other is residual and negatively defined. That is, it is marked by the absence of these properties. At its extreme, it represents a class essentially marginalized by innovation. If the first is functionally significant because it includes all those connected to information creation, the "knowledge workers," the other consists of marginals who are in this sense functionally superfluous. Of course, neither represents a class in the strict sense because both have multiple alliances, associations, and affiliations. Moreover, links are possible between the two. One almost never finds a class struggle between them. What replaces class struggle in a Marxist sense is, under certain conditions, a growing predisposition to violence. I want to use violence as a problemmatique for the discussion of a next stage of developmental theory.

Historically, the violence I have in mind is associated with development. Indeed, as Arendt has suggested, the idea of revolution begins with the French revolution. Violence and development have gone together and modernization theory is only a variant of the classic problem of rendering violence into order. Violence, however, also can result from successful development. Take, for example, the unforeseen consequences of land reforms in certain Latin American countries where progressive reforms contributed to a remarkable increase in the efficiency of agricultural sectors. They also contributed to a surge in primary products production resulting in oversupply and surpluses (especially agricultural) in international markets. Among the negative results were indebtedness, rural displacement and the growth of squatter populations, loss of income in world markets, and the overburdening and overwhelming of social services. With a middle class at the center, polarization at the extremes, and rural guerrillas, military coups d'etat are not hard to predict.

Caught between the growing power and prestige of a bureaucratic and technologically sophisticated elite and downward mobility pressure, mobility displacement rather than incorporation occurs in sectors close to marginalized groups. The more a bourgeoisie is subject to such pulls, the more it will change from a class in itself into a class for itself, a circumstance favoring authoritarian political regimes.[57] Many such battles begin in the educational system, whose installation according to modernization theory is the chief requisite instrument for socialization and integration into functional roles. Serving instead as a venue for polarizing tendencies, pupils are caught between pressures to perform well and join the functional elites, and pressure toward marginalization. Secondary and higher educational facilities will also reflect these cleavages and tensions in society.[58]

More and more frequently it is the marginalized groups, especially those *dispossessed* of their lands and *displaced* from their communities, who form into semiorganized groups and press demands on governments under circumstances, economic and political, that the latter are unwilling or unable to satisfy. In a zero-sum political situation, a typical response is to borrow from outside, thereby increasing indebtedness. Another is to offer special inducements to outside investors in hopes of stimulating growth and generating new employment opportunities both in new industries and service occupations (thereby increasing dependence). But, in many cases, available labor in developing countries is so poorly trained and motivated and its skill structure so low that outside firms consider it too inefficient for labor-intensive industry. Not surprisingly, labor-intensive industry is declining everywhere. The "cheap labor" theory of capitalism applies less and less. If one puts together the decline in agricultural and basic commodity prices with a declining labor force, "contradiction," and social polarization, one can see ahead increasing political protest, a more generalized climate of unrest, and tendencies for political controls at the expense of democracy.

With these and other political uncertainties creating a climate of very high risk, only firms powerful enough and sufficiently multinational in scope to be immune to the vagaries of politics are likely to be the instruments of development able to survive, and they will survive best in highly technical fields where "production workers" are less needed than "knowledge workers." In any case, the kind of investment most likely to be realized under such circumstances will not be in the traditional industrial manufacturing sections that characterized industrial growth in the past.

It is now an old story that in certain poor societies such marginalization also can radicalize "peasants" who become dispossessed of their holdings, displaced from their communities, and become rural guerrillas, as historically in France, China, or today in the Philippines. In urban areas, the original radicalizing thrust was by means of a revolutionary proletariat. Today under prevailing social, subcultural, and motivational conditions, the prospect is instead a self-perpetuating condition of marginality, rural and urban. Moreover, the functionally superfluous often serve as coconspirators in their condition. Most violence is self-inflicted and internal, as among severely marginalized Blacks in the United States, a condition extremely difficult to break out of. Hence, the extremes—of organized insurrectionary or terrorist movements as in Argentina in the 1970s, or in Peru and Ireland today. Indeed, because marginals are very difficult to mobilize, many of the most successful movements define marginality in racial, religious, ethnic, linguistic, and similar terms to create primordial movements as in Lebanon, Sri Lanka, and elsewhere.

There are important exceptions, of course. Where the labor force is compliant and efficient and labor unrest minimal (as in Taiwan, South Korea, Singapore, Hong Kong, and Malaysia), labor-intensive industry has been profitable, and indeed has led to shifts in industrial growth that threaten industry and manufacturing in advanced countries. But even in these countries, the transition today is to high technology enterprise and, with it, an emphasis on innovation and capital intensive modes of production.[59]

More important for our purposes, however, some of these contradictions of development characteristic of Third World countries are manifesting themselves in advanced industrial states, but not for reasons advanced by dependency theorists. The problem is not caused by the growing dependence of industrial countries on primary producers. Quite the contrary—they have become increasingly uncoupled from them while less developed countries have become more dependent on and vulnerable to Western metropoles than ever before.

The point is that in both Third World and advanced industrial countries, the productive system and world economy are changing in ways that confound conventional liberal modernization and dependency theorists. Innovation leading to growth also generates polarization, marginalization, functional displacement, dispossession, and with them a growing predisposition to violence in advanced industrial systems. This pattern of modernization II takes different forms but certain outlines are becoming clearer. Industry shifts to more profitable pursuits. Social overhead costs are reduced. The need for savings for investment grows. The pressures to innovate intensify. The more productivity depends on the effective translation of new design into industrial outputs, the more favored will be a technocratic elite.

Hence, it is not surprising that today countries as diverse as Britain, France, and the United States confront these tendencies in the contexts of "deindustrialization" and zero-sum growth.[60] All have experienced rising unemployment and marginalization. In all, per-man-hour efficiency has declined relative to wages, despite restrictions on wage increases. All have experienced severe fiscal crises.[61] The pressure to "modernize" has become almost ineluctable and that means increasing productivity by means of innovative enterprise, eliminating unprofitable and subsidized firms, while relying increasingly on market forces to ascertain, define, and determine functionality. It also means that in countries such as France, more effective collaboration between government and industry in research and development has become a high priority, placing even greater emphasis on high technology information and capital-intensive growth.

Indeed, France is a good example of what we are describing. Technocratic elites have been given broader scope in both public and private sectors. They are increasingly able to set political agendas even at the expense of party programs. For example, technocratic considerations came to prevail over the original "110 theses" of the socialist Mitterand government. Forced to reverse course drastically, retrenchment policies pursued between 1983 and 1985 were not so different in consequence from those of Prime Minister Thatcher in England or President Reagan in the United States.

As for the United States, which for a time had seemed to handle the problem of job decline fairly well, recent congressional studies have shown that from 1979 to 1984, out of 11.9 million workers who lost jobs, only 61% found new ones and that, on the whole, skilled workers who did find new jobs found them in service industries at far less pay.[62]

Indeed, two-thirds of those reemployed earned less than 80% of their former income. Among Blacks, the displacement was disproportionately worse and the opportunities for reemployment substantially less. A permanent underclass now exists that is not only unemployed, but basically unemployable. Despite all this, no clear understanding of underlying changes in the productive process has emerged. In a single recent issue of the *New York Times*, one article could speak of the economy in 1986 as similar to the "roaring twenties," the "postwar boom," and the "soaring sixties," while another could point out that "millions are bypassed by economic recovery." The point is that growth and development under conditions like those just described will not only continue to omit certain sectors of the population, but that unemployment is increasingly being transformed into marginality. This is a far more complicated and difficult social condition, which stimulates rising social overhead costs, places increasing burdens on the state, and often under circumstances in which the economic and political consequences can no longer be mediated.

Even in industrial countries that are not becoming "deindustrialized," the impact of design change on the labor force has been heavy. Increasing manufacturing production goes hand in hand with decreasing blue-collar employment. According to Drucker, for the past 30 years, manufactures have remained at a steady 23%-24% of total GNP in the United States and in other industrialized countries. In the United States between 1973 and 1985, "manufacturing production (measured in constant dollars) . . . rose by almost 40 percent. Yet manufacturing employment during that period went down steadily. There are now five million fewer people employed in blue-collar work in American manufacturing industry than there were in 1974." The prospect is that industrial labor will drop to about 5%, or roughly the same proportion of the labor force found in agriculture today.[63]

Moreover, there is a growing discrepancy between the declining industrial labor force and its absorption into an expanding service industry. Reemployment of the displaced worker becomes more and more difficult. It is precisely here that marginality becomes important over time, and as a consequence of innovation generated in the most successful industrial societies by the small, but increasingly important, functional elite.

Such problems have, of course, had very different political consequences. In most Western societies, as industrial labor has become marginalized, support for trade unionism has declined.[64] Also there have been marked increases in primordialism, racism, and discrimination against Arabs, Turks, Blacks, Jews, West Indians, Africans, and Asians. Indeed, one sees in all parts of the world tendencies toward primordial revivalism, zenophobic, often fascist. And the more that social polarization leads to political polarization, the more extremes of right and left create their own "discourse" and a common predisposition to violence although their reasons may differ. It is not surprising, then, what has been a Third World phenomenon is now a daily aspect of life in certain advanced industrial states. So much so that one can say that the spread of terrorism is a function of development itself, and in global terms. The question is whether violence is becoming the "postmodern phenomenon."

To summarize, the "disposition to violence" results from the contradiction between innovation and marginalization. Innovation is a process essential to industrialization. Because of its centrality, it has the power to define the functional value of roles, classes, and individuals in a community. It also, and increasingly, serves as the legitimizing basis for hierarchies of access to resources and political power. It represents, too, knowledge as science and order rationally conceived. Marginality is just the opposite. It represents those effectively excluded from participation in that knowledge. It is outside the discourse and legitimacy it represents. Hence, violence by, on behalf of, and in favor of those marginalized, dispossessed, or displaced in some fashion constitutes an antilegitimacy. In terms of the modern state, it is against the state. Produced by development, it is both "premodern" and "postmodern" at the same time. It raises the question of the social limits of growth.[65] It is the ultimate cost of innovation.

VII. TOWARD A
NEW FRAMEWORK

Before introducing some new ingredients into the argument and, as well, shifting the focus to development and violence, I want to show briefly how these themes came to concern me. Mainly they derive from fieldwork that forced me to modify my views in theory. Indeed, how to enlarge modernization theory to deal with such matters in politically significant ways was the original object of *The Politics of Modernization*. There the emphasis was on strategic modernization roles and class differentiation, with categories provided that could be used to operationalize tendencies toward both mediation and polarization in a context of political types. Further elaboration of these categories in terms of systems analysis was the purpose of *Choice and the Politics of Allocation*. The object there was threefold: to construct a formalized model of the reciprocities of power, to translate these into operational categories, and to suggest tendencies toward contradiction, which, in turn, became the political problématique for developmental politics.

Interest in such matters was first stimulated by field studies in Ghana and Uganda. Originally, I shared many of the assumptions of modernization theory, applying a modified version of structural-functional analysis to the problem of political institutional transfer, that is, how a nationalist movement used parliamentary means and party politics to make the transition to independence, and, subsequently, how it changed to a more mobilizing system and a single-party state.[66]

The second case study was more ethnographic. A political anthropology, it dealt with ethnic and religious pluralism and tribal separatism in a society moving toward independence without the integrative force of an overarching nationalist movement. It was in this context that I became interested in primordial revivalism and, as well, developed the consociational model, which was modified and popularized by Lijphard and others.[67]

Fieldwork in these countries and others in Africa dealt with political problems in countries at very low developmental levels. It was subsequent research in Latin America that suggested how, with development, social contradictions could worsen rather than improve. This contrasted sharply with the more hopeful positive correlations between developmental growth and democracy anticipated and proposed by most modernization theorists. It was in the context of work on Argentina, Chile, and, to a lesser extent, Peru, that most of the ideas about marginalization and functional polarization were worked out. Many of these ideas were similar to but independent of radical dependency theory. When I began research on these three countries, all of them had democratic political systems. In each case, for reasons suggested here, all three were overthrown.

In two of the three, Argentina and Peru, violence was endemic. In Chile, the problem was radicalization from above and below, which resulted in competing pulls on a middle class. The latter—originally a class "in itself"—later responded as a class "for itself." In different ways, each of the three paid a heavy political price for that kind of innovative modernization that resulted in marginalization, with social contradiction leading to conditions favoring violence. In each case, but for different reasons, the more responsibility the state assumed, the less effective it was in mediating those contradictions.

It was work in Latin America that turned my attention to violence. I began to work on it in Europe, the Middle East, and Japan. Japan was in some ways the most curious case because there modernization seemed to have been most successful with developmental contradictions least in evidence. Yet paradoxes of development were there even in Japan. With several Japanese collaborators, I turned to a different kind of fieldwork, more phenomenological, the characteristics of which will be outlined below. The framework was developed in the field around the problem of extrainstitutional protest and in a contest of violent episodes, antistate in character. Here we found a particular variant of marginalization, the dispossession of small farmers by government decree and the self-marginalization of militants of various left-wing radical sects. In a small setting, one could examine in detail a movement whose symbolic importance contrasted greatly with its small size, raising questions about the state as an obstacle to mediation, in terms of both policy and practice.[68]

It was in the Japanese context, too, that concepts such as retrieval and projection, narrative and text, and so on (drawn from Levi-Strauss, Barthes, Bourdieu, Habermas, Ricoeur, Jameson, Lyotard, and others) were applied in a field setting—what I refer to as a "mobilization space." Two intersecting crossroads represented two political economies. One, consisting of rural households and local exchange, was becoming "marginalized" and rendered functionally superfluous by the other, an airport representing industrial, commercial, and international exchange, a world of functional elites. When the second crossroads was imposed on the first, the resulting violence formed a narrative and a text, a history and a logic that remains to this day.

This brings me back to the general hypothesis that connects the earlier focus on development to the more recent one on violence. I have suggested that liberal modernization tradition emphasizes linear growth and its integrative and pluralistic social and political consequences. The dependency tradition, although using a more Marxist or unilinear emphasis, replaces the "proletarianization" hypothesis with a "marginalization" principle.

As suggested above, the present theory is a more "curvilinear" one, combining the two. Contradiction results when innovation creates both a generalized middle, as liberal modernization theorists suggest, reduces proletarianization (which most Marxists refuse to recognize), but also creates a functional elite. Marginalization and what might be called incipient marginalization generate a predisposition to violence. This, a consequence of modernization II, is what I regard as a "postmodern" political condition.

VIII. VIOLENCE AS A POSTMODERN CONDITION

If we consider violence as a postmodern problemmatique, what is required to understand it is (1) certain developmental tendencies that I have described as modernization II; (2) the interpretation of violence as a discourse and a semiotics; and (3) a phenomenology in which violence is itself a mode of interpretation, with interpretation leading to violent events: protest, insurrection, terrorism. These events in their different ways constitute an antitext, the object of which is to challenge or supersede legitimacy, explode conventionality, and "deconstruct" that developmental "structuration" that expresses the functional rationality of ordinary life.[69]

Violence of these sorts is also postmodern in the sense that it is an unanticipated consequence of modernization. An increasingly generalized phenomenon, it differs from typical social movements of the past insofar as these latter were for the most part simply demands for more participation. In liberal theory, development, plus participation and the more equitable allocation of resources and opportunities, is the solution to violence. The more democracy in this sense, the more able governments will be to mediate conflict.[70] But if the structural reasons for violence suggested above are systemically valid, they would certainly cast doubt not only on the benign teleologies of modernization theory, but also on the wishful thinking of the dependency solutions that rely on the state itself as the appropriate venue for solutions.

This suggests a whole new area for inquiry, one that treats violence as a diagnostic phenomenon rather than the activities of mad, irresponsible, or misguided people. Because we cannot say when or where violence will actually occur, there may be a huge gap between a predisposition to violence and its actual occurrence. We need to locate the several strategic variables in between. For example, multiple forms of marginalization under conditions of castelike pariah status may dampen tendencies toward violence even where predisposing conditions for it would seem to exist in extreme form. Take South Africa, for example. There one would have expected apartheid to have caused massive and widespread violence years ago. Only now it is occurring on a large scale. One would expect, too, that in the United States the predisposition to violence would be greater than in Western Europe but the increase in terror, the growth of the extreme right, is greater in many European countries than in the United States. Answers are not clear. Each case requires specific analysis.

What experience does show, however, is that once unleashed, violence generates its own dynamism. Or, to put it in a more theoretical way, it generates its own discourse. Such a discourse will have certain characteristics. It will retrieve and project. It will be linked to memory and nostalgia. It will convert previous affiliations into commitments and obligations, and more—to solutions, millennial in character, often utopian. Such a discourse can make use of those precise materials, primordial mixtures of racial, ethnic, linguistic, and other similar ingredients, which in the context of modernization theory are supposed to disappear but show a remarkable propensity to revive under conditions of polarization. Hitched to radical formulas, they can allow marginalized groups to speak for the whole society, even while defining themselves as unique and special, and to use the margin to evaluate the whole in moral terms.

Carried far enough and with sufficient mobilized supports, the dynamic of violence defines moral moments whose symbolic effects spread out to the wider society. At their most extreme, such groups become agents of the disjunctive moment, the break, revolution, redemption, the founding of a new state, the dynamics of which are transformation, purification, rebirth. The search for the disjunctive moment through violence reconstitutes language as performative discourse, shattering conventional modes, a mixture of narrative and theater.[71]

Wherever functional polarization takes place in highly modernized societies—industrial ones and potentially socialist systems as well— violent protest can be expected to grow. Moreover, such violence tends to be an antistate phenomenon even when the ostensible object is *for* the state, that is, the carving out of a new state from an existing one on grounds of ethnicity, language, or a religion as in separatist movements. Marginality then attaches a certain dubiousness to the state that allows marginalization to occur.

This suggests that the real importance of violence is as symbolic capital.[72] It is the functionally equivalent opposite to economic capital. What I mean by *postmodern* is in the reemergence of symbolic capital as an independent source of power. It changes the discourse of meaning. It "deconstructs" economic capital as rationality, that is, as the developmental basis of authority. It "brackets" ordinary terms of politics to create a "common sense" of radical intentions. Violent events form into "language games" different from those that represent conventionality. If innovation leads to marginalization and the latter predisposes to violence, it is violence that forms an antidiscourse. As a disordering and reordering *mytho-logics*, it "develops" into symbolic capital and the struggle between good and evil.[73]

Although the violence we have in mind can come from above (i.e., the state), or below, the main concern here is with the latter. It should be clear too that the emphasis is on organized rather than random violence. True enough, the violence that breaks out in a more or less destructive episode or emotional explosion may be very important in the terms we have been using, that is, as a "discourse." Nevertheless, it lacks the sustaining power of particular objectives. If it is not to be a mere epiphenomenon, violence, to be significant, must be a project of intentionalities. As symbolic capital, its discourse is important to the extent that it unites diverse and particular intentions of individuals within a common semiotic system, signs, codes, signals, and so on.[74]

This "discourse approach" has as a starting assumption the notion that people have an inveterate predisposition to storytelling, which is the first step toward collective interpretation. Storytelling is a form of narration in which certain predicaments and situations are presented. Crucial is the identification of a negative pole, the overcoming of which is the object of dramatic enterprise. Such stories work best when they contain something of the fabulous. The truly remarkable is logic-defying, magical. Moreover, the magic requires that the narratives are authorless.

But if people are disposed to storytelling as a way of "ordering" and the rendering of experience into dramatic narrative, so they are equally disposed toward logic and explanation. We mean the kind of explanation that translates experience into events, events into facts, and facts into evidence. It is through the observation and interpretation of facts as evidence according to explicit logical principles that leads to "theory." Theory then is the product of reflection and interpretation arising out of the relation between event and text, experience and abstract knowledge. In this respect, events constitute a social text. Read, interpreted, and made coherent in terms of broader principles, such a social text stands on its own. It represents interpretation as a form of evidence on its own.

A phenomenology of violence then consists of placing acts that violate conventional rules and behavior and form into a sequence of episodes that, part narrative and part text, represent a double discourse. At one level, aimed at exploding prevailing political codes and structural forms, social and "mental," the two discourses intersect to form a mutually reinforcing mytho-logics of their own, a displacing order. Each discourse starts with the same events and the same negative pole. Each follows different but parallel rules for the transcendence of that negative pole. The parallelism is crucial because the two discourses need to be transformable, one into the other: a narrative that recounts heroic acts, remarkable feats, and arranges episodes into a dramatistic mode, giving coherence to events that explode against the power of the orthodox. In turn, the narrative must be transformable at each point into a text.

Not any text, of course. The text must show a connection between episodes of the narrative and the logic, the necessity of it as history or projection. When the logic of overcoming is linked with an intentional morality, the two discourses at one and the same time represent modes of interpretation and performative utterances. In this sense, violence serves as a language that creates structure out of events, and events out of structure. The connection is a matter of recitation, recounting, repetition. It follows certain rules of narrative as myth and theory as logic.

At another level then, violence, which one thinks of as disordering, is also a reordering phenomenon. Symbolic turbulence is where it begins. Its structuring appeal grows when authorless myth finds voice and agency. Agency, in turn, requires an agent through which events pass, or better—a moral architect who forms them into symbolic capital, power, or antipower. Moreover, the practical ingredients of this symbolic capital need to be ready at hand, recognizable. It is when ordinary things are suddenly charged with meaning and stand for larger devices— retrieval and projection, narrative and myth, logic and theory—that an enriching process occurs, a reinforcing particularity so that icons, markers, traces, can be mobilized to endow a mytho-logics of terror, insurrection, protest with symbolic density.[75]

It is in this sense that violence as a postmodern phenomenon refracts virtually everything ordinary. It turns the ordinary on its head. It represents a "dedoublement," a double discourse of inversion, the hero as antihero, the prison cell as redeeming agent, the thief as prosecutor, the madman as judge.[76]

Put in such abstract terms, violence may seem artificial. This is what happens when commentary is converted into more systematic language. The intellectual problem is to maintain a sense of a dual perspective, one structural, the other phenomenological. The first will regard a social text as a series of events and episodes in terms illustrative or paradigmatic of what is already "known," or contained in the form of mythic narrative as an ordinary device. At the same time, those episodes in a narrative signify a range of meaning in which they themselves serve as surrogates for a "real" text (one that reveals or contains the "real" meaning of history). To put it another way, on the structural "side" of the discourse, each event is both signifier and signified, metaphor and metonymy, the one as myth, the other as theory. On the phenomenological "side" of the discourse, the same events have meaning in terms of the intentionalities attached to them by participants. As shared experiences articulated in the form of common intentions, the more "structural," the more singular the interpretation, the more phenomenological, the more the discourse is "moral."

These points can be represented schematically. Between the two discourses, "structural," on one hand, and "phenomenological," on the other, the ingredients can be arranged as seen in Figure 1.3.

Seen from below, the phenomenological perspective begins with an immersion in episodes. It proceeds to interpretation using retrieval, memories, resonances of past events, all placed in a continuing historical context. Parallels with the past help establish a pedigree, reinforce the present struggle as authentic. There is, too, the identification of a specific but generalized negative pole, moral in character, to be transcended by means of mythically significant metaphors.

In turn, the same events so formed are surrogates for established metonymies. They illustrate a known text, particularly an ideological one. Both are incorporated ("objectivized") in a single ideology, the one as a story, a recounted tale, including elements of the fabulous; the other as a logic, structure emerging as an ordering system, as myth and as theory. Both are composed of binary structures. Theory demonstrates

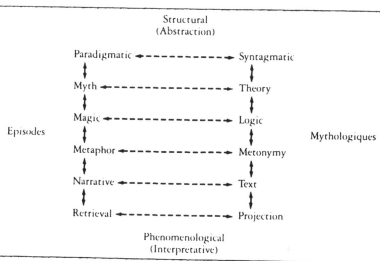

Figure 1.3 Modes of Discourse

syntagmatic properties. Myth demonstrates paradigmatic properties. The first projects as an expression of rational power. The second retrieves, layering the present with the past. What begins as episode thus ends as mytho-logics, a form of symbolic capital, a form of power.

Whether or not episodes of violence succeed in their purpose may or may not be important. But even if not important immediately, they have consequences for the future. The symbolic layering that such interpreted events leave behind may be retrieved as evidence at another time. So, symbolic capital as violence enters history as memory and inheritance. It remains a potential ingredient for reordering. On the other hand, if it "succeeds" and makes a "break," it realizes the disjunctive moment and, becoming symbolic capital, serves as the basis for a new orthodoxy.

For example, the Long March in China and the Yan'an period that followed it constitute a series of mytho-logical events. The first is a biblical narrative of a journey against all odds, struggles against the enemy, extreme physical hardship, covering thousands of miles through alien lands, over high mountains, across dry deserts, and so on. Miraculously, a tiny band survives. It forms an instructional "republic of the caves" in Yan'an. There one finds the Socratic and dialectical vision of the revolutionary agent, Mao. A projective logic is added to the miraculous events. The survivors become representatives of historic destiny. They go from the periphery to the center, from the caves to the commanding heights of power. They become testimonials, witnesses to their own mytho-logics, a good example of symbolic capital created from below establishing the orthodoxy of the state.

Violence is about break, disordering, and ordering. It can do these things because it also has about it a certain starkness, a minimalism that, utterly shocking, pulls away the fabric of decency. It defies and disrupts ordinary rationality. Its episodes are uniquely visual. Senseless acts of human and physical destruction have, after all, their own totality. The final testimony of the dead is their eloquent muteness. Their silence is the absolute deconstruction.

As a postmodern phenomenon, then, violence has become so widespread that even the protected observer has come to know the proximity of fear. A good deal of violence today, even when far away, has a dissolving effect—an alien intimacy—personal yet impersonal, like rape. One experiences it alone. When its unknown presence becomes intense, violence will mask and unmask. It is in this masking and unmasking that it becomes the ultimately significant postmodern phenomenon.[77]

IX. CONCLUSION

Symbolic capital as violence, violence as a postmodern phenomenon, both place renewed emphasis on the remaking of social worlds. They open up the concept of "superstructure." They bring into a single frame experiences that have spread from developing countries to industrialized ones, and treat both as a structural unity, a unity of mutually interactive contradictions.

Among the ingredients of our discussion, three kinds of structuralism have been employed. The first, deriving from modernization theory, is basically a theory of equilibria, a set of mutually responsive structures that, as a grand design, have been duplicated, replicated, or established as the basis for a successfully generalized model of industrial society. It constitutes an *outcome*.

The second, radical dependency theory, is essentially a theory of contradictions, a set of mutually incompatible circumstances that show why the outcome projected by modernization theory will be impossible.

The third, ideational structuralism, is the organization of contradictions into a logic of binary oppositions, the mediation of which is a projective and mythological task the aim of which is to establish a logic for mythic narrative, and a narrative for a logical theory—a second ordering performative task that we commonly refer to as "ideology."

We began with development and the importance of economic capital and its role as the "science" of development, that is, the scientific discourse of projection. We concluded with the significance of symbolic capital. But if we impose the last on the first, this brings us back to science and modernization. How can we follow the effects of violence in terms of roles and networks, multiple and overlapping affiliations, symmetrical and asymmetrical reciprocities, and the interactive ramifications of these in a context of deep structures rather than surface ones? What has been the impact of violence on beliefs and ideologies, norms and values, on the internalization of norms, and the consequences of their "externalization," the "spitting out" and rejection of them? What effect will conflicting norms have on motivations, instruments of socialization, the nurturing process, familial, educational, and the state itself? These are the kinds of questions that arise when "structuralism" is imposed on modernization I and II.

Such a perspective also emphasizes the importance of the wide rather than the narrow perspective of power, transforming symbolic capital into a total and interactive process in society with the state revealed simultaneously in normative, structural, and behavioral breaks. The question in each case is how well mutually compensatory responses work to sustain prevailing patterns of internalization, socialization, and institutionalization. If ruptured, these political requisites of the state will signal its decay, downfall—violence is the disjunctive moment. Applied in terms of radical dependency theory for which the logic of developmental contradiction counts, the dynamic of polarization should reveal how, why, and when the actions taken by the state to improve its condition and mediate contradiction will actually intensify both, and worsen its condition to the extent that it too will require alteration in design.[78]

This way of framing development suggests that while each type of theory commits terrible crimes of omission, each not only has something to offer in a renovated "developmental" theory, but is essential to the other. On the other hand, the result will not be a theory of benign outcomes. It suggests instead that through rethinking of politics in a contest of developmental violence, postmodernism throws open all the political conventions and customary ways of thinking.

To recapitulate, radical dependency theory condensed the social structural aspects of Marxism into political economy and the state, and emphasized the conception of political power where modernization theory had enlarged and extended the social aspects of liberal political economy, institutions, and the distribution of political power. "Concentration" emphasizes contradiction, "distribution" pluralism. Using both instead of treating them as wholly different and alternative developmental tendencies, one can consider them as simultaneous processes, as developmental hypotheses to be applied to cases, to concrete situations.

Hypotheses that center on polarization and the state emphasize disjunctive moments, foundings, revolutions, theocratic revivals, and so on, in short, transformative emphases. Modernization theory will emphasize the complex and interactive networks of relations that constitute—if not a kind of Sartrean practico-enert—at least the multiple ways in which family, kinship, interest group, institutions, and the variety of networks that constitute the building blocks of various societies (not to speak of the norms embodied in them) will act to normalize, adapt, mediate.

In turn, radical dependency theory turns attention from top to bottom, to attacks on authority and power rather than on how to establish and maintain them, and against the state rather than for it. Here, the emphasis is on protest and violence: random, extrainstitutional, insurrectionary, terrorist. In the literature, generally these phenomena are not linked to developmental polarization except in the case of insurrectionary or revolutionary activity. Violence is generally treated as the pathology of a few twisted individuals, or something that breaks out in rashes for no good reason. In this view, violence is both structural (and in that sense fundamental) and a discourse of its own—a language, a strategy of ordering and disordering. These and similar themes dealt with in the second half of this book are about developmental disordering, myth creation and destruction, with both a function of lived experience, interpreted, retrieved, and projected.

NOTES

1. Donald Winch, *Classical Political Economy and Colonies* (London: G. Bell, 1965). See also Henri Baudet, *Paradise on Earth* (New Haven: Yale University Press, 1965).

2. Leo Panitch, *Social Democracy and Industrial Militancy* (Cambridge: Cambridge University Press, 1976), pp. 7-40. See also Maurice Dobb, *Capitalism, Development and Planning* (London: Routledge & Kegan Paul, 1967).

3. Albert O. Hirschman, *The Strategy of Economic Development* (New Haven: Yale University Press, 1958). See also Eugene Staley, *The Future of Underdeveloped Countries* (New York: Harper, 1954).

4. S. N. Eisenstadt, *Tradition, Change, and Modernity* (New York: John Wiley, 1973). See also David C. McClelland, *The Achieving Society* (Princeton, NJ: Van Nostrand, 1961); and Marion J. Levy, Jr., *Modernization: Latecomers and Survivors* (New York: Basic Books, 1972).

5. David E. Apter, *Choice and the Politics of Allocation* (New Haven: Yale University Press, 1971). See also Samuel Huntington, *Political Order in Changing Societies* (New Haven: Yale University Press, 1968).

6. Bert F. Hoselitz and Wilbert E. Moore, eds., *Industrialization and Society* (Paris: UNESCO-Mouton, 1963).

7. P. T. Bauer and B. S. Yamey, *The Economics of Underdeveloped Countries* (Cambridge: Cambridge University Press, 1957). See also Amartya Sen, *Resources, Values and Development* (Cambridge, MA: Harvard University Press, 1984), pp. 485-508. See also Robert F. Arnove, *Philanthropy and Cultural Imperialism* (Bloomington: University of Indiana Press, 1980).

8. G. Bingham Powell, Jr., "Functionalism as a Paradigm in Political Science," in *The Paradigm Problem in Political Science*, ed. William T. Bluhn (Durham, NC: Carolina Academic Press, 1982), pp. 141-60. Also, Raymond Bauer, *Social Indicators* (Cambridge: MIT Press, 1966); James M. Beshers, ed., *Computer Methods in the Analysis of Large-Scale Social Systems* (Cambridge: MIT Press, 1968); Bruce M. Russett et al., *World Handbook of Political and Social Indicators* (New Haven: Yale University Press, 1964); Charles Lewis Taylor and Michael C. Hudson, *World Handbook of Political and Social Indicators*, 2nd ed. (New Haven: Yale University Press, 1972); Richard L. Meritt and Stein Rokkan, *Comparing Nations* (New Haven: Yale University Press, 1966); and Mattei Dogan and Stein Rokkan, eds., *Quantitative Econological Analysis* (Cambridge: Harvard University Press, 1974).

9. Tony Smith, "Requiem or New Agenda for Third World Studies?" *World Politics* 38, no. 4 (July 1985), pp. 532-61. See also David E. Apter, *Introduction to Political Analysis* (Cambridge: Winthrop, 1977), pp. 453-527; and Bertrand Badie, *Le development politique* (Paris: Economica, 1984).

10. Kenneth J. Arrow, *Social Choice and Individual Values* (New Haven: Yale University Press, 1951). Also Joan Robinson, *Essays in the Theory of Economic Growth* (London: Macmillan, 1964).

11. Ludwig Wittgenstein, *Philosophical Investigations* (New York: Macmillan, 1958). Also Edmund Leach, *Culture and Communication* (Cambridge: Cambridge University Press, 1976).

12. Claude Levi-Strauss, *The Savage Mind* (Chicago: University of Chicago Press, 1966), pp. 18-26.

13. Harry G. Johnson, *Economic Nationalism in Old and New States* (London: George Allen & Unwin, 1968). Also Ernest Gellner, *Nations and Nationalism,* (Ithaca: Cornell University Press, 1983).

14. In modernizing societies, the perspective is one of "marginalization." In industrial societies, the same process is often described under the general rubric of "deindustrial-

ization." See the special issue of *Revista Latinoamericana de Sociologia* 5, no. 2 (July 1969), "La Marginalid en America Latina" (Buenos Aires: Centro de Investigaciones del Instituto Torcuato Di Tella). Also Frank Blackaby, ed., *De-Industrialization* (London: Heinemann, 1978).

15. Gullermo A. O'Donnell, *Modernization and Authoritarianism* (Berkeley: Institute of International Studies, 1973).

16. Aristide R. Zolberg, *Creating Political Order* (Chicago: Rand McNally, 1962).

17. Colin Leys, *Underdevelopment in Kenya* (Berkeley: University of California Press, 1974), pp. 1-27.

18. Daniel Bell, *The Cultural Contradictions of Capitalism* (New York: Basic Books, 1976). Also Claus Offe, *Contradictions of the Welfare State* (Cambridge: MIT Press, 1984); and Peter Gourevitch et al., *Unions and Democratic Crisis: Britain, West Germany and Sweden* (London: George Allen & Unwin, 1984).

19. Peter Berger, Brigitte Berger, and Hansfried Kellner, *The Homeless Mind* (New York: Random House, 1973).

20. Marion J. Levy, Jr., *Modernization and the Structure of Societies*, vol. 1 (Princeton, NJ: Princeton University Press, 1966).

21. Talcott Parsons, *The Social System* (New York: Free Press, 1951). Also T. Parsons, "The Present Status of 'Structural-Functional' Theory in Sociology" in *Social Systems and the Evolution of Action-Theory*, T. Parsons (New York: Free Press, 1977). See also William Buxton, *Talcott Parsons and the Capitalistic National State* (Toronto: University of Toronto Press, 1985).

22. Jean Viet, *Les methodes structuralistes dans les sciences sociales* (Paris: Mouton, 1965).

23. Lucien Sebag, *Marxism et Structuralism* (Paris: Payot, 1964).

24. Nicos Poulzntzas, *State, Power, Socialism* (London: Verso Editions, 1980).

25. Levi-Strauss, *The Savage Mind*, p. 130.

26. David E. Apter and Nagayo Sawa, *Against the State* (Cambridge: Harvard University Press, 1984).

27. Jürgen Habermas, *Communication and the Evolution of Society* (Boston: Beacon Press, 1976). Also J. L. Austin, *How to Do Things with Words* (Oxford: Oxford University Press, 1962).

28. Jean-Paul Sartre, *Critique of Dialectical Reason* (London: New Left Books, 1976).

29. Paul Ricoeur, *The Symbolism of Evil* (Boston: Beacon, 1969). Also Hans-Georg Gadamer, *Truth and Method* (New York: Seabury Press, 1975); and Fredric Jameson, *The Political Unconscious* (Ithaca: Cornell University Press, 1981).

30. Martin Jay, *The Dialectical Imagination* (Boston: Little Brown, 1973).

31. Habermas, *Communication*.

32. Pierre Bourdieu, *Outline of a Theory of Practice* (Cambridge: Cambridge University Press, 1977).

33. McClelland, *The Achieving Society*. Also S. N. Eisenstadt, *The Protestant Ethic and Modernization* (New York: Basic Books, 1968).

34. Joseph A. Schumpeter, *Capitalism, Socialism, and Democracy* (New York: Harpers, 1947). Also Robert A. Dahl and Charles E. Lindblom, *Politics, Economics and Welfare* (New York: Harper, 1953).

35. Charles E. Lindblom, *Politics and Markets* (New York: Basic Books, 1957).

36. Anthony Downs, *An Economic Theory of Democracy* (New York: Harper, 1957).

37. Kenneth J. Arrow, *Social Change and Individual Values* (New Haven: Yale University Press, 1951).

38. James M. Buchanan and Gordon Tullock, *The Calculus of Consent* (Ann Arbor: University of Michigan Press, 1967).

39. Steven Lukes, *Power* (London: Macmillan, 1974).

40. Gabriel A. Almond and Sidney Verba, *The Civic Culture* (Princeton, NJ: Princeton University Press, 1963). Also James S. Coleman, ed., *Education and Political Development* (Princeton, NJ: Princeton University Press, 1965).

41. Claus Offe, *Disorganized Capitalism* (Cambridge: Polity Press, 1985).

42. See the useful discussion of radical dependency theory in Leys, *Underdevelopment in Kenya*. Also Gary Gereffi, *The Pharmaceutical Industry and Dependency in the Third World* (Princeton, NJ: Princeton University Press, 1983), pp. 3-49.

43. Herbert L. Sussman, *Victorians and the Machine* (Cambridge, MA: Harvard University Press, 1968).

44. Most of the critical theory in the dependency tradition has its origin in Paul Baran's *The Political Economy of Growth* (New York: Monthly Review Press, 1962), which was extremely influential in Latin America.

45. Leonard Binder et al., *Crises and Sequences in Political Development* (Princeton, NJ: Princeton University Press, 1971). Also G. A. Almond, Scott C. Flanagan, and Robert J. Mundt, *Crisis, Choice, and Change* (Boston: Little Brown, 1973).

46. Immanuel Wallerstein, "Modernization: Requiescat in Pace" in *The Uses of Controversy in Sociology*, ed. Lewis A. Coser and Otto N. Larsen (New York: Macmillan, 1976), pp. 131-35.

47. Clifford Geertz, *The Interpretation of Cultures* (New York: Basic Books, 1973).

48. Gabriel A. Almond and James S. Coleman, eds., *The Politics of the Developing Areas* (Princeton, NJ: Princeton University Press, 1960), pp. 3-64. Also David Easton, *A Systems Analysis of Political Life* (New York: John Wiley, 1965).

49. Robert T. Holt and John E. Turner, *The Political Basis of Economic Development* (Princeton, NJ: Van Nostrand, 1966).

50. See the discussion of this point by Thomas McCarthy in "Complexity and Democracy, or the Seducements of Systems Theory," *New German Critique*, no. 35 (Spring/Summer 1985), p. 47.

51. Charles Tilly, *Big Structures, Large Processes, Huge Comparisons* (New York: Russell Sage, 1984).

52. See the critique of dependency theory by Colin Leys, "African Economic Development in Theory and Practice," *Daedalus* (Spring 1982), pp. 99-123.

53. Karl Marx and Frederick Engels, "Manifesto of the Communist Party" in *Marx and Engels, Selected Works* (Moscow: Foreign Languages, 1962), pp. 34-45.

54. Smith, "Requiem or New Agenda," p. 549.

55. For all its significance for identifying larger scale structural change, the danger of world system theory is to eliminate any sense of discretionary power on the part of groups, societies, and states. See Immanuel Wallerstein, *The Modern World-System I* (New York: Academic Press, 1974), and *The Modern World-System II* (New York: Academic Press, 1980). Also the critique in Tilly, *Big Structures, Large Processes*.

56. Leys, "African Economic Development."

57. Fernando Henrique Cardoso and Enzo Faletto, *Dependency and Development in Latin America* (Berkeley: University of California Press, 1979). Also Michael Lipton, *Why Poor People Stay Poor* (Cambridge, MA: Harvard University Press, 1976).

58. For a study of the "coding" consequences of such polarization, see Basil Bernstein, *Class, Codes and Control* (London: Routledge & Kegan Paul, 1971). Also Samuel Bowles and Herbert Giutis, *Schooling in Capitalist America* (New York: Basic Books, 1976). Also the *New York Times*, 20 October 1985, "A New Generation of Poor Youths Emerges in U.S."

59. Peter F. Drucker, *Foreign Affairs* (Spring 1986), pp. 768-69.

60. Blackaby, *De-Industrialization.* Also Lester C. Thorow, *The Zero-Sum Society* (New York: Basic Books, 1980). See also Jean Leca and Robert Papini, *Les Democrates, Sont-Elles Gouvernables?* (Paris: Economica, 1985).

61. James O'Connor, *The Fiscal Crisis of the State* (New York: St. Martin's Press, 1973).

62. *New York Times*, 6 March 1986.

63. Drucker, "The Changed World Economy," p. 776. Drucker points out that where deindustrialization has occurred, that is, in Britain, it is because the number of blue-collar workers went down more slowly than in all other non-Communist nations, although Britain also had the highest rate of unemployment—above 13%.

64. Gourevitch et al., *Unions and Democratic Crisis.* Also Alain Touraine, Michel Wievorka, and Francois Dubet, *Le mouvement ouvrier* (Paris: Fayard, 1984).

65. Fred Hirsch, *Social Limits to Growth* (Cambridge, MA: Harvard University Press, 1976).

66. David E. Apter, *Ghana in Transition* (Princeton, NJ: Princeton University Press, 1973).

67. David E. Apter, *The Political Kingdom in Uganda* (Princeton, NJ: Princeton University Press, 1971).

68. Apter and Sawa, *Against the State.*

69. Jean-Francois Lyotard, *The Postmodern Condition* (Minneapolis: University of Minnesota Press, 1984).

70. Francois Furet, Antoine Liniers, and Philippe Raynaud, *Terrorisme et democratie* (Paris: Fayard, 1985).

71. Jameson, *The Political Unconscious.*

72. Bourdieu, *Outline of a Theory.*

73. Roland Barthes, *Mythologies* (New York: Hill and Wang, 1983). Also Georges Bataille, *Literature and Evil* (New York: Urizen Books, 1973), pp. 145-79; and Ricoeur, *Symbolism of Evil.*

74. Leach, *Culture and Communication.*

75. Levi-Strauss, *The Savage Mind*, p. 19. Also his "The Structural Study of Myth," *Structural Anthropology* (New York: Basic Books, 1963), pp. 206-30.

76. Jean-Paul Sartre, "Foreword" in *The Thief's Journal*, Jean Genet (New York: Grove Press, 1964).

77. David Moss, "The Kidnapping and Murder of Aldo Moro," *Archive for European Sociology* 22 (1981), pp. 265-95.

78. Offe, *Disorganized Capital.*

PART I

FOR THE STATE

TOWARD A THEORY OF MODERNIZATION

Camus makes Sisyphus his hero. Sisyphus, returning again and again to roll his rock up the hill, may appear absurd. Yet on each occasion he is happy. How odd that seems! And how like our own times. The work of modernization is the burden of this age. It is our rock. It is an objective that is not confined to a single place or region, to a particular country or class, or to a privileged group of people. Modernization, and the desire for it, reaches around the world. No matter how difficult the labor, or even, at times, how fruitless, the rock is shouldered once again, eagerly and with hope. Perhaps it is the element of hope that allows Camus to conclude his essay on the Greek myth with the words, "One must imagine Sisyphus happy."[1]

Modernization is a special kind of hope. Embodied within it are all the past revolutions of history and all the supreme human desires. The modernization revolution is epic in its scale and moral in its significance. Its consequences may be frightening. Any goal that is so desperately desired creates political power, and this force may not always be used wisely or well. Whatever direction it may take, the struggle to modernize is what has given meaning to our generation. It tests our cherished institutions and our beliefs. It puts our country in the marketplace of ideas and ideologies. So compelling a force has it become that we are forced to ask new questions of our own institutions. Each country, whether modernized or modernizing, stands in both judgment and fear of the results. Our own society is no exception. Democratic representative government is clearly an appropriate means by which highly complex and advanced industrial societies have solved serious and perplexing social and moral problems. It has been a dramatic achievement in the West to devise suitable mechanisms for resolving the twin political problems that all governments encounter: orderly change and peaceful succession in office. Much of the study of Western government has been concerned with how to improve these mechanisms. Only recently have social scientists, and more particularly students of politics, directed their attention to similar problems in modernizing societies. Most of such studies, however, have accepted the point of view that representative government, with a few alterations in form and accommodations in spirit, is the most suitable form for all societies.

Events have clearly changed this assumption. Democratic institutions, as we know them, have undergone such radical transformations in most modernizing societies that it would be sheer blindness on our part not to recognize that they have become something else. Yet how should we regard such countries as Indonesia or Egypt, Ghana or Tanzania? Or, for that matter, India, where the spirit of representative government remains embedded in a Congress party that dwarfs and overwhelms its opposition? There is no comfortable answer. What we are witnessing in the world today is a range of accommodated political systems. Even the toughest of them is weak. Even the most monolithic in form tends to be divided in its practices and diluted in its ideas. Few are totalitarian. Almost all are populist and, in a real sense, mainly *pre*democratic rather than *anti*democratic.

Such systems require both sympathy and understanding. The language of politics needs to be adjusted in part to account for them. All lie somewhere between familiar extreme categories of political forms. To approach such societies as predemocratic allows us to view certain institutions of coercion as perhaps necessary to the organization and integration of a modernizing community. We need to confront the possibility that representative institutions may fail to work in most modernizing societies and, therefore, will be discredited. The preoccupation of political studies with the strengthening of democratic practices has obscured the need for an examination of the role of predemocratic forms of government, which, as a result, has received little attention. The politics of modernization requires us to examine the uses of predemocratic and nondemocratic institutions so that we can make a realistic appraisal of those structural principles likely to lead to representative government.[2]

The dynamic aspect of modernization for the study of politics can be expressed in the general proposition that modernization is a process of increasing complexity in human affairs within which the polity must act. This is why it creates severe political problems. Politics becomes, in large measure, the business of coping with role differentiation while integrating organizational structures. Political actions that arise from such increasing complexity, however, are not pure responses by political leaders outside a political context. The question is, what is the *political context*? In the sense in which the phrase is used here, it refers to the particular arrangements by which government exercises authority. As these structures change, so will political responses, and as political responses change, so will structures.

The translation of general approaches in systems theory into an empirical study of modernization is itself a major problem of research. It involves, first, determining the level of reality to be observed and, second, relating the formal system to a set of empirical categories.[3] These are arbitrary decisions, but the research enterprise itself depends on them. Here we will consider "reality" in terms of the ways in which people identify themselves and achieve and express emotional bonds. This is expressed symbolically in the literature and art of a group of people, in their ideology, and in their religious forms of expression. Moreover, such bonds exist in a commonsense world in which everyday events are translatable into abstract forms, for motive and meaning, in much the same way that abstract and geometrical designs may express shared symbolic values in such folk arts as pottery or weaving.

But there are other levels of reality. One common level in the post-Marxian tradition is social stratification. For observers trained in the Western tradition and concerned with problems of modern industrial society, a useful way to order social and political relations for purposes of comparison is through the study of stratification. Not only does this imply sets of positions in a hierarchical arrangement and an examination of the elite-mass relationships that result from such a hierarchy, but it also leads to the differentiation of strata in terms of interests and thus implies a theory of motivation—for example, that people are socially aware and upwardly mobile. Hence, competitive mobility becomes the motive of politics.

This view may serve to exclude an equally valid conception of the community as a reinforcing set of cohesive roles in which the meaning of the self is determined by the collectivity rather than by the hierarchical arrangements of roles. For example, when one examines a Latin American community after studying North American urban society, it makes sense to compare hierarchical relations with a view to discovering how much access and mobility exist. This is a useful comparative approach and a common one. But when one examines a Latin American community after studying African societies, one is inclined to seek some underlying principle of coherence as well. What are the core roles that constitute the meaningful center of the community? How do departures from the meaningful center affirm or deny the central values of the society? This kind of study requires more of an anthropological approach, an abstraction (in the range of reality) from a set of segregated roles, less on the basis of hierarchy than on the basis of meaningfulness (for example, kinship). Such a study can stress aspects of roles that help reveal the stability of a system no matter how much change is under way.

Personal meaning and social meaning; the rhythm and pace of social activity; the roles of the misfit and the innovator; the hierarchy of power and prestige; concern with interpersonal associations, political ideology, religion—each of these implies a different pattern of desire, motive, and choice. Knowledge of these patterns lies between that revealed by structural and behavioral analyses of any given social system. For these meanings and levels of reality, we need to screen individuals in their roles, identify congeries of roles in which individuals act, understand the mechanisms by means of which the regulation of roles takes place, and be aware of the symbols by which unities and disunities in roles are articulated.

Perhaps the most important consequence of the study of modernization is that it brings us back to the search for first principles. By this I mean that it requires the unity of moral and analytical modes of thought. Not the study of modernization alone, of course; the rapid-fire developments in social theory and the breakthroughs in the biological sciences, not to speak of the retreat of philosophy into linguistics, have combined to render us philosophically defenseless and muddled. The two most characteristic responses to this state of affairs on the meeting ground between social theory and philosophy have been, first, Marxism, with its insistence on the material plane of reality (which involves the unfolding of historical necessity and the obliteration of the idea of freedom and that can only be genuinely "known" through action), and a second response that does not have a convenient name. The latter involves theories of choice that arise from the analysis of alternative situations in normative, structural, and behavioral terms. This second view depends on a probabilistic rather than a deterministic universe, and its central principle is that there is a relationship between freedom and choosing and that the understanding of this relationship is the object of social analysis. Freedom, in such a view, lies in the critical awareness by the chooser of both the moral and the material consequences of choice.

If the Marxian point of view seems faintly old-fashioned as a philosophy, as an ideology it has force and freshness, especially for those living in developing areas. One reason for this is Marxism's insistence on an evolving material universe that proceeds from a lower to a higher plane. Modernization, in this view, can be understood as a series of altering material relationships out of which a more abundant (and kindlier) world will eventually emerge. Indeed, Sartre speaks of Marxism's appropriateness as a philosophy of scarcity, in the sense that it derives its political relevance from the explanation of scarcity in terms of class conflict and exploitation. He has also dared to challenge contemporary Marxism by adding to it the idea of freedom. Freedom, for Sartre, consists of the ability to understand a relationship between the being of the self and the process of the material world, that is, its functioning. For him work is the means by which the material world and the process of being are coordinated. It is in work, and the projects that man sets for himself, that he becomes part of the material world itself and acts upon it. Sartre's position would appear to take him far away from Marxism despite his stated intention to remain within its doctrine.[4]

One important criticism of Marxism is that it cannot present the universe as a contrived reality. Such a criticism may sound surprising. If one accepts the view that there is more than one layer of reality, however, then the idea that there is a single layer, the material, on which items of knowledge may be grafted is unacceptable. From a probabilistic view, the choice of a layer of reality is arbitrary. Selection and definition of appropriate levels are determined by the questions one is asking. Moreover, each level embodies its own theories and contextual rules. A normative plane of reality, for example, demands the use of particular rules for understanding normative evaluations. This type of evaluation is part of the analysis of behavior. Separate analysis of structural and behavioral layers of action result in the derivation of different kinds of theories. They can be examined on their own terms, as when the psychologist studies motivational aspects of behavior, and they can be unified into an integrated body of ideas. The latter is what we call a general theory.

If one accepts the notion that there are different layers of meaning relevant to the understanding of choice, one must also take a further step and accept the implicit idea of the observer. By this I mean that the probabilistic approach to reality requires one to occupy the role of observer rather than participant, a passive rather than an active role for the analyst *qua* analyst (as distinct from citizen, revolutionary, reformer, or whatever activist role he may choose to play as an individual rather than as a professional). The probabilistic universe is one in which we are *observers* rather than *workers*.

One difficulty with this approach is that it is better in providing criteria for evaluating what is already consciously known that it is in exploring new layers of consciousness. The latter processes are, at the present state of knowledge, most mysterious ones. Not much is known about how new insights and levels of consciousness are formed. We do know that action can be a way of creating new forms of consciousness. But if this is so, will we not be required to change our role from observer to worker?

One answer is that in practice we move back and forth between these two roles—between observer and worker, between a passive and an active form of observation. Our movement between social philosophies is similar—between some new form of Marxism (stripped of its ideology) and a probabilistic approach to reality. Indeed, one can argue the existence of an interesting dialectic between the two that is a reflection of the movement from the role of observer to that of worker, with the resulting multidimensionality that provides a good basis for viewing both the self in action and the self's action in a wider context. Just as the existentialist wants to locate new layers of meaning between man and his universe through the study of his work, so the probabilist wants to translate these meanings into more rigorous analytical systems that may lead to experimental and operational (contrived) forms of analysis.

Separately, each approach implies different modes of interpretation. The Marxian-existential leads to a single place of reality, the material. The probabilistic leads to a factoring of truths observed at each layer of reality—a probabilistic consensus (not truth but likelihood). The Marxian-existential, by virtue of its emphasis on "totalization" (synthesis), makes that single reality all-encompassing and, therefore, too gross to provide answers to questions that lie within it. Is it really useful to study class today, or is it more interesting to study the total situation of choice and the role of class in that situation? Indeed, we need to know more than the ways in which the instruments of competitive conflict reflect material aspects of life—rather, we must see them in the context of our understanding of choice and the precise nature of the relationship involved in choice. This brings me to the concept of choice itself, which I regard as the focal point of the social sciences, uniting normative, structural, and behavioral theory.

MODERNITY AS CHOICE

Some would place the origin of inquiries into modernity in ancient Greece. There, certainly, the distinction between Greek and barbarian comprehended many of the ideas that help us discriminate between the modern and something else, in particular, the idea of the self-conscious pursuit of human ends within a context of critical scrutiny and moral questioning. But can it be said that in this sense the Greeks were any more modern than the ancient Chinese? I doubt it. Indeed, both venerated education, which is an indication that culture was for them a self-conscious concern. Concern with culture in itself, however, is not necessarily modern, even though modern societies are preoccupied with it.

We would perhaps need to look elsewhere for origins of the critical complex of meanings we call modern. One possible view is that modernity began when men gained insight into their economies. With measurable units (money), they found ways to assess preferences, controlling them within a context of a rapidly changing technology. With such concerns, there emerged the desire to make explanations and predictions about social and political life. Certainly, the late mercantilist economists and the early laissez-faire theorists, the physiocrats, and above all Adam Smith, abstracted the mechanisms of choice and exchange from the range of activities of which daily life was composed. Thus modernization as the process leading to the state of modernity begins when man tries to solve the allocation problem, just as social science was born with the study of choice and preference.

In my view, modernization as a noneconomic process originates when a culture embodies an attitude of inquiry and questioning about how men make choices—moral (or normative), social (or structural), and personal (or behavioral). The problem of choice is central for modern man. This is the reason political scientists have so often called Machiavelli the first of the modern political writers and the reason classical and antique civilizations, no matter how noble their conceptions, are nevertheless not modern. To be modern means to see life as alternatives, preferences, and choices.

Self-conscious choice implies rationality. Men will in principle see more than one alternative as plausible. Preferences include the ranking of priorities, and about these reasonable men may differ. Therefore, debate and discussion are characteristics of modernity. In fact, to my mind, they are the critical and minimal conditions of modernity. The

Greeks came close, as did the Romans, which is one reason they fascinate us. But as Fustel de Coulanges shows, the essential features of their cultures were set within the frameworks of religion and kinship, and to impute modernity to them is to forget this.[5]

More important, perhaps, self-conscious concern with choice has led to an attitude of experiment and invention that has changed man's entire outlook. Nature became controllable. Human affairs could be seen as ultimately explicable. The cumulative effect of innovation through industrialization in those parts of the world that became the most dynamic and explosive was to make it clear that modernity was not the property of the few, or of a scientific elite, but rather a fact of culture. Hence, in these times, more than ever before, it is not only interesting but also important to recognize this characteristic of modernity: choice. Societies are now able to choose a direction and means of change. For this reason, theory that can explain how men choose is important. For this reason, too, the normative aspects are critical.

To carry this point of view about choice one step further: a political system becomes a system of choice for a particular collectivity. Government, which I will define in greater detail later on, is the mechanism for regulating choice. Different political systems will not only embody different ways of choosing but vary in their priorities. Governments will vary in the ways they regulate choice. Thus there are different systems of choice, and there are choices between systems. One of the characteristics of the modernization process is that it involves both aspects of choice: the improvement of the conditions of choice and the selection of the most satisfactory mechanisms of choice.

IMPLICATIONS OF CHOICE

The outermost significance of choice is not methodological in any narrow sense but moral. Choices by an individual define his moral personality. Choices by governments constitute the moral aims of society and reflect the ambitions of those within it, thus constituting that measure of satisfaction that will lead ultimately to a stable order. The efforts to find such a moral condition, however, may lead to the most violent and unstable human conditions. The most dramatic of these results from a change in political systems. In such periods, the loftiest human purposes may be expressed in violence. Whatever the situation, it is in such times that men make explicit those core values they hope will lead to both a moral community and moral individuals. Perhaps this is the ultimate secret of political life. It is an endless search, sometimes through violence and often in fear of it, for a moral community through which man hopes to realize his individual moral personality. Perhaps, too, it is the ceaselessness of the search itself that gives man his claim to humanity.

Within a general framework that embodies moral "intentionality," we want to know the direction in which society is headed in order to understand the basis on which its authority rests. We seek clues as to whether nations will confound their moral purposes or realize them through modernization, and we generally accept some well-entrenched values as universals, not because they are embodied in natural law or natural rights, but because they are sufficiently widespread to seem rooted in common sense—such values as the respect and dignity accorded to individuals, and the opportunities provided for each to realize his potentiality. No modern societies today deny these ideas, although some have strange ways of attempting to achieve them.

These concerns, although they are important for comparative studies in general, are particularly interesting when applied to modernizing and new nations (those that have emerged from colonial status), which must wrestle directly with problems of equity and authority as a matter of survival. Countries recently removed from subject status, only to confront grave problems, may have little time for moral abstractions. (It is presumed, however, that when people take their first sturdy steps toward an independence of spirit and mind and an improved political condition they will do so in the manner that suits them best.)

THE NORMATIVE APPROACH

Perhaps the simplest way to summarize the discussion so far is to try to translate the distinctions that have been used into types of legitimacy. We can then show the problems that arise when legitimacy and political forms are fitted together into a type of political system.

The Western ideal of government is based on the primacy of the libertarian principle. The moral purpose of government is to maximize the condition of freedom. But freedom must lead to equity. One alternative form, the communist, emphasizes the fulfillment of potentiality. This emphasis, a developmental one, is the main reason for the moral attractiveness of Marxism to many people in modernizing societies. This is a surprising view of Marxism given that it is far removed from the original analysis of Marx. For him, it was the libertarian system under capitalism that achieved development through revolutionary changes in technique and technology; in fact, for him, this was its main accomplishment.

The developmental objective as a principle of legitimacy is very difficult to evaluate. Some would argue that the most efficient forms of economic growth can be realized by adding the objective of liberty to that of development. Others would argue that the Marxist idea that the potentiality of the citizen is realized only through the actions of the collectivity is the most significant contemporary means of development.

However we treat these principles of legitimacy, they are clearly related. If the explicit moral rationale for a modernizing society is development, it is ordinarily expressed in terms of realizing potentialities, human and social. I will argue that as such potentialities come within range of achievement, so will the libertarian ideal. At least that is my hope.

The political link between equity and liberty, on one hand, and equity and potentiality, on the other, has been, historically, the ideal of equality. In modernizing societies, it remains a powerful moral force. Because it remains largely unrealized, the management of tensions is often a considerable problem in the new nations. This is one reason they have frequently relied on autocratic and personal rule. When, on the other hand, they have adopted a more democratic approach to government, they have often been plagued by instabilities. One reason for this is that unplanned development results in social inequalities, which can easily harden into more or less permanently organized classes, each with its own subculture, as has occurred in many parts of Latin America. Here, then, are some of the main problems that a normative view of modernization identifies. Can democracy work for modernizing societies? If it fails to work in particular cases, what alternative systems will replace it? In order to answer these questions, we need a better idea of what we mean by different kinds of "systems."

Although it is unfair to judge modernizing societies from the peculiar standpoint of our own political forms, we must nevertheless put their efforts in a universal moral cast; otherwise we would demean their significance. It is no service to the modernizing nations (or ourselves) to judge their policies purely on the basis of utility. Government is, after all, a reflection of the nobler as well as the mundane purposes for which people live in society. In this sense, no government is better than its moral standards, and no valid moral judgment is premature.[6]

If we accept the view that government actions must be judged in moral terms here and now (and as the realization of morally valid goals), what are useful criteria to employ? This is a difficult but crucial question. Asking the moral questions compels us to find appropriate forms of inquiry. In this sense, it is morality that impels us to science, not the reverse. In politics we have some old and still serviceable standards: government should not be capricious; its politicians should not misuse public power; they should remain deferential to their trust; and so on. How far is it possible to extend these questions to matters of political form as ordinarily conceived? Probably not very far. It is no good evaluating governments on the basis of their organization. A single-party state, for example, may be meaningfully democratic. A supreme court may not be decisive in developing the rule of law. Concrete forms of rule have many functional consequences, and there is no simple relationship between organization, form, and substance.[7]

This point of view lies at the heart of political science, which, as distinct from the other social sciences, begins with the moral aspects of choice. Difficulties arise for comparative studies because we have enshrined moral principles in models that have served well in a Western political context. The models we derive from concepts of justice, equity, and the good society may be quite inappropriate for modernizing societies. In our haste for political science to take on the attributes of a science by employing analogies inspired by investigations in the natural sciences, we may confuse form and substance.

Specifically, what I reject are the comfortably formulated descriptive models that are assumed to embody abstract principles of virtue, when, in reality, they embody our preferences and prejudices—for example, the definition of democracy as the operation of a two-party or multiparty system because "totalitarian" systems exclude more than one party. If we reject descriptive and simplistic models, however, with what can they be replaced?

My analysis will try to answer this kind of question. All around us new moral communities are being established, and the context of moral fulfillment is modernization. Different authority systems modernize by allocating mundane and sacred rewards and promises. Some are more directly devoted to the allocation of the mundane in the hope that individual morality will be encouraged by the satisfaction of mundane wants and that political morality will be reflected in the summation of individual moralities. Others are more interested in seeing an ideal of the moral community realized and mundane satisfactions restricted except as they serve long-run opportunities for achieving the moral community. The one emphasizes the present, and the other the future. If these assumptions are correct we might even say that the way in which man copes with uncertainty is his individual test as a moral personality; and differing political systems offer different solutions to the uncertainty of man—the most demanding of contemporary problems.

This moral basis of politics, I suggest, determines the meaning of legitimate authority. *Authority* can be said to be a definition of political morality in a particular setting. In the final analysis, it is the problem of the individual or, to use an old-fashioned phrase, a matter of conscience. It is linked to such personal dimensions as immortality, purpose, and meaning. Politics is peculiar insofar as principles of legitimacy are normative first and structural second. Indeed, this relationship of the normative and the structural underlies the theme of analysis employed here as follows. The two normative principles described above, liberty and potentiality, become principles of legitimacy; the first we associate with democracy, and the second has been linked historically with the ideal of the evolution of a community. The forms of government most frequently associated with the types of legitimacy are, in the first instance, constitutional representation, embodying what can be called pyramidal authority and decentralization of power to critical subunits of the system, and, in the second instance, centrally controlled systems, embodying hierarchical authority (see Figure 2.1). These categories will lead us to the development of universalized types of political systems, each of which deals differently with the problem of modernization.

THE STRUCTURAL APPROACH

Structural analysis is concerned with the limits within which particular choices take place.[8] To gain some understanding of these, we need to compare units with one another. Hence, the structural aspects of this study begin in comparison and classification, in a search for basic principles around which to cluster data. Beginning with a concrete unit of analysis, we ask, What functions must be performed to ensure the survival of that unit and all others of the same type?

Principles of Legitimacy	Form of Government
Equity—"democracy"	Constitutional representation (pyramidal authority)
Potentiality—"community"	Centrally controlled system (hierarchical authority)

Figure 2.1 Legitimacy and Structure

A structural approach is useful for comparison partly because it avoids the problem of dealing with the unique. For example, we are accustomed to regarding democracy as uniquely related to a multiparty form of competitive politics. If, however, we consider democracy as a system of rule, a function of which includes public checks on arbitrary power, then it is possible to conceive of situations in which a single party, through its internal factions, serves much the same purpose. Structural analysis, then, helps avoid the familiar fallacy that whatever is is necessary.

As another example, we ordinarily think of government as a specialized instrument of rule. Society X has no such specialized instrument. We then conclude that it functions without a government. But what we really mean is that certain societies are without a formal governmental organization. Because the functions of government can be met in diverse ways, our attention must then logically be directed to other instruments of social life to see if they perform a political role. Government can thus exist where no formal structure exists, and may be found in kinship systems, religious bodies, or other organizations that we are not accustomed to thinking of as government but that, in fact, are carrying out the functions of government.

Still another reason for using a structural method is that, by means of its requisite-analysis form, we may delimit the conditions within which a given system can continue to operate. Structural studies assign significance to activities in such a way as to separate the crucial from the epiphenomenal. Structuralism allows us to apply logical tests (experiments in the mind, as it were) to macro-problems that cannot be neatly controlled in the laboratory.

Structural analysis is itself a comparative method, in a form that directs our attention to an analytical level of thought rather than a descriptive level. The object is to see functional meaning in many diverse activities. Functional equivalences in different actions do not mean, of course, that one action is really like another. There is functional uniqueness, just as there is functional similarity. The principle to be followed is an old one. First, we observe many cases in order to find and exhaust functional similarities; then we proceed to uniqueness. Structural analysis must, therefore, be seen in stages: from the general to the particular, from the universal to the unique. At each succeeding stage, what was residual and left in the interstices of the previous stage now becomes central. This descending order of procedure is cumbersome (comparison is not a very efficient method of building theory) but extremely interesting.

What stages of analysis are involved? Three might be demarcated. The first of these, as we have already suggested, is typological but goes beyond classification to an analytical clustering of characteristics against which concrete systems may be evaluated. This is the basis of "ideal-type" analysis, used so effectively by the late nineteenth-century historical sociologists. Ideal types qualify for the appellation "scientific," for they are essentially statements of system, that is, an ordered and coherent relationship between parts. Essentially intuitive and non-experimental, they nevertheless engage our attention because they arrange experience in a useful manner. Indeed, Carl G. Hempel has argued that ideal types can be regarded as significant only if they are interpreted as theoretical systems, that is, by (1) specifying a list of characteristics with which the theory is to deal, (2) formulating a set of hypotheses in terms of those characteristics, (3) giving those characteristics an empirical interpretation that assigns to the theory a specific domain of application, and (4) as a long-range objective, incorporating the theoretical system, as a "special case," into a more comprehensive theory.[9]

This first stage of the analysis requires, at the start, the delineation of boundaries of the units. The selection of units depends on the nature of the problem, but a useful rule of thumb is to look for the largest membership group that meaningfully encompasses the activities we want to examine—in our case, the nation-state.

The second stage of analysis involves us in the problem of meaning. What intrinsic consequences do the activities performed by the unit, arranged in some classification, have for the system? What would happen if some major category of activity was no longer performed? Would the system be able to remain stable, that is, could the boundaries maintain themselves? These questions lead to the form of structural analysis known as requisite analysis, in which the functions that have been delineated are considered as a minimal and irreducible set necessary to the maintenance of the unit. From the functions so selected, the structures are established by a series of logical and empirical exercises. The activities are examined again in order to determine the means by which they deal with the functions. Functions stress meaning in the sense that they indicate the significance of some activities and their equivalences in diverse activities. These functions are the core problems that all systems of a similar type need to handle. Structures are ways to handle the functionally defined problems.[10]

The third stage in structural analysis is the derivation of theories about the data. It is this last aspect of structural analysis that preoccupies us. Our theories will be made explicit, although in this study I make no attempt to marshal supporting data.[11]

Structural analysis, then, is useful for several reasons. It reduces the risk of ethnocentrism. It delineates changes in systematic terms and forces the observer to examine meanings of the basis of function. It points up the core problems facing systems. It provides an orderly way of examining large numbers of cases in order to develop comparative theories.

THE BEHAVIORAL APPROACH

Behavioral analysis is concerned with a different level of explanation. Whereas structural analysis is mainly concerned with delimiting the conditions within which social choices are possible, behavioral analysis is concerned with which social choices are made and why. The behavioral looks inside the actors. This method is similar to Weber's category of *Verstehen*. What he regarded as unique to the human sciences, as distinct from the natural sciences, was the capacity of the observer to put himself in the position of someone else and ask questions about motivation. This, however, involves us in a different level of analysis. The structural approach, we have suggested, is an effort to find general properties of systems that limit the range of action open to individuals. This range of action will vary from system to system. The gross behavior delimited is particularly useful for large-scale comparative studies. What is sought is analytical or qualitative, logical rather than quantitative. In contrast, behavioral analysis, which emphasizes quantitative methods, takes us directly into the study of motivation, symbolic behavior, and, in particular, moral conduct, as these aspects affect individual choice.

Most of the theoretical questions we confront here fall in an area between structural and behavioral theories. There have been many efforts to close this gap; every general theory tries to do do. In this book I will incorporate several structural and behavioral ideas into a single system for the comparative analysis of political modernization. The analysis can be seen as an inquiry into the conditions that establish and maintain authority during modernization. One approach is to consider the relationship between authority and support. When we consider this set of conditions as analogous to the marketplace, we can observe that individuals maximize benefits by supporting authority. The alternative analogy, the community as an organism—a collectivity with a life of its own—emphasizes the nonempirical ends of supporting authority. The emotional warmth, the sense of creativity, and other "feelings" and states of mind produced by the leader may be sufficient to retain loyalties for a very long time in the absence of concrete benefits. Why? Explanations will in some measure lie in behavioral theories of how loyalties are formed.[12]

It is important to remember that normative aspects of systems are embodied in both structure and behavior. For example, roles are differentiated on the basis of publicly accepted notions of subordinate and superordinate relationships. And the behavior of individuals reflects norms that have become part of the motivational system of individuals. Indeed, many important areas of inquiry, such as the analysis of political socialization, deal with the way norms are absorbed and internalized through the blending of structural and behavioral principles in concrete instrumentalities (like schools) by concrete individuals.

CHOICES BETWEEN
POLITICAL SYSTEMS

The analysis that follows brings together the three approaches—normative, structural, and behavioral—by centering on models of government described in terms of two main criteria: degree of hierarchy and type of values. The first is the measure of stringency of control and is structurally visible in the degree of centralization of authority. The second criterion is the degree to which ultimate ends are employed in action, with ultimate ends understood as "religion" and intermediate ends as "secularity," following Durkheim's distinction between sacred and secular ends. The extremes of these factors combine to form four models, of which two, the secular-libertarian and the sacred-collectivity, are the most interesting. These two normative models are in perpetual conflict and are constantly in danger of being transformed into each other.

Although we insist on the normative characteristics of these models, with all that that implies in terms of types of authority, the distinctions we will use here accord with most of the comparative schemes that have gained currency today that are based on the degree of pluralism. What might be called the "plural-monism" continuum has proved to be a better basis for determining types of politics than the "democracy-totalitarianism" continuum because it is somewhat broader and is based on forms of differentiation rather than on the explicit method of government. Competition is another useful criterion. As James S. Coleman has suggested: "Competitiveness is an essential aspect of political modernity, but not all competitive systems are 'modern.'"[13] Edward A. Shils has developed a similar classification in which the modernization process is described as a progressive sharing by the public in an understanding of modern life in such a way that, no longer passive agents acted upon by outside forces, they can utilize their potentialities and their creativity.[14]

These two factors, pluralism and participation, form the basis of almost all the typologies of "political systems" or "polities," and each student adopts some variant of these to suit his particular purposes. Morris Janowitz, for example, in his study of the military in the developing countries, notes five types: (1) authoritarian-personal control, (2) authoritarian-mass party, (3) democratic competitive and semicompetitive systems, (4) civil-military coalition, and (5) military oligarchy.[15]

The typology I have used accepts the same principles and to that extent is not different from the others. By stressing values and hierarchy, however, I want to emphasize the way people organize society and feel its pull in terms of durable proprieties, rights and wrongs. This approach will reinforce the point that has been made by Gabriel Almond and Sidney Verba in their study of the civic culture. The importance of their book for me lies in its advance from typologies based purely on matters of structural differentiation to a typology based on the forms of cognition and meaning that exist in a particular culture. This leads them to the analysis of "fit" or congruence between the ideals and values of the community and the forms by which it is organized.[16] The problem of congruence, which emerges most clearly in roles, has been the central point of my analysis. Given that roles are institutionalized forms of behavior defined by function, both the structural and the behavioral approaches are employed in analysis. The structural deals with the organization of roles and their functional relationships. The behavioral deals with the ideas of right conduct embodied in the roles and the consequences of those ideas in the formation of personalities.[17] Any complete analysis necessarily includes both these aspects. As I use the terms, the *behavioral approach* deals with *which* choices are made by groups or individuals and *why*; the *structural approach* delineates *what* choices are possible.

To incorporate both structural differentiation and cognitive evaluation in a highly generalized manner is a difficult task. The following approach seems feasible. If we consider the two main variables discussed above, hierarchy and values, we obtain the typology of authority types given in Figure 2.2.

Types A and B are derivative of the pure normative models, the sacred-collectivity and the secular-libertarian, and are the polar opposites in this general formulation. As I have already suggested, they are more often than not in conflict with one another. The other two, C and D, may be described as historically significant, and perhaps practical, alternatives to the two major conflicting forms. Type A may be called a mobilization system, and type B a reconciliation system. Category C does not have a convenient name. Subtypes might be called modernizing autocracies, neomercantilist societies, or bureaucratic systems. Category D is equally difficult to label, but its subtypes may be called theocracies. The last model is most helpful in analyzing traditional societies, whereas the other three can be used in the study of most modernizing cases. Type C, for example, would include "Kermalism" and "neo-Bismarkian" types now gaining considerable currency in the literature. Type D includes feudal systems.

Each of these types is first a normative system organized around certain structural features and incorporating particular styles of political life and civic action. Most important of all, each of these political systems defines the conditions of choice differently. The approaches used to examine such conditions—normative, structural, and behavioral—each impose a different evaluative criteria. The first consists of the values and priorities that combine in a moral consensus, the second elaborates certain conditions of choice, and the last embodies the conditions under which individuals and groups make particular choices.

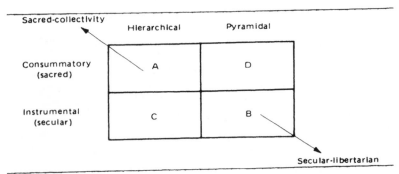

Figure 2.2 Authority Types

These three elements, which are present in all political systems, operate within a set of general boundaries—the human and physical resources available at any given time. Inside the boundaries, we can see alternative types of political systems that approach the problems of modernization somewhat differently. The extreme model, type B, may, as we have said, be called the secular-libertarian; *it is a perfect information model.* Its opposite, type A, is the sacred-collectivity, *a perfect coercion model.* Between these two extremes, the other types have proved to be accommodated or mixed systems of choice.[18]

Let me consider type B as a normative system. It can be observed to be analogous to the marketplace. Individual minds within the system become independent units that act upon the external world in order to make it conform to their perception of meaning. Individual minds are, in summation, the means by which the external world is given subjective meaning; yet the objectification of these subjective meanings is the basis of scientific knowledge. Toleration, leading to debate and competition in ideas, is the way to discover truths. Policy is a form of truth for the members of a community. Just as one's person is property and must be safeguarded, so one's mind is sacred and must be free. Ideas are derivations from empirical phenomena and must be tested competitively with other ideas in order to establish truth. And the establishment of truth is the aim of science. Hence, the libertarian model is essentially an extension of the rationalism of the marketplace, with the atomistic, competitive, and free play of ideas controlled only by a legal constitutional mechanism that prevents any group from obtaining a monopoly of power.[19] Its principle of legitimacy is *equity,* and its main emphasis is on allocation.

The limits on this normative type are many. Just as the pure theory of competition in economics does not accurately describe the real world, neither does the secular-libertarian model correspond to an existing political system. Just as, in the first instance, there are monopolies and oligopolies through which a few firms control the market, so, in the case of politics, there are classes and interest groups that wield superior power and give exceptional opportunities to some at the expense of others.

The structural defect in this normative type in large-scale and complex societies is the ineffectiveness of individual representation. Indeed, the liberal critique of modern society is that modern industrial enterprise has created such conditions of political inequality that individual representation is rendered meaningless. Early Marxism, for example, is essentially an attack on inequalities; it ascribes the failure of the representational system to inequalities arising in the economic sphere. Workers have become subdued to the discipline of the machine, subordinated in political as well as in economic terms, brutalized, and alienated from society. Marx's fame was instantaneous because his critique of the prevailing system was not only drastic but intellectually very powerful. For him, the problem was not merely that the liberal market system did not work in practice; he came to feel it could not work, in either economic or political life. Indeed, even the ethic appeared a vast deception—not scientific but antiscientific. Accordingly, the new science would begin by formulating certain principles of political and social conduct that would serve as universal rules for analyzing the evolutionary aspects of history. The morality of society was to be realized in an evolutionary way when economic groups were deprived of their special privileges or, more specifically, when economic classes disappeared. Indeed, liberal toleration of other systems than the libertarian begins with this critique. Today we can see that there are other problems than the ineffectiveness of the representation system.

In fact, the Marxist critique created a new moral ideology that concedes that some men, having gained a superior insight into themselves and their institutions, both as scientific and moral beings, must realize this superior knowledge in a system of authority. Men of superior intellect who emancipate themselves from the limitations of their own class outlook and the knowledge of their day—by having a scientific understanding of social life—are the ones who must establish the new collectivity. To be scientific is to know these principles and to work for their realization.

This is the basis of the modern collectivist community (the sacred-collectivity type): the generation of new power through unity, the unfolding of a moral and scientific personality through the mystique of developing toward a higher plane. Politically, one would not want to represent the people as they are, because "as they are" is debased by the imperfections of the society. Here the principle of legitimacy is *potentiality*, and its main emphasis is on development. It is not surprising, therefore, that many political leaders of modernizing nations are attracted to the Marxian view.

THE SECULAR-LIBERTARIAN MODEL

Underlying Western concepts of democracy is what we have called a secular-libertarian model of polity.

Behaviorally, the secular-libertarian model consists of units that possess two capacities: the ability to reason and the ability to know self-interest. These are the universal behavioral characteristics of human beings according to Locke, for example, who grants them even to individuals in a state of nature. *Structurally*, the system must allow maximum opportunity for the exercise of rationality and the pursuit of self-interest. Hence, the emphasis is on a framework that will prevent coercion and provide limited government. The usual realization of this need is a system of representative government with checks and balances designed to prevent tyranny. *Normatively*, such a system takes certain fundamental properties as given. Locke, for example, assumes that ultimate ends of conduct will be expressed primarily in terms of religion. Indeed, he suggests that without religion there can be no social contract, which he sees as the foundation of structural constitutionality, without which there can be no political basis for equity.

The secular libertarian model is thus the classic liberal picture of a political such community. But we must distinguish between the model and the ideology that stems from it. For example, if the model fails to work because of certain monopolistic practices arising in group political life, or if religion begins to decline and the contract to fail, the result may be the growth of solutions that, although designed to restore the model, appear to attack it. In this sense (and on a purely theoretical level), Marxian theory is designed to create a new rationale for a liberal universe that would be a benign modern equivalent of Locke's state of nature. In practice, however, Marxism as an ideology tends to be employed by systems that at present are opposed to the liberal ideology and the liberal political community.

The more common form of the secular libertarian polity, however, is the liberal utilitarian model. Such a model derives from the classical deist period and emphasizes *mechanical* harmony or equilibrium. The polity is like a vast marketplace. Government represents the sellers, with incumbents and candidates for political office actively engaged in producing policy or in discussing anticipated policy. Citizens are the buyers. The citizens are politically equal, as in the concept on one man, one vote. Power and loyalty are constantly being exchanged for benefits and privileges. The voting mechanism is the equivalent of the market. Preferences are rationally registered by the citizens as choices in the political arena. In this model, the primary value is liberty.

This concept of the polity parallels the pure theory of economic competition and accepts the same values.[20] Citizens registering their preferences act in their political role. In their economic role (as consumers) they register economic preferences in the marketplace. In both, the sum total of private wants emerges as public good. In the political sphere, the attempt of each person to realize his personal benefits on a plane of political equality with others generates power, just as consumer preference manifested by a willingness to spend money in the market generates wealth. Whereas money is the measure and expression of wealth in the market, votes are the measures and expressions of power in the polity.

There are other similarities between the economic and the political forms of the secular-libertarian model. Information is freely available to voters and officials just as it is to buyers and sellers. On the basis of information, rationality is possible. Hence, political freedom is first a condition of frankness. Knowledge of the product and knowledge of the policy assume an informed public. Knowledge of the public assumes an informed government. The emphasis on education is not solely because of its functional value (that is, to increase our technical skills or for any other utilitarian reason). Rather, education becomes the precondition of information, and information is the basis on which the relationship between public and policy is maintained. Harmony and stability result.

In such a system, it is implied that the values of the community are already enshrined in law and custom and that they will maintain the political conditions we have already suggested. Hence, just as in the pure theory of competition there should be no monopoly, so in the secular-libertarian polity there should be no monopoly of power in the political sphere. Power needs to be dispersed, and various systems have been devised to ensure its dispersal. These include the formal checks and balances of our own system and the principle of parliamentary sovereignty in Europe.

How does the secular-libertarian model fail? Interference in its working may come from either side of the polity, citizen or governor. Citizens seeking to maximize their power by organizing into groups can generate special powers, which in extreme cases may render the government helpless. Or the government may seek to minimize the controls exercised over it by various groups. The study of comparative politics of democratic societies concentrates on discovering possible improvements that will prevent both of these occurrences (much as in the economic sphere, government seeks to prevent large-scale combination through antitrust legislation).

Competition between politically equal units is the basis of the system, with competition in ideas reflecting competition of interests, the constellation of which represents the desires of the multitude. Such, briefly, is the ideal of Western libertarian government. It has a high commitment to rules and laws. When the discrepancy between theory and practice is great, individuals become lonely and divorced from the system. If too many withdraw from the political marketplace, a general condition of alienation from the society results. The libertarian model is vastly different when realized in the real world, where there are many special claims to power. Political parties are quite often anxious to limit rather than increase the range of intellectual discourse by focusing on a few issues with symbolic appeal (rather than offering intellectual choice); and we find the same efforts to produce automatic behavior that advertising companies use to encourage our addiction to trade names. Political packaging may produce moral cynicism in the same way that economic activity generated by advertising induces economic skepticism. We can see how, if this should result in alienation, people may draw away from the secular-libertarian model to something else. The theme of alienation runs through the history of secular-libertarian models.[21]

THE SACRED-COLLECTIVITY MODEL

The sacred-collectivity model in its broadest implications contains essentially three elements. *Behaviorally*, it is made up of units whose singular characteristic is potentiality. Individuals, for example, are perceived as nothing more than potentials. *Structurally,* the political community is the means of translating potentiality into some sort of reality. Hence, the society is the key to social life. Moreover, as the primary instrument of socialization, the political community is essentially an educational body. It exists for the improvement of the community itself. The individual is merely derivative, a derived personality. *Normatively,* the sacred-collectivity is an ethical or moral unit. Thus the morality of the individual depends on the morality of the system, which embodies those higher purposes that may be enshrined in kinship, political ideals, and so on. Included under the rubric of this essentially Aristotelian view of the political community would be most traditional societies, theocracies, and certain modernizing ones as well. It is the modernizing societies that are most interesting to us and on which we will concentrate.

Seen as a modernizing force, the sacred-collectivity model stresses the unity of the people, not their diversity. It depends less on the free flow of ideas than on the disciplined concentration upon certain political and economic objectives. It claims a "higher" form of morality than that of the secular-libertarian model, because social life is directed toward the benefit of the collectivity rather than toward that of the self. It is more disciplined because more is concentrated on the priorities of the polity. Equality in the economic sphere is often regarded as a goal to be achieved by the eventual elimination of private property, although not all collectivity systems are socialist. Political inequality exists, but for equalitarian ends.

Operating on very different principles from those of the secular-libertarian model, the sacred-collectivity has its origins in the idea of society organized as a corporation. In the medieval theory of corporations, inequality and status were embodied in legal entities (such as guilds) and classes of individuals (such as noblemen and clergymen).[22] Today the corporation is the state, and the parts of it are functional groupings such as workers and farmers.

The sacred-collectivity model is significant for our purposes because it is an alternative to the secular-libertarian model, which may break down if loyalty to and consensus about the polity are lacking. If, for example, the economy fails to function and mundane satisfactions are unequally distributed, the alienated men who may be produced by these conditions may well look for revolutionary reform under a new moral discipline. This moral discipline will be able to justify inequality and reduce the significance of unequal distribution of mundane satisfactions.

We can call this model nonrational because it does not presume a free-flowing pattern of exchange of information between rulers and ruled. The rulers need to be in a position to coordinate and discipline the ruled in order to achieve certain objectives, which tend to be highly diffuse, utopian, and spiritual.

This emphasis is particularly strong in hitherto predominately commercial societies in which inequality is exceedingly great and lifestyles range from the most primitive to the most technologically luxurious. To integrate them into a single system is extremely difficult without wholesale alterations in social strata. One means of integration is to introduce socialism in order to restrict social differences. The objective is moral discipline, consensus, and similarity of outlook. Planning, rationality, and progress become associated with the sacred-collectivity model; and individualism, private gain, and the market become little more than other names for egotism and opportunism, and are seen as parochialism and a narrowness of outlook.

A COMPARISON OF
THE MODELS

It is necessary to recognize that the two normative models aim at quite different moral ends. The secular-libertarian model essentially accepts society as it is and suggests a framework that will allow modest change over time. It contains a set of presuppositions about the way in which representative government ought to operate: (1) There should not be a monopoly of power any more than there should be a monopoly of corporate enterprise. (2) The same rules apply to all; hence, as legal personalities, all are equal. (3) Preference can be realized within a framework of law in which those exercising power are checked by legal means—by control over the executive, and so on. Law, the constitution, and the actual mechanisms of government are seen as a seamless web in which the symbol of authority is the social contract (even the term *contract* is taken from law) or a contract between the people that lays out the conditions of government.

The sacred-collectivity model is opposed to conditions as they are. It cannot assume, as can the secular-libertarian model, that an educational system, for example, should create a level of understanding of current problems sufficient to support opposing points of view and that opposing views should be tolerated as long as the problems are shared and communication about them possible. The sacred-collectivity model prefers to cope with such problems politically, through a system of authority that enforces selective communication between people about certain key political problems. If the original aim was to direct people to a common social language, the end result is the establishment of conformity in communication. That is why the political language employed by systems conforming to the sacred-collectivity model is always so important; key terms are continually reinforced and come to define political orthodoxy. It is a system in which consensus cannot be taken for granted but must be built—a directly opposite situation to that obtaining in the secular-libertarian model.

These two models are at opposite ends of a continuum of political systems. What determines the distance between them, however, is not merely their particular forms of government but rather two related components. The first of these components is made up of values and purposes. The secular-libertarian model is rooted in the ideal of individual liberty. The conditions that maximize liberty represent the central purpose. Modern group politics is a step away from the pure type. Pluralism consists not in the number of individual participants (one man, one vote) but rather in groups in competition. These groups (political) try to maximize their power, and individuals give over their loyalties to them. Group-oriented democracy is to the classic libertarian tradition what large-scale enterprise is to the pure theory of economic competition, and in theory has the same relationship to the libertarian model as monopolistic competition has to pure competition.

At the other end of the continuum political groups, not individuals, make up the system. The all-embracing political group is the state, from which subgroups derive their corporate personalities. Individuals exist only as the elementary "particles" of which the corporations are composed. With the emphasis on highly centralized authority, any dispersal of it is seen as dangerous to the whole. Such a system can be based on equality—but equality does not have the same significance it has in the first model, because it does not lead to the realization of individual wants. The secular-libertarian model assumes that equilibrium is produced by means of a policy representing a summation of the wants of its members, carried out within the framework of given values of rationality, freedom, and competition. The sacred-collectivity model assumes that any such policy would be inadequate because of deficiencies of knowledge among the people. Instead, the system must express values of unity, growth, and development. The collectivity type creates authority and carefully allocates it within a community. It can be seen as a community-creating process. The libertarian type caters to an established system of authority, using power within already defined legitimate limits for diverse purposes. It is interesting to note that the secular-libertarian type, awkward in dealing with the problem of establishing authority, resorts to myths of compact such as the social contract to do this.

Historically, we can see a relationship between these two approaches. All libertarian systems have evolved from earlier collective systems, during which authority was established. In this sense, it is possible to consider the two types as concretely interrelated systems that first must cater to the problem of authority and then at a later stage can cater to the problem of equity.

Of course, there are problems with this view. Is the secular-libertarian model incapable of establishing authority? This is clearly not the case. But as this model does not set up authority easily, what are the conditions favorable to it, and which conditions favor the alternative form? And if there is a relationship between the two, and the ultimate goal is the secular-libertarian system, is it not perfectly justifiable to favor a militant, organismic, collectivist society if that seems to be the precondition out of which a secular-libertarian model will emerge?

A host of questions arises when the matter is put this way. If a libertarian system is proposed for a new state in which the odds are that it will fail to establish authority, should the attempt be made? Ought nation-builders form the collective variety from the start? The question is not abstract. Since 1945, colonial territories have been provided with libertarian constitutions, many of which disintegrated within a few months of independence. Not one began as a collectivist system. Perhaps this only serves to underline how drastically different the central problems are in these two systems: equity or authority.

SUBTYPES

A more empirically useful departure from the pure secular-libertarian model I call a reconciliation system; and a similar departure from the pure state of the sacred-collectivity model I call a mobilization system. In reconciliation systems, given values and purposes generate legitimate authority. Conflicts between individuals and groups trying to realize those accepted values give rise to governmental policy. Policy thus reinforces values. In mobilization systems, new values are being created. This means that political leaders are trying to work out a moral system of authority. In between these types are some interesting combinations. One of these combinations I have called a modernizing autocracy, another is a military oligarchy, and still another a neomercantilist society. These three types are confusing because of the similarity of their basic components. Each of them is a special variant of hierarchical authority and instrumental values. The particular characteristics of each ought now to be made more explicit.

The modernizing autocracy tends to have a traditionalistic ideology associated with a monarch or king who represents the nation. Authority remains at the top, although, in fact, it may be shared through a variety of instrumentalities such as councils, parliaments, party groups, and so on. Examples are Thailand, Morocco, and Ethiopia.

The military oligarchy shares some of these characteristics. It has hierarchical authority and instrumental values, but a military leader (or junta) takes the place of the king. It, too, may decentralize power. The curious problem of the military oligarchy is its inability to deal with politics. Sudan is one testimonial to this failure, Vietnam is another, and Argentina is perhaps another.

The neomercantilist society also shares many of these characteristics but is ordinarily headed by a "presidential monarch." In order to support authority, it uses a mixture of private and public enterprise in which the critical rationale of economic activities is political. In this it fits the description of mercantilism employed by Eli F. Hecksher. Many mobilization systems turn into neomercantilist societies in practice, particularly when they employ traditionalist ideologies in an attempt to ritualize authority and change charismatic leadership into a more institutional form.[23]

Our analysis will be concerned with specifying the implications of these subtypes and in demonstrating some of their consequences for government. Most modernizing nations are combinations of these types, accepting at least some of the paraphernalia of the reconciliation system (most often a rudimental parliamentary form).

Our concern in the study of a particular nation's efforts to modernize is not only where the nation may be placed on a continuum but the systemic changes that occur during various phases of modernization. Some countries begin with a framework established by colonial officials who have sought to realize as closely as possible the libertarian ideal.

The result is not the ideal but a reconciliation system in which group pluralism soon breaks down into a monopoly of power by one group. It thus becomes a mobilization system—characteristically, a single-party state with a militant leader. At this stage, the mobilization system may change either in the direction of the collectivist model or toward some new synthesis such as a neomercantilist society.

Many theories may be employed as we try to examine the patterns of movement within the modernizing nations. One widespread assumption, however, ought to be made explicit at the beginning, because it is held by many of those who study modernizing nations: The implicit assumptions and values underlying the libertarian model will continue to exist in all the other systems, although in a hidden and disguised way, and will emerge even in the collectivist systems after they have succeeded in building some kind of unity, in developing the material standards of the society, and in providing a sense of identity and worth for individuals. If this is correct, then the long-term prognosis for democracy is hopeful.[24]

STRUCTURAL DYNAMICS

So far our discussion has centered on the problem of choice and its political implications during the modernizing process. Policymaking is the process of making choices, and the various elements of the process, which have already been described, are present in every system of choice. Perhaps a diagram will incorporate the various elements more explicitly (see Figure 2.3).

Two sets of propositions may now be made explicit. The first set deals with the relation of the four types of political system to modernization.

(1) Of the four types of operating models, the reconciliation system is the least likely to serve as a satisfactory basis for establishing a new, modernizing polity.

(2) Reconciliation systems are likely to attempt to realize modernization through a process of localized initiative and individual entrepreneurship, including private and private-public forms of enterprise. In contrast, mobilization systems are likely to see modernization as a process of centralized planning and governmental enterprise.

(3) Mobilization systems are most successful as "conversion" systems, that is, in (a) establishing a new polity and (b) converting from late modernization to industrialization.

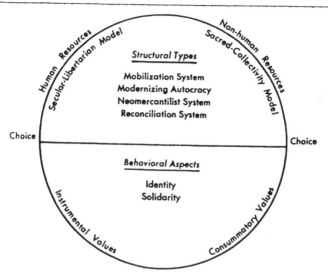

SOURCE: Adapted from Marion J. Levy, Jr., *The Structure of Society* (Princeton, NJ: Princeton University Press, 1952), p. 11.

Figure 2.3 An Approach to the Analysis of Choice

(4) Modernizing autocracies and neomercantilist societies are optimal political forms for long-term modernization, in particular, for the conversion from the "early" to the "late" stages of the process.

(5) Reconciliation systems are optimal forms when the conversion to early industrialization has been completed, that is, for a modern industrial society.

The second set of propositions restates the first set in somewhat more generalized form. One central functional hypothesis is that *different polities employ different mixtures of coercion and information in trying to maintain authority, achieve stability, and increase efficiency.* I posit, for analytical purposes, an inverse relationship between information and coercion in a system: that is, high coercion systems are low information systems.[25] The political form that achieves an equilibrium between information and coercion will achieve maximum efficiency and authority. Not only will it achieve its goals, but it will produce goals proximate to its economic and social resources. Given that political forms have their own dynamics by means of which the relationship between coercion and information is determined, we can treat political form, or polity, as an independent variable, with coercion and information as intervening variables and modernization the dependent variable.[26]

If this hypothesis could stand alone, however, proving correct in each case, there would be little reason for governments to engage in coercive practices. In fact, high information systems have a problem of "overloading."[27] That is to say, the decision makers may receive so much information that they have difficulty acting. Moreover, the information may be preselected and uneven in its sources and emphases. Hence, the difficulty in high information systems is evaluation. This leads to uncertainty. A corresponding hypothesis, then, is that high information systems are uncertainty systems, whereas high coercion systems are deterministic systems. Only if the high information systems have a political framework that can handle probabilities, that is, cope with a probabilistic universe, can they function well. High coercion systems operate with less information. Especially during periods of transition, when uncertainty is frightening, there is a widespread urge for control and a deterministic outlook associated with particular goals.

A third hypothesis combines these two. *Modernizing societies and industrial societies can utilize information only when they possess sound interpretative mechanisms.* Hence, the direction of modernization will be toward a probabilistic universe—and away from a deterministic one—through what I will call a reconciliation system (eventually arriving at representative government), if this is the most satisfactory means of handling and evaluating information. Hence, although one type of political system does not change into another in a unilinear or evolutionary fashion, modernization and industrialization do result in a secular tendency toward increasing differentiation and complexity. From this secular tendency, we may infer, on the basis of our hypotheses, a long-run series of political changes leading toward high information and low coercion, that is, to some form of reconciliation system.

CONCLUSION

Predemocratic polities become significant for the study of politics through the analysis of political systems and forms and through the study of legitimacy. Also important are public aspiration and belief. Hence, ideology, motivation, and mobility become critical areas of discussion. The general process of modernization provides a useful setting for revealing these complex political matters.

Modernization may be described in nonindustrial societies as the transposition of certain roles—professional, technical, administrative—and the transposition of institutions supporting these roles—hospitals, schools, universities, bureaucracies. Nonindustrial modernizing societies, however, lack the powerful integrating thrust found in industrial societies. Social organizations are more chaotic and confused. Politics becomes the mechanism of integration, and authority is the critical problem confronting the leaders.

This conclusion leads to a consideration of the political forms most appropriate to producing and coping with modernization. Indeed, modernization emphasizes certain types of authority. The particular combinations of right that, embodied in authority, we call legitimacy are quite often determined by the goals of the polity. Failure to achieve such goals is thus prejudicial to authority. This means that in many modernizing societies, the polity can only be secured by its successes. The efficiency of a regime determines the quality of its authority.

NOTES

1. Albert Camus, *The Myth of Sisyphus* (New York: Random House, Vintage Books, 1955), p. 91.

2. That is the long-range object of the research undertaken here. Indeed, it may even be premature to discuss topics for research or to formulate research strategies about politics in modernizing societies until these broader issues have been made more explicit. The following four structural variables are not dealt with here:

(1) Equality: Is there an increase or decrease in equality during modernization in relation to different political forms?

(2) Role distribution: What is the distribution of modernized roles in the system?

(3) Rates of economic growth: What are the comparative rates of economic growth, and what are the mechanisms of planning?

(4) Degree of stability: What is the relationship between stability and growth? How much coercion is required?

These four variables become meaningful for political theory only in the context of very important political issues. It is necessary to examine these larger issues before undertaking research on the variables themselves.

3. See A. Schuetz, "On Multiple Realities," *Philosophy and Phenomenological Research* 5 (June 1945).

4. See Jean-Paul Sartre, *Search for a Method* (New York: Knopf, 1963).

5. By *culture*, I mean the learned symbols and artifacts in a system.

6. If we accept this line of reasoning, we must admit that most governments are not very "good" and that some are worse than others. The analysis of some may suggest possibilities of rapid improvement. For others, where a moral rhetoric disguises acts of force, violence, intimidation, and deception, we may simply be compounding these deficiencies if we fail to apply moral criteria. If we cannot discriminate between governments, it would be a better alternative to lay aside all judgments in favor of judicious silence. How comforting to divert our attention to the consideration of purely historical events (and regard contemporary judgments as premature until the system has already gone through its main evolution and its outlines become so fixed, its practices so decided, that little further change can be expected). But this would be to substitute expediency for judgment. See Benedetto Croce, *Politics and Morals* (London: George Allen & Unwin, 1946).

7. But matters of form are at stake when they embody matters of principle. We need to suggest types of developing societies, if only to point to the forms of misconduct to which they are heir. How else can we demonstrate their moral potentialities in relation to modernization? Behind any utilitarian judgment of the role of government lies the larger question of moral potentiality.

8. Structural analysis is used here to include all forms of systems analysis that refer to unit change. It includes functional analysis as a method of identifying significant variables in a system.

9. See Hempel, "Symposium: Problems of Concept and Theory Formation in the Social Sciences," in *Science, Language and Human Rights* (Philadelphia: University of Pennsylvania Press, for the American Philosophical Association, 1952), p. 84.

10. See Marion J. Levy, Jr., *The Structure of Society* (Princeton, NJ: Princeton University Press, 1952).

11. In practice, structural analysis has been largely intuitive and speculative. This is perhaps as it should be. There is nothing inherent in the nature of this method of analysis that causes this; but when it is applied to macrounits like societies, precision becomes more a matter of logic than data because there is too much material to handle.

12. This general approach incorporates different aspects of the following forms of theory: functional and processual, structural and behavioral.

13. See Gabriel Almond and James S. Coleman, *The Politics of the Developing Areas* (Princeton, NJ: Princeton University Press, 1960), p. 533.

14. See Edward A. Shils, *Political Development in the New States* (The Hague: Mouton, 1962). A useful variant of the pluralism-monism continuum is Chalmers Johnson's typology for situations of radical change; see his *Revolution and the Social System* (Stanford, CA: Hoover Institution on War, Revolution, and Peace, 1964), no. 3.

15. See Morris Janowitz, *The Military in the Political Development of New Nations* (Chicago: University of Chicago Press, 1964), p. 5.

16. See Gabriel Almond and Sidney Verba, *The Civic Culture: Political Attitudes and Democracy in Five Nations* (Princeton, NJ: Princeton University Press, 1963), chap. i.

17. The best discussion of the explicitly structural aspect of roles is S. F. Nadel, *The Theory of Social Structure* (New York: Free Press, 1957). Discussion of the behavioral aspect is to be found in T. M. Newcomb, *Social Psychology* (New York: Dryden Press, 1950), chap. x. The most important effort to combine these two dimensions of analysis remains Talcott Parsons's, *The Social System* (New York: Free Press, 1951); and T. Parsons, Robert F. Bales, and Edward A. Shils, *Working Papers in the Theory of Action* (New York: Free Press, 1953).

18. The best short introduction to the immediate problems of analysis is contained in Karl W. Deutsch's *The Nerves of Government* (New York: Free Press, 1963). See also Wilbert E. Moore, *Social Change* (Englewood Cliffs, NJ: Prentice-Hall, 1963). The most important and explicit statement of structural-functional requisite analysis is in Marion J. Levy, Jr., *The Structure of Society* (Princeton, NJ: Princeton University Press, 1952). See also Juan L. Linz, "An Authoritarian Regime: Spain," in *Cleavages, Ideologies and Party Systems*, ed. E. Allardt and Y. Littunen (Helsinki: Westermarck Society, 1964), pp. 291-301.

19. The idea of power in this system is the zero-sum approach. There is a given amount of it in the system, and if one group gains more, that of others decreases correspondingly. See Talcott Parsons, "On the Concept of Political Power," *Proceedings of the American Philosophical Society* 107 (June 1963).

20. See Anthony Downs, *An Economic Theory of Democracy* (New York: Harper, 1957).

21. See Robert Tucker, *Philosophy and Myth in Karl Marx* (Cambridge: Cambridge University Press, 1961). See also the discussion in Philip Selznick, *The Organizational Weapon* (New York: Free Press, 1960), chap. vii.

22. See Otto Gierke, *Natural Law and the Theory of Society*, ed. E. Barker (Cambridge: Cambridge University Press, 1950); and O. Gierke, *Political Theories of the Middle Ages*, ed. F. W. Maitland (Cambridge: Cambridge University Press, 1927). See also Ewart Lewis, *Medieval Political Ideas* (London: Routledge & Kegan Paul, 1954).

23. This usage is derived from the description of mercantilism in the introduction to Heckscher's *Mercantilism* (London: George Allen & Unwin, 1955), p. 22. Heckscher describes mercantilism as an "agent of unification."

24. Western policy is predicated on the assumption that this is true, just as Soviet policy vis-à-vis the modernizing nations is based upon an opposite viewpoint, namely, that mobilization systems will eventually build up those forms of unity essential to the collectivist society as conceived in Marxian terms. I hold to the first view as an article of faith. But I also hope to show the superior utility of the libertarian system in its handling of complexity. In this sense, I believe that modernization ultimately produces libertarian systems.

25. There are many complicating factors in this hypothesis. One of the most interesting is the usefulness of corruption as a political device to increase information without reducing coercion.

26. Any system of analysis that purports to examine such complex matters needs first of all to be classificatory and then analytical. Radcliffe-Brown has pointed out most persuasively that the

basis of science is systematic classification. It is the first task of social statics to make some attempt to compare forms of social life in order to arrive at classifications. But forms of social life cannot be classified into species and genera in the way we classify forms of organic life; the classification has to be not specific but typological, and this is a more complicated kind of investigation. It can only be reached by means of the establishing of typologies for features of social life of the complexes of features that are given in partial social systems. He continues, although typological studies are one important part of social statics, there is another task, that of formulating generalisations about the conditions of existence of social systems, or all forms of social life. . . . The study of social dynamics is concerned with establishing generalisations about how social systems change. It is corollary of the hypothesis of the systematic connection of features of social life that changes in some features are likely to produce changes in other features.

See A. R. Radcliffe-Brown, *Structure and Function in Primitive Society* (New York: Free Press, 1952), p. 7.

27. See Wilbur Schramm, *The Process and Effects of Mass Communication* (Urbana: University of Illinois Press, 1955), pp. 16-17.

—3—

SOME CHARACTERISTICS OF MODERNIZATION

Modernization first occurred in the West through the twin processes of commercialization and industrialization. The social consequences of these processes can be summed up in the following rather paradigmatic categories: the growth of lending and fiscal devices, the need to support modern armies, the application of technologies in competitive market situations, and the influence of trade and voyages on the scientific spirit—all of which are evidence that modernity in the West attacked religion and superstition, family and church, mercantilism and autocracy. Indeed, we have come to consider science as the antidote for faith, with Galileo as a kind of folk hero of modernization. His triumph is the triumph of reason, and reason as applied to human affairs is the foundation of modernity.[1]

In many non-Western areas, modernization has been a result of commercialization and, rather than industrialization, bureaucracy. Some of the same values appropriate to industrial countries have been spread by enterprising men, sometimes in the context of politics and trade and at other times in the context of religion and education. Modernization can thus be seen as something apart from industrialization—caused by it in the West but causing it in other areas.[2]

Behind these large considerations are smaller ones. Consider what it means to establish a small shop near a traditional market at a time when there is no regularized system of bulk purchasing or wholesale buying, few distributive outlets, and a largely illiterate clientele, many of whom buy on credit. Quite often the Syrian or Lebanese trader in West Africa, or the Indian or Arab in East Africa, or the Moslem in Indonesia represents a crucial prototype for modernization. Suppose our shopkeeper finds that his shop has become a central meeting place, with the more successful customers gathering on the stoop to pass the time of day. Perhaps he will serve drinks and later open a restaurant or a hotel. If he is enterprising, he may try to make his shop the local post office. Exchange of the written word and the cash nexus go hand in hand.

Or the village party organ may establish a reading room and provide literacy classes for adults. A bare office with tattered books comes to mean learning. Clerks in offices formerly represented modernity; but today it may be the uniforms of the youth: Boy Scouts, Young Pioneers, or other local derivatives. Ideologies link the heroes of the country with others, Western and Eastern. Names such as Lincoln, Marx, Lenin, Roosevelt, Gandhi, Sukarno, Mao are all modernizing symbols, linked to particular modes of reform. It is the politicians who are symbols in the developing countries and notably not the inventors or craftsmen. Whereas the famous technological inventions changed the nature of "our" society, such innovations are virtually a natural feature of modern society for the people of the developing areas. Indeed, Western society has little meaning apart from its technology for these countries, and its institutions are inextricably linked together—politics and science, inventions and parliaments.

DIVERSE SOURCES OF INNOVATION

Who are the modernizers? A growing literature indicates how curious we are about the personalities who are the agents of modernization. Some argue that they are the marginal men, as in the case of the Chinese in parts of Southeast Asia. Quite often they have been born of marriages between persons from two culturally or ethnically unrelated groups, are at least to some extent multilingual, and are products of an educational system that drew them away from home. Elements of marginality can thus be regarded as a critical factor in the development of modernization skills.[3]

A second factor is the accessibility of innovative roles, a condition that affects youth primarily. In particular, education in the form of either apprenticeship or more formal schooling has been important in stimulating an interest in the roles of modernity, as have the power and prestige consequences of the roles themselves.

Third, the mass media and, as Lerner has shown, the growth of communications in general have made it possible to conceive of modernity even in the absence of many of its qualities.[4] Nor does it require a large group of those who define themselves as intellectuals, or technicians, to have an enormous "aura effect" in a community, because they, in order to make themselves more secure, are the very ones—journalists, writers, teachers, civil servants, engineers, and so on—who need to substantiate themselves with larger rural groups and pre-moderns.

These three factors do not exhaust the conditions that stimulate people to become modern. Quite often it is the organization of traditional society itself, its immobilities and its adaptive qualities, that generates a force for modernization. Often, too, the strength of the motivation depends on the personalities in the society, their creativity and their general buoyancy.[5]

Whatever the quality of the personalities involved, it is clear that modernization creates a catch-up psychology and a sense of being placed at disadvantage that generate the motivation for change. Any material improvements in a community create a demand for more. As Bernard Lewis has suggested in the case of Turkey,

> In the neighborhood of the towns, bus services, piped water, electricity, daily newspapers, and access to urban amenities heralded the dawn of a new age; even in remoter places, a local road, a daily bus, and a few battery-operated wireless sets brought new contacts with the outside world, a new awareness of membership of the larger community, and the beginning of a new process of far-reaching social change.[6]

The roles created are those of the bus driver, the wireless repairmen, the reporters, and all the rest whose halo effect is significant. At the same time, the condition of change, the roles of change, the personalities for change need to be fitted together in such a way that their tentative efforts bring results. Otherwise a small degree of modernization may bring despair and bitterness—a knowledge of attempting to be modern but failing at it—as the Banfields show in the case of a southern Italian village.[7]

Quite often it is the main job of government to prevent the population that has tasted modernization but cannot quite cope with it from slipping back. Egypt was plagued with this problem for years. There were more wealth and efforts at modernization in Egypt than in any other Middle Eastern or North African country. Under British adminis-tration, there had developed large urban areas, a small but significant factory culture, a larger artisan group, and a highly rationalized civil service. The latter, recruited mainly from the urban population (74.2%), were able to go to the university and complete their first degrees (77.1%); most of them were the sons of civil servants, white-collar employees, and landlords (62.4%).[8] Despite the efforts of the civil service, however, it was not until relatively recently that the effects of modernization created that climate of buoyancy and hope that would attract personalities with the capacity for both innovation and self-discipline. This has been one major achievement of the present Egyptian government.

Quite often the first modernizers have been those who realized that if they did not change their roles they would be forever barred from political power. In Africa, for example, some of the earliest modernizers were chiefs whose traditional prescriptions of office clearly delineated a religious rather than a secular role. Yet they could turn their hands to modernization at times, and, if not they, then their sons. In almost every major African territory, there were schools for the sons of chiefs, and it was to ensure their participation in modern government that they were recruited.

In the case of Ghana, some of the chief-modernizers were treated poorly by the authorities. King Aggery of Cape Coast was first rewarded for his spirit of modernity in prosecuting court cases and public works and later attacked for his political independence and stalwartness, deposed and deported.[9] Similar treatment was given King Jaja of Opobo in Nigeria. After his recognition as a chief by the British, according to Sir Alan Burns, "Jaja's energy and acumen had full scope. His wealth was considerably increased by trade, and this permitted him to acquire sufficient force to strengthen his position and establish a monopoly in the districts claimed by him." Arbitrator, merchant, shipping agent, and general entrepreneur, Jaja tried to control the trade along the creeks and inlets near Opobo. He, too, was deported.[10]

These examples are cited because, although somewhat unusual, they are quite typical of a certain period in the modernization of a colonial country. More frequently, the educated elites were singled out for particular abuse by an ambivalent colonial government, which regarded them, on one hand, as a product of forward-looking colonial policies in education and, on the other, as a cause of persistent trouble and complaint. The "scholars," as they were often called, were regarded as mischievous, arrogant, and dishonest. Their efforts at modernization were seen as parodying Western institutions and aping the mannerisms and characteristics of their "tutors." Such attitudes can still be found among Europeans in South Africa.[11]

More recently, conflicts between generations have inadvertently produced a similar situation in modern guise. In order to identify comfortable modern roles for themselves, youthful aspirants need to challenge the form and order already established—whether imposed from the outside or not. The clearest example of this is in India, where the Congress party has become so venerable (yet controlling all the main modernization posts) that the youth cast about for party alternatives that will provide them better opportunity to apply their skills and innovative capacities. This is one reason why the Communist party of India continues to recruit young educated Indians despite the conflict with China. (Indeed, for many developing societies, communism has been attractive as a form of modernizing system that will provide stability and control during the difficult period of role search and definition.) Where the obstacles in modernization are great, creative, frustrated, or innovative personalities may seek out the most powerful, drastic, and contrasting system of politics and give it their loyalty. In the Middle East, for example, the disavowal of parliamentary governments that occurred after the 1930s led both to "military socialism," as Laqueur calls it, and to an interest in communism.[12]

In an attempt to summarize the diversity of roles through which modernity spreads, Lucien W. Pye has used a typology that includes several functionally defined types: mediators, transmitters, conveyers, and so on. He has arranged these in terms of tendencies that, although opposite to each other, nevertheless have a modernizing consequence: the *administrator*, who emphasizes rational bureaucratic norms, as opposed to the *agitator*, who awakens dormant demands; the *amalgamate*, who combines both old and new roles in one, in contrast to the *transmitter*, who tends to represent only the new roles; the *ideological propagandist*, who strives to establish a common ideology with the *political broker*, who aggregates special interests.[13]

Whatever the problems with such a typology, it does point up the diversity of modernizing roles with a direct reference to politics, which must be examined in any empirical evaluation of modernization. Of particular significance is the way in which such modernizing roles are linked to those of high status. Role, status, profession, and occupation all need to be examined in order to identify the reinforcing elements of role change and the incompatibilities as well.

Quite often the urge toward modernity is the same as that which produces new forms of art or exotic techniques in painting. Indeed, some of the young Communists in China, for example, mixed poetry with politics in a very explicit way. Even the most sorry demonstration and the most ineffective acts of the party came to arouse the same sense of pride and achievement as a major victory.[14] Both modern nationalism and communism have this much in common; for the youth they represent cultures of modernity, cast in a political mode, through which their supporters seek the liberation of the human spirit.

COLONIALISM AS A
MODERNIZING FORCE

Whatever we may think of this practice, colonialism demonstrated the role of commerce and bureaucracy in modernization. By stating this, I do not mean to deny the developmental aspects of precolonial systems. Traditional societies were not all subsistence economies—for example, the ancient trade in salt, kola, gold, and slaves between North Africa and West Africa. Various forms of money were in use long before European intervention. Ports and markets were often very elaborate. The traditional Dahomean port of Whydah, for example, was administered by the king of Dahomey, and although Dahomeans did not participate to any great extent in commercial activities, their military requirements were such that they allowed foreigners to operate what became a major entrepot along the coast.[15] The rise and fall of empires in West Africa— Mali, Ghana, Songhai, Gobir, Bornu, and others—were largely determined by trade and the organization developed to further it, despite large subsistence sectors. Long before the European presence, trading sectors became highly developed, that is, part of the traditional network of trade and commerce, and began to change rapidly. Many of them began to participate in commercial activity in earnest. Once the Europeans set up their trading factories, however, the pace and techniques changed. First came the pioneers and then the trading families. Factories or trading houses were set up in Dakar, Freetown, Monrovia, Accra, and Lagos. Extensive intermarriage took place between the local peoples and the Dutch, Danes, Brandenburgers, French, Corsicans, Italians, Spaniards, and others.[16] Hence, it was the direct line between a metropolitan country and an overseas territory that helped to build a set of relationships that were manifested not merely in "old" and "new" roles, or in traditional or modern ones, but in a wide range of intermediate roles.

Because commercial and some industrial enterprises established in the colonial territories had their markets and main source of investment in the home countries, there is a correlation between the rising economic status of the metropole and the increase in commercialization and modernization of the overseas territory. Overseas development occurred between periods of war or depression. In the period immediately after World War I, for example, investments overseas, capital development projects such as railways, harbors, and schools, and other forms of primary development were characteristics of British territories, where the prevailing philosophy was to place the colonies on a pay-as-you-go basis as quickly as possible and thus end parliamentary subsidies. To some extent, the same was true of French colonies, although the overseas investment of France was much smaller.

During the 1930s, when overseas funds were unavailable, colonial territories were forced to retrench drastically. This quite often took the form of reduced expatriate staffs, with much more direct administrative control in order to maximize efficiency. Social services were restricted. The growth of local councils, treasuries, and the like was stunted, largely because of their cost, to be renewed once again on a much larger scale after World War II. It is the uneven application of modernizing programs, not the lack of modernization itself, that is the characteristic of different colonial systems. Obviously, different metropolitan powers employed different patterns of modernization; some did remarkably little—the Portuguese in Africa—others did a very great deal. Indeed, with the exception of programs of mass modernization by drastic political methods, colonialism at its best has been one very useful mechanism for modernizing.[17]

Political modernization came to have two meanings in colonial systems. First, it meant that there had to be a "Westernized" secular elite that could participate in political life; and, second, there had to be "Westernized" forms of government so that the elites could be represented. This was characteristic of the British pattern of political evolution in colonial territories, although there were some profound exceptions to the general rule and the rule itself is of very recent origin.

The desire to foster a brood of Westminster models as a legacy of British rule has been a comparatively recent, even brief and passing, phenomenon in British policy. Exact identity with the British model was neither desired nor demanded: it was repudiated as inconvenient or inhibiting by both rulers and ruled. Imperial and colonial politicians quoted British example or precedent only where it was useful to their case.[18]

It was, of course, useful to the extent that it encouraged the evolution of self-government and independence through conciliar government.

There were numerous variations on the theme of political evolution in the British territories, fewer in the French system, and many fewer in the Belgian, Dutch, and Portuguese systems. France applied a very broad pattern of political evolution throughout large regionally organized groups of territories, such as French West Africa. Within this general pattern, there were very complex adjustments to local conditions.[19]

A description of various colonial systems, however, would divert us from the main purpose at hand. We are concerned here with various colonial systems only as primary instruments of modernization (even though they were transitional political forms). The most general structural variables that may be applied in a comparison of colonial systems over a period of time are, first, whether the colonial government was mainly autocratic or conciliar and, second, whether leadership was personal or impersonal. If we consider various colonial territories— British, French, Belgian, Dutch, and Portuguese—in terms of parallel stages cutting across the usual distinctions between colonial systems, we can see colonialism as a modernization process proceeding through four main stages: the pioneering, bureaucratic, representative, and responsible governmental stages.[20] These need not follow a linear progression (see the diagram in Figure 3.1).

What this diagram emphasizes are the structural changes in colonialism that coincide with policies leading to modernization. Political modernization is a cause of further change. The uniqueness of government as a modernizing instrument can thus be demonstrated by treating it as an independent variable (as a creator of a different environment for itself). Hence, political modernization is both consequence and cause of modernization, and this is reflected in an appropriately changing governmental system. Some of the colonial systems went through all the various stages leading to independence. Some never really arrived there. The Congo, for example, was in the very first stage of representative government when it became independent; Indonesia was still in the bureaucratic stage; India had had a reasonably long period of representative government; and Ceylon, which was one of the first to do so, had gained responsible government. It should be added that postindependence governments are also subject to the same stages of transition.

	Personal	Impersonal
Autocratic	Pioneering	Bureaucratic
Conciliar	Representative	Responsible

Figure 3.1 Stages of Colonialism

Probably the most exciting period in the transition from dependence to independence is the representative stage because, although there are legislative bodies, the responsibility for government remains outside the colony. It becomes an outrageous political condition for many potential politicians, stimulating them to organize followers and to capitalize on grievances. This is the period in which what we will call "Robin Hood" roles are formed—and played by semicharismatic figures who can rally around them the disadvantaged and confused. Lacking the controls of the impersonal but autocratic patterns of government of bureaucratic colonialism, the representative period often coincides with conditions described by Norman Cohn as characteristic of the late medieval period, and with similar results.

> There were however many who merely acquired new wants without being able to satisfy them; and in them the spectacle of a wealth undreamt-of in earlier centuries provoked a bitter sense of frustration. In all the over-populated, highly-urbanised and industrialised areas there were multitudes of people living on the margin of society, in a state of chronic insecurity.[21]

So in the period in which personal politics and conciliar forms coincide, a period in which there is widespread unrest and political irresponsibility, the conditions are ripe for nationalist movements, which have as their object the achievement of some new and higher synthesis of modern life, free of the enslavement of race, of subservience, and of inferiority. It is in this context that nationalism emerges with particular sharpness in the colonial societies and attacks government, an alien fortress.

Colonialism is an interesting historical phase. It illustrates a particular sequence of transition, a pattern in which modernization has been universalized and in which some of the important roles of modernity have been acquired. It is replaced in the period of independence by systems that change in response to modernity and that manipulate modernity itself. It will be useful, however, to discuss modernization more specifically to indicate its relationship to traditionalism, on one hand, and to industrialization, on the other.

TRADITIONALISM AND DEVELOPMENT

It has been suggested that modernization is the process of consciously directing and controlling the social consequences of increased role differentiation and organizational complexity in a society. The most interesting cases are those in which such differentiation and complexity of organization are not merely products of size, or population growth, but rather results of an increase in technologically significant functional roles.[22] Putting the matter this way leads us to speculation on the origins of modernity.

We have discussed some of the conditions that led to a change from traditionalism to modernity. Much of our thinking about development, and indeed, the contemporary interest in social change, has been centered on this transition. Nonetheless, attempts to analyze modernity have not handled traditionalism well. The reason is not hard to find. The historical cases are so involved and varied that it is difficult to separate the strands of traditionalism from those of modernity. Even recent attempts to prevent the distinction from becoming blurred by the complexity of the process (by a combination of functional methods and ideal-type analysis) treat traditional societies as composed of a particular set of ingredients, all of which share a certain static quality. Conservatism is thereby linked with traditionality, implying that kind of equilibrium (or delicate balance of social practices and beliefs) that is embalmed within a religious framework and that, by virtue of its sanctity and immemoriality, defies change.

This kind of analysis uses traditionality as an ideal type not to be found empirically in pure form. Problems arise when we examine the traditional society itself. Too often there is a tendency to reify, that is, to take the ideal type as real and static. In practice, traditionality in its various forms and patterns is an essential part of the study of modernization (particularly its political aspects) precisely because it, too, changes. How many of the practical problems of politics, and the more serious challenges to authority, stem from the remaining strongholds of traditionality within the modernizing society? And how often, by challenging traditionalism head on, do political leaders cause grave and serious conflicts in their society when they would like to avoid them?

Such issues are not new; many theorists have tried to show differences between traditional and nontraditional societies by citing institutional variations. Maine, for example, emphasizes the peculiar significance of kinship in "primitive societies" by stressing the strategic role of agnatic relationships (as compared with cognitive relationships) in modern society, and links these forms of relationship by means of an evolutionary theory of development. Kinship not only has important effects on status, property, inheritance, and the like, but, as a pattern of relations between men, is "conceptually" different.

> We saw one peculiarity invariably distinguishing the infancy of society. Men are regarded and treated, not as individuals, but always as members of a particular group. Everybody is first a citizen and then, as a citizen, he is a member of his order—of an aristocracy or a democracy, of an order of patricians or plebeians or in those societies which an unhappy fate has afflicted with a special perversion in their course of development, of a caste. Next, he is a member of a gens, house, or clan; and lastly he is a member of his *family*. This last was the narrowest and most personal relation in which he stood; nor, paradoxical as it may seem, was he ever regarded as *himself*, as a distinct individual. His individuality was swallowed up in his family. I repeat the definition of a primitive society given before. It has for its units, not individuals, but groups of men united by the reality or the fiction of blood-relationship.[23]

For Durkheim, too, the differences between primitive and modern societies are very great. As with Maine, the juridical rules of the community indicate the prevailing form of social relationship and, in particular, the basis of solidarity.[24] In primitive society, which he calls "mechanical," there is a high degree of repressive law, in which similarity of conduct is ensured by the authorities' classification of any significant departures from custom as crimes. These crimes, symbolic acts against community solidarity, exact the most extreme penalties (mainly death). Organic solidarity, that is, "modern" society, on the other hand, is characterized by complex forms of interactions between individuals and groups. Functional interdependence is the key to this solidarity. Repressive law is only a small part of the juridical system. Restitutive law is the main part. Like Maine, Durkheim gives us a concept of evolution of social systems from lower to higher forms. The *deus ex machina* that provides the transition from one to the other is the division of labor.

These distinctions, although powerful, turned *tradition* into a blanket term to cover all forms of social life other than the modern industrial type.[25] They, and others like them, are subject to the criticisms applied by Firth in his analysis of Maine. "His ideas of social development in terms of polar opposites: family to individual, status to contract, penal legislation to civil law, are too arbitrary and naive by modern standards of analysis."[26] This criticism would also apply to theoreticians like Weber, Sombart, Tönnies, and Durkheim and to some of the more recent ones, like McClelland and Hagen. The latter see in the universalization of modernity an outlook that is necessarily anti-traditional (with *traditional* meaning a fundamentally closed, personalistic way of life, relatively fixed and not easily amenable to development).

ROLES AS INDICATORS
OF MODERNIZATION

Viewing the change from agrarian to industrial society from a nineteenth-century perspective, the historical sociologists were mainly concerned with the effect of the process on the civic community, with politics seen largely as the evolution of morals. What happens to the family and to the work group when the ties of kin and oath are no longer binding? What forms of normative regulation replace the cross-pressures of the intimate environment? From these questions grew the interest in urbanization, personality, the factory, and culture change and the links these factors have with the regulatory mechanisms of the society.[27]

Today an analysis of society proceeds in terms of professionalization, skill, technology, rationality, and functionality—all terms that we associate with modern society. We identify these abstractions in terms of particular strategic roles in the society, for example, the civil servant, the hydraulic engineer, the community development expert, the university lecturer. How sharp is their contrast to traditional roles—the chief, the priest, the queen mother, the bearers of the king's patrimony!

Putting the matter in terms of roles, however, only makes us aware how complex the process of modernization is. New roles emerge at every point. In a sense, that is what change really is—the formation of new, adaptive roles in a system. Modernization employs particular roles that have been drawn from various industrial societies (and ordinarily associated with Western industrial society, although modernization can no longer be claimed as peculiarly Western) and that embody choices between life-styles and the idea of "career."

Roles, new or old, modified and adapted, given new meaning by changes, ought to be the beginning point for the analysis of modernization. They provide much of the data for the analysis of politics. They embody new notions of morality. In forming modalities of interaction, they illuminate the actual problems that arise in the social sphere, which can be seen as problems of mobility and of direct conflicts in values as well as problems of relationships between people at the workplace and at the place of worship. What Banfield describes as "ethos" in the southern Italian village of Montegrano can be translated into "roles." And as S. F. Nadel has suggested, the way roles are put together reveals something of the moral basis of the community and the structure of the society as well.

> The advantages of role summation lie in the strengthening of social integration and of social control. For the more roles an individual combines in his person, the more is he linked by relationships with persons in other roles and in diverse areas of social life. Equally, any additional role assumed by an individual ties him more firmly to the norms of his society.[28]

To illustrate these remarks, let us take the proposition that modernization is a slower and less ruthless process than rapid industrialization. In terms of roles, this means that during modernization a large number of intermediate roles come into being whose primary functional significance is to mediate between old and new. We can speculate that such roles will in some measure act both to facilitate innovation and to resist it. In the case of industrialization, however, the intermediate roles that have come into being during modernization are swept away, as they have become only obstacles and are no longer of use. For example, commercialization, as an aspect of modernization, may be acceptable to particular groups of individuals who can act as middlemen in all alien community and at the same time resist changing their family habits and their living arrangements. Retaining a brokerage relationship between town and country, they may rely on familial rather than contractual ties to undertake commerce and may hoard their money (or distribute it in the bazaar to innumerable relatives) rather than invest it for development. Thus such brokerage roles may at one stage serve as modernization instruments and at another may deter modernization.

There is no such thing as a purely modern role. The lawyer

represented modernity in Latin America in 1930. Today it is the economist. Tomorrow it may be the engineer. Certain roles are strategic indicators of modernity at one point in time but not at another. Clearly, then, we must locate meaningful sets of roles that include the most functional careers for a particular level of innovation and that are recognized as most significant by change-oriented members of the community. These may include technical-bureaucratic careers, political careers (when government or party is employed as a modernizing instrument), and so on. How such careers are placed in a society indicates the society's choice of organization and its ways of manipulating organization. A comparative study of modernization begins in the comparison of strategic career profiles in relation to stratification.

THE MANAGEMENT OF ROLES

The complexity of the problem of roles links modernization to politics. The expectation that political leaders will advance their countries from one status to another, as from dependence to independence, is only part of a generally more widespread demand for innovation in the community, including the universal desire to raise living standards. Even raising living standards requires such radically new attitudes of hope and daring and a willingness to tinker and meddle with already established roles that most political leaders are forced to alter the hierarchy of power and prestige and to set their sights on some new corporate image of society in which the modernization roles will fit together, make sense, and work.[29]

Such an environment of changing roles results in a sense of hope as well as grievance. Modernization is often associated with breaking dominance-submission relationships and the repugnant analogies that have been associated with them. Modernization means, from this point of view, the establishment of agencies and instruments of modernity that allow independent rather than dependent relationships. As a result, the development of skills, the awareness of new patterns of time, participation, mastery over nature, and so on, are transformed into a search for personal integrity, worth, and self-respect. These are, of course, well-known observations, but they are worth repeating, because they may somehow help us render more accessible the instruments and institutions of present highly developed countries without being offensive. This is difficult, however, given that modernization is linked to a wide range of adjustive emotional attitudes that assert personality, cultural autonomy, and political independence.

In many societies, the intensity of belief is not based on blindness and superstition but on a deep-rooted fear that personal identity will be destroyed if religious or political practices are changed. This is why, in the effort to reorganize their societies today, many political leaders rely on the connections they can make with tradition. These connections help to create an inheritance. Israel, for example, in addition to wishing to reinforce her historic claims to the site, is preoccupied with archaeology as more than an academic pastime. In Senegal, research by some indigenous scholars is devoted to linking ancient Egypt as a black kingdom with sub-Saharan Africa.[30] In the Convention People's Party headquarters in Accra, there were to be found large murals depicting Africans as the founders of ancient law and medicine. The desire to modernize without losing tradition necessitates a search for a new moral synthesis in which the individual can be related to authority.

Modernity and traditionalism are linked together in fundamental ways, even in the context of modernization. The synthesis between them serves as a primary moral focus. Michael Polanyi's description of science can be applied to the relationship between tradition and modernity. He commented that science, reflecting the modern mind, is in a paradoxical condition.

A new destructive skepticism is linked here to a new passionate social conscience; an utter disbelief in the spirit of man is coupled with extravagant moral demands. We see at work here the form of action which has already dealt so many shattering blows to the modern world: the chisel of skepticism driven by the hammer of social passion.[31]

Both in the modernizing nations and elsewhere men have refined their moral sensibilities along with their skepticism. At no time in history had the world been so sensitive to moral subtleties and more likely to take transgressions seriously. This sensitivity is expressed in the search for new political forms, in the public's desire for reform, and in the willingness to apply research and science to human problems. A paradox arises in that the more people desire to ameliorate their ills, the more these crowd in upon them. Each fresh solution only uncovers more problems.[32]

These remarks should also suggest that political development is no mere reciprocal of economic development but rather a complex of factors that results in systemic coherence. This "urge to coherence" may not necessarily materialize successfully. But in the effort to create a more effective integrated system, economic factors will most frequently come to serve political and social needs. The criteria for the economic proposals and programs involved in the development of modernizing nations are first political.[33]

Two related and important concerns that arise from the study of development in general, or economic development, more specifically, and that might be added to the factors already mentioned are, first, the problem of how development gets started. That is, what preconditions are essential to initiate development? And second, once begun, does development come to an end? This is an important question, because it involves some examination of retraditionalization, which is another way of suggesting that a new coherence of values, institutions, and organization must be established near the end of a development period and, indeed, that they are part of it. This question is not only important because of the relationship between traditionalism and modernization but also because of the effects of industrialization on both. So dynamic is this latter form of development that we tend to think of it as preventing a new institutionalization of social life, as causing a malintegration in the institutional and organizational spheres (during the conversion from modernization to industrialization), papered over by ideological beliefs that give the appearance of integration without its social reality. Many modernizing societies thus became vulnerable to totalitarian ideologies as they seek to industrialize. Failure to "retraditionalize" poses a continuous political problem in the sphere of basic legitimacy, which no amount of technological achievement can resolve.

Hence, great tension exists in the lives of modernizing men. Schools and universities can hardly be expected to pass on the accumulated values of the community when these are in constant flux. The socialization process becomes a tension-creating system. Moreover, such tension is a key feature of the creative process in modern developing societies. Status conflict, value conflict, marginality—these have all been recognized as having important consequences in producing creative and innovative individuals. In such a condition (when an entire system is regulated by its marginal relationships), the political dimension becomes the focal point of stability, supplying a framework in which conflicts can be worked out. To that extent, government becomes the strategic instrument of development, and the result is a high degree of government regulation of social life in order to introduce greater coherence of values and institutions and to cater to creative tension.[34]

OVERLAPPING CHARACTERISTICS OF DEVELOPMENT, MODERNIZATION, AND INDUSTRIALIZATION

Development, modernization, and industrialization, although related phenomena, can be placed in a descending order of generality. Development, the most general, results from the proliferation and integration of functional roles in a community. Modernization is a particular case of development. Modernization implies three conditions—a social system that can constantly innovate without falling apart (and that includes among its essential beliefs the acceptability of change); differentiated, flexible social structures; and a social framework to provide the skills and knowledge necessary for living in a technologically advanced world. Industrialization, a special aspect of modernization, may be defined as the period in a society in which the strategic functional roles are related to manufacturing. It is possible to attempt the modernization of a given country without much industry, but it is not possible to industrialize without modernization.

It is possible for a modernizing country to have a large manufacturing sector and yet fail to develop an industrial infrastructure because its industry is merely an extension of the industrial system of another country. This is a common problem in many Latin American countries. They have a large number of foreign firms involved in processing, assembly, and light industry. These activities build up a local body of workers and technicians, whose operations, however, are integrated with the system of the metropolitan country rather than with their own. This is a normal characteristic of late modernization and represents a classic case of imperialism. Nationalization of such foreign-owned industries is, therefore, an increasingly common feature of the transition from late modernization to industrialization. Recent examples are Yugoslavia, where the rupture in political relations with the U.S.S.R. effectively broke a semicolonial economic relationship, and Cuba, where the same process occurred vis-à-vis the United States.

It is now necessary to link these comments to those made earlier about development. At its broadest, development is the process by which secular norms of conduct are universalized. These secular norms can be thought of in terms of the distinctions introduced by Maine (between status and contract); Durkheim (between mechanical and organic solidarity; sacred and secular beliefs); Weber (between instru-

mental and consummatory ends; traditional and legal-rational authority); and Tönnies (between *Gemeinschaft* and *Gesellschaft*). They have
been elaborated by Parsons in his pattern variables and by Levy in his
analytical structures of aspects of relationships (both of which have been
modified by Moore by his corrective emphasis on the dynamic
properties exhibited by social systems at all stages of the developmental
process).[35]

How is modernization, a particular case of development, different
from industrialization? Industrialization is that aspect of modernization
so powerful in its consequences that it alters dysfunctional social
institutions and customs by creating new roles and social instruments,
based on the use of the machine. More dynamic than modernization, it
is also more narrowly consistent in its processes.

The comparative study of modernization is conceptually more
cloudy and in many ways more difficult than the comparative study of
industrialization. However, the study of modernization is at present
more important to us, especially as a means of identifying those social
arrangements that help or hinder industrialization and as a means of
observing how changes become adjusted or lead to further change.
Clifford Geertz has suggested that

> though it may be true that, as an economic process, development is a
> dramatic revolutionary change, as a broadly social process it fairly clearly
> is not. What looks like a quantum jump from a specifically economic
> point of view is, from a generally social one, merely the final expression in
> economic terms of a process which has been building up gradually over an
> extended period of time.[36]

Included in this judgment is an emphasis on the importance of human or
social capital, which seems to be more significant for modernity than
material resources. These points appear more obvious after industrialization has become a political objective of government, and decisions
and arrangement are made to further it.

ROLE SETS AND GROWTH INDEXES

As I have said, it will be a long time before most of the modernizing
nations are in a position to industrialize, even if they continue to
modernize strenuously. A modernizing country needs to take part in the

international division of labor, so that exogamous industrialization roles may form the support-structure of the country's modernization roles. Modernization roles in Nigeria, for example, depend upon foreign industrial roles. It is not surprising, therefore, that political leaders try to minimize this dependence through the internationalization of dependence, that is, by spreading out international exchanges with a variety of industrialized countries and by efforts at internal industrialization. Efforts to promote the latter may be premature and result in great expense and waste of resources.[37] Modernization, not industrialization, will be the key to development in most new countries for some time to come.

The comparative mode of analysis directs us to those changing forms and values of human institutions that require the patient arts of government. Comparative data available today are rich in examples covering a broad range of political types, races, and cultures.[38] The main guides to modernization that can be compared most easily are the following key sets of modernization roles and growth indexes: career and entrepreneurship roles (numbers and pervasiveness), and technology and per capita income.

Obviously, these four factors vary in degree of explicitness. Administration may be treated as a key form of career, and roles in the civil service, including technical services, may be analyzed. It is more difficult to study entrepreneurs if only because their talent is quite often latent, depending for its appearance on propitious circumstances. Moreover, if we extend the notion of entrepreneurship to include political entrepreneurs, that is, those who organize a following in order to gain access to state resources, then we will have to include a number of political leaders in our figures.

With respect to per capita income, the figures are obtainable, although quite often misleading. Such figures have been used as rough guides for the comparison of countries engaged in economic growth, with or without correction for the special characteristics of each country.

Measurements of technology are less easily obtainable. Efforts have been made to use kilowatt hours as one measure. Probably the energy-employment factor is as useful as any.[39]

What do such indicators show? Rather different things. Career and entrepreneurial roles imply a set of values based on the degree to which rational decision making—with universal standards of judgment and predictable and standardized rules governing conduct—has become pervasive. As institutions, these roles are more widely comparable; levels of training, skill, and experience are useful measures. Doctors, for example, can be compared across national boundaries on the basis of their performance, knowledge, and standards of ethics, as can civil servants.

Entrepreneurship, as has been suggested, poses some difficulties in analysis. The ability to innovate and challenge accepted forms of practice must be directed toward a desired goal. In both modernizing and industrializing societies, creativity may be evaluated by examining entrepreneurship. Entrepreneurship implies other qualities than mere individual skill. It suggests that in the society there are means of training people who have the potential for imaginative choice, who enjoy exploring alternatives and testing feasibilities.

Per capita income also implies certain values. That such figures are available suggests the existence of a previously developed, complex standard of measurement of income and expenditures, investment and consumption. Both gross and net national products have been calculated. The ideas of planning, growth, estimated depreciation on physical plant, and so on, have already become regular items of bookkeeping.

The fourth main factor in modernization, technology, is a measure of the degree to which nonhuman energy is employed in the conduct of complex tasks. For this reason, it is the most strategic test of modernization, because it implies planning, allocating, and organizing resources around abstract principles that, when applied, will lead to desired results.

THE SPECIAL PROBLEM
OF EQUALITY

Modernizing roles, both institutionalized and innovative, are normally associated with very different styles of life from that of the ordinary public. Residential patterns are observably different. (Civil servants, for example, are quite often provided with government estate housing.) A successful entrepreneur may try to show his success by naming an office building after himself, by building a large residence, or by displaying other outward manifestations of success. In countries where modernization problems are severe, these differences in life-styles become points of tension. They distinguish the rich from the poor, the more modern from the more traditional, and the urban from the rural. Here then is an interesting puzzle. Development creates inequality; modernization accentuates it.[40]

This tension between equality of access and extension of the social hierarchy is one stimulus to continual modernization. If the stimulus stems from the original assumption that the discrepancies in life-styles and roles characteristic of modernizing societies are temporary, systems able to employ the tension caused by inequity will be able to generate a continuous developmental process. Hence, inequality can be seen both as a cause of modernization and as a result of it. This is particularly the case when government is being used to enlarge the modernized sector. As T. H. Marshall has suggested, inequality in the context of citizenship produces a constant agitation for equality in every sphere. Successful pressure for equality will compress both ends of the scale of income distribution, extend the area of the modernizing culture and experience, and enrich the universal status of citizenship.[41]

Although it is a central feature of the modernization process, the tension imposed by the lack of equality may be extremely awkward to manage. Attempting to manage it provides government with some of its most important work. The adjustment of roles and systems of roles is always difficult, even when inequality is accepted as a norm. How much more difficult it is when modernity and the expectation of equality go hand in hand. Nor do material conditions of equality suffice, for psychic inequalities may remain.[42] The most important point to keep in mind, however, is that such tension contains the principles of legitimacy, that is, equity and potentiality.

The achievement of equality is an ever-spreading moral objective in the modern world. Few modern societies, even if they institutionalize inequality, regard it as a good thing. The desire for equality grows, covering more and more social attributes. Race can no longer serve as a ground for inequality, nor can religion, ethnic association, or other attributes. One might say that as secular beliefs associated with the modernization process are universalized, there is a corresponding peeling off of different layers of belief associated with inequality.

The urge to equality is invariably translated into matters of practical political doctrine. Colonialism, which postulated a relationship of inequality in the political sphere, has largely disappeared. No matter how wise an enlightened official may have been, his presence in an alien territory violated egalitarian values. Claims to equal treatment by Blacks in the American South are based on the belief that pigmentation should have no relevance to social hierarchy.[43] Gone, too, is the notion of the lowly but worthy servant or the yeomanlike laborer. There are few countries nowadays where servile positions are regarded as inherently rewarding; nor is a man's worth based entirely on generalized social qualities like self-respect, devotion, thrift, or personal honor.[44]

The "predicament of equality" causes governments to indulge in some rather interesting ideological and structural maneuvers. One advantage in stressing the political condition as the primary expression of egalitarianism (by equating citizenship and equality) is that political hierarchy (and, therefore, inequality) may then be defined as an organizational device through which the political elite becomes the instrument of the citizenry. Differences in rewards, both in power and in prestige, can be explained in terms of the need to modernize and, particularly, to attract into the organization individuals most functional to the modernization process, that is, planners, technicians, training officers, community development specialists, and the like. When political hierarchy is defined in functional terms as a corps of technicians, with specific roles and circumscribed spheres of competence, it thus becomes a mechanism to achieve equality—a postponed and somewhat illusory but important norm.

General authority is limited to a few highly diffused, all-purpose roles. By emphasizing change and development, present inequalities may be seen not only as temporary but as necessary for further change. Hence, the public can be led to regard political inequality as a device for gaining equality.

EQUALITY AND THE ROLE OF
THE INTELLECTUALS

During the modernization process, the intellectuals have a special role to play, for they are most inclined to respect the culture of freedom. At the same time they remain exceedingly vulnerable to an egalitarian-minded public. If they help to make a revolution in the name of the people, they cannot also be expected to be effective in restricting the excesses of the people. In their attempt to identify with the public, intellectuals quite often accuse each other of having inflated egos, of being pompous, and, in fact, of being divorced from the people. In arguing for equality, they often downgrade their own enterprises to the point where no one need have any respect for them. People who are denied entry into the clubs of the intelligentsia, for example, are often pleased to take the latter at their own public evaluation.[45]

These tendencies have been particularly evident among intellectuals during revolutionary periods. Shils has discussed the deep politicization of the intellectuals:

> The high degree of political involvement of the intellectual in under-developed countries is a complex phenomenon. It has a threefold root. The primary source is a deep preoccupation with authority. Even though he seeks and seems actually to break away from the authority of the powerful traditions in which he was brought up, the intellectual of underdeveloped countries, still more than his confrere in more advanced countries, retains the need for incorporation into some self-transcending, authoritative entity. Indeed, the greater his struggle for emancipation from the traditional collectivity, the greater his need for incorporation into a new, alternative collectivity. Intense politicization meets this need. The second source of political involvement is the scarcity of opportunities to acquire an even temporary sense of vocational achievement; there have been few counterattractions to the appeal of charismatic politics. Finally, there has been a deficient tradition of civility in the underdeveloped countries which affects the intellectuals as much as it does the non-intellectuals.[46]

And Lipset has pointed out that the leadership of the intellectuals in new states does not survive the first revolutionary generation.

Three points become clear from these comments. First, the intellectuals are clearly politically engaged. They manipulate the intellectual side of any modernization movement and represent its brains. Second, the postrevolutionary political culture is quite often the creature of the intellectuals; but they are only a precondition of it and not in themselves a sufficient basis for it. Nowhere is this more clearly illustrated than in the American experience, in which a numerous intellectual political leadership created the civic culture that in broad outline has been sustained to the present time.[47] Third, intellectuals are extremely vulnerable to populism and quite often contribute to their own vulnerability in trying to identify with popular groups. Indeed, in countries that take socialism at all seriously, the ambiguity surrounding the role of the intellectual is a good token of the status of political freedom in the country. The most frequently encountered socialist intellectuals are less than brilliant; and if they miss excellence by a wide margin, they are often punitive and resentful. Some overtly compromise with nationalists in order to secure their status, finally losing their moral strength. Others may adopt the "necessities of the revolution" as an article of faith and become willing the faithful cohorts of any regime in power.

Modernization is thus a trying phenomenon for intellectuals; they are bearers of the culture of modernity and at the same time are vulnerable to the forces they help unleash. This is particularly the case in systems in which the ideology is blindly naive or utopian, as in the Soviet Union directly after the revolution and in many of the developing countries today. Consider a typical statement in the early stages of the Soviet Union:

> But if one then thinks of the schoolmasters of this present day, the absolute unfitness of the bourgeois intellect for the new society, the necessity that this entire generation of intellectuals should disappear in the transitional process of the dictatorship of the proletariat, become evident. The annihilation must be definite, for the type cannot be tolerated even in a modified form. It is evident that the very notion of teacher, professor, etc, must be obliterated. The ideal can be approximated only if all co-operate towards "education," considering this as a natural part of their daily work.[48]

There is often a similar emphasis in contemporary modernizing societies. The lowering of educational standards to increase recruitment and to make it more egalitarian can have the effect of weakening the position of the intellectuals and forcing them to the periphery of their society. The emphasis on technical education (to obtain much-needed skilled and trained manpower) may disguise a deeper political objective, namely, a more professionalized and pliable elite, antiseptic in its role and unwilling to engage in the moral issues posed by modernization. This elite, like the civil service, has obedience built into its positions.

Obviously, the question of the intellectual's role in political modernization is a complex one. It is easy to find fault with the obstinacy and blindness of intellectuals and to root this in the social distance that exists between the educated—the "black Englishman" or "Balliol-Indian"— and the noneducated. But these are hackneyed examples and caricatures. Quite often those who seriously wrestle with the deeper aspects of the politics of modernization (and whose sensitivities are aroused by so ruthless a process) are destroyed by the forces of populism; when this happens, an important part of the yeast of modernization is lacking, and the civic culture is to that extent diminished.

Modernizing revolutions are not mindless; nor are they raw mass movements striking out blindly against injustice. They are complexes of individuals and groups that are seeking solutions to particular problems and see hope in change. But a modernizing revolution, whether bland or bloody, has no subject matter other than that provided by its interpreters and its thinkers, its writers and pamphleteers, its orators and proclaimers. Public meaning is, after all, a political matter and not merely a symposium of private views. In creating this public meaning and identifying the interconnections and directions of change, the intellectuals play a critical role. The regime that can make use of them in this way helps its own cause. When they are alienated, debased, or corrupt, the process of modernization becomes politically more precarious.

One can, of course, overstate the role of the intellectuals. It is important, however, to distinguish them from the elite in general and, more particularly, to separate them as individuals, wrestling with the world as they see it, from their skills or roles.

Most intellectuals have had considerable education and are found in intellectual roles. They are not scattered, like leavening, in all social bodies at all layers of a community. Furthermore, they tend to live adjacent to one another and to intermarry. This reinforces them as a group, on one hand, but also sets them apart. How the intellectuals are balanced with other groups determines the political form modernization is likely to take and also the state of morality during the process; for ultimately, intellectuals are drawn to the moral implications of political conduct. The role of the intellectual, then, is a key indicator of the nature of the polity during modernization.

YOUTH AND THE INTELLECTUALS

If intellectuals represent one special indicator in modernizing societies, youth represents another. The former may desire equality, but they are in danger of being destroyed by it. Youth wants equality as a right, as a way of succeeding to adulthood. Both groups are dissatisfied, and the one may express the hostilities of the other.

A modernization process depends heavily on youth precisely because the members of this group are ordinarily the most eager to adopt modern roles. They have less to "unlearn," as it were. Modernization is thus a universalizing process among youth that transcends nationality. Youth movements are likely to build fraternal links with one another in many countries just as intellectuals are likely to be known by one another across national boundaries. Congresses and meetings of youth are as much a feature of modern life as are schools and factories. Modernizing youth are deeply politicized, and such politicization is an important part of growing up.

There is a peculiar rhythm to this universalizing process among youth, dependent in large measure, of course, on the shape of politics and the form of authority in a country. We must not forget, however, that youth cannot be considered an undifferentiated group. Some will fill the roles of the modern community and at a senior level. Others may fall by the wayside to become disgruntled and angry young men. Still others may form cadres in the community, which blindly accept an official line. Indeed, once the first political phase of a modernization revolution has passed, succeeding generations of youth may become more rather than less parochial—more wedded to local party cadres than to the wider world, and more provincial than the intellectuals, leaving the latter isolated, at times abused, and rendering them anachronistic and, therefore, unable to serve the process they helped create. Occasionally, when the youth are cut off from the intellectuals, the resulting process may be modernization by technicians, with the accompanying danger that the less provincial visions of society will disappear. Indeed, the extent to which the youth culture becomes cramped and limited, or turns away from the wider intellectual stream, depends directly on the degree to which the youth and intellectuals become mutually alienated.[49]

NOTES

1. See Giorgio de Santillana, *The Crime of Galileo* (Chicago: University of Chicago Press, 1955), p. 11.

2. The characteristics of modern industrial societies have been usefully summed in an article by F. X. Sutton, as follows:

1. Predominance of universalistic, specific, and achievement norms.
2. High degree of social mobility (in a general—not necessarily "vertical"—sense).
3. Well developed occupational system, insulated from other social structures.
4. "Egalitarian" class system based on generalized patterns of occupational achievement.
5. Prevalence of "associations," i.e., functionally specific, non-ascriptive structures.

See Sutton, "Social Theory and Comparative Politics," reprinted in H. Eckstein and David E. Apter, eds., *Comparative Politics: A Reader* (New York: Free Press, 1963), p. 71.

3. See Lea A. Williams, *Overseas Chinese Nationalism: The Genesis of the Pan-Chinese Movement in Indonesia, 1900-1916* (New York: Free Press, 1960), pp. 138-39.

4. See Daniel Lerner, *The Passing of Traditional Society* (New York: Free Press, 1958).

5. See Kurt W. Back, "The Change-Prone Person in Puerto Rico," *Public Opinion Quarterly* 22 (Fall 1958). Back points out that for the urbanized and lower economic stratum in which his survey was conducted, personality tests and attitude indices distinguished change-prone from other individuals.

The modernism index has a central place in this complex, showing high relations on the one side to the personality measures and on the other to behavioral indices. This index is made up of two questions, (a) belief in and relation to the new generation, and (b) active planning for improvement of the situation. It shows that the key ingredient in modernism is orientation toward the future. We can conclude that this attitude is based on a somewhat general personality disposition (p. 340).

6. Lewis, *The Emergence of Modern Turkey* (London: Oxford University Press, 1961), p. 472.

7. See Edward and L. F. Banfield, *The Moral Basis of a Backward Society* (New York: Free Press, 1958).

8. These figures are taken from Morroe Berger, *Bureaucracy and Society in Modern Egypt: A Study of the Higher Civil Service* (Princeton, NJ: Princeton University Press, 1957), pp. 42-27.

9. See the description of Aggery in David Kimble, *A Political History of Ghana, 1850-1928* (Oxford: Clarendon Press, 1963), pp. 215-20. See also J. E. Flint, *Sir George Goldie and the Making of Modern Nigeria* (London: Oxford University Press, 1960); P. D. Curtin, *The Image of Africa* (Madison: University of Wisconsin Press, 1964), chap. xvi; and R. Robinson, J. Gallagher, and A. Denny, *Africa and the Victorians* (London: Macmillan, 1961), chap. xii.

10. See Burns, *History of Nigeria* (London: George Allen & Unwin, 1951), pp. 141-42.

11. See Mary Benson, *The African Patriots* (London: Faber & Faber, 1963).

12. See Walter Z. Laqueur, *Communism and Nationalism in the Middle East* (London: Routledge & Kegan Paul, 1961), pp. 18-21.

13. See Pye, "Administrators, Agitators, and Brokers," *Public Opinion Quarterly* 22 (Fall 1958). See also D. A. Rustow, *Politics of Westernization in the Near East* (Princeton, NJ: Princeton University, Center of International Studies, 1956). For an examination of the problem of the representation of such roles, see the excellent study by Reinhard Bendix, "Public Authority in a Developing Political Community: The Case of India," *European Journal of Sociology* 4 (1963). For a study of role change in the context of local government, see Ursula K. Hicks, *Development from Below* (Oxford: Clarendon Press, 1961); and for a general commentary on "the will to economize," which in many ways represents the beginnings of modernity, see W. Arthur Lewis, *The Theory of Economic Growth* (London: George Allen & Unwin, 1955).

14. See the interesting discussion of this in T. A. Hsia, *Enigma of the Five Martyrs* (Berkeley: University of California, Institute of International Studies, 1962), pp. 74-75.

15. See Rosemary Arnold, "A Port of Trade: Whydah on the Guinea Coast," in *Trade and Markets in the Early Empires*, ed. Karl Polanyi, Conrad Arensberg, and Harry Pearson (New York: Free Press, 1957). See also Paul Bohannan and George Dalton, *Markets in Africa* (New York: Doubleday Anchor Books, 1965).

16. There is an interesting literature on West African stratification. See D. Westermann, *Autobiographies d'Africaines* (Paris: Payot, 1943); Jacques Charpy, *La Fondation de Dakar* (Paris: Larose, 1958); M. Banton, *West African City* (London: Oxford University Press, 1957); and Arthur Porter, *Creoledom* (London: Oxford University Press, 1963). Many others could be cited.

17. Such generalization are always open to criticism because they are excessively broad. For one thing, there is no colonial "system" except in the very loose sense of the subordination by one country of a noncontiguous territory whose political status is legally defined as inferior to the metropolitan country. In some instances, political reform meant providing greater and greater warrants of autonomy and an enlarged share in political life to the modernized elite within the territory, looking toward the time when representative bodies, which in constitutional practice embody legitimacy, could be established. When a colony could pay its own way and when representative self-government was securely established, then political independence for the territory logically followed.

18. See Frederick Madden, "Some Origins and Purposes in the Formation of British Colonial Government," in Kenneth Robinson and Frederick Madden, eds., *Essays in Imperial Government* (Oxford: Basil Blackwell, 1963), p. 2. For an astringent view of colonialism, see Paul A. Baran, *The Political Economy of Growth* (New York: Monthly Review Press, 1962), pp. 163-300.

19. Even gross distinctions between French and British colonial practice (direct and indirect rule) have turned out to be schoolboy distinctions that are almost useless for analytical purposes. But there are still some important comparisons that can be made. For some time, the French ideal of political evolution overseas was to raise a territory or group of territories to a status similar to that of a department of France, with gradually greater warrants of authority resulting in increased participation in the institution of French politics—the National Assembly, the Cabinet, and the like. Some overseas territories were in fact governed as departments. Of course, this pattern was not unambiguous, and such ambiguity can perhaps best be seen in the institutions of the French Union, which would eventually have diverted overseas territories from French metropolitan institutions, which, in turn, would increasingly have become instruments of overseas rather than metropolitan deputies. France did not relish the prospect of becoming a captive of her territories. Still, the emphasis on the metropole, its legal structure, the uniformity of its educational system, the forms of overseas aid, and the fiscal and financial structure (which was more closely linked to the metropole than in the British system) all helped to create quite different attitudes toward politics. The French educational system, for example, helped to spread both Catholic and socialist forms of universalism as political ideologies, whereas the bewildering array of English forms of education—the various mission schools, government schools, and private and public schools—were geared more directly to local political life, local councils, and local problems.

20. For a detailed discussion of these types in an East African context, see my book, *The Political Kingdom in Uganda* (Princeton, NJ: Princeton University Press, 1961), pp. 447-59.

21. See Cohn, *The Pursuit of the Millennium* (New York: Harper Torch Books, 1961), p. 28.

22. Less interesting are the cases where complexity occurs as a result of more population increase, but even in these cases, the effects may be of significance. This is one reason why ancient societies are of interest to us. Moreover, the whole question of the relationship of differentiation and growth to the formation of high cultures, traditional in form, is one that has barely been explored.

23. See Henry Sumner Maine, *Ancient Law* (Boston: Beacon Press, 1963), pp. 177-78.

24. Durkheim says, "Our method has now been fully outlined. Since law reproduces the principal forms of social solidarity, we have only to classify the different types of law to find therefrom the different types of social solidarity which correspond to it" (Emile Durkheim, *The Division of Labor* [New York: Free Press, 1949], p. 68).

25. What all these distinctions, primitive-complex, sacred-secular, folk-urban, mechanical-organic, and *Gemeinschaft-Gesellschaft*, have in common is their implicit notion of development as moving from the simple to the complex—the complex forming an elaborate network of mediating and integrating points in political life, in religion, or in religion, or in the economy—a notion that I share.

26. See Raymond Firth's "Preface," in Maine, *Ancient Law*, p. xxx.

27. Emerging now as a significant from of analysis is the study of the polity as the mechanism of change, with the morality of change embodied in the state itself. Durkheim, in a rather surprising passage, says, "The fundamental duty of the State is laid down in this very fact: it is to persevere in calling the individual to a moral way of life. I say fundamental duty, for civic morals can have no pole-star for a guide except moral causes" (mile Durkheim, *Professional Ethics and Civic Morals* [New York: Free Press, 1958], p. 69).

28. Nadel, *The Theory of Social Structure* (New York: Free Press, 1957), p. 71. See also Banfield and Banfield, *The Moral Basis.*

29. Willie Abraham has put the matter as follows:

When one culture borrows some of its industrial technique and institutions from another culture, one can expect that, depending on how central these are in the matrix, they will already be controlled and permeated with other cultural elements, even if these only take the form of tea breaks. It could certainly happen that these borrowed items are in their native setting surrounded by ideals, attitudes, relationships, inter-human habits, which include design of buildings, amenities, types and method of control of labour, relationships between employees and managers and employers, attitudes of labour to work, and happen to be repeated in their new setting. But even when this is so, the borrowers may still feel considerable pain at their own institutions and techniques having been replaced. This is sometimes due to the mistaken but natural belief that the new institutions cannot be serving the same purpose writ large, or are not informed by the same ideals. But this belief, though sometimes mistaken, has an opportunity of being correct from the very fact that it is natural. Indeed, that this is a distinct possibility is a consequence of the corrosive effect of material culture on the value aspect of culture. The possibility that certain techniques and institutions are already infused with cultural elements of the people from whom they are lifted, may well make it impossible to effect a simple transplantation. It may become necessary to carry out an operation more in the nature of a graft.

The Mind of Africa (Chicago: University of Chicago Press, 1962), pp. 33-34. This kind of concern, expressed politically, is one basis for the direct political control of innovation.

30. See Cheikh Anta Diop, *Nations Negres et Culture* (Paris: Editions Africaines, 1955).

31. Polanyi, *The Logic of Liberty* (Chicago: University of Chicago Press, 1958), p. 4.

32. This paradox is reflected in attitudes to modern ideologies. None seems able to capture the public imagination for long, either programmatically or morally. In the developing areas, interestingly enough, it is the heroic individual or leader, rather than his

ideas, around which the many rally in order to organize themselves. There, leadership and progress can be seen to go together. In the more developed areas, it is more complex than that. Offended morality leads to outrage. We still do not know where outrage will lead.

33. Perhaps the most consistent efforts to explore the relationship between economic and political development have been in the work of the Social Science Research Council's subcommittee on economic growth. Joseph Spengler, Wilbert Moore, Bert Hoselitz, and others have been trying to establish the conditions surrounding it. There are many others. See Joseph J. Spengler, "Theory, Ideology, Non-Economic Values, and Politico-Economic Development," and Wilbert E. Moore, "The Social Framework of Economic Development," in *Tradition, Values and Socio-Economic Development*, ed. Ralph J. D. Braibanti and Joseph J. Spengler (Durham, NC: Duke University Press, 1961); Wilbert E. Moore and Arnold S. Feldman, "Commitment of the Industrial Labor Force," in *Labor Commitment and Social Change in Developing Areas*, ed. Moore and Feldman (New York: Social Science Research Council, 1960); Wilbert E. Moore, *Industrialization and Labor* (Ithaca: Cornell University Press, 1951). Hoselitz has been more concerned with a historical-economics approach than with a sociological one; see "Main Concepts in the Analysis of the Social Implications of Technical Change," in *Industrialization and Society*, ed. Bert F. Hoselitz and Wilbert E. Moore (The Hague: Mouton-UNESCO, 1963), and "Theories of Stages of Economic Growth," in *Theories of Economic Growth*, ed. Bert F. Hoselitz (New York: Free Press, 1960).

34. See Frank Barron, *Creativity and Psychological Health* (Princeton, NJ: Van Nostrand, 1963).

35. See, in particular, Moore's criticism of the simple model of development that begins with a static notion of preindustrial society, delineates a dynamic transitional period, and ends with the system coming to rest, as it were, in a "developed" but static period once again (Wilbert E. Moore, "Industrialization and Social Change," in Hoselitz and Moore, *Industrialization and Society*, chap. xv). See also Wilbert E. Moore, *Social Change* (Englewood Cliffs, NJ: Prentice-Hall, 1963), p. 42.

36. Clifford Geertz, *Peddlers and Princes* (Chicago: University of Chicago Press, 1963), p. 2. For a case study of this approach in a different setting, see Walter Elkan, *Migrants and Proletarians* (London: Oxford University Press, 1960). See also Claude Tardits, *Porto-Novo: Less nouvelles generations africaines entre leurs traditions et l'occident* (Paris and The Hague: Mouton, 1958).

37. Industrialization, however, will be a symbolic objective and, as such, will be maintained by bringing overseas investment from many different sources into competitive and, therefore, manipulatable circumstances.

38. Indeed, with respect to the last, one of the nice questions is whether high civilizations modernize more quickly than primitive ones. Quite often it is the highly complex and ancient civilization that shows more resistance to industrialization and the consequences of a machine technology (even when this is held to be a desirable political goal) than the simpler cultures that are embodied in delicate relationships between myth, religion, and social practice. It may prove easier for traditional African societies to become modern than for ancient societies such as India, where the blending of old and new produces great intellectual and social anxieties. One is struck by the disproportionate number of "Western" men in Nigeria and Ghana as compared with India, perhaps not in political beliefs, but in general social conduct and outlook. However, one cannot jump to the conclusion that high cultures resist modernity because of some presumed "anti-commercial" virtues or some similar reason. Milton Singer has suggested that Indians can

be as commercially minded as any other people (see "Cultural Values in India's Economic Development," *The Annals* 205 [May, 1956]). I cite this question only to show how wide a sweep there is to the political compass and to show many different areas we must demarcate for research.

39. See Karl W. Deutsch's efforts to develop transactional indicators that reflect functional interdependence in *Nationalism and Social Communication* (New York: John Wiley, 1953) and "Social Mobilization and Political Development," *American Political Science Review* 55 (September 1963).

40. This is one of the reasons why the desire for socialism in many modernizing nations is important—and also why it fails. Socialism, with its emphases on equality and modernity, ends in new forms of inequality.

41. Marshall, "Citizenship and Social Class," in *Citizenship and Social Development* (New York: Doubleday, 1964), p. 116.

42. *Psychic equality* denotes a condition in which each man feels confident of his worth on the same plane as his neighbor, with all traces of psychological deference or servility in conduct totally removed. Equality of opportunity may exist in objective terms, however, and individuals continue to feel unequal, reflecting a hangover of older class attitudes and having the effect of crippling individuals, debasing their worth, and making some act and feel lower in the scale of human values than others.

43. See St. Clair Drake, *The American Dream and the Negro* (Chicago: Roosevelt University, Division of Continuing Education, 1963), pp. 51-64.

44. Christian doctrine was always ambiguous on this score. On one hand, the meek were to inherit the earth; on the other, those who became rich and powerful through their own enterprise were the models of the community. Calvinism was never comfortable in the face of meekness.

45. See C. Vann Woodward, "The Populist Heritage and the Intellectual," *American Scholar* 29 (Winter 1959-60).

46. Edward Shils, "The Intellectuals in Political Development," *World Politics* 12 (April 1960), reprinted in John H. Kautsky, *Political Change in Underdeveloped Areas* (New York: John Wiley, 1962), p. 205.

47. Lipset points out that Philadelphia was the second largest city in the English-speaking world at the time of the American revolution. The educational level of the political leaders was high. Their literary output was very large. Their self-awareness of their role, that is, to establish a style of politics as well as a form of government, was very much in evidence in their statement and published writings. See *The First New Nation* (New York: Basic Books, 1963), pp. 66-74, 90-98.

48. S. J. Rutgers, "The Intellectuals and the Russian Revolution," in V. I. Lenin et al., *The New Policies of Soviet of Russia* (Chicago: Charles H. Kerr, n.d.), p. 106.

49. How important these interrelations are can be seen in India, where modernization is accepted as a slow process, directed only in part by government and requiring many forms of adaptation and modification. Industrialization is the eventual objective. With a new *Stand* deliberately cultivated by the British, an intelligentsia was built, apart from the pietistic, religious forms that were traditional in Taksasila, Naland, Vallabhi, and other centers of classical learning (where astrology, astronomy, logic, philosophy, history, and law were taught). The modernizing intellectuals were provided with English forms of education to make the Indian officers of government intellectually and morally fit to perform their duties with efficiency and probity, especially in the judicial and revenue branches of the public service where their responsibilities and powers were rapidly

growing. What prevented a generational conflict in real and open terms was the continual role of the intellectual in political life and a wider expansion of the intellectual culture into the emotional system. See B. B. Misra, *The Indian Middle Classes* (London: Oxford University Press, 1961). See also Philip Woodruff, *The Men Who Ruled India: The Founders* (London: Jonathan Cape, 1953-54), vol. I, *Introduction*.

4

NOTES FOR A
THEORY OF NONDEMOCRATIC
REPRESENTATION

The discussion so far lends itself to a consideration of nondemocratic representation. Need for such a theory has been apparent for some time, particularly in relation to the process of development, which changes the context in which we are accustomed to consider representative institutions and their functions. As suggested, most (although not all) nondemocratic representation is better seen as "predemocratic," rather than as alternative or hostile to democracy. Such representation is also functionally varied, depending for its relevance on the stage of development obtained and the prevailing type of political system. Indeed, different political systems stress forms of political participation relevant to the immediate context of their social situations. Given that a political type is a means to solve problems, each system type has its advantages and disadvantages. None is permanent any more than the context of social life is permanent. Representation is a variable thing, and its forms and consequences are different in each type of political system. I offer these remarks to challenge the more commonly accepted view, which evaluates all representation as it approximates our own Western experience or some ideal type of it.

Our analysis begins with an effort to describe the changing character of social life by focusing on the special relationship between government and society formed through some form of representation. Three main types of representation are emphasized: *popular*, as associated with "one man—one vote" and a conciliar form of decision making; *interest*, as associated with special corporate groupings seeking special and parochial attention; and *functional*, as associated with technicians, planners, civil servants, and the like. Each type represents a moral claim, so to speak. Popular representation is based on the rights of *citizenship*.[1]

Interest representation is based on some presumed social significance or contribution to society from a particular type of group, primarily *occupational*, such as trade unions or business, or professional organizations. Functional representation is based on presumed or recognized expertise useful to society, primarily *professional*.[2]

The framework just indicated implies some main lines for analysis: (1) a developmental social context imposing conditions within which representation occurs; (2) a set of political types, each of which emphasizes alternative modes of representation; (3) a competitive relationship between each type of representation—popular, interest, and functional—in terms of a set of functions that we call the functions of representation; and (4) the functions themselves, which are *goal specification, institutional coherence*, and *central control*. (We assume that representation has these three functions as a significant minimum.) Hence two models emerge. The first, a general model, specifies the relationship between society and government in terms of stratification and political systems-type variables. The second, a model of representation, is based on types of claim to access and functions of a representational elite. This representational model is an intervening variable in the general model.

Although the concepts employed can be applied to any concrete system, our concern here is to elaborate them in the special context of predemocratic, development politics. We will attempt to illustrate their use in a series of short synoptic descriptions, which are intended to be suggestive of some possible future lines of application. Although these illustrations are purely descriptive and impressionistic, it is possible to operationalize the entire approach by identifying the main groupings of social actors (clustered in the present stratification categories) and determining empirically and over time their type of claim to representation (popular, interest, and functional), the "weight" of that claim, and the elite functions they perform (goal specification, central control, and institutional coherence).

ON THE CONCEPT
OF "NONDEMOCRATIC"

As already indicated, these comments are designed to refer to predemocratic, rather than *anti*democratic, systems. Special attention is warranted because the association of representation with democracy is so close that to speak of nondemocratic forms of representation seems somehow a travesty. Certainly there is an "incompleteness" about predemocratic representation, as if somehow in waits for "fulfillment." This is because our Western conception of government implies an integrated political system in which needs (motives), access (participation), and goals (purposes) are balanced through representatives popularly elected and brought together in a conciliar decision-making body.

But predemocratic forms of government are not simply imperfect forms of democracy. They imply a different form of integration, perhaps coercive, in which needs are more arbitrarily defined, access is restricted, and goal priorities are realized within a public context. Public and private tend to be the same. However, representation exists here too, as we shall see. To discuss it, however, we are required to assess both the political form of government and the general underlying complexity and structural characteristics of society by identifying groups that demand government recognition in many ways: by expressing needs, demanding access, and identifying goals that governments may or may not acknowledge.

In general, we can say that representation implies a permanent relationship between a government and its society. The limits of authority each can impose on the other change, however. Because these limits are in some measure determined by "social capabilities," they are best evaluated in a context of development and modernization. Analysis of the evolving bases of social life leads to identification of the particular representational claims that form that tension between society and government common in all systems and that are ultimately manifested in a changing equilibrium between discipline and freedom as follows.

Concretely, in order to identify the group representational basis of society in a developmental context, I use certain stratification categories that seem to correspond to a particular developmental stage. These categories are preclass, for example, caste and ethnicity; class in the sense of the formation of occupationally based classes; class in the sense of the emergence of multibonded forms of class; and finally, postclass, for example, the growth of specialized functional status groupings. Generalizing from these categories gives a picture of the developmental process in which multiple and overlapping claims to representation result from a mixture of traditional social clusters and contemporary innovative ones introduced from industrialized systems.[3]

Analytically, the relationship between discipline and freedom provides a more directly political concern. It makes a difference whether society is the independent variable and government is dependent, or government is the independent variable and society is dependent. In the first instance, the claims of the society become the boundaries within which a government needs to act; in the second, society is to be molded and changed by governmental decision. To handle this set of political problems, we have developed four types of political systems: two in which government is the independent variable, the *mobilization system* and the *bureaucratic system*, and two in which society is the independent variable, the *theocratic system* and the *reconciliation system*. None of these systems needs to be "democratic" in the sense of Western representative government, which is, in fact, being excluded from this discussion.[4]

It should be clear from the discussion so far that the representational variables that link stratification to political system are central to this analysis. We are able to treat the relationships between society and government in terms of those elite formations that compete for priority performance of three main functions: *goal specification, central control*, and *institutional coherence*. If the general proposition that emerges is that where society is the dependent variable and government the independent one, these three functions are more likely to be performed by government-sponsored elite formations, such as party leaders in a single-party system. In contrast, where society is the independent variable, competition between private and public bodies for the performance of these functions is likely. In both cases, however, the ability of particular groups to take a priority position vis-à-vis these functions will be seen to depend upon the stage of development in terms of the group structure that prevails. How these elite functions are distributed determines the participant basis of the society. Today, when these functions are seen in the context of modernization and development, we describe the result as a "participation explosion." This "explosion" includes greater access to roles in the modernized sectors of society as well as the spread of such roles in the society itself. Hence the wheel comes full circle. Greater proliferation in the modernized role sector means more modernization, which, in turn, changes the pattern of prevailing needs in the system.

THE DEVELOPMENT PROCESS
AND THE GENESIS OF NEEDS

So far we have referred to the concept of *need* derivatively in terms of modernization and as made visible in the form of political demands. It is obvious that needs in traditional societies will differ in many important respects from those in industrial societies. During modernization, however, old needs will continue long after new ones appear. Need seen in developmental terms becomes progressively more complex. It has two aspects: the concrete demands produced, and the mechanisms by which these demands are represented. The first is a series of events of a day-to-day sort. The second is a set of institutional arrangements. The latter aspect concerns us at the moment.

Representative institutions are based on claims to representation by interest, functional utility, or equality of right. They derive their complexity from the overlapping qualities of traditionalism, modernism, and industrialism.[5] To diagram these, we describe the system aspects of development in terms of the continuum in Figure 4.1.[6]

Each general stage of development corresponds to a particular cluster of defined needs arising from social displacement and the formation of new tasks and objectives in the society, in combination with an overlay of "obsolete" ones. The result is cumulative and affects whichever roles are appropriate. However, a set of roles appropriate to one developmental stage is never completely abandoned. It continues to remain significant in the next stage, sometimes serving a useful purpose and sometimes producing negative consequences. More important, the combination of need with role creates an integrative problem of the greatest importance, both in terms of the stratification system and of effective decision making as well. If the institutional arrangements for linking need and role are visible in the particular combination of representational claims prevailing in the society in question, then the opportunities these provide for competitive elites to perform elite functions become a central empirical concern; such competition creates information for government, and more generally results in participation in decision making precisely in the most sensitive areas of developmental change, such as, the alteration in the hierarchy of power and prestige in a system. We can now turn from the concept of need to the analysis of stratification.

	Traditionalism	Modernization	Industrialization
	interest	interest	interest
CLAIMS TO REPRESENTATION	function	function	function
	right	right	right

Figure 4.1 Developmental Continuum and Representation

THE STRATIFICATION CATEGORIES

Each stage of development has been described in terms of social mobility. The most limited preclass case is caste (or castelike), in which portions of a population are separated into distinct and separate groupings (whether religious, ethnic, or racial). Boundaries here emphasize primordial attachments or an exclusivism that goes beyond ordinary prejudice.[7]

More complex stages of development enlarge *class* access. Mobility here is greater than with caste but is still clearly bounded (as in a Marxian sense). It includes a subjective awareness of membership in a semipermeable group, the life chances of whose members are similar and primarily determined by occupation. This notion (similar also to the one held by Weber) makes class dependent on the relation to the means of production. Much less restrictive than caste, it is not "primordial" in identification, although it tends to transform its class interests into general values for a whole society. Its boundaries are fixed when opportunities for occupational mobility are limited. With this type of class, one can also speak of the formation of class "consciousness." Demands for class representation here include seeking redress for grievances arising from limited access to mobility. We will refer to this class as type A.

At a more advanced stage of development, class is a more multi-bonded affair, and attributes of membership derive from many factors: religion, occupation, income, residence, family background, style of leisure, and so on. Class in this more Marshallian sense, which we refer to as type B, puts forward claims that, also based on interests, *transform issues of value into negotiable interests.* The result is the opposite of class type A—it breaks up rather than creates solidarity.[8]

Finally, we have postclass status differentiation based on types of status clusters, particularly those associated with industrial skills and embodying a degree of professionality. These create claims for functional representation and include private as well as public bureaucratic status groups and technocratic groups. The latter are specially characteristic of highly industrialized countries.

We can restate the argument so far by combining the developmental and stratification variables.

During industrialization, not only does the multibonded class type (class B) come to predominate, but also the new types of status elites based on a functional role in industrialization or its related activities. These groups form an organizational elite. Using highly germane functional criteria (education, training, professional skill), such groups represent an intellectual "class" in the limited sense that they create information and knowledge that becomes the basis for innovation within industrial societies. Innovating status groups are found not only in industrialized societies, where they occupy central power and prestige roles, but, more derivatively, they are also established in late-stage modernizing societies. Indeed, such groups are part of the modernizing process, linked, too, to their counterparts in industrial systems. *Hence, while we speak of development as a process along a continuum from traditionalism to industrialization, in practice, modernization is a process that moves from roles originating in an industrial society, which we recreate in a nonindustrial setting.* The consequence of this "reverse" overlapping of roles leads to the "embourgeoisement" hypothesis.

THE "EMBOURGEOISEMENT" HYPOTHESIS

If our analysis is correct, this reverse formation of roles (reverse in a historical sense) describes both a process and a tendency, which at the most general level can be called the "production of pluralism." By the "production of pluralism," I mean the proliferation of roles and role sets organized around primarily instrumental ends. Class B and status relationships are thus common even in early stages of modernization, converting conflicts over values into conflicts over interests. This allows us to suggest that the behavioral consequence of the growth of functional representation is the instrumentalization of need, which

		AUTHORITY	
		Hierarchical	Pyramidal
NORMS	Consummatory Values	Mobilization systems	Theocratic systems
	Instrumental Values	Bureaucratic systems	Reconciliation systems

Figure 4.2 **Political Systems**

results in preferences for immediate gains rather than postponed gratifications. Such a consequence produces a predicament in non-democratic systems precisely because, in varying degrees, they operate on the basis of a higher component of "postponed" satisfaction than do representative democratic systems. Modernization, then, produces "embourgeoisement," which in turn creates a plurality of instrumental ends located unevenly in the stratification system and creating a tug-of-war between popular, interest, and functional claims.

This situation leads to a central proposition underlying the present analysis. We have already suggested that the greater the degree of modernization, the more the modernized roles in the society gain predominance, proliferate, and expand. These roles are predominantly instrumentalistic in consequence. In the absence of an industrial infrastructure, however, such roles are not integrated around a central allocating focus; hence, they create a severe "management" problem for government. The reason follows from the explanation suggested above, for example, that while representation on the basis of modernized roles may take the form of demands for popular representation, remnants of traditional roles may outnumber them.

Popular representation then leads to a struggle for power. Those leading demands for a genuine popular representational system are the traditional or near traditionals, while the modernized sections supports a doctrine of the "weightier part." More often, "populism" is the result, with popular participation channeled into purely formal conciliar bodies lacking functional substance, as in most "single-party" systems. Claims may be made on the basis of interest groups formed in the modern sector. Functional claims may also arise. Whatever the form of representational need, however, the proliferation of modernized roles creates such ambiguity, coalitional possibilities, and competition between principles of representation by various elites that not only does the management problem become great, but the possibilities for both conflict and stagnation also tend to grow. The greater the problem of such role conflict, the more likely is a drastic nondemocratic political solution. *Hence, the greater the degree of modernization, the greater the possibility of multiple claims to representation, and the greater the possibility of restrictive and authoritarian political solutions.* We can explore this proposition a bit more fully.

In the period of traditionalism (despite the variation in political types), the relationships between systems were both horizontal and vertical caste, or castelike (ethnic), in the sense of a high degree of exclusiveness. In Africa, Europeans were at first virtually a caste group (cultural, racial, and religious primacy) imposed vertically on hitherto horizontally related ethnic caste groups (tribes). Subsequently, in most territories, the Europeans became a class group. In Latin America, vertical caste-caste relationships tended to harden in terms of Spaniards and Indians. In the African case, the dominant caste-status group was expatriate; in Latin America, it was first Spanish, then Creole, and eventually aristocratic and nationalistic. In the latter case, the typical form of caste-caste relationship was the patron-client relationship to sustain rural power. (Conflicts over federal or unitarian rule commonly erupted with this relationship.) Methods of cutting across such exclusiveness could also be found. Empire was one practical way whereby a dominant ethnic group could create political links and, by imposing hegemony, change caste into status, that is, slave, warrior, and so on. Perhaps the most common links that in varying degrees reflected traditional social organization were based on kinship.[9]

In the early stage of the transition from traditionalism to modernization, these caste-class or caste-status relations change. Caste tends to remain primarily in rural areas (especially in the form of patron-client relationships, as with the *haciendados* and *campesinos* in Peru or Chile), while in urban areas a "middle class" of the A type emerges, sandwiched in between the caste or castelike status groups. (Such a middle class also represents the commercial and mercantile development characteristic of modernization.)

This stage two phenomenon shows similar characteristics in many parts of the world. In Africa it included occupational groups, such as clerks, teachers, and others related particularly to commercial life. At this point, political factions representing class interests arise. Caste and status groups may also form into factions with restrictive but primordial ideologies of primitive nationalism. (In Africa, these were usually concerned with widening the possibilities of representation in local and, more particularly, municipal councils.)

At a still more advanced stage of development, status groups may survive as a sector of an aristocratic class. The most rapidly growing group is a middle class of the multibonded type, lacking class consciousness, but aware of the self-rewarding characteristics of modernization, and very much preoccupied with social mobility.[10]

Finally, during the transition to industrialization, this multibonded class begins to draw in both upper- and lower-class groups of the A type (as when campesinos move toward and into *barriadas* to become lower-middle-class groups).[11] Toward the end of the modernization period, the A type class disappears. Modernization thus favors a class structure that is similar to urban middle-class life in industrial societies, the characteristics of which are increasingly accessible to all. In addition, because modernization today takes place through links with highly industrialized societies, the transportation of key roles creates salient points for the spread of "middle-classness." Hence modernization brings about the "embourgeoisement" of developing societies.

This "embourgeoisement" accounts for the fact that even under conditions of high modernization with extreme inequality, as in Latin America, there is little radical working-class activity of the class A variety. Even peasant movements succumb to the lure of the cities. The multibonded notion of class does not lead to polarization of groups into ideological extremes showing ideological propensities. Instead, issues of values are translated into issues of interest. Issues of interest result in demands for representation on the basis of corporate groupings, including well-entrenched interest groups that can function best within the context of the formal pattern of one man—one vote while using special advantages to rig elections and sustain group representation. True, frustrations of some of the middle class of the type B variety, especially the intellectuals, may take the form of a radicalization, especially among youth or university students, but it is the middle class that shows these radical offshoots, not the working class.[12] Indeed, a country reaching the final stage of advanced industrialization is characterized by such a proliferation of multibonded class roles that it is difficult to speak about class at all; it is preferable to refer to interest groups and competing status roles, that is, popular and functional.

Our point is that if we see development in structural terms, we can define a functional pattern of increasing need differentiation. The "embourgeoisement" phenomenon changes the demand for access from collective caste or class claims to personal status advantages by means of multiple organizational groupings. Thus conditions are created for competitive elites that cater to increasingly fractionalized interests.

As suggested earlier, each stratification category—caste, class A, class B, and functional status—indicates a type of need and demand. We have emphasized the point that these needs and demands will overlap and reinforce each other, just as the different stratification groups themselves will overlap. Hence, the "symposium of needs" and the coalitional linkages possible in the society—which become more complex and differentiated as a society moves from a more traditional to a more industrial footing—create the "pluralistic" problem for government. The key question about representation for nondemocratic governments is how they will confront and manage this problem.

POLITICAL SYSTEMS TYPES AND THE FORMS OF ACCESS

We have discussed public need in terms of developmental patterns of stratification. Before going on to a discussion of representation itself, we must first examine the problem of *access*. We see access as a function of the political system. The political system as used here is formed as the result of a relationship between the norms of a society and the prevailing patterns of authority. On the first axis, norms may be expressed symbolically in ideological or religious terms, in ethical precepts, or in terms of concrete goals of society. The most effective political systems combine in a linked system both intermediate and ultimate ends, such as was the case with Calvinism in the seventeenth and eighteenth centuries or with socialism in modern China, with powerful motivational results. On the second axis of the relationship defining a political system—authority—we refer to the degree of accountability of leaders to those led. *In theory, perfect accountability would exist where there was perfect representation.* Both sets of variables define four possible political types, each involving different types of access. Systems emphasizing ethical (consummatory) values and hierarchical authority result in "mobilization" systems. Those emphasizing concrete (instrumental) values and pyramidal authority are "reconciliation" systems. Systems with instrumental values and hierarchical authority can be called "bureaucratic" systems. Those with consummatory values and pyramidal authority can be called "theocratic" systems. We diagram these in Figure 4.2.

Concrete applications of each type are as follows:

(1) *Mobilization systems*, such as Communist China, have a universalizing political ideology in which issues of interest are converted into issues of value. A command system of control comes closest to the pure type.[13]

(2) *Reconciliation systems* are not necessarily democratic, although they are representative. Examples include democratic countries, as we know them, as well as "single-party" states such as Senegal, and possibly socialist countries such as Yugoslavia. Consummatory values exist, but they are relegated to the private sphere, and are believed to be inherent in the individual. Public behavior is seen in terms of instrumental ends.[14]

(3) *Bureaucratic systems* tend to result from a change from one of the other systems. For example, the military subtype of the bureaucratic system would be of a "Kemalist" or possibly "Nasserist" type, in which the main problem would be the accessibility of the elite. Here the danger of institutional formalism would arise in the fashion described by Crozier. The advantage of this type of system is that it sustains specialized instruments of political control in order to maintain integration. Examples include Egypt, Argentina, and post-Nkrumah Ghana. Subtypes other than the military form are also common.[15]

(4) *Theocratic systems* were seen classically in feudalism, when, by virtue of the local pattern of government based on proprietary and manorial rights and local and reciprocal allegiances, they were held together through lines of unstable kinship. The entire feudal system was infused with devotional extremism and a religious ideology. The problem with this type of system is that its stability depends heavily on ideological or religious unity, and this dependence contradicts the realities of local power, with consequent conflicts ensuing over the proper roles of church and state. There have been stable theocracies, however, such as small New England religious communities.[16] Iran is perhaps a contemporary example.

We should point out that these types of political systems are not real or concrete in the sense of membership groups; instead, they must be seen as analytical models and applied as ideal types (although they are not ideal types in the Weberian sense). More important, each system tends to give priority access to different kinds of claims to representation. Mobilization systems, although they may be populist in character as

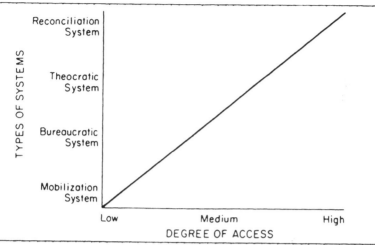

Figure 4.3 Representational Access by System-Type

suggested earlier, tend to favor functional claims to representations. However, such functional claims may not be restricted to purely development functions, but may also include catering to party organization. Bureaucratic systems will tend to favor claims to representation based on interest and will regulate these according to recognized and institutionalized standards. Theocratic systems (and here we have in mind only historical cases, not contemporary ones) tended to favor popular claims to representation in the context of a widespread religious reform or messianic movement, yet allowed scope for interest claims by means of which the more instrumental qualities of social life were realized. In reconciliation systems, all three claims to representation—popular, interests, and functional—tend to compete with industrial subtypes, with considerable conflict between the first and third. We diagram these propositions in Figure 4.3.

(1) Mobilization systems respond to pluralism and "embourgeoisement" by restructuring society along political lines in which popular representation becomes a symbolic gesture of unity, interest group representation is made public, and functional representation is bureaucratized.

(2) Reconciliation systems respond to pluralism and "embourgeoisement" by oligarchical manipulations, corruption, and the use of economic advantage to restrict popular representation, and to expand interest group representation with functional representation subordinate to interest group representation.

Stage of Development	Stratification Relationships	NON-DEMOCRATIC POLITICAL SYSTEMS TYPES			
		Theocratic	Bureaucratic	Mobilization	Reconciliation
Industrial	Class B Functional status Residual class A	Representational claims (popular, interest, and functional)			
Modern	Class A Class B Residual caste	''	''	''	''
Traditional	Caste (ethnic)	''	''	''	''

Figure 4.4 The Developmental Typology as a General Model and Representational Claims

(3) Theocratic systems respond to pluralism and "embourgeoisement" by allowing popular representation, interest representation, and functional representation to occur as long as none threatens the sanctity of the religious values, thus ensuring a good fit between consummatory religious values and popular belief.

(4) Bureaucratic systems respond to pluralism and "embourgeoisement" by manipulating interest group representation and functional representation and restricting popular representation.

To translate these propositions into more operational terms would require ranking the type of claim and the degree of significance within that claim of various concrete groupings in the system. Hence, we could rank representative groupings from the various sectors of the stratification system in terms of their significant access on the basis of right, on the basis of function, and on the basis of interest. A number of interesting hypotheses would emerge almost immediately. For example, in the case of Argentina, it is possible to show over time how various groups, such as landowners or trade unionists, shifted from popular representational significance to interest representational significance as the system of government changed from one type to another, when the bureaucratic government of Peron changed to eventually become a reconciliation system. Hence, differential access on the basis of claims, although it may occur for a variety of reasons, needs to be seen in the context of changing patterns of stratification on one hand and alternative model types of government on the other. As we already suggested, both "systems" are linked by representation.

The result is a sequence of differentiation reflecting the proliferation of need and the instrumentalization of ends embodied in the development process as it moves from a state of traditionalism to industrialism. Each stage of the process presents a problem for each type of government, namely its response, by virtue of its own "systems-properties," to the problem of managing and controlling pluralism and "embourgeoisement." To summarize the discussion so far, the variables are arrayed in diagrammatic form in Figure 4.4.[17]

THE FUNCTIONS OF ELITE REPRESENTATION AND THE GENERAL MODEL

So far, we have concentrated on the evolving relationships between changes in stratification resulting from development and government according to system-type. These have been linked by representational access on the basis of access claims. The precise nature of these claims and the rights and properties they imply form an important part of the normative dimension of politics. Moreover, they define what kind of information government should have at its disposal by recognizing the legitimacy of the claims implied. Much political struggle has been precisely over the degree of access each type of representation can be allowed in a political system.

However, we have said nothing about the various types of participation in decision making by virtue of these claims. To do so, we need to turn to the analysis of elites and the competition between them. Elites, as used here, constitute a set of variables intervening between society and government that have significant subsystem properties of their own. By representational elites, we mean those with special access to power and prestige by virtue of the wider grouping they represent in society or the functional significance of the role they perform for some object of government.[18]

We can now turn to the functions themselves and define them as follows:

(1) *Central control*: the ordered maintenance of discipline in a political system on a day-to-day basis.

(2) *Goal specification*: the identification and priority ranking of policies; hence, a sharing in policy formulation on the basis of a longer term.

		Theocratic System			Reconciliation System			Bureaucratic System			Mobilization System		
Stage of Development	Types of Stratification and "Embourgeoisement"	Central control	Goal specification	Institutional coherence	Central control	Goal specification	Institutional coherence	Central control	Goal specification	Institutional coherence	Central control	Goal specification	Institutional coherence
Industrial	Class B Functional status Residual class A												
Modern	Class A Class B Residual caste												
Traditional	Caste (ethnic)												

TYPES OF POLITICAL SYSTEMS AND FUNCTIONS OF ELITE

NOTE: Shaded boxes refer to illustrative cases discussed later.

Figure 4.5 The General Structural Model and Representational Functions

(3) *Institutional coherence*: the continuous review, reformulation, and adaptation of the fit between boundaries of subsystems, including the regulation of overlapping jurisdictions, and including, as well, ideological adjustment.

With such a formulation it is possible to determine in each case whether the concrete organizational elites are specialized vis-à-vis these functions or whether they are engaged in a constant conflict to extend their degree of access.[19]

By combining these categories with those already employed, we obtain the diagram in Figure 4.5.

Just as it was possible to operationalize the access claim of various groups in terms of their claim to representation, so it is possible to evaluate the significance of an elite in terms of its degree of access in decision making by functional significance. Particular elites, such as landowners, members of government, civil servants, businessmen and merchants, trade union officials, and the like, can be seen in the context of their access to decision making by means of their ability to perform functions of central control, goal specification, and institutional coherence. For example, it is quite possible for businessmen in the United States, with claims to access based on interests, to take part in goal specification and institutional coherence to a very high degree. Their degree of access will be limited, however, by competing claims based on popular and functional claims from other elite representatives of the system. Because the United States is a democratic subtype of a

FUNCTIONS OF A REPRESENTATIONAL ELITE

		Central Control	Goal Specification	Institutional Coherence
TYPES OF REPRESENTATIONAL ACCESS CLAIMS	Popular			
	Interest			
	Functional			

Figure 4.6   A Matrix for a Theory of Representation

reconciliation system, the general pattern of competition is built into the political system and is quite acceptable. In a quite different situation, as in a mobilization system such as Guinea's under Sekon Touré, the claim to representation from the same group (whether public or private) would be far less acceptable; even if the claim were acceptable, the group's share in functional access to decision making would still remain less.

Assuming we could find numerical values for these rankings, what would we be able to factor as significant but derived theories from the data? One answer is that we should be able to account for many specific structural relationships within society and between society and government. Moreover, as ours is a predominantly structural model, we should be able to determine the major sources and gains and losses of information in a system. This is of far-reaching theoretical significance, because the general efficiency of a type of political system can be related to various levels of development. If the theory is correct, we should be able to make some predictions about the capacity of different political systems to handle integrative and developmental tasks at different stages of development—a useful object in its own right, which also sets the stage for further studies concentrating on behavior within the structural context.

We can now review the dimensions of this model:

(1) The traditional-industrializing continuum is a statement of the growth in complexity of social need leading to demands.

(2) The differentiation in stratification indicates the group basis of competitive claims to access—popular, interest, and functional—that arise from social need.

(3) The degree of hierarchy in a system indicates the differential pattern of access that government will allow in terms of the functions of the elite.

(4) The degree to which ends are consummatory and empirical, or instrumental and empirical, will determine the quality of political response.[20]

We can now restate the central proposition as follows: *The greater the degree of hierarchy, the narrower the participation in central control, goal specification, and institutional coherence.* To which, we can add one further point: *the lower the supply of information available to government.* In other words, we used the functions of the organizational elite to indicate the amount of information available in the system that the government is able to obtain. This leads to another proposition: *Where the amount of information available to government is small, coercion will be applied in order to maintain the balance between government and society. Coercion is a substitute for uncertainty.*[21]

Coercion, which we define as the application of violence or the threat of violence by the state, in turn causes a loss of information. It does so by using the organizational elites as a coordinating and punitive arm of government. Hence, the following proposition: The more advanced the system in developmental terms and the greater the degree of hierarchy, the more the organizational elites will be used to *control* the sectors of society. The greater the degree of development and the smaller the degree of hierarchy, the more the organizational elites will be used to *coordinate* the sectors of society. The first set of conditions implies coercion through the elites. The second implies a sharing in power through the application of information.

Our main points should now be clear. When representation is viewed as the link between social need and government decision making, it defines the relationship of public need to access in government. The pattern of representation will vary with the system-type, both in terms of participation and function.[22]

In mobilization systems, where government is the independent variable and society the dependent variable, representation is, therefore, a control device "representing" government to society through the organizational elites. The result is minimum information and maximum coercion. In a reconciliation system, where society is the independent variable and government dependent, the organizational elites share in power, provide information to government, and help coordinate society through participation in decision making. Information is at a maximum, coercion at a minimum. In both cases, the intervening variable is representation. Thus by determining how well social need combines with political effectiveness, it is the most sensitive general indicator of structural balance in a system.

THE REPRESENTATIONAL MODEL

We have attempted a development approach using stratification to indicate the formation of group needs and interests by means of which representative elites can be identified in a general model and organized separately in a representational model. We have seen that such needs produce three types of representation: popular, interest, and functional. Access has been defined in terms of legitimate claims (popular, functional, and interest) operating within each governmental type: mobilization, reconciliation, theocratic, and bureaucratic. The role function of the representative elites varies in each. These functions are central control, goal specification, and institutional coherence. Because we have treated representation as an intervening variable, the three types of representation and the three functions will result in very different consequences and purposes of representation in each political system as well as in each stage of development. Operationalizing representation in these terms thus emphasizes its multiple purposes, its many different aspects, rather than the habitual although often implicit assumption that a particular combination of representational forms or functions leads to a particular political type of pattern of balance.

My emphasis has been entirely the other way around, primarily in order to enable us to develop a true theory of representation. To do so, we should be able first to correlate certain types of representation with certain functions; second, to universalize the correlations; and third, to find a generalized explanation of why the correlations appear. It would then be possible to make representation the independent variable, with political system and developmental stage as intervening or dependent. Hence, my object in these notes, though this is perhaps only the first step, has been to specify the conditions under which a theory of representation is possible, namely, to establish the matrix for empirical correlations. The matrix is shown in Figure 4.6. At the present stage, however, we can see only the variable consequences of each box in Figure 4.5, rather than correlations or syndromes.

These remain entirely problematical. Still, the possibilities are interesting; and we can speculate, as I will now attempt to do, about which relationships are significant. I realize that proper speculation would require much more systematic work. The applications that follow are merely "trial runs" on a purely descriptive and impressionistic basis for illustrative purposes.

A PRELIMINARY APPLICATION
OF THE TWO MODELS

Applying so many variables presents severe problems of language. Not only is it difficult to handle the simultaneous relationships involved without distortions imposed by our ordinary notions of sequences, but also, in this case, we are dealing with two "sets." In one, the development process is the independent variable, the functions of the elite and government are intervening variables, and "political balance" or the stable relations between rulers and ruled is the dependent variable. Here we want to know how, in the absence of freely representative relationships in a political system, governments manage the growing complexity of need and provide suitable satisfactions to the members of a society. In the second "set," government is the independent variable, the functions of the representative elite are intervening, and the development process is the dependent variable. In the first "set," we find concrete systems that fall predominantly in the pattern of theocratic and reconciliation systems. In the second are those systems that fall mainly in the pattern of bureaucratic and mobilization systems.

Using these differences as our guide, we can now discuss the dimensions of the model employed in terms of its implications for nondemocratic representation as well as for different stages of development. We will not discuss all the possible types but will use several for illustrative purposes.

A Traditional Theocratic System
and Change to a
Traditional Bureaucratic Type

Stratification in traditional theocratic systems was based on caste relations determined by kinship, that is, tribal ethnicity. Such systems tend to link kinship with ancestors, in which case ancestral obligation is a form of shared central control between the living and the dead. Conflicts between ethnic groups define the central political problem; elites emerge from kin groups. Institutional coherence derives from priests and others, such as elders, who ensure the propriety of religious beliefs. Representation thus combines lineage and kin or clan leaders with ancestors in the form of kin "interest" and client "function." Government is not separate or distinct from the kinship elites, but rather, the central figure. Indeed, priest, king, and lineage merge. The combination results in the performance of the central control function by government.

What ensures the balance of the system is stability in the stratification sphere and the harmonization of social relations with sustained belief in imminent practices by a kinship elite with popular links through clans or other familial units. There is a minimum emphasis on functional representation. Popular forms of pluralism are managed on the basis of reciprocal kinship or ethnic relationships. This arrangement is accepted as a divine expression. The problem of control is, therefore, to sustain the relationship between consummatory and instrumental values. Kinship representation combined with priestly authority is the general method employed.

We have chosen as an illustration the case of the Arab caliphate, because it was in our terms "traditional" in its developmental stage, that is, organized on caste-ethnic lines (Semitic tribes) that originated in a theocracy (founded by the Prophet), and transformed itself first into an expansionist mobilization system (the Arab conquest) and then into a bureaucratic system (the Arab Empire). Our primary purpose is to use the typology first in a dramatic, historical way to illustrate some of the categories suggested above.

The Arab caliphate was organized for war in order to spread the faith. Its first phase was purely religious. After the death of Mohammed, a military organization developed, which represented hierarchical authority but with instrumental values subordinate to religious values. This combination has frequently been a compelling force in history. Ibn Khaldun notes that "religious propaganda gives a dynasty at its beginning another power in addition to that of the group feeling it possessed as the result of the number of its [supporters]."[23] (The quotation notes the temporary quality of this form of religious power.) Bernard Lewis, commenting on the caliphate after the death of the Prophet, suggests that those who elected Khalifa (the deputy of the Prophet) "can have had no idea of the later functions and development of the office. At the time they made no attempt to delimit his duties or powers. The sole condition of his appointment was the maintenance intact of the heritage of the Prophet."[24] So established, the Arabs, organized along military lines, began the twin tasks of conversion and conquests.[25] If the early caliphate was hierarchical in its system of authority, its very imperial successes meant that military commanders and governors could exercise increasing autonomy and control. The principle of election to the caliphate by powerful governors was followed. In theory, at any rate, the Muslim community as such was represented.

The forms of representation during the early expansion period of the Arab empire were extremely limited. Important family dynasties exercised influence in court. Administrators, tax collectors, and other officials associated with the organization of public lands and rents occupied central decision-making positions. The key to representation was military, administrative, or familial power, with each serving as a claim to wealth. In Mecca a wealthy class of patricians dominated the elections to the caliphate. Their representation, based on political skill supported by great wealth, quickly turned them into an oligarchy, which, in turn, led to a decline in religious commitment. Subsequently, conflicts arose between civil administrators and the oligarchy. Competition for support from non-Arab converts to Islam, who were anxious to obtain advantages as well as the financial success of the empire, caused the priority to shift away from consummatory toward instrumental values. "The assumptions of this system were the identity of Arab and Muslim and the maintenance of the religious prestige by which the Caliph exercised his authority. Its breakdown became inevitable when these assumptions ceased to be valid."[26] The result was a growth in oligarchical corruption and nepotism, which eventually led to civil war.

> The administration of the Empire was decentralized and in disorder and the resurgence of nomad anarchism and indiscipline, no longer restrained by a religious or moral tie, led to general instability and lack of unity. The theocratic bond which had held together the early caliphate had been irrevocably destroyed by the murder of 'Uthman, the civil war that followed it, and the removal of the capital from Medina. The oligarchy in Mecca was defeated and discredited. Mu'awiya's problem was to find a new basis for the cohesion of the Empire. His answer was to start the transformation from the theoretical Islamic theocracy to an Arab secular state, based on the dominant Arab caste.[27]

What were the dominant groupings to be represented? They were first organized around war and administration by means of appointed chiefs who came to have territorial jurisdictions. Their importance to the caliphate was so critical that they formed a "court" in which intrigue was a key characteristic, particularly against the Mecca castes. Functional "representation" based on administration was thus arrayed against group "representation" based upon caste. The former prevailed, resulting in the secular, bureaucratic Arab state.

A Traditional Reconciliation System and Its Consequences

Traditional reconciliation systems are organized in stratification terms around kinship. Kin groupings clustered into castelike relationships are entered by marriage, adoption, or co-optation. Coalitions of caste relationships hover somewhere between caste and class A and are characteristic of historic European reconciliation systems about which we have some knowledge, such as Athens, the Roman Republic, or the Florentine city-state. In each of these cases and within the general category of caste-type relationships, there was to be found a dynastic pattern of stratification. However, such general characteristics hold for more than antique European prototypes and would even include those age-grade segmentary systems in Africa in which entry is on the basis of generation. Central control in such reconciliation systems is normally through a king in a council dominated by senior castes, coalitions of castes, or age-grades. These last may vary in type from dynastic familial organizations to other groups that maintain stewardship over land and possess other property rights not easily attainable by the ordinary public. Goal specification consists primarily of special protection for the various major economic and ethnic groupings. Institutional coherence rests with the consultative and conciliar procedures worked out, including courts and councils, magistrates and priests, and shared participation of overlapping castelike groupings in the reconciliation of conflicting interests. The traditional reconciliation system thus emphasizes representation on the basis of familial seniority. For a more complete illustration, we will analyze the case of the Roman Republic.

The Arab case demonstrates how systems change from theocracy to mobilization to bureaucratic representation. Another case of a traditional system is better known because it is closer historically to the European experience, namely, the traditional reconciliation system of the Roman republic, particularly at the time of the attempted reforms of the Gracchi. Government of the republic had been primarily aristocratic, with the burgesses dominated by the old senatorial families. During the expansionist phase of the Roman empire, this type of government worked reasonably well. But, at the height of Rome's glory, as Mommsen suggests:

> The government of the aristocracy was in full train to destroy its own work. Not that the sons and grandsons of the vanquished at Cannae and of the victors at Zama had so utterly degenerated from their fathers and grandfathers; the difference was not so much in the men who now sat in the senate, as in the times. Where a limited number of old families of established wealth and hereditary political importance conducts the government it will display in seasons of danger an incomparable tenacity of purpose and power of heroic self-sacrifice, just as in season of tranquility it will be short-sighted, selfish, and negligent—the germs of both results are essentially involved in its hereditary and collegiate character.[28]

The Roman case would indicate a shift from claims to popular representation on the basis of a narrowly limited definition of citizenship to rural interest representation on the basis of clanship estates. Struggles over access to decision making resulted in a corresponding decline in institutional coherence (and in the formulation of a religious vacuum that prepared the ground for the successful entry of Christianity at a later stage), struggles over central control and goal specification between various clans, and in the development of different classes.

Attempts to prevent the senate aristocrats from plundering the system and to make them recognize the needs of the public gave rise to conflict between "optimates," who wished the rule of the best, and "populares," who favored the will of the community. The result was conflict over and struggles between rival "classes" as well as between "estates." Attempts to create major reforms, first by Tiberius and subsequently by Gaius Gracchus, ended in their deaths.

The Roman example is interesting because it demonstrates the difficulties as well as the typical problems of reconciliation systems that are not democratic, that is, that exclude part of the community from effective representation. The Roman system excluded slaves, foreign burgesses, and, in effect, the urban poor, yet, nevertheless considered them part of the society. The civic community was thus only a part of the whole. Magistrates, for example, were chosen from a relatively small number of families. Nevertheless, the citizens could record a vote on important issues, and politicians, in order to be elected, needed to have a faction behind them. The basis of faction was in the *gens*, the family. Hence, family connection and political marriage were extremely important.

Personal obligation and the resulting patron-client stratification system were also important. Faction, intrigue, and personal connection are all characteristics of representation in reconciliation systems that provide for accountability through conciliar bodies that represent the "weightier part" of the community but not necessarily the most functionally significant part. What H. H. Soullard suggests for Rome is certainly true of reconciliation systems more generally:

> It is this far-reaching nexus of personal and family relationships and obligations that underlies the basis of Roman public life, a fact which the nobles themselves may have sought to obscure. Its form naturally will have varied at different periods of Rome's history. Thus in the early days the tie of the clan was probably the predominant factor; families would group themselves around such leading patrician clans as the Fabii, Aemilii, and Claudii.[29]

The Roman case merely illustrates in a historically familiar context a general phenomenon found in many modernizing societies today. If we take the same characteristic case, the separation of society from the effective civic community, and place it in the context of modernizing nations—whether old ones as in Latin America, or new ones as in Africa—we see many of the same problems arising again. In the Latin American case, the result has been the growth of class A conflict and class B coalitions, thereby providing various oligarchies with manipulative control over representative organs. Representation has been on the basis of family. Although such representation was originally based primarily on rural landowning wealth, it has expanded laterally in the form of controlling dynastic commercial and industrial oligarchies. Hence, there has been overrepresentation of the "weightier part," and the patron-client relationship has extended into every aspect of political life.

The Modernizing Reconciliation System

Modernizing reconciliation systems are likely to be extremely unstable in the primary stages of modernization because of the survival of many traditional practices. Overlapping caste, class A and class B relationships provide the basis of competing coalitions. Here interest representation predominates; central control is weak and bureaucratic;

goal specification of the developmental variety is manipulated by politicians with only marginal participation by technocrats; and institutional coherence is based on corruption, mobility, and payoff. If there is popular representation, it militates against developmental planning. Uneven access to power accentuates inequity and social discrimination. Many Latin American countries fall into this category.

In later stages of modernization, with the growth of class of the B type and its intermediary status clusters between class A structures, central control tends to become more organized around a bureaucracy. Goal specification is shared by competing class and status groupings, while institutional coherence is sustained through multiple and overlapping institutional groupings. This pattern is likely to lead to organized plunder, with repeated interventions by the military. The combination of political and economic stagnation, popular representation in voting, and functional representation through the bureaucracy, army, and developmental agencies creates conflict between popular and functional principles of representation.

As we have suggested, reconciliation systems are not necessarily *democratic* in the Western sense of the term. Caste, class A, and class B relationships are linked to familial and personal ties. Such overlapping role sets combine within a single community elements of caste opportunism and class conflicts (as in campesino movements), so that the development of multibonded class and status relationships uses the structure of representative government as an umbrella to protect its interests from demands produced by caste and class A types of conflict. Moreover, when such conflict gets out of hand, the class B elites, faced with a management problem, tend to favor military intervention leading to a new constitutional framework.[30] Such efforts attempt to link by political means the structure of social relationships and roles established in each sector of the stratification system with government on the basis of interest representation. A new round of corruption occurs, as well as a new tendency to plunder the system in the absence of more positive representational links and associations. The crisis in central control soon repeats itself; hence, the predicament. Sharing power through popular representation by means of the proliferation of voluntary associations, committees, and local governments, and by means of general participation in assemblies and councils throughout the structure of pyramidal authority, only intensifies the conflict between popular and interest claims to representation; but in the exercise of their functions, the elites emphasize distribution rather than development.

This exaggerates a "plunder" psychology with few possibilities for managed and enforced savings in the community. Representational access in terms of any organized interest—whether based on class or function—becomes dominant at the expense of the others.

The problems of the nondemocratic reconciliation system are thus accountability without constraint and political participation for short-term gains. The result is likely to be political and social stalemate, punctuated by periods of conflict.

An Industrializing Reconciliation System

The third type of reconciliation system—a type that occurs in industrialized countries—represents the most acute stage of the "crisis of meaning" inherent in the model itself. In this type of reconciliation system, class conflicts have given way to status coalitions, each supporting popular and interest representation in competition with functional representation. Central control has become a function of conflict between bureaucrats, technocrats, and politicians. Goal specification is a tug-of-war between interest and functional representation. Institutional coherence is based upon popular representation. Here lie many of the familiar problems confronting pseudodemocratic societies, such as the inadequacy of representative mechanisms and restricted access.

Representation in an industrial society is much the same as in the modernizing society, except that in the former case either a party, a bureaucracy, or a military group is responsible both for central control and for goal specification, while institutional coherence is left to whatever class and associational groupings are found available, perhaps those surviving from the previous system. In other words, nondemocratic reconciliation systems in industrial societies tend to be "tolerant" of the social system and to allow institutional coherence to be handled by the community itself, while functional access is increasingly prominent.

Modernizing Mobilization Systems

Characteristic cases of modernizing mobilization systems would include Guinea, Ghana, and Mali immediately after their independence. The stratification relations of such systems are of both the caste and the class A types. In other words, we find a typical traditional caste/colonial or expatriate caste stratification system alongside a "middle class" conscious of its position and performing modern tasks.[31] A mobilization system tries to eliminate the colonial caste root and branch and to integrate class and remaining traditional caste relations around new political clusters—a political "class" of the A type, which embodies the community, such as the P.D.G., the Union Soudannaise, or the C.P.P.—while manipulating populism as a substitute for popular representation.

Party organization creates representative clusters and attempts to define participation in functional terms: the socialization function (youth movements); the production function (trade unions and corporations); the rural innovation function (cooperatives and farmers associations); and the ideological function (ideological institutes). Interest representation is likely to be suspect and regarded as "neo-colonialist" or imperialist. Attempts to alter caste relationships are made by changing the principles of representation and by modifying sources of mobility—both politically, through a "single party," and by bureaucratic co-optation. Central control is likely to be in the hands of a party-government coalition in which the key posts in each are occupied by the same individuals. Goal specification is expressed in terms of planning based on a combination of ideological and technical goals in which technocrats, engineers, economists, statisticians, and the like play a large part, normally in some conflict with political leaders. Institutional coherence is based on increasing bureaucratization, again with a high ideological component. Two characteristic principle conflicts exist between government-sponsored elites and the remnants of traditional elites, and between ideological specialists in the party and civil servants and technocrats. Here we find representation on the basis of function ideologically linked with relevant groupings in the society. Counterelites are excluded, but even these may not necessarily be restricted in terms of social mobility within the system.

The principle differences between the traditional and modern forms of mobilization systems are, first, that populism is used to support functional representation in the modern forms, and, second, that populism requires a consultative base, while functional representation requires a special access to functional elites. Populist and functional elites contend with each other for power. Popular representation is limited to being of the testimonial variety of populism. Access to central control and goal specification is restricted to those concerned with development or maintenance of support. The institutional coherence function is restricted to programmatic ideology, with organizations modified according to the degree to which they fit the ideological pattern.[32]

In general, we can say that even where there is a minimum of popular representation, growing competition between populist and functional elites for access to central control and goal specifications produces considerable accountability. Even the functional elites seek to expand their competitive access by broadening their recruitment base in society. The tendency is to move downward through the restratification of the public into corporate functional groupings relevant to development and systems-maintenance. Not class, but *corporate* grouping, is characteristic; hence, a kind of "corporate representation" in primary stage modernizing mobilization systems is seen as the means of reconciling populism with functional expertise.

The solution just mentioned is rarely achieved, however, because of the appearance of the "embourgeoisement" phenomenon, which breaks up the stratification along corporate-functional lines. Moreover, even caste elements prove difficult to eradicate, not to speak of class A type groupings. The middle class of the B type, growing as modernization proceeds, makes demands based on wider needs. Thus central control needs to be even more tightly organized in a military or paramilitary type of formation. The result is government versus the elites. Goal specification then relies more heavily on systems-maintenance than on development. Institutional coherence tends to be a combination of ideological orthodoxy and coercion. Government-monopolized central control is allocated on an appointive basis to administrators.

Goal specification is toward a future objective. An elite of ideological specialists is required both to create such goals and to ensure their status as consummatory values. Institutional coherence is handled by administrative magistrates or tribunals dedicated to the preservation of ideological uniformity. The functions of an elite are joined within a narrow circle, closely associated with government and hostile to other groupings, particularly other caste groupings in the system. When there is a weakness or failure in the performance of any of the elite functions, government is likely to apply coercion. Hence, "embourgeoisement" creates the conditions for mobilization and also prevents the mobilization system from working.[33] Under such paradoxical conditions, popular representation in the form of a party elite would collide with the governmental functionaries or technocrats over an increasingly restricted access to elite functions.

The Industrializing Mobilization Systems

During industrialization, the problem of the decline of consummatory values in combination with the primacy of instrumental values tends to fit directly with a structural pattern of differentiation, in which class conflict gives way to multibonded class with coalitions and groups forming on the basis of functional significance. Party leaders and technocratic elite are likely to compete for central control, as in the case of the modernizing mobilization system; however, party leaders and bureaucrats are likely to handle goal specification by means of consultative instruments, while institutional coherence is similarly dealt with by party leaders and plant managers. The industrial system injects new and mutually opposing elements into the picture: On one hand, there is the need for decentralization of command units (as the complexity of the system grows), and, on the other, there is increasing bureaucratization occasioned by the effort to retain command over a decentralized decision system. Representation is thus likely to be functional on the basis of the productive system and consultative on the basis of the hierarchy. We can call the resulting subtype *consultative* (as distinct from popular) representation, as exemplified in China by the direct contact between cadres and the masses.[34] But even in China, the emerging stratification pattern creates an interesting problem, namely, the "embourgeoisement" phenomenon, which breaks up society into competitive status groupings, making it difficult to treat the population in terms of any given class or corporate interest, but rather as representative of elaborately distributed needs.

Breaking up the class pattern into multibonded class emphasizes competitive claims to popular representation under the guise of consumer interests. If a few technocratic elites, crucial to the developmental process, gain supremacy over the party elite, central control would be shared by administrators, civil servants, and managers. Goal specification would be decentralized with a corresponding depoliticization of many aspects of social life. Institutional coherence would be provided by the shared and overlapping organizational pluralism associated not only with production and distribution, but also with local government. At this point, consultative representation may be transformed into popular representation. If this should occur, then the political system could become democratic.

The industrializing mobilization system is of great importance because it seems to produce a contradiction between political and economic needs. In highly industrialized societies, the multibonded pattern of class spreads throughout the system. It becomes virtually meaningless to speak of classes in the Marxist or Weberian sense.[35] The new types of status groupings, each with special claims to representation and power, are competitive in terms of the function of the elite and their type of claim to representation. Most important is the role of the new technocrats, whose functional value is based upon knowledge or innovation. They are opposed by the bureaucrats, whose claim is based upon continuity and efficiency, and by the politicians, whose claim is based on instrumental or consummatory values of a populist variety. The conflict arises because of the role of information. The modernizing society has a model to follow and a goal, industrialization. It can afford to be imitative. The principal difference between modernization and industrialization is that the latter creates a revolution in innovation and technique. In industrial systems, it is necessary to reconcile representation of interests and function with new knowledge (innovation). Each of these types of representation involves a form of information that government requires during industrialization. Hence, the effect of high industrialization is to diversify need as a basis of information, setting up the following causal chain: *The need for information results in more diverse representation on the basis of complex interests. This emphasizes instrumental values. As consummatory values decline and the need for information grows, the mobilizing industrial system will move toward a reconciliation system.*

SOME TENTATIVE GENERALIZATIONS

By putting so much emphasis on development, we have related system-type to representation in terms of changing needs and information. Our formulation does not deal with democratic systems, but could include them. In modern predemocratic developing societies, and some industrial ones as well, democracy is a goal based on developmental priorities rather than an independent normative aim, based on a prior, if implicit, agreement on popular representation. The maintenance of representative government in democracies over time is partly a function of an ability to convert potential conflicts over values into conflicts over interests, *without, nevertheless, allowing interest representation to become dominant. This implies an effective blend of consum-*

matory and instrumental values and high accountability on the basis of
popular representation, both of which imply agreement over the balance
of representational claims with regulated competition of functional
access by elites. Such a system is subtle, complex, and delicate.

In a mobilization system, on the other hand, consummatory values
clearly dominate. There are few overt challenges to hierarchical
authority and there is minimal popular representation. Indeed, pluralism
is the enemy. The corporate community is, at least formally, highly
unified, and dissidents are silent. However, over time there is a tendency
toward functional representation. During the early stages of development, particularly in premodern systems, these functional representatives include military and administrative figures in bureaucratic
roles.[36] In mobilization systems at the highest stage of development—
industrialization—these roles tend to become more specialized around
those most germane to generating information and technique, and the
clusters of functional roles facilitate central control and goal specification.

We conclude with the following propositions:

(1) Both mobilization and bureaucratic polities are limited accountability systems, with government the independent variable and society
dependent. Emphasis in the former is on functional representation. In
the latter, functional representation is mixed with various forms of
patron-client interest relationships.

(2) Both reconciliation and theocratic polities are high accountability
systems in which society is the independent variable and government
dependent. Emphasis in the former is on a mixture of interest,
functional, and popular representation; emphasis in the latter is on
popular and interest representation personified in a religious/ethical
authority.

Although representation is treated here as an intervening variable, it
does have several generalized subsystem characteristics. First, information is created through the functions of the elites. The greater the
access to central control, goal specification, and institutional coherence
by the elites, the more broadly is power distributed, the more likely are
the elites to engage in competition to represent diverse groups, and the
greater is the degree of information available to decision making. When
the system begins as a mobilization system, the competition among
elites constitutes a disciplinary problem for government; elite functions
are reduced and information is lost. The proposition that emerges then
is as follows: *When a society of the mobilization type is at the stage of*

late modernization or industrialization on the development continuum, it develops a multibonded/status social system. The competition for access by elites leads to decentralization of power but to no change in the principle of hierarchy, thus posing an authority problem for government likely to lead to coercion on one hand and intrigue on the other. Intrigue will be the main activity of the elites competing for access to central control, goal specification, and institutional coherence. In the absence of good information, government will apply coercion.

In reconciliation systems, such competition between elites is likely to lead toward a greater degree of elite participation by wider sectors of the public, with two main tendencies emerging: representation on the basis of multibonded class, or *popular* representation; and representation on the basis of modern status, or *functional* representation. Competition between elites consists of conflicts over the role of experts (civil servants and technocrats) versus politicians (elected representatives). Such competition profoundly affects the effectiveness of participation by the public. Under conditions of high industrialization, a sense of power-lessness can lead to public feelings of alienation as well a to a decline in the overarching-shared consummatory values of the systems; in this case, the conversion of issues of values into conflicts of interest produces an excessive fractionalization of power, which renders effective decision making impossible. Under the circumstances, freely available information becomes unusable. The proposition that thus emerges is that *in reconciliation systems, if the competition between elites for access to elite functions and the differing claims to representation produce an excessive fractionalization of power resulting in the privatization of wants and randomization of ends, then the rules of the system themselves become vulnerable. Such systems produce increasing amounts of information and little coercion, but the communications net is so overloaded, and the claims to participate in central control, goal specification, and institutional coherence so competitive, that the systems tend to be ineffective.*

The conclusion to these notes is really to state a problem, namely, that the long-term process of industrialization polarizes social structure into groups that are counterposed against each other in a competition for representation that is imposed by the need for information. Although I believe that these conditions produce a long-run tendency toward a reconciliation system, the likely possibility is a "dialectic" between a modern form of the corporate state, with a high emphasis on functional representation, and a democratic state, with a high emphasis on popular and interest representation.

In sum, we have attempted to identify the types of representation that are functionally distributed to particular elites under conditions of variable access and growing need.

NOTES

1. Although there is an elaborate numbers game that can be played with representation, particularly the form known as electoral geometry, we incorporate in this notion two main types of popular representation that may or may not involve electoral machinery. The first is direct representation, where citizenship becomes a shared condition or a common property of the members of a community with defined obligations and rights requiring direct participation on a Rousseauean standard. Where because of size, numbers, and complexity, direct democracy is impossible, and citizens cannot participate directly in the decision-making process, some "representative" must do the job. Representation in this sense requires a manageable elite speaking on behalf of a wider public. This second form of popular representation is most common, and it is the latter situation that primarily concerns us.

2. Functional representation derives from the more technical aspects of social life, opening up special access to decision making on the basis of particular utility. Administrators and civil servants, governors and soldiers, specialists of various kinds in public works, such as irrigation, public health, and even religious or ideological matters, gain key access in proportion to the need for their skills by government. See Harold Wilenski, *Organizational Intelligence* (New York: Basic Books, 1967), pp. 94-129.

3. Interesting combinations of roles result, which affect permissible behavior, such as a Latin American economist (functional status membership) living in an upper-middle-class community (multibonded class) descended from an aristocratic family of landowners (caste origin changed into occupational class). Such a role is likely to be linked with planners and economists from the United Nations and other international bodies, yet it is associated, in a reasonably comfortable manner, with all other social groups in the system.

4. For a more detailed discussion of these types, see my book, *The Politics of Modernization* (Chicago: University of Chicago Press, 1965).

5. The contrast between modernizing and industrializing in social terms is that modernization is a process in which roles appropriate to (integrated with) an industrial society are established in the absence of an industrial infrastructure. Industrialization, on the other hand, means that the economy has passed beyond the stage where resources are used directly to produce technically simple products for export or direct consumption and has reached a stage of complex application of resources and technology—all within "a pattern of intersectoral flows involving capital and intermediate products." See R. H. Green's review of Szereszewski's "Structural Changes in the Economy of Ghana, 1891-1911," *Journal of Modern African Studies* 4, no. 1 (May 1966), p. 126.

6. The continuum is a common one. It is often used in comparing modernizing countries. There are some special problems here, however. If we set the continuum on an axis, we find that while traditionalism can give way to modernization, it is a contradiction in terms to say that modernization gives way to industrialization. The point is that

modernization does not end in industrialization but is, rather, continuously defined by it.

7. Such exclusivism extends this concept well beyond its ordinary usage in India so as to include ethnic and all other exclusivist boundaries difficult to penetrate except through kinship. Hence, intratribal relationships in Africa, even in the same contemporary political framework, can be regarded as a form of caste relationship as the term is employed here. Caste may, of course, vary independently of hierarchy. See Clifford Geertz, "The Integrative Revolution," in *Old Societies and New States*, ed. Clifford Geertz (New York: Free Press, 1967) for a discussion of "primordial" attachments.

8. See T. H. Marshall, *Class, Citizenship, and Social Development* (New York: Doubleday, 1964), pp. 138-43.

9. Tribal or ethnic-ethnic forms of caste, as in precontact Africa, can be described as horizontal linkages. Caste in terms of political and culturally defined groups can be described as a form of vertical linkage.

10. This is essentially what has already happened in Latin America. The broad public remained a residual caste (for example, Indians in Peru) or a peasant class. In Africa, on the other hand, in few areas has an aristocracy emerged. The old caste (ethnic) groupings have been rendered increasingly obsolete. No status elite has emerged aristocratic in quality, but rather a new type of elite, based on universalistic criteria: civil servant, technocrat, that is, professional, trained abroad, but with strong middle-class associations.

11. The aristocrat class becomes obsolete, with some of its members becoming members of the technocratic elite and others gradually becoming submerged in the elite section of the middle class.

12. Some of the late stage countries in Latin America have more in common with the highest stage of industrialized countries than with early stage industrializing ones, with this exception: many of the former tend to have the atmosphere of industrial societies during depression. Of primary concern in both is distribution in the face of frustrated production.

13. Mobilization systems do not need to be of the "left"; they may be of any political persuasion. Peron's Argentina began with an effort to create a mobilization system combining both "left" and "right" characteristics. It failed, especially in the second half of its tenure. Guinea, Ghana, and Mali attempted to establish mobilization systems around a universalized political elite (African socialism), but they had limited developmental capacities. Characteristics of a mobilization system include a charismatic or prophetic leader, who is outward-looking and employs a proselytizing ideology. The main problem, as Weber first pointed out in terms of charismatic authority, is the ritualization of leadership and the decline in belief leading to self-interest rather than community interest, which proves inimical to the latter.

14. The problem is that the instrumental ends are in danger of becoming completely separated from consummatory ends, so that the latter are randomized. The resulting conflicts strain the legal framework or mechanism of bargaining by affecting the sanctity of their rules. A high degree of self-restraint in behavior is required. The emphasis on instrumental ends tends to wear this away, and a loss of generalized meaning ensues.

15. One we have called the "neomercantilist" subtype, with civilian bureaucratic control; and the other, which (like Afghanistan, Thailand, or Morocco) employs monarchical leadership and components of a military, party, or army bureaucracy for political rule, we call a modernizing autocracy.

16. To reject the publicly defined consummatory norms would normally mean expulsion from the community, or constitute grounds for terminating any meaningful

participation. Control in the system is in the hands of those claiming a special quality of religious or devotional inspiration.

17. It must be pointed out that the variable of access and type of claim is not merely a function of the type of political system that prevails, but also the degree of development. Hence, early stage reconciliation systems may show some popular representation; however, representation tends to be limited to "citizens" who represent only a small part of a total population, excluding slaves and other categories of "noncitizens" from participation, as in the Greek city-states.

18. By organizational elites, we refer concretely to a wide variety of roles including administrators, chiefs, army officers, civil servants, priests, businessmen, and so on, behind which stand particular organizational groupings, administrative bodies, clans or castes, armies, bureaucracies, churches, and industrial enterprises. How elite functions are distributed is not only the key to nondemocratic representation, but it is in conflicts over which groups shall monopolize these functions that the case of nondemocratic policies can be isolated. In bureaucratic systems (with government the independent variable), priority is given to functional elites relating to discipline and administration, that is, armies and civil servants. In mobilization systems (where government is the independent variable) popular representation cannot only be expected to be restricted within a single-party framework (in which party serves to distribute the elite functions and allocate access at the request of government), but it is also nonfunctional. In theocratic systems (where society is the independent variable), popular representation needs to be managed by religiously organized functional elites, who thereby restrict government policy and shape it. In reconciliation systems, the manipulation of popular, interest, and functional elites is a basis of political bargaining and negotiation.

19. In the first instance, the claim to legitimate access is likely to be on the basis of functional expertise. In the latter instance, functional expertise and representation by virtue of public participation are likely to be employed.

20. These four propositions suggest a relationship in which empirical patterns emerge from the analysis of real or concrete units through developmental-time and between systems-types. It is thus possible to use them for heuristic comparative purposes.

21. On the variables of coercion and information, see the discussion in *The Politics of Modernization*, p. 40, and *Choice and the Politics of Allocation*.

22. It would be possible to devise a scale of participation and a scale of functional access in each general type of political system at each stage of development (including the variable access between those who claim technical knowledge, that is, technocrats, and those who claim information about public needs). We can ask how effective is the role of the expert in monopolizing the functions of the elite, and how competitive with popular representation.

23. See Ibn Khaldum, *The Muqaddimah*, trans. Franz Rosenthal (New York: Pantheon, 1958), I, p. 320.

24. See Bernard Lewis, *The Arabs in History* (New York: Harper & Row, 1960), p. 51.

25. Ibid, p. 52.

26. Ibid, p. 59.

27. Ibid, p. 64.

28. See Theodore Mommsen, *The History of Rome* (New York: Free Press, n.d.), III, p. 297-98.

29. See H. H. Soullard, *Roman Politics 220-150 B.C.* (Oxford: Clarendon Press, 1951), p. 3.

30. See the interesting theory of military intervention advanced by Jose Nun in "America Latina: La crisis hegemonica y el golpe militar," *Desarrollo Economico* 6 (July-December 1966), pp. 22-23.

31. In this usage, I would reject the notion advanced by those who claimed that there was no "class" in Africa. Vertical caste (European/African) was followed by class A/caste (African elites versus tribal groups) and class A/class A relationships relatively quickly.

32. See Aristide R. Zolberg, *Creating Political Order* (Chicago: Rand McNally, 1966), pp. 93-125.

33. Ibid, p. 127.

34. See James K. Townsend, *Political Participation in Communist China* (Berkeley: University of California Press, 1967).

35. The concept of false consciousness seems merely a presumptuous convenience, adopted by messianic intellectuals as a warrant of superiority in a world that otherwise largely ignores them.

36. It is important to stress that quite often the role is created by the individual, that is, a trusted lieutenant is made an administrator. If he, as occupant, can be replaced, but the role is retained, then role institutionalization has occurred, and it is possible to consider the role independently of the occupant.

5

EQUITY AND ALLOCATION IN MODERNIZING SOCIETIES

The three central hypotheses that so far have been mentioned can be summarized as follows: (1) As modernization proceeds, the potentiality for embourgeoisement increases, and as industrialization increases so does the potentiality for radicalization. (2) The greater the degree of industrialization, the greater the need for information by decision makers, and the greater the degree of modernization, the greater the need for coercion. (3) The greater the degree of coercion, the smaller the amount of information available to decison makers. These three hypotheses are linked to the dynamics of development and constitute universal paradoxes that can usefully be considered in terms of two stages, modernization and industrialization.

Taking these hypotheses one further step, we will argue that as development proceeds, the pressure for embourgeoisement comes from "below," whereas the pressure for radicalization comes from "above." Moreover, our proposition that there is an inverse relationship between coercion and information is based on the assumption that risk varies inversely with knowledge; that high risk implies low knowledge (or high stakes with some knowledge); and that coercion is a political consequence of high risk. Finally, embourgeoisement and radicalization will result from changes taking place at the normative and structural levels of societies as they develop. Coercion and information will result from the more specific responses emphasized by particular types of political systems as they seek to establish order.

MODERNIZING SOCIETIES AS DERIVATIVE

Opportunities for choice are a function of development, and development takes two forms, industrialization, which is dynamic and innovative as a consequence of the allocation of new information of technology, and modernization, which is derivative. In general, development offers choices between higher and lower rates of savings (with consequences visible in types of economic growth) and long-term or short-term priorities (insofar as the system becomes rationalized and predictable rather than magical and demonic). Preferences need to be clarified and priorities established for investment in heavy or light industry, durable or consumer goods, and so on. In addition, development means social choices. Individuals have more opportunities to choose their styles of life with respect to geographical location, housing, education, occupation, financial autonomy, membership in voluntary associations, and so on. Growth in opportunities means continuous changes in allocation. Certain powerful coalitions, for example, may skew the allocative process so that development is itself inhibited, a common condition of many Latin American countries in a late stage of modernization. As a source of variation, then, industrialization is dynamic, universalizing, and continuously disruptive. Industrial societies are innovative in the sense that their central activity is the production and utilization of new forms of information; modernizing societies, because of their derivative character, are in a continuous state of dependence. They may improvise with great skill, but they will not change until they are able to become innovative. By this criterion, only two countries in the past generation have passed completely from the modernizing stage of development to industrialization—Japan and the Soviet Union.

Accepting the view of development as a linear progression allows us to divide the choice variable into three stages. The stage corresponding to the highest choice can be described as industrial. (Postindustrial societies, a fourth stage, exist only as some special characteristics of a few very highly industrialized countries in which they form a particular "value-problématique." In them there is a decline in choice and a feeling of powerlessness.) The lowest choice stage, which is characterized by the absence of development, we call traditional. The various choice stages in between we call modernizing.

Figure 5.1 suggests a sequence in which the increasing spread of roles and changes in sets of roles lead a society from a traditional system to an industrial one, a process that can take many forms. In the nineteenth century, the form was mainly commerce, and it led to various types of colonial center-periphery relationships. Such linkage roles as those of educator, civil servant, and professional helped to mediate both between the industrial center and the modernizing periphery and between the traditional and modern sectors of society. This was true everywhere in Asia, Africa, and Latin America, although, of course, the relations with the center differed in each case.

A universal pattern with complicated consequences is to be found in middle-stage modernization. The expatriate quality of modernizing roles disappears with the appearance of a large and growing reservoir of mobile and aspiring local candidates. Mixed role sets produce a wider choice of alternatives and result in role ambiguity, particularly in the cases of modern roles such as civil servant and technician, which may lack functional relevance in a nonindustrial environment. As roles split, subdivide, and lose their boundaries, it becomes difficult to maintain standards of performance, and values not necessarily related to role performance are emphasized. Functional criteria may be less important in the middle stage of modernization than in earlier or later stages.

In the later stages of modernization, however, functional criteria reappear and are crucially important. Increasingly, the boundaries of roles become relevant preconditions for industrialization. Certain roles become strategic. As functional significance becomes important as a result of the growth of opportunities for the employment of skills, there is likely to be a normative shift toward instrumental values of functionality and consummatory values of development change. The proportions of these values will vary from case to case, but in all societies some tendencies or pressures for appropriate remedial alterations in the relationship between government and society will be created. Hence, as modernization proceeds, both potential structural antagonism and the number of normative claims increase.

If these stages of modernization have such characteristic differences, it should not be difficult to identify the stage of a particular society. The chief indices would be modernizing roles and their proportion and distribution in a system. Roles with the most durable boundaries, such as those in business, bureaucracy, and education, would be the most suitable indicators. In later stages, another important index would be the proportion and distribution of technocratic roles, particularly those associated with planning and development. Both sets of roles provide a modernization profile, although, for a comparative analysis, a weighting system would have to be devised.[1] With such role criteria in mind, most countries of sub-Saharan Africa may be placed in the first stage, and most Latin American countries in the second, with a few—Brazil, Argentina, Mexico, Uruguay, Chile, and Cuba—about to enter the

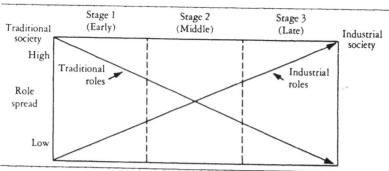

Figure 5.1 Stages of Modernization

third stage, the point of transition from later modernization to early industrialization. Countries that have made the transition are Poland, Yugoslavia, and possibly Taiwan—all of which have become technologically innovative and have begun to export industrial surpluses. Countries such as Argentina, Brazil, and Mexico remain stuck on the border between derivative and innovative societies.

Such late-stage modernizing societies remain in a disadvantageous position.

With very few exceptions, these countries must depend, initially at least, on outside investment for capital. Some internal savings from a more efficient agriculture are theoretically possible but are seldom realized in practice. Most modernizing societies first generate savings by exploiting some useful primary product, where their comparative advantage is greatest. Producing an export commodity appears to be a first step in the right direction, especially if demand is inelastic. With the development of an exportable commodity comes a rise in internal demand. The expansion of the domestic market increases demand for educational and training facilities, the elaboration of a transport and distributive network, better communication, and so on. All of these activities increase investment opportunity. In most former colonial countries, expatriate farmers, trading companies, or other entrepreneurs have been quick to identify profitable fields for investment, in spite of the vulnerability to the money markets of primary industrial centers, with their leads and lags and the drastically fluctuating prices of the international commodities market. This dependency on foreign capital should not matter if industrialization is the goal; in fact, it may be both politically and economically useful. In this sense, the pejorative use of such terms as *colonialism, neocolonialism, imperialism,* and *neo-imperialism* is not appropriate. Industrial centers create the international capital market that allows modernization to proceed by generalizing economic growth.

But in other senses, the pejorative use of these terms is appropriate. They do have a sociological and political relevance that is more significant than mere ideological or informal use would imply. The survival of such organic links of economic dependency can prevent political equity. Production and consumption, for example, have somewhat different meanings in modernizing and industrial societies. In industrial societies, production and consumption are viewed as two aspects of the same process, the manufacture and distribution of goods and services. It is possible to analyze the interdependence and complexity of, say, the factory system, the pattern of distribution deriving from it, the level of technological innovation, and the reinvestment of resources to achieve the next stage of development. But if we apply the same economic analysis to modernizing societies, because of certain political and sociological factors, the comparison with industrial societies breaks down. One factor is the vulnerability of modernizing countries. Another is the growth of social inequality within them.[2]

In the derivative modernizing society, consumption largely consists of overseas purchases of finished products or of finished components to be assembled locally. On the whole, import substitution does not reduce dependency. In rare cases where the volume of exports is great, the dependence of modernizing societies on any one foreign country may be reduced by selective purchases from many sources. But the typical modernizing society remains simply one customer among many and subject for its economic health to the health of the industrial society from which it buys. Industrial societies are occasionally dependent on modernizing ones for some products (e.g., Middle East oil), but such days of dependency are numbered, with the number of irreplaceable items steadily being reduced. Industrial countries, then, rely less and less on modernizing ones for raw materials, but their own overseas markets continuously expand. Modernizing countries, in contrast, remain in constant danger of a balance of payments crisis against which there are few internal reserves or alternative resources. Increasing indebtedness results. For these and other reasons, such as growing unemployment, modernizing societies exist in a world environment that in spite of outside aid and multilateral alliances is essentially hostile. Furthermore, they have few mechanisms of defense to maintain equilibrium.

The derivative character of modernizing societies has many consequences. In political terms, it allows an industrial society to play a "monitor role" at the expense of modernizing countries. It also assures that many of the problems of industrial societies will increasingly arise in modernizing ones, the more so as the latter approach the point of transition to industrialization. The adaptive strains produced by combinations of internal and external inputs create political problems that can never be adequately resolved by centralized planning, because the modernizing society has little control over the externally induced pressures of industrialization. Development may occur, but the relationship between allocation and equity may be upset and may produce a threat to order.

The predicament is difficult to resolve. Given the great costs of economic growth, few countries can be autarchic. Indeed, the alternatives open to a society that wants to develop are few. If a country exports primary products in order to generate capital, its short-run rationality is likely to produce long-run irrationalities as the process of development continues. Given that demand for its primary products is relatively elastic, expansion of production is likely to cause prices to drop. Increased investment in such products will, therefore, increase vulnerability rather than reduce it; hence, the need for "political" rather than economic solutions.

The pursuit of what appears to be an economically rational course of action may also result in "social" dysfunction. Development policies that maximize income in order to sustain a good balance of payments position and stimulate the flow of investment capital are usually designed to stimulate internal growth. They are likely to increase consumption as well and enlarge the market. Larger incomes are often directed toward consumption of imported goods or investment in industrial countries rather than toward investment in domestic industry. The fortunate individuals whose personal incomes are rising characteristically are more concerned about minimizing the consequences of underdevelopment to their style of life than about using their increased capital for socially useful purposes. The economic consequence of this concern for status consumption is a slower rate of industrialization. The sociological consequence is embourgeoisement. The political consequence is greater and greater inequality, accompanied by skewed allocation of the expanding opportunities for choice. These, then, are some of the internal responses to externally induced modernization.[3]

The vulnerability of modernizing societies thus tends to be self-perpetuating. Investors distrust a vulnerable economy. Public and private domestic investors, eager to improve their living standards, favor high and quick returns, a preference that tends to produce inflationary pressures that in turn stimulate the demand for consumer goods and further diminish funds available for domestic industrial growth.

Under these circumstances of disorderly development, political instability is the characteristic outcome. Often, governments respond with grandiose plans that attempt to solve all problems at once. In the face of increasing socioeconomic inequality, they must allocate an ever higher proportion of income for social welfare in order to placate a public increasingly aware of "relative deprivation." These costs, once incurred, are politically difficult to limit. Efforts to shift the balance of expenditures in the economy toward production would realistically require political restrictions on welfare, government expenditures, and public consumption, along with strict controls to prevent inflation; but few governments take these measures. Long-term developmental planning is also costly, because, as modernization increases, so do the opportunities for gross errors in planning. Hence, the pursuit of a short-term rational development is likely to create long-term political difficulties, while long-term planning may be impossible under such frangible circumstances.

If this description is applied to two of our types of political systems, it is clear that a reconciliation system's approach to equity-allocation imbalances will lead to stagnation, exploitation, and corruption, slow growth in the industrial sector, and gradually increasing external vulnerability. A mobilization system's approach will lead to misallocation, waste, and error. In both, roles functional to industrialization will continue to emphasize consumption over production except when high modernization already exists. The one will show political inequality through the skewed allocation of power, whereas the other will show economic inequality through the skewed distribution of income.

In both cases, the high proportion of modernized occupational roles in bureaucracies and the proliferation of government services will have the effect of shipping off funds from production into social welfare and other services. This kind of allocation, a form of normative appeasement, creates its own difficulties. A large and parasitical "pseudo-bourgeoisie" grows. Yet how can this be avoided? Few leaders are able to afford the political consequences of restricting consumption in favor of major investment, particularly when the immediate industrial climate is not favorable. Long-term plans, where there are shortages of trained manpower, minuscule domestic markets because of inadequate purchasing power, and gaps in the basic infrastructure, are likely to lead to waste, inefficiency, and demoralization.

These and other real limitations, such as the lack of skilled middle managers and entrepreneurs, confront most modernizing societies at a time when they are most vulnerable to industrial ones (although they may be less dependent on them because of a lower degree of embourgeoisement). A highly modernized society is dependent because large government expenditures, heavy overhead costs, huge recurrent expenditures for social services, inflationary pressures, and costs of import substitution. All of this makes it difficult to jump into industrialization. Whatever the stage of development, a derivative society can never be independent as an innovative society can.

These, then, are some of the political problems induced by modernization: increasing dependence resulting from the superior technology and knowledge of industrial countries; embourgeoisement resulting from randomization of intermediate roles and proliferation of role sets; overemphasis on consumption and short-term bargains rather than on long-term solutions, interspersed with periods of drastic remedial planning. This manner of describing the complex process of modernization embodies a point of view. It emphasizes the continuous subordinating pressure by industrial systems on nonindustrial ones.

The basic problems posed by modernization can be identified here without invoking certain theoretical shibboleths that have become part of the literature of modernization. For example, some "radical" theories of modernization suggest that the spread of functional industrial roles at the expense of traditional ones is accompanied by a growing contradiction between rich countries and poor ones. This contradiction sharpens the poor population's awareness of relative deprivation. Modernization then increases alienation, resulting in the progressive radicalization of the mass and particularly of certain strategic marginals whose number and strength increases as modernization proceeds.[4]

Modern conservative theories suggest that there is a "trickle-down" effect produced in hitherto traditional societies by outside investment, leading to domestic commercialization and the growth of a middle class, which combined with democratic political mechanisms ensures stability, the prime condition for further growth.

Something is obviously wrong with both approaches. For a variety of reasons, those who should be radical because of deprivation are quite often among the most conservative in a population. Or, perhaps more frequently, they are able to hold conflicting ideological positions simultaneously. Nor is the response of a modernizing society to inputs of foreign investment generally equable. Indeed, increasing modernization is most often associated with rising unrest.

Taking a different view, we suggest that modernization produces an embourgeoisement of the population resulting in its deradicalization. Embourgeoisement produces structural complexity and stagnation requiring a radical political method of change. Both are based on the relationship between development and allocation and can be presented graphically (see Figure 5.2). These hypotheses can now be combined in terms of allocation or access to resources. By this means, it should be possible to explain our hypotheses about role randomization and conflict during modernization and to make projections about the consequences for stratification.

MULTIFUNCTIONALITY AND STRATIFICATION

The descriptive surrogate we use for allocation is stratification. Simple functional theories tend to be based on reciprocity, a principle that may be useful for analyzing small-scale traditional societies but does not serve for studying modernizing ones. Reciprocity notions fail to describe class relationships during modernization, because at that time functional specificity combines with multifunctionality and no single set of functional attributes can be applied to a particular class. This is especially true during late-stage modernization, which is characterized by a high degree of "intermediate functional substitutability" (below the level of highly generalized functional requisites), as well as by a variety of mechanisms able to fulfill the same functions. For example, there are many appropriate and visible alternative ways of providing transportation and communications. Such a wide range of social strategies is available in highly developed choice situations that any strictly functional definition of reciprocity or class conflict is simply not applicable.

Highly modernized systems embody a multibonded system of class that includes competitive clusters of groups that may be mutually hostile and at the same time related in diverse functional ways. Multi-

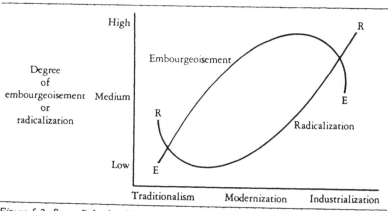

Figure 5.2 Some Behavioral Consequences of Development

functionality, not reciprocity, is the key to this concept.[5] Thus our four main stratification categories are seen in terms of two variables, *mobility* and functional significance, or *germaneness*.

Segmentary stratification. This preclass situation is characterized by a permanent boundary around each group, or a lack of mobility, and criteria other than germaneness for membership. It may be "horizontal," as with African tribal groups occupying adjacent geographical areas, in which case we call it "ethnic." Or it may be "vertical," or layered, as with the hierarchy of Indian castes, in which case we call it "caste." Both have highly ritualized boundaries, with ritual expressing primordial attachments deriving from race, language, and religion. Ritualized norms reinforce the structural character of caste by reinforcing solidarity within and hostility toward those outside.[6]

Fused stratification. In this condition, a boundary exists between groups through which some mobility is possible, but difficult, and considerable functional germaneness is accepted as a criterion for group membership. As a result of common work and life chances, occupationally determined membership in a group or class produces a subculture with shared outlook that is clearly identifiable and in sharp contrast and conflict with other groups or classes. Not only is it difficult to move from one class to another, but once achieved, the move exposes the actor to ridicule and hostility from both his new and old classes. Class consciousness, then, is a characteristic of this type of stratification.

In a "class system" (in the Marxian and Weberian usages of the term), each class is engaged in sometimes hostile but also reciprocal relations with other classes based on the integration of their roles in the productive systems. Today the fused system is typically found where there is early-stage modernization with large rural classes, a small industrial proletariat (a somewhat larger subproletariat in urban areas), a large urban bourgeoisie, and a small aristocracy. Often the aristocracy and the rural peasantry form one set of reciprocal relations (patron-client), the subproletariat and the urban bourgeoisie a second set, and the industrial proletariat employed in expatriate industries along with the reciprocals (owners) of these industries, a third set.[7]

Differentiated stratification. This type of stratification implies greater diversity in a society that rests on a more functionally complex and more "distributive" set of group relations than did the systems discussed so far. Membership criteria do not necessarily stress germaneness to a greater extent than in a fused system, except in the sense of giving greater significance and power to professionality and skill. Mobility is based on competition. Occupation is still crucial, but recruitment is by education for positions functionally relevant for the society as a whole rather than narrowly related to the process of production. As the society becomes more industrial, membership in a class is not dependent upon any one factor, such as occupation (place in the productive process), but many: education, place of residence, cultural attainments, religion, income, travel, and so on. Once the transition to industrialization is made, education becomes the most important qualification. Although some nongermane residual caste-ethnic characteristics (such as religion or race) may continue to be important, in general the trend is away from such "anachronistic" aspects of social stratification and toward an emphasis on instrumental values.

Structurally, differentiated classes lack stability. They are continually being broken up so that their boundaries are blurred. Small groups are arranged and rearranged in order of increasing professional power, and prestige is more narrowly differential as more and more positions proliferate. The groups on which this system is based are mainly interest groups. Hence, instead of solidaristic classes, there develop functional interest groups that favor instrumental values. This is why we say that the differentiated system is competitive, mobile, antisolidaristic, and pluralistic. In such a system, class is multibonded and Marshallian.[8]

Functional stratification. This type of system is a postclass phenomenon. It is founded at the apotheosis of modernization—industrial or postindustrial society—when roles of critical functional significance have come into being. Many of these roles are found in specialized status clusters involving those creating information, such as scientists, research workers, and mathematicians, and those applying it, particularly in government, such as highly trained technocrats acting in supervisory, mediating roles.[9] In modernizing societies, they are also to be found in groups whose status is based mainly on germaneness (expertise). Such roles are in practice the most closed and in theory the most open; that is, they are ordinarily open to all capable of going through the elaborate education and training required. These special status groups are characterized by their own technical languages (jargon), a sense of the boundaries of knowledge in their fields, and some sense of their wider significance in the social structure, particularly as the transition from late-stage modernization to industrialization begins. Normatively, they are completely instrumental except when obstacles to their role performance arise. They tend to see the universality of their expertise, with the result that professional solidarity is combined in them with instrumentalism. Structurally, they form professional groups and sustain supporting links and associations with their counterparts in other industrial societies through various international bodies (see Figure 5.3).

By juxtaposing the characteristics of the types of political systems and the stratification categories, we should be able to evaluate the effects of modernization on political systems, and vice versa. Only structural characteristics will be discussed here. We deal later with claims to representation by elites.

An important distinction between stratification categories can be made in terms of their bases of solidarity. The solidarity of the fused stratification system is based on similarities of predicament that lead to shared sentiments and bonds, the phenomenon described as "class consciousness." It can only occur when class boundaries are so hard that an individual who passes from one class to another is conscious of it and is proud or ashamed of his change.

In a differentiated system, there is little fraternal loyalty to class as such, but instead there are practical attachments to friends, associates, and acquaintances. Such attachments may be quite superficial, but they help to determine status with a class. However, more important than class to the members of differentiated groups is the immediate social unit that limits and defines their conduct. General standards are important, including civic postures. Manner and style, then, are substitutes for the class consciousness and the feeling of general responsibility to a particular class found in fused systems.

In fused systems, even when class boundaries are a bit vague, there is

| Stratification | Characteristics | |
type	Structural	Normative
Segmentary	Set boundaries Fixed membership No mobility	Primordial attachments (e.g. race, tribe, religion)
Fused	Well-defined boundaries Limited mobility Solidarity	Ideologies
Differentiated	Weakly articulated boundaries Lack of solidarity	Interests
Functional	Well-defined boundaries Ease of mobility for those with germane attributes Solidarity within the social unit	Professional expertise

Figure 5.3 Normative and Structural Characteristics of Stratification

an identifiable awareness of class position, which is mainly indicated by occupation. Groups may bear descriptive names such as "proletariat" and "bourgeoisie." Whatever the division, awareness of class may accompany a sense of disjunction between equity and allocation. This sense of inequity need not lead to class conflict; indeed, it may help to break up fused relationships. Coalitions not polarizations are the result of development advancing far enough for education to be the key to "reallocation." Occupation is also a distinctive characteristic of differentiated systems, of course, but in them social mobility depends to a much greater extent on education. As a society moves toward differentiated stratification, we assume that the role of education becomes increasingly important. Only a highly modernized system, however, can absorb its educated elite.

The progression of segmentary, fused, differentiated, and functional stratification categories is linear in the sense that each type is the result of the society's degree of development. But the particular mixture of types in any given case gives rise to different and nonlinear political inputs. Ethnicity, for example, seems to count in functional status hierarchies in Latin America and Africa and to be present but less important in the United States. Tribe, race, caste, and religion may be present in societies in all stages of development, in many possible combinations. In a situation of fused stratification, where occupation and income constitute the main criteria of membership, there are many other possible secondary distinctions between rural and urban persons, large landowners and peasants, owners and workers, combines and small businesses, and so on. In the differentiated type, the situation is even more complex. Although differentiation is based on certain standardized criteria, education being the most important, this system is also the most open and, because of its multibonded character, contains some residual aspects of segmentary or fused situations. In Nigeria, for example, an Ibo Catholic surgeon is generally of somewhat lower status on a differentiated scale than a Yoruba Anglican surgeon. And as we have seen in the other categories, such distinctions are not restricted to modernizing countries. In Britain, a man recognized as a gentleman on the basis of residual fused criteria who occupied a differentiated schoolteacher's post would probably be higher on a differentiated scale than a doctor in a fused system Welsh mining community.

Hence, although criteria germane to class become most important with differentiated stratification (and later with functional stratification), the criteria for this type are not necessarily simplified by this fact or even limited by it.[10] Because distinctions in this category are extremely subtle, their measurement becomes complex. Such complexity is increased by the frequent reevaluation of status rankings that occurs in a differentiated system. Particularly in industrial societies, distinctions of rank are revised vis-à-vis the frontier of knowledge, with theoretical scientists ranking higher than applied scientists.

Our discussion of modernization suggests that development produces a kind of allocational or stratification lag. Ranking that originated with caste or ethnic associations may retain not only a sentimental attachment based on primordial loyalties but also power based on the role of these associations as organizational boundaries for interest groups. Hence, a stratification system may endure in spite of drastic changes in collective mobility and a host of phenomena that inevitably accompany development.

Comparison of fused and differentiated types of stratification should not imply a conflict between them. For example, the fused type is not necessarily "working class" and the differentiated, "middle class." Nevertheless, conflict between types is possible. Fused-system groups of all levels, "upper" and "lower," may see the growth of differentiated groups as a threat. A particularly obvious example is the alliance of fused-system businessmen and workers against differentiated and functional status groups that form an educational elite. Education and style are then objects of envy, anger, and abuse, and are seen as threats to a class system based on occupation. In various early-stage developing societies, it is possible to find a fused-system upper-middle class composed of teachers, journalists, businessmen, civil servants, and lawyers, conscious of their vulnerability, cultural as well as economic, existing alongside rural ethnic groups such as tribes and urban marginal groups loosely organized along caste or ethnic lines. Alternatively, the marginal groups may show many differentiated characteristics, including subgroup competitiveness and an acceptance of gradations between occupational alternatives based mainly on degrees of education. For this group, clerkships, storekeeper posts, junior civil servant positions, and other lower-level jobs have class corollaries in residence, education of children, changes in church affiliation, and so on.

There is no inevitable stratification pattern of allocation for each degree or stage of modernization. Nor is there a hierarchy appropriate to each development type. As a general tendency, however, the greater the degree of development, the more the differentiation phenomenon becomes a function of the upper levels of society rather than the lower. Even here there are problems of formulation. For example, a differentiated structure may change into a fused one, particularly under conditions of late-stage modernization. The range of mobility of lower-level differentiated groupings, such as those found in the barriadas outside Lima, may become restricted by the limitations of geography, which formerly provided new opportunities for population shifts from rural to urban centers, mountain to valley areas, and so on. As the boundaries grow rigid, real or pseudosubproletarian fused groups are likely to grow out of the former differentiated groupings.

Whatever the changes in rank or position of various classes, distinctions based on the relevance of occupation and education continue to hold because of the strategic role of information and knowledge, new or derivative, in modernization. Even in early-stage modernizing societies, education is widely accepted as the main route to mobility. In highly industrialized societies with differentiated stratification systems, its role is even more decisive. In early-stage modernization, education may actually lead to unemployment, particularly in countries with high levels of illiteracy and few occupational alternatives. An individual may be prohibited from entering the labor market by virtue of his superior education, in part because he will not do the work of the uneducated but also because an insufficient number of posts are available for the educationally qualified. "Educational unemployment" is a common occurrence in early-stage developing countries with lower-level differentiated stratification. Such a predicament confronts many African countries today, not least because of the derivative character of their economies.[11] In industrial societies, as the competition for upper-level positions in the differentiated hierarchy increasingly is decided on the basis of education, advantages derived from an earlier fused system playing a smaller and smaller part, the opportunity to be part of the "meritocracy" will be based on equal entry and unequal dropout.

As a society becomes more industrialized, then, it moves away from caste toward functional status groups, and away from the Marxian fused system toward the Marshallian differentiated groupings. Extensive overlapping will always occur between segmentary, fused, differentiated, and functional status groups, because one type does not necessarily disappear as another appears. Multiple membership is possible. Newly differentiated groups, showing great mobility as a result of functional germaneness, can coexist with segmentary and fused groups. This coexistence produces the complexity without coherence that we described earlier; it may or may not be characterized by conflict between classes within each type of stratification or between the types themselves.

This brief discussion of the multiple and overlapping aspects of stratification should help to clarify the pattern of pluralism that is produced by development and that may be explained in terms of allocation. In any of the stratification systems, there is the possibility of challenge from the traditional and agricultural caste groupings, whose leaders are skilled at the manipulation of primordial or class normative attachments. There is also the possibility of conflict from industrial workers whose experience occupied in commerce may also hamstring the new status elite, which is interested in more efficient means of development, by their antiplanning, short-term entrepreneurial propensities. Thus in order for development to proceed, pluralistic coalitions must exist between diverse groups.

Multiple access to functionally significant roles is another potential source of conflict. Similar groups, instead of working together, are likely to become competitive with each other, as well as with older, less functionally significant groups that have nevertheless retained popular support. Thus there is a continuous need during modernization to search for convenient affiliations and mutual support. For example, roles associated with types of agricultural or industrial labor that have become visibly residual during the later stages of modernization do not disappear. Rather, those who occupy these roles look for new leaders to mobilize other forms of "relevance." If labor-saving devices minimize the need for an unskilled labor force, this search for relevance may, for a time, cause featherbedding and other protective activities. Of course, as industrialization proceeds and substantially fewer industrial workers are required, there will be role attrition, not only because roles have become residual but also because the functional significance of some industrial positions, particularly managers and technical personnel, will grow even if their proportionate numbers do not, thus creating a new rank of roles. These roles are likely to be separated from residuals of a fused system or others involved in the basic production process.

Agricultural roles tend to become more functionally significant in one sense and less in another. Their significance grows if agricultural productivity is a major source of investment funds for development. However, no matter what form the organization of agriculture may take, it is ordinarily more efficient than it appears on the surface, whereas the social system associated with it is less efficient especially insofar as it remains traditionalistic. Improving agricultural efficiency by introducing modern machinery and techniques may, therefore, also change the social structure. The enormous capital expense of modernization will rock the economic structure; unskilled farm laborers displaced by machinery will be forced to undergo rapid urbanization in a situation in which inadequate numbers of jobs await them. Agricultural roles are extremely varied. They may be seen in terms of patron-client relationships or involved in various types of corporate, community, or communal holdings. Membership in these groups may be based on caste or ethnic characteristics, on the nuclear or extended family, or on shareholding.

In contrast, commercial roles are much less varied. In early-stage modernization, they form preponderantly fused middle or upper classes that seek to generalize their significance by pressing the claims of their interests. Hence, the ideology of nationalism in early-stage modernizing societies is associated with expanding opportunities for a local bourgeoisie. This fused middle class enlarges as development occurs. Related ideologies of nationalism view middle-class commercial roles as the stabilizing centers of gravity in new nations. At this stage, education counts for less than occupation, because command over resources, human and national, is embodied in an occupational role.[12] In this view, the middle sectors expand at the expense of the aristocratic and rural patron sectors.

This is the classic definition of development: not that a fused system becomes differentiated, but that all fused groups eventually blend into an "extended middle." Indeed, much American overseas aid policy is based on this notion. Our contention, however, is that modernization, instead of throwing all classes into one, is more likely to produce another pattern[13] in which civil service roles proliferate and come to embody more and more of the specialized attributes of functional status groupings plus highly instrumental values. Given that the major structural problem during modernization is a lack of organizational skills, especially at the middle and lower levels, the expanding network of bureaucratic roles is actually a way of organizing resources. What does *not* occur is a class struggle between fused groupings, for group alignments are more complex than that. Nevertheless, this proliferation of the civil service creates a perpetual pull in favor of a bureaucratic type of political system. Pluralism plus bureaucracy rather than class conflict is the result.

Figure 5.4 emphasizes the overlapping pattern of relationships that are continually becoming more complex, the changes in the functional germaneness to industrialization of each type, and the decreasing likelihood of conflict. Turning now to the normative dimension of choice, we find that the picture is also interesting. Modernization is accompanied by a shift away from primordial attachments of race, religion, and language, all nongermane to development and associated with more or less ritualized boundaries. At the fused level of groupings, there is growing solidarity and class awareness involving the articulation of moral issues within a political subculture. These fused groups do not form a "working class," however, but a commercial middle class or, in the classic sense of the word, a bourgeoisie. As modernization continues, the normative emphasis on solidarity and class awareness changes to an emphasis on instrumental values, reflecting the growth of interest groups and an increase in the types of activities leading to accommodation rather than conflict, and reconciliation instead of persistent hostility. Lower-level fused groups remain small even after industrialization has begun because new technologies are not labor-intensive. Competition arises for various germane attributes. A permeable differentiated system recruits from residual fused and segmentary types on the basis of educational attainment. As the society moves closer to industrialization, certain highly instrumentalized functional status roles become strategic. The normative consequence of structural pluralism accompanied by instrumentalization is the conversion of values into interest and the creation of groups that support or challenge this conversion: the condition of embourgeoisement. This is why we suggest that modernization produces embourgeoisement in a bureaucratic form.

EMBOURGEOISEMENT AND BUREAUCRACY

The preoccupation with occupation, mobility, short-term coalitions, and consumption creates a frame for the response we call embourgeoisement. It should be clear from the start that this is by no means a condition limited to capitalistic forms of modernization; it applies equally to socialist forms. It leads to bureaucratism, opportunism, and corruption, to efforts to provide for family, friends, and associates, and to reduce risks in what is seen as a hostile and demanding environment. But embourgeoisement does not necessarily imply irresponsibility. It is possible to find the most responsible elements in a society involved in coalitions that will favor their work. For example, engineers, plant managers, and other technicians in socialist societies, in a desire to regulate and make more predictable the immediate world of their expertise, may attempt to reduce actions that are a response to ambiguity. This may have politically dysfunctional consequences, although it may be highly successful economically, as when the most productive managers of an industrial plant in China are judged, from a political point of view, to be irresponsible bourgeois elements, opportunists, or worse.

Embourgeoisement occurs when there is an intersection of instrumental values with functionally accommodated roles. A certain degree of role stability is necessary, and the perpetuation of such stability soon becomes a goal. The result is an emphasis on rewards, including respect, dignity, and a style of life that underscores traditional virtues. Expenditure on items to symbolize these virtues, such as houses, furnishings, and clothes, is a familiar characteristic of embourgeoisement. This is why the "consumption function" is important for our analysis.[14] If there is corruption in the bureaucracy, it leads not to satisfaction but to a self-righteous, even angry, defense of bureaucrats who blame the confusion in society for their behavior.

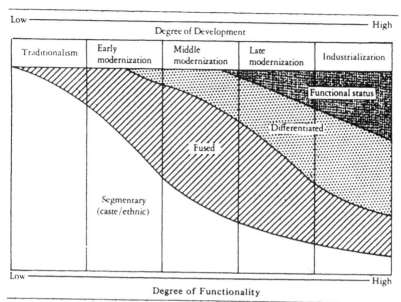

Figure 5.4 Stratification and Pluralism

Obviously, there are different styles of embourgeoisement, each determined by the society in which it occurs. In countries in the early stages of modernization, embourgeoisement tends to emerge in political and business roles. In middle-stage modernization, embourgeoisement is frequently found in professional roles, such as those of doctor, lawyer, teacher, professor, and senior civil servant. In later stages of modernization, it touches the new technocrats. This progressive quality of embourgeoisement should not be understood to imply that those affected first become less bourgeois as more and more roles are involved. Rather, we suggest that the process is progressive and cumulative.

Embourgeoisement is an important aspect of modernization for more than stylistic reasons, however. It has the effect of exaggerating the consumption function without correspondingly affecting the production function.[15] It occurs as classes become multibonded (based on a variety of criteria), as group boundaries become increasingly fluid, and as fixed identifications or loyalties are replaced by competitive group affiliations—that is, when society is divided not by powerful antagonistic classes but by competitive interests. In a fused system, conflicts of interest are likely to be converted into conflicts of values (primordial or ideological, as the case may be). In a competitive, pluralistic, and multibonded class system, however, the process is reversed: conflicts of value are likely to be converted into conflicts of interest.

The embourgeoisement hypothesis can be restated as follows: the greater the degree of modernization, the larger the number of pluralistic and competitive instrumentalistic groupings in the system and the less likely a successful revolution. What results is not polarization but pluralism. A contrary hypothesis, however, is equally plausible: the greater the degree of modernization, the more extensive the proliferation of roles originally derived from an industrial setting, the less effective the government's ability to coordinate social life and cope with the growing chaos. In this hypothetical situation, pressure for a revolutionary solution must come from above.

SOME POLITICAL CONSEQUENCES

We have said that, in general, the growing significance during modernization of differentiated groupings and embourgeoisement does not eliminate other groupings. Where castes remain, they constantly seek to extend their relevance. If this fails at the structural level, it may still succeed at the normative—where primordial loyalties to race, religion, culture, and language are represented. If the normative relevance is supported by some strategic role advantages, these advantages are likely to take the form of either roles appropriate to primordial attachments (e.g., in the church or in the army) or residual claims to property (e.g, like those of fused-system landowners). Which of the two forms emerges will depend on whether the residual segmentary stratification system is horizontal or vertical.

If the segmentary system is vertical, it is likely to be transformed from a caste to an estates system, in the sense that its component parts have legally defined boundaries, rights, and obligations. If our theory of embourgeoisement is correct, as modernization proceeds, caste norms shift from consummatory to instrumental values—in other words, from primordial rights to interests. As instrumentalization increases the vulnerability of traditional groupings to modernization, the vertical system tends to rely on its special institutional supports to resist. Surviving reciprocal class and caste relations prove useful for this purpose. When the highest castes are linked solidly with the lowest classes in patron-client relationships, as in southern Italy and many Latin countries, a united front is created to combat the threat of modernization.[16]

Caste relationships of the vertical type are based to a great extent on kinship. By means of a virtual monopoly on cosmopolitan education, higher castes have often retained access to government more successfully than their numbers of functional significance would suggest. When these higher castes form an aristocracy, it is possible for them to manipulate political life so as to deflect modernization insofar as it threatens them. Obstacles to modernization may thus be inherent in the vertical caste system.

The horizontal segmentary system for the most part is composed of ethnic or tribal groupings occupying the same political space. Examples are Nigeria and the Congo, where such horizontal groupings pose the problem commonly known as tribalism—competition between tribes at the expense of the larger society to which they all belong. The result of tribalism in times of modernization may be civil war or secession. And tribalism can have other effects on modernization through its tendency to allocate political offices, fellowships and university places, and other positions to fellow tribesmen, for example. On the normative level, this type of system puts tribe above nation and thereby casts doubt on the legitimacy of the nation. On the structural level, it causes basic cleavages in social allegiances, so that each new strain divides society along the same lines.[17] Hence, conflicts over development, local government, education, and so on, which inevitably accompany modernization, reinforce separatism and pose the political problems of unity and legitimacy. In sum, the threat posed by modernization to the primordial loyalties and functional significance of ethnic groupings results in the attachment of their members to groups of individuals whose normative status is given precedence over that of society as a whole and whose structural status is separatist and exclusive.

In our fused stratification category, the contemporary modernizing situation is very different from the Marxian notion of reciprocal functional relations between increasingly polarized occupational groups. It has already been suggested that in the early and middle stages of modernization it is likely that the fused system will lean more toward the middle class (defined as a modernizing group with roles drawn directly from an industrial setting and with caste as its reciprocal) than toward other classes of the fused type. In short, modernization does not provide a dramatic confrontation between a powerful group of industrial captains on one side and a large group of industrial proletarians on the other. Instead, the class that comes to preeminence is urban, commercial, familial, and solidaristic to the extent that it feels vulnerable to downward mobility (that is, to falling into the ever-present reservoir of lower castes and classes) and is in an ambiguous position vis-à-vis higher castes and classes. The dominant middle group in the fused stratification pattern is likely to desire upward mobility into a "modern" style of life and will ask that other groups identify its success with the general development of the country. (Liberal and religious normative values support this group's view.) At a later stage of modernization, this is the class most likely to turn into a differential group, with a small fused group of the proletarian sort standing in opposition.

When a large nonsolidaristic bourgeoisie is confronted with a small solidaristic working class, the working class is more likely to search for a place on the general differentiated mobility ladder by the threat of revolutionary disorder than to undertake a revolution that would actually create sufficient opportunities for upward mobility. Moreover, opportunities are slow to expand when a particular combination of segmentary, fused, and differentiated groups exists, resulting in a stratification stalemate imposed by pluralistic group activity and competition; in such a situation, lower groups must settle for short-term gains on the basis of temporary coalitions. To put the matter differently, as the number and type of groups multiply, marginal gains become more difficult to achieve and the society reaches an allocation stalemate.

Finally, we come to the new status elites, those occupying what we have called "career roles." Among the most important of these are the technocrats, whose functional significance becomes greater as modernization proceeds, and certain bureaucrats. Technocrats are underemployed in most modernizing societies because of the lack of supporting facilities, material and human, that would enable them to contribute to development. As a result, they lose heart and tend to abuse their roles or to become politicians. Bureaucrats are also likely to follow this course, but for opposite reasons; they most often have too much to do and become resentful. There are exceptions, of course. For example, the old Indian civil service could draw from a middle class of the fused type and thereby sustain its high quality even after the original conditions favoring its historical evolution had diminished.

We can also mention another role that has political consequences of great significance—that of the intellectuals, who represent universalized ideological norms and differentiated class references, or, in some cases, residual caste references that they reject. Most intellectuals in modernizing societies come from bourgeois groups of the fused or differentiated type, but they reject the competitive instrumentalism of the differentiated system. Hence, it is the intellectuals who become the carriers of consummatory values and represent revolutionary innovation. Their ideologies, all-embracing to be sure, are particularly designed to link them to lower caste or residual fused groups, as when young radicals in Buenos Aires adopt Peronism or the cause of "the workers." Quite often, though, their ideologies and activities mobilize residual caste groups against them, resulting in the appearance of polarization without its substance, in the sense that upper "residuals" are posed against lower "marginals" while the bulk of the population continues to move toward a differentiated type of competitive mobility situation. The problem for government is how to avoid becoming imprisoned in the various maneuvers of such groups. If it fails, it becomes exposed and vulnerable to a takeover by any organized group with the capacity to move quickly and immobilize its opposition. Not mass revolution but coup d'etat is the consequence of modernization, and not by a mass public but by an elite. This is what we mean by revolution from above. Late-stage modernization thus contains the possibility (it is no more than that) of both stagnation and coup. It is an interesting predicament for both populist revolutionaries (especially those among the radical bourgeoisie) and all governments of the nonmobilization type.

Our comments may be summarized. In the most general terms, the structural processes just described involve the adoption of function as the principle of role allocation at the expense of reciprocal obligation; the normative processes involve secularization at the expense of the sacred. All of our stratification types tend to follow this sequence, but the transition is never clear-cut. The particular modes of differentiation and values will vary from place to place. In addition, the secularization of traditional values opens up a normative space into which new norms can be introduced, although (from a behavioral point of view) not very easily. The resulting political problem of society is a lack of solidarity, a high degree of competitive bargaining among members with few internalized restraints, and an emphasis on short-term gains. This is the classic situation of the reconciliation system.

The political problem of the modernizing society is thus posed on two levels. First, how will modernization be achieved? Second, what political system is it likely to support? According to our discussion, political instability may be the most favorable condition for further development.

We are now in a position to state what is perhaps the most important paradox of the modernizing society, particularly in its late stages. These in turn have exercised a pull toward a reconciliation system. But a reconciliation system would limit development because it does not allow the concentration of resources for rapid growth. The most appropriate type of political system for development would be the mobilization system. *Thus development pressures tend to produce a dysfunctional political system, and the system that would be most functionally useful is very difficult to put into practice.* The most common resolution of this problem in modernizing societies is through some variant of a bureaucratic system.

If our assumptions about embourgeoisement are correct, we should be able to specify certain propositions about the process at various stages. In the case of industrialized societies, the spread of embourgeoisement coincides with the resolution of the allocation crisis: increases in the social product are accompanied by greater opportunities to exercise choice over roles, together producing a collective mobility for the entire system, including an increase in access to various status roles. In late-stage modernizing societies, however, this mobility occurs primarily between differentiated roles; there is little increase in the opportunity for movement from fused to differentiated groupings. The result is a shifting of the allocation crisis downward, with the following effects. Differentiated groups confront fused groups more sharply. Fused groups develop a particular set of counternorms. Differentiated groups become instrumentalized and try to form alliances that cut across residual segmentary and fused stratification lines. Revolution from below becomes increasingly less likely, but revolution from above, which seeks to bridge fused and differentiated group differences and conflicts and which makes particular use of status elites functionally related to industrialization, becomes more acceptable. Thus the likely effects of embourgeoisement during late-stage modernization are revolution from above, with tendencies toward a mobilization governmental form, or the emergence of a bureaucratic system. If a bureaucratic system materializes, it will be vulnerable to many of the same pressures that gave rise to it in the first place, and it is likely to be replaced by a system closer to a reconciliation type under which the allocation crisis will continue more or less as before.

A mobilization system is most likely to succeed at the point of maximum embourgeoisement in late-stage modernization, but not by mass revolutionary action. Its leaders are likely to be bourgeois radicals, whose links are with status elites (technocrats) and whose ideologies are populist, socialist, nationalist, or national-socialist. Modernizing societies, then, become revolutionary through bourgeois radicalism, a phenomenon frequently commented upon but insufficiently analyzed. A mobilization system, however, is least likely to be able to cope with embourgeoisement. Hence, the political paradox of modernization: embourgeoisement creates the conditions both for a mobilization system and for its demise. This we regard as the crucial political predicament encountered by governments in all modernizing countries.

What these comments suggest is that revolutions from below in the form of people's revolts that begin in armed rebellion and end in general social disruption are less likely than we might assume. Popular rebellions or mass movements are more a nineteenth-century phenomenon than a contemporary one. In our view, normative and structural conditions during modernization are much more likely to result in an aggressive, highly instrumentalized, and increasingly mobile population that may not necessarily be productive or entrepreneurial in the real sense of the term but may be dominated by narrow self-interest, commercialism, and the desire for mobility. Looking for security rather than for innovation, the population will tend to live off commercial activities of the type common to derivative economies. Such results of modernization are fostered by large urban areas with small industries at the periphery and a rural hinterland, conditions that are found on a relatively modest scale in Dakar, Accra, Lagos, and Nairobi, and on a larger scale in Buenos Aires, Santiago, Mexico City, and Lima.

A second proposition about revolution and radicalization becomes relevant when purposeful developmental goals are frustrated by functional randomness and normative polarization. Functional randomness or even role incompatibility as a consequence of modernization paves the way for revolution from above, particularly if a normative vacuum accompanies randomization. The coups d'etat and forays from any organized source are more likely to succeed. Long-run success, however, is possible only if the new regime can generate enough popular support to create an effective restructuring of roles along more immediately functional lines and normative system that affects motivation. Ideologies of revolution from above may be of any political shade. There might be a revival of "corporate" normative theories, not dissimilar to fascist ideologies, based on a dialectical tension between nationalist and socialist ideological pulls; the structural units of such a system would be functional corporate groups possessing external institutional support.

Indeed, fascism (stripped of some of its more atavistic characteristics, perhaps) might reappear as an ideology with considerable relevance, to be preferred to some of the more anarchic theories of socialism.

RADICALIZATION FROM ABOVE

The analysis so far makes certain assumptions about the normative and structural consequences of development during modernization. Choice is enlarged. The range and number of roles potentially open to members of society increase. Competition for these roles intensifies. Institutional groupings mediate the growing competition either by trying to monopolize and control entry or by eliminating it. Such change wears away at established notions of equity. Older and more traditional ideologies are broken or die and are revived in new forms. Those appropriate to a more fixed and stable order give way. There is a general downgrading of consummatory values in favor of instrumental values more relevant to development and to competition between interest groups. Under such circumstances, if the equity-allocation relationship is at all responsive to expanding choice, embourgeoisement should combine successfully with a reconciliation system to minimize the difficulties of transition to industrialization, liberating many sources of participation and involvement, stimulating growth and activity. That, of course, is the liberal ideal. It lies behind such programs as the Alliance for Progress, not to speak of other types of aid designed to expand choice, make allocation more flexible, and allow greater public participation on the basis of instrumental values related to development. According to this ideal, development is its own reward.

But if other assumptions are also correct, the success of this pattern is exceedingly rare. For one thing, the equity-allocation relationship is characteristically different from the responsive ideal, with previous advantage leading to a more or less successful monopolization of increased allocation opportunities rather than to an expansion of choice. Institutionalized mediating groups restrict the downward flow of role allocation, not in simple class terms but by means of coalitions that limit immediate benefits to the cooperating parties. The smaller the coalitions, the greater the benefits for their participants. No fixed membership is necessary, however, and the pattern of coalition can include representatives of all groups able at one point or another to generate populist, interest, or professional sources of power. As modernization increases, so do the possible coalitions, and although it can be argued that in the long run this is in itself a form of reallocation, it may be the very long run indeed.

Moreover, such bargaining between groups creates conditions of corruption. Groups become gamblers, with equity determined entirely by highly instrumentalized and short-term bargains. In terms of general social norms associated with choice, there is lack of trust in others and a minimum of reliance on law, courts, and other civil procedures. A consummatory space is likely to appear alongside such extreme instrumentalism, representing a longing for some sort of moral rejuvenation, a new beginning. Hence, when development follows this pattern, one behavioral consequence is the need for innocence—the desperate desire to be fresh, to have direct relationships between individuals, and to do away with the hypocrisy and the atmosphere of fraud that permeate political life. This is particularly the case among those whose fundamental roles, as civil servant, technocrat, or university lecturer, have about them some generalized commitment to the future and to the development of the society as a whole (that is, to the industrial part of the modernizing society). These persons are likely to be the most corrupted by such a situation because they are inevitably co-opted in one way or another by various interest groups or coalitions. But not always; it is interesting that a significant proportion of the radicalized leadership in modernizing countries consists of teachers, doctors, lawyers, and civil servants. When they in effect "jump" their roles to form counterelites in which highly consummatory values require selfless devotion to the state and to the objectives of development, a radicalization process has begun. These elites embody different ideas of equity to be realized by a reclassification of roles according to criteria of germaneness to industrialization or some other objective standard. These are the sources for the mobilization system. The ideological pulls come from groups that are unwilling to strike the bargains offered to them and that resist being co-opted.

In general, two factors militate against the mobilization system. One, as we have suggested, is the flexibility of the coalitions that can offer immediate benefits and advantages to all with some education and a bit of following. The other, a characteristic weakness of the mobilization system, lies in the relationship between development and allocation, namely, the limited accountability of those controlling choice to the elites created by development. Except as bands, guerrillas, or other small underground groups, where camaraderie and hierarchy can be successfully combined, a lack of political participation prevents involvement in the society. Even the most successful mobilization system is plagued by the problem of pseudoparticipation, which in turn creates an imbalance in the relationship between norms and structures. The consummatory values associated with revolutionary purity soon give way to instrumental values, and the pressures to return to some form of reconciliation system grow.

At this point, it is interesting to consider cases in which the response to development has in one way or another been kept within bounds, so that the development-order relationship has not been upset. Two notable cases are the Philippines and India. In India, the British legacy of a powerful civil service plus the extension of instrumental values to include the proprieties of government provide the most interesting illustration of two types of political systems (reconciliation and bureaucratic) operating effectively, one inside the other.

The great difficulty with the purely bureaucratic system is its combination of hierarchical authority and instrumental values, which increasingly requires reliance on coercion (unless it is possible to revitalize primordial racial or religious or nationalist values to reinforce the instrumental ones). Under some circumstances, this is possible; Egypt, for example, relies periodically on intensifying the conflict with Israel for this purpose. Without such dramatic confrontations, however, the normative tendency is in the other direction. It becomes impossible to obtain the necessary public response to government-defined development policies. Bureaucratic systems are not capable of generating any "big push" into industrialization unless they receive unusual amounts of outside assistance, as, for example, did Taiwan.

In general, then, we can suggest the political tendencies that are most pronounced in the transition from early to late modernization (see Figure 5.5). Systems originating in the mobilization form (such as Ghana, Guinea, and Indonesia) or reconciliation form (such as Nigeria, the Congo-Kinshasha, and Sierra Leone) show periodic tendencies in the early stages of modernization toward bureaucratic systems, in a military or some other form. Bureaucratic systems show a continual tendency toward the reconciliation type, producing a pattern of instability characteristic of late-stage modernizing societies. However, some bureaucratic systems (Peru) also generate tendencies toward the mobilization type (Cuba, China), which in turn shows bureaucratic tendencies.

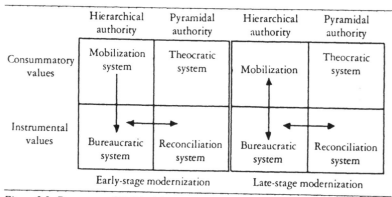

	Hierarchical authority	Pyramidal authority	Hierarchical authority	Pyramidal authority
Consummatory values	Mobilization system	Theocratic system	Mobilization	Theocratic system
Instrumental values	Bureaucratic system	Reconciliation system	Bureaucratic system	Reconciliation system
	Early-stage modernization		Late-stage modernization	

Figure 5.5 Responses of Political Systems to Modernization

These varying tendencies during modernization when combined with the embourgeoisement hypothesis lead us to a tentative conclusion about political response to development. Continuous variation in the type of political system is itself an important characteristic of modernization. It has the effect of altering the relationships between society and government and by this means opening up, for a short time, at any rate, a new set of options. Hence, with respect to modernizing societies, political instability, seen as the continuous rearrangement of political relationships, may itself be both a result of modernization and a cause of further development.

NOTES

1. This need for weighting raises a practical question about the appropriateness of treating roles that are functional in an industrial system as if they must have some necessarily similar functions in a nonindustrial setting. The point is a good one because our theory does contain implications of functional teleology that in fact can scarcely be avoided. On one hand, we do not intend to make roles into substitutes for some set of functional imperatives. On the other hand, if we treat roles as having some institutional persistence, then it seems fair to expect them, like Pirandello's six characters, to search for ways to perform functions for which they were originally intended, even though the scene may be different.

2. Marx had a remarkable insight into this problem very early. See Karl Marx, *The Grundrisse*, ed. David McLellan (New York: Harper & Row, 1971), pp. 43-46.

3. If we illustrate the consequences of the derivative character of modernizing societies in the context of entrepreneurship (whether individual or corporate), we find that

the rationality of the entrepreneur or the rationality of the firm may be quite perfect. One does not need to look for an absence of Calvinist ethics or for some nonrational traditional preference to account for this. The pursuit of rationality under conditions of a derivative society may result in nonrationality from the point of view of the system as a whole. Hence, a corollary of our notion of modernization is that increased vulnerability is the result of attempts to balance international payments, allocation of expenditures into quick and safe sources of capital return, and high emphasis on consumption expenditures. Some of these consequences are discussed in René Dumont's *False Start in Africa* (London: Andre Deutsch, 1966).

4. This is the approach contained in the idea of a peasant or campesino revolt as a means of radical modernization, and also in the "strangle the cities" theory and organizational Leninism, occurring (conveniently enough) under the hegemony of the radical intellectuals (à la Gramsci). We doubt that the peasantry (replacing the working class) will be headed by a dictatorship of the intellectuals.

5. It is not that the older notion of class should disappear but that it ought to be applied as originally intended and not tinkered with too much. That is, it should refer precisely to the common membership in a group that derives from a relationship to the means and models of production, the consequence of which is a consciousness of life chances and normative proprieties, reciprocally defined. Such a notion of class, Weberian as well as Marxian, is at base a liberal one in which class, class interest, and motivation are considered to be different functions of the same phenomenon.

6. In a case hierarchy within a single system, it is possible that shared norms will define some castes as "chosen people" and others as ritually unclean, or what Weber called "pariah people." Normative religious situations may involve negative and positive reciprocities. Something of this sort may extend to other stratification situations, such as those involving patron-client relationships (for example, haciendados and campesinos in Indian areas of Peru). We could then speak of the relationship between patrons and clients as similar to that between castes. See T. Shibutani and K. M. Kwan, *Ethnic Stratification* (New York: Macmillan, 1965), pp. 82-115.

7. See Barringon Moore, *The Social Origins of Dictatorship and Democracy* (Boston: Beacon Press, 1966).

8. See T. H. Marshall, *Citizenship and Social Development* (New York: Doubleday, 1964).

9. See my discussion of career roles in the *Politics of Modernization*. It should be pointed out, if it is not already obvious, that the present set of stratification categories utilizes the more recent work of many writers on the subject. Perhaps the most important for our purposes is that of Ralf Dahrendorf. See his discussion of quasi-groups and the relation of these to imperatively coordinated associations. Dahrendorf makes the point that social classes and class conflict are present wherever authority is distributed unequally over social positions, a position with which I agree. See his *Class and Class Conflict in Industrial Society* (Stanford, CA: Stanford University Press, 1959), p. 247. See also Suzanne Keller, *Beyond the Ruling Class* (New York: Random House, 1963).

10. We might also suggest that fused-system prestige is collective, that is, class determined, whereas in differentiated systems, prestige is individualized.

11. Behavior in differentiated systems is very similar at lower and higher levels, although the style and manners in each case may be different. There is preoccupation with education on one hand and with consumption on the other. The scale of consumption is lower in developing societies, but its manifestation in conspicuous waste is similar to the

phenomenon of discarded automobiles and elaborate mansions of highly industrialized societies.

12. This was particularly characteristic of very early-stage development, such as that undertaken by West African nationalism in the 1920s and 1930s.

13. See Morris Zelditch and Bo Anderson, "On the Balance of a Set of Ranks," in *Sociological Theories in Progress*, ed. Joseph Berger, Morris Zelditch, and Bo Anderson (Boston: Houghton Mifflin, 1966), pp. 248-49. See also Alain Touraine, "Management and the Working Class in Western Europe," *Daedalus*, Winter 1964, p. 332, in which he speaks of "conflict participation" as the characteristic of a "new" working class.

14. See, for example, Pi-chao Chen, "Individual Farming after the Great Leap: As Revealed by the Lieu Kiang Documents," *Asian Survey* 8 (September 1968), pp. 724-91.

15. The reason for this effect of embourgeoisement is by no means simple. It has both functional and dialectical aspects to it that have not been properly explored except in some very superficial ways (as in Milovan Djilas's argument about the rise of the "new class" and in writings as diverse as those of Trotsky and Burnham). As a practical matter, however, the way modernization proceeds determines in some measure the results.

16. See Michael Parenti, "Ethnic Politics and the Persistence of Ethnic Identification," *American Political Science Review* 61 (September 1967). See also Sidney Tarrow, *Peasant Communism in Italy* (New Haven, CT: Yale University Press, 1967); and Edward Banfield, *The Moral Basis of a Backward Society* (New York: Free Press, 1957).

17. Perhaps the best illustrations are to be found in Africa, with the Biafran war being the most dramatic and tragic.

6

EQUITY AND ALLOCATION IN INDUSTRIAL SOCIETIES

The analysis of modernization so far has led us to define certain stratification systems through which we might operationalize the allocation variable. By stressing the more derivative characteristics of such systems, we were able to suggest certain structural tendencies. The relationship of norms and structures is continually changing, with each part in some measure varying independently of the other, and it provides an important focus for empirical research on concrete societies, particularly for comparative research dealing with the responses of different types of political systems to highly generalized problems.

How far norms and structures can diverge is an open question. In all concrete systems, the mechanisms of adjustment are ordinarily flexible enough to respond to changing needs. In addition, the dialectic over norms most often occurs when there is a threat to legitimacy. If such threats can be met by reviving old consummatory values or instrumentalizing basic value conflicts, the political system may be preserved even when there is dissatisfaction with its structures. Precisely because of the wide range of possible strategies and combinations, we need to penetrate below the surface of events, instrumentalities, and techniques of rule to identify analytically some limits to the alternatives.

INDUSTRIALIZATION AS A DYNAMIC PROCESS

Industrialization is dynamic in the sense that industrial societies generate new knowledge at an exceptionally rapid rate, apply it to all aspects of social life, and at the same time produce exportable industrial surpluses. Although a country such as Israel may have very high research potential, if that potential cannot be utilized at home, the country is still not industrialized. If a country produces an exportable industrial surplus only because of the presence of the branch of a foreign industrial firm as in Latin American countries, it is not industrialized, although it may be industrializing.

An industrial society is already bourgeois (whether in socialist or capitalist terms is irrelevant). Insofar as modernization and industrialization proceed together, the conditions of embourgeoisement are present. However, because the occupational structure of an industrial society reflects a hierarchy of roles based on their relation to knowledge and information functions, the result is not only bourgeois but meritocratic. A bourgeois meritocracy embodies a functional definition of merit that combines open recruitment with unequal role distribution. Consequently, any rejection of roles functionally related to information triggers a search for new meaning and contributes to a continuous redefinition of equity. This is because roles related to information creation are, in industrial societies, self-legitimating. Rejection of them by those eligible for such roles creates the bourgeois radicals. The greater the degree of industrialization, the more meritocratic the stratification system and the more widespread the search for meaning.

The continuous redefinition of a society's consummatory values is evidence of what we mean by radicalization; the legitimacy of the system is being questioned. Like embourgeoisement, radicalization is caused by a normative-structural imbalance. The hypothesis we suggest is that the more industrialized a society becomes, the greater its crisis in meaning. Because an industrial society is based on high information, the type of political system best able to facilitate information formation would appear to be a reconciliation system. But this type is the very one that because of excessive instrumentalism is always in danger of losing its legitimacy; as a result, it is vulnerable to pulls from other types (particularly bureaucratic and mobilization systems). This political vulnerability highlights the fundamental predicament of highly industrial societies, namely, that high degrees of embourgeoisement produce radicalization. Moreover, this predicament can confront governments in all highly industrialized societies whether they are capitalist, socialist, or guided by a combination of ideologies.

The continuous crisis in industrial society is puzzling primarily because it is difficult to conceive of industrialization as a predicament rather than as an achievement. It is as if those who live in industrial societies see their past not as a landscape studded with monuments to their accomplishments, but rather as a combat zone littered with casualties. The political effects of this disillusionment are just beginning to be visible both in countries like the United States and in slightly less industrialized ones like Japan and the U.S.S.R. The phrase "post-industrial society" expresses a sensitivity to the need for new and different political solutions to the problems of industrialization.

Consciousness of a predicament is one of the distinguishing characteristics of an industrial society. Within modernizing societies, a widely accepted view—particularly by leaders—is that industrialization is the final solution to the problems that plague them. The advantage of such a view is a certain programmatic innocence in which general agreement is easily reached about policy objectives and developmental goals. Few such illusions persist in highly industrial societies. The competitive pace of new knowledge contributes to the functional vulnerability of roles; they are no longer linked together in groups based on solidarity but are locked into networks in which the parts are as replaceable as those of machines. The vulnerability of the individual is increased; new marginals are created as old ones disappear; political inequities multiply.

The multibonded character of differentiated classes in an industrial society contributes to status incongruities but also makes them less important. Although there may be many routes to a particular rank or status, one route may have been crucial for obtaining other characteristics. Occupation was in this category for roles in the old fused system. Education is similarly salient for differentiated roles in industrial societies. Hence, we can pick out salient (and, therefore, desirable) roles and use them not only to determine a wide range of other class characteristics but also to define mobility within the stratification system. Of the changes that may occur in the shift from modernization to industrial society, therefore, two will stand out; the increase and spread of status incongruities and the expansion of salient roles.

The stratification picture is complicated by the fact that no industrial nation is without its modernizing sector, which, in the context of stratification in an industrial society, is composed of marginals. The issues of political life are confused because the needs of both sectors are so different. The modernizing sector wants embourgeoisement—in particular, greater social mobility. It does not, however, challenge prevailing concepts of equity unless mobility is denied it. At the far end of the spectrum, at the top of the industrialized sector, the new technocratic elite shows signs of becoming antibourgeois. That is, its radicalization has begun, accelerated by increasing concern over the dehumanizing consequences of a functional universe, created, of course, by its own activities.[1] Between these two sectors, modernizing and industrial, is a wide range of groups, each of which defines equity in a different way. The result is a curious dialectic on the normative level between opposite structural groups: prosystem marginals versus antisystem bourgeois radicals. Hence, the same forces that generate embourgeoisement in modernizing systems produce the opposite result in industrial ones, where the difficulties are compounded by the way industrial countries coexist with modernizing ones, by the way industrial countries coexist with each other, and by the fact that neither system follows in a simple manner the tendencies just described.

CHARACTERISTICS OF INDUSTRIAL ROLES

A truly instrumentalist society is impossible without complete internalization of shared norms by members of the system (if only because of the randomization of ends). Complete internalization of norms requires an effective socialization process built on a stable structural base.

Until recently it was widely believed that knowledge was open-ended and that information, applied through an expanding educational system, was capable of extending the area of rational control over empirical problems. Thus industrial society appeared to possess the secret of self-validating moral purposes and a view of knowledge so dynamic that it created its own demands and its own categorical imperatives.

But new knowledge does not necessarily replace old knowledge. Nor does knowledge follow narrow grooves of expertise. As it expands, it creates new paradigms, signal systems, word sets, and overlapping theories. Input-output models, stimulus-response models, the concept of feedback, and other types of systems theory spread from research to applied fields as diverse as engineering, psychology, and business planning and marketing. With the application of knowledge, a mutually comprehensible language makes its appearance. Although it is useful, it creates insiders and outsiders. Generalized models become core theories that can be borrowed and applied from subject to subject. Eventually, this process gives rise to metalanguages. Metatheories also form, establishing boundaries of participation for special elites that have gained access to power by monopolistic control of technical knowledge. Such functional elites are the ultimate result of concentrating on instrumental ends. Knowledge, therefore, extends the process of instrumentalization but at the expense of consummatory values.

Traditional democratic theories are becoming obsolete because they are based on the assumption that any normative problem can be solved by enlarging political participation, leaving questions of meaning to chance. Unfortunately, the solution is not that simple. The industrial process, by generating new knowledge, continuously superimposes multibonded and functional elite classes and groups on an existing network of groupings based on ideologies and interests. Antagonisms and coalitions with complex political consequences result.

Because of its strategic role in industrial society, then, knowledge creates a functional hierarchy and multibonded classes composed of small nonsolidaristic groups defined by multiple criteria. It also creates unique sets of marginals.[2] These marginal groups are likely to be found in residual areas of society such as castes or among newly debased fused or differentiated groupings. For them, opportunities to participate are severely limited. Some never attempt to participate. Those who try and fail are likely to fall back on primordial norms to fill the normative vacuum and to respond to populist appeals. It is the marginals' attachment to primordial norms that enables politicians to manipulate them in order to attack technocrats or other intellectuals who represent rationalistic instrumentalism and, derived from it, liberal economic presuppositions. This conflict over instrumentalism increasingly identifies the main areas of political controversy. Its dialectical forms are knowledge versus anti-intellectualism and elitism versus populism, which are incorporated in a specific ideological package appropriate to the political culture of the society. The growing instrumentalization of values is accompanied by a search for simplistic, consummatory formulas. Not the end of ideologies but their proliferation is the chief normative problem of this stage, heightening the instability already engendered by science and technology and the substitution of new knowledge for old. If our assumptions are correct, the industrial society is characterized by increasing instrumental clarity and power based on new information and by greater consummatory confusion and power based on populism. Occupants of nonfunctional criteria are attracted to radical or revolutionary norms. That is the main point of the present discussion of radicalization as a crisis of meaning for highly industrial societies. The *industrial society becomes a universe of calculation for its elite and a universe of chance for its mass.*

If the liberal tradition underlying the democratic ideology of representative government (capitalist or socialist) accepts that instrumentalization is capable of creating its own self-validating and universalized ends manifested in a stable set of rationalistic consummatory norms, our discussion suggests several reasons to doubt this view. The instrumentalization of norms produced by an increasingly rationalistic universe of information leaves too great a meaning gap. Purpose and action are divorced. Preoccupation with short-term objectives, the breakdowns of moral constraints, and the personalization of failure are some of the consequences of this divorce.

Pluralism, a structural imperative of highly complex systems, becomes the instrument of false values and slipshod solutions. Many ardent advocates of purer forms of democracy attack pluralism because it increases the structural coherence of a system at the expense of its normative coherence. For example, growing instrumentalization may result in the proliferation of interest groups that cater to a range of more or less functional demands; if the elites of these groups have access to decision making and their sources of power are hardened into fixed stratification categories, this in itself becomes a source of inflexibility in the system that seriously weakens its ability to develop. Hence, the response to development in industrial society is twofold: it results in the establishment of functional claims as the basis of allocation; it fosters instrumentalization at the expense of consummatory values. The modernizing sector of an industrial society holds to such values if increased social mobility is possible for its members. The industrial sector responds by dividing into two main groups—one that favors instrumentalization and intensifies it by performing certain roles and the other that rejects instrumentalization and seeks either to revive fading consummatory values or to create new ones. These two groups arise to fill the normative space created both by immobilities in allocation and by equity conflicts resulting from excessive instrumentalization. Although industrial society should be a situation of wide choice for any individual, this normative confusion turns opportunities for choice into an illusion.[3] Disorderly development is thus endemic in an increasingly rationalized universe.

EMERGING ALLOCATION PATTERNS
IN INDUSTRIAL SOCIETY

This interpretation of the industrial crisis can be linked to our form of structural analysis more specifically. We have defined information as a key variable in determining hierarchy, a meritocratic hierarchy that divides society into three main clusters—functional status groups, multibonded class groups, and functionally superfluous groups. As we go from the most functionally relevant to the least, the role of information changes. Each group has a different information function. The first group provides professional information. The second provides interest information, and the third provides populist information. The three groups overlap and are linked in various ways to form the concrete basis of alterations in a society's notions of equity, allocation, and order. Each group is capable of internal subdivision. At the highest level, the functional status elites include those who produce information through research, such as physicists, medical research workers, computer research scientists, and, increasingly, social scientists, particularly economists and psychologists. These roles create new concepts and new techniques of research, and they are also concerned with application of research. They are institutionalized in universities, independent research complexes, and academies of science.

Closely associated with the highest functional status roles are the applied scientists and administrators of scientific knowledge. These include experimental scientists—space engineers, for example—and a variety of specialists closer to the production side of industrial life than to research but dependent on new knowledge and techniques, such as technocrats, high-level administrators, and highly specialized entrepreneurs. Such roles are often interchangeable between universities, commercial enterprises, and governments. Indeed, one can identify them by their relative closeness to university centers, given that the academy is the most institutionalized corporate group concerned with both research and recruitment of candidates for all roles pertaining to knowledge.

The multibonded class groups can be similarly subdivided, although they comprise a much wider range of positions and roles. The roles are differentiated either in terms of the functional significance of a role vis-à-vis the industrial process, particularly whether it is declining or becoming more significant, or in terms of the degree to which education allows nonfunctional aspects of life to become important. The first criterion is a means of judging whether a role has industrial importance, and the second, whether a role is part of a fused or differentiated class.

Division among the functionally superfluous groups tends to take caste-ethnic forms. These groups are marginal. One of the consequences of industrialization is the continuous creation of marginal groupings. The marginalization process does not mean simple downward mobility. It is possible for individuals to move downward in a ranking of roles without becoming marginal. The concept of marginalism is related to the problem of functional superfluousness in which, in terms of societal needs, an individual can make no recognized contribution by means of his roles. In modernizing societies, this often occurs as the functions of chiefs, religious figures, elders, and others are displaced (i.e., when formerly useful roles lose their original purposes). In industrial society, this is more a result of such occupations as those of unskilled laborers. However, there are more complicated ways in which marginalization occurs. Engineers or physicists may become functionally superfluous when their skills become outmoded or when they fall behind the theoretical advances of their fields. In other words, marginalization may be a function of obsolescence in terms of specialized knowledge. This is "high-level" marginalization. The person involved may or may not find it possible to be reabsorbed in a different functional role.

Marginalization needs to be distinguished from collective downward mobility, which occurs when a set of roles become less functionally significant. Such collective downward mobility has occurred among such professional roles as those of doctors, and commercial roles such as salesmen, small businessmen, brokers, and the like.

The most salient groups in industrial society are those most closely related to the creation of knowledge and its application. These groups consist of scientists (pure and applied) and technocrats (including entrepreneurs and senior organizational leaders). The next level of groups is involved in the translation of knowledge into industrial and commercial life; in highly industrial societies, the roles in these groups are mainly of the differentiated type and are ranked according to social distance and functionality. At the opposite end of the scale, the functionally superfluous groups represent marginals in the system.

In postindustrial societies, a new group has arisen between the functional status groups and the differentiated groups—the bourgeois radicals, who reject the functional standard of ranking. If they are reactionaries, they attempt to revive fading or historical consummatory values, as have Stalinists in the U.S.S.R., nationalists in Poland, and right-wing conservatives in the United States. If they are revolutionaries, they create new consummatory values or provide old ones with new meaning, as have poets, students, and writers in the U.S.S.R. and the bourgeois radicals in the United States, Britain, and France.

Coalitions are increasingly viable between bourgeois radicals and technocrats. In Czechoslovakia, for example, the economic reforms suggested by Ota Šik and others were designed to improve industrial performance. Support from high-ranking technocrats for the reforms also opened the way for a reinterpretation of consummatory values. Thus instrumentalization is not a one-way process. It can result in a decline in consummatory values, but it can also call forth a new consummatory-instrumental synthesis.

What does the meritocracy look like in terms of our structural theory? Let us compare it briefly with earlier descriptions, such as those of Marx or Weber, that used objective categories denoting a class type together with an expected form of action, or that of W. Lloyd Warner, which used statistically significant characteristics to establish class rankings including social prestige and style. Marx and Weber suggest categories such as subproletariat, peasantry, proletariat, bourgeois, haute bourgeois, and aristocracy, each constituting a distinct subculture, a source of consciousness, and a particular relationship to the mode of production. The pattern of reciprocal exploitation between classes, as they become polarized, is set during a system change. But in this specific prediction, Marx was wrong. And he was wrong insofar as he based his revolutionary theory on a simple theory of polarization.

Marshall and Warner were concerned with the multiple characteristics of class in a highly industrial society. Particularly in the case of Warner, these characteristics were subjectively defined by the members of the unit under analysis. Statistically significant points of reference included various social structures, family, clique, voluntary association, and kinship, which were then combined in a descriptive ranking—lower, upper lower, lower middle, middle middle, upper middle, lower upper, and so on. Using this approach, Warner paved the way for a new evaluation of the concept of class that allowed Lipset and others to focus on the reverse of the Marxian hypothesis of class polarization, namely, an all-embracing middle.[4]

If the early Warner approach (and much of the later literature on stratification, which represents variations on his model) has many weaknesses, it does not ignore the qualitative changes that take place in the character of stratification as industrialization proceeds. Although the specific Marxian thesis was wrong, the dynamic use of class categories was valid. Combining both approaches should create a new pattern that does greater justice both to the actions of classes involved in modernization and to qualitative changes in social life. Our criteria of functionality and mobility (or weakly articulated boundaries) establishes a general progression from segmentary to fused to differentiated to functional status stratification types occurring as a result of modernization. Because modernization works from the industrial center to the traditional periphery, the progression today does not follow the same pattern it followed in Western Europe, for example. Most modernizing societies have a small proletariat and a large commercial class of the fused type. They may have small numbers of functional status elites that are nevertheless extremely important because of their functional control of the sources of power.

What is the emergent pattern for industrial society? It is the meritocracy. If our categories are valid, ranking within the meritocracy is as follows. Marginals, continuously replenished and redefined, are at the bottom, barely participating in the system. Their share in the allocation of resources is minimal and their functional utility zero. Next are the fused groups, whose collective mobility is downward because the groups are derived from occupation rather than education and whose hierarchy is based on functional significance (e.g., doctors and entrepreneurs at the top, salesmen in the middle, workers at the bottom). Differentiated groups come next, consisting of multibonded classes. Within the category, there are "miniclasses." Whereas fused groups are solidaristic and engaged in reciprocal relations (whether in the form of polarized conflict between workers and management or of mutual dependency between patrons and clients), differentiated groups are competitive. Beyond the multibonded differentiated groups are three divisions within the functional status category. The first is composed of bourgeois radicals who repudiate the entire system but who by virtue of high education have potentially high functional significance. They redefine functionality. Next is the administrative elite whose function is transformation, that is, the transformation of new knowledge into corporate or institutional form. These two groups are competitive. At the top is that part of the functional status elite that creates new information. It can be divided into two, the pure and the applied. This gives us a pattern, presented in Figure 6.1, that includes the older patterns within it, utilizes the implications of the Marxian theory, and

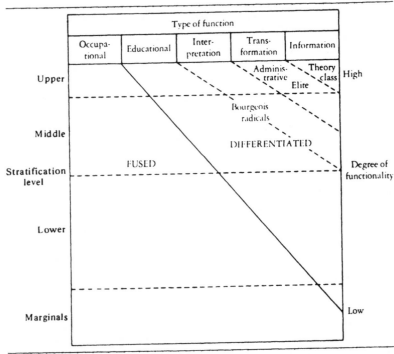

Figure 6.1 Allocation in the Emergent Meritocracy

takes into account the limitations of the Warner approach.

This formulation suggests that with increasing embourgeoisement in the middle sectors of the fused and differentiated stratification systems, two types of bourgeoisie appear (one solidaristic, the other competitive). Fused groups can either move up into fused ranks or differentiated ones or be pushed into marginal status. The tendencies of this marginal group are toward embourgeoisement if the movement is upward and radicalization if it is downward, the latter taking the form of primordial loyalties and a reemergence of caste-ethnic affiliations (nativism, Christianity, primitive Stalinism, and so on). The process at work in the fused sector is the redefinition of functionality; occupation is being divorced from a relationship to property or ownership, and education (the acquisition of technical skills) is being given priority over occupation.

The functional status elites are open to radicalization, whether toward the left or the right. They do not need to search for functional significance but for a wider context of meaning for their skills. The radicalization of this elite is likely to occur as instrumentalization reaches excessive levels and leaves a consummatory vacuum. Innovation in the arts, and the criticism of society that that often implies, becomes important in the process of radicalization. Some governments attempt to defend themselves against these radicals by making them marginal, while others co-opt them through commercialization.[5]

Allocation in industrial societies is based on competition between functional claims. The marginals have the least functional relevance and the theory class, with its information function, the most. The administrative elite has a transformation function that is necessary to society in order to generate an output or a project. The bourgeois radicals have an interpretative function, ranging from criticism to revolutionary rejection. The competition between classes in a fused system is perhaps less and less significant in an industrial society, where it is replaced by competition between fused and differentiated groups (or, in other words, between occupation and education).

STRUCTURAL SOURCES
OF RADICALIZATION

Industrial society offers many opportunities for choice but in doing so distorts allocation in ways that violate universalized egalitarian norms. In socialist countries, allocation is skewed by political power (particularly by that embodied in party and bureaucracy). In capitalist countries, it is skewed by unequal access to wealth. Both conditions are self-perpetuating. The question of public or private ownership, although important, is not crucial. Conservatism and radicalism manifest themselves (and for similar reasons) in both the capitalist and the socialist systems.[6]

Given the emphasis on new knowledge as a key characteristic of industrial society and the basis of its continual innovation, it is not surprising that education and educational institutions become strategic for the balancing of norms and structures. Precisely because competitive inequality is built into educational achievement, the more egalitarian the access and the less egalitarian the results, the greater the "violation" of ideas about equity and the more "perverted" the actual pattern of allocation. We say "violation" because in all industrial societies there is a normative pull toward social leveling in comprehensive or integrative schools that competes with the structural tendency to rank on the basis of achievement. Ability determines rewards in indirect proportion to its functional value for industrial society. The value changes: for example, the overpowering functional need today is for creative skill and imagination, so these talents are at a premium and are the new sources of inequality.

The ways inequity and skewed allocation are manifested are many. In political terms, arbitrary powers may be applied in the name of egalitarianism. The present tentative trend toward liberalism in some socialist countries, for example, the abortive tendency toward reconciliation systems in countries such as Czechoslovakia, is apparently in response to the sorry record of arbitrary actions. In the United States, economic not political misallocation is the core problem among the urban poor and the black population.

That both kinds of inequality are anachronistic in any highly industrial society should go without saying. The liberal solution favored in the West relies on the notion that wider political participation by underprivileged groups will improve the situation (through changes in taxation and increases in services, welfare, and educational opportunities). But this solution has little hope of success unless it is combined with a different consummatory emphasis. Structural changes, too, have not been sufficiently rapid to repay patience with greater collective mobility. Even in Britain, for example, after successive Labor governments, some nationalization, and enlarged social services, the distribution of private wealth helps to sustain a skewed system of allocation in which roughly 7% of the population owns 84% of the wealth.[7]

Normative interpretation of these startling figures is more complex than it appears. Taking a rather traditional socialist position, Robin Blackburn cites the Vauxhall case—in which workers, hitherto regarded as generally positive, "calculating," and reciprocal (instrumental) in their relations with the firm, "exploded" in a militant (consummatory) conflict with management—as evidence that coercion and exploitation were in reality the bases of worker relations with their employers. From our standpoint, Blackburn's interpretation is incorrect; the events do not support an either-or proposition that the workers were either cooperative or coerced. Both are possible. Indeed, it may be that a calculating and highly instrumentalized relationship based on reasonable and reciprocal gains had actually stimulated feelings of coercion and exploitation by emphasizing, in normative terms, the crisis of equity. The radicalization process occurs in industrial societies because events generate intensities of passion that are translated into powerful ideological expression. These political ideologies may wax strongly only temporarily. In other words, in industrial societies, crises can arise not only because of narrow conflicts of interest but also because of the erosion of consummatory values by instrumental ones and the structural proliferation of interest groups that combine to generate a search for new and drastic solutions.

Action—strikes, mass confrontations, violence—may itself be sufficient to assert or redefine meaning in a satisfying way, and the revolutionary moment may pass. (This is the likely result of much student activism.) We should not be tempted, therefore, to build our notions of political equity on the superficialities of mass action. Nor should we be lulled into assuming political stability. Industrial societies confront a permanent crisis of a sort largely absent in modernizing ones. Dialectically, the crisis is brought about by the instrumentalization of values, which encourages competition to fill the consummatory vacuum. Functionally, it is a result of the proliferation of competitive and pluralistic groupings, which becomes counterproductive.

With reference to whether there is any justification for considering instrumentalization a problem in socialist systems, the Czechoslovakian experience would be relevant, but little empirical data is available. As the most highly industrialized socialist country, one that was embarking on a liberalization program (interrupted so dramatically by the Soviet invasion), it would have been a perfect case study. However, considerable data is available from Yugoslavia, which in our view moved from a modernizing stage to early industrialization in the last decade.[8] One of the most important norms of specifically Yugoslav socialism was worker participation in management. A self-validating consummatory value, it was based on the idea that fulfillment came from working in a situation free of exploitation, whether from capitalists or managers. But from 1960 to 1964, the relative importance of work as motivation declined sharply in favor of wages, and self-management remained the least valued single objective.[9] In addition, management, whose significance had originally been based on its revolutionary role and an involvement with consummatory values, was seen simply as a barrier to greater efficiency.[10] Growing instrumentalization produced circumstances in which a system of beliefs failed to validate empirical actions.[11] The Yugoslav case also shows that ideologies that presume an identity between the larger rationality of nature and the particular requirements of social life create so many problems at the consummatory level that they cast doubt on the original synthesis.

Whatever the form taken in Yugoslavia, instrumentalization prepares the way for such normative dialectical confrontations as those between Catholicism and Calvinism, capitalism and socialism, socialism and revisionism. Although they are perplexing, they invariably follow a particular sequence. First, a comprehensive normative synthesis represents legitimacy. It links instrumental actions with consummatory values, associating nonempirical and empirical ends in the context of proprietary limitations on conduct and behavior. The result is a validated set of ends defining equity. Second, when over time this comprehensive system begins to break down into its consummatory and instrumental parts, the instrumental becomes more important and the consummatory more perfunctory. The gap between them can be covered over for a time, but eventually opportunities arise for the creation of a new set of consummatory values. If these new consummatory values are to be successful, they have to correspond more adequately to changes in structure and functional needs than the set they are to displace. This final stage in the sequence defines radicalism.

In the context of our emergent meritocracy, such a sequence illuminates a predicament of all industrial societies: that except for moments of equilibrium, the functional needs of society based on industrial life remain in conflict with the normative needs of society based on consummatory principles of equity. Thus permanent contradiction is the characteristic condition of industrial society. Ideologies introduced to resolve contradictions often end in solidifying them. Ideological conflicts, then, seem to be perpetual, though their venue and their intensity but never their vitality may change.

STRATIFICATION GROUPS
IN INDUSTRIAL SOCIETY

Having identified a characteristic predicament of industrial society, we turn now to an examination of the groups that vie for roles in this society.

The functionally superfluous caste and ethnic groups, or marginals, comprise tribal, ethnic, language, and nationality clusters that have a pronounced identity or classification and are encircled by ritualized constraints on their mobility. These constraints may be partly due to subcultural solidarities based either on primordial consummatory values, as in the German communities in Russia, Canada, and the United States; or on cultural prejudice, as against Blacks or Indians in the United States; or, more likely, on a combination of both, as with Jews in Western Europe.

In the process of industrialization, upper caste and ethnic stratification rankings lose even residual functional relevance, theoretically making way for open entry. A differentiated type of system emerges, with the top rank based on functional relevance and continually expanding as choice expands. Thus individual mobility and collective mobility are simultaneously possible. However, few members of segmentary groups can make the transition to a differentiated group. Functional irrelevance is their more likely destination. Ethnic boundaries persist, especially when a fused pattern of upward mobility is the only sort available. Blacks can move into top-level positions in the United States, for example, only if they have had access to education and housing in areas that permitted their enculturation in White society. Those who are functionally superfluous are cut off from active competition by the negative qualities of ghetto existence and the related behavioral consequences of discrimination. The closer equal access appears to be, the more devastating their condition. As industrialization increases, these caste and ethnic residuals become increasingly hostile to one another, unless they can find some common enemy. Because a single class enemy is impossible to find in industrial societies, which are formed along multibonded class lines, anger is unstructured, highly generalized, and random. In a meritocracy, no matter how democratic, there is no comfort in being at the bottom. Indeed, even solidarity disappears entirely at that level. Functional significance is negative— violence, crime, sexual challenge—and contrasts so strongly with the norms of the rest of society that this lowest common denominator is viewed by some as the moral center of society, with a monopoly on a certain kind of truth.[12] When this occurs, *the functionally superfluous marginals become a key group for normative, not structural, reasons.* They are able to define negative or positive values for the rest of society.

In industrial society, class identify is undermined as roles emerge for the upwardly mobile. *Residual fused groups*, which are collectively immobile, lose their position by standing still. When this happens, fused groups become politicized, the stimulus being the threat of their own irrelevance in the face of increasing specialization. The most important example is the old fused bourgeoisie in the United States, the group that for generations had its functional base in occupations essential to industrial society—businessmen or bureaucrats whose success was based not on special training but on hard work, skill, thrift, and all the notions of how wealth and well-being should be won. For this group, occupation determined place in the social structure. Organized in various corporate bodies, devoted to shared concerns, such fused groups seemed to be permanently balanced against other fused groups-for example, employers and trade unionists. The key to the fused form of industrial society was enterprise not education. Opportunities created by enterprise furnished the meaning of society itself.

It is precisely this group that suffers most in the late-industrial period. Missing are such clear demarcations as blue or white collar, by which class reward and position were distributed. Less important is the assembly line, that bogey of earlier forms of industrial enterprise, with its presumed alienating characteristics. Instead, specialization occurs in a "situation chain" in which infinite hierarchical gradations involving minute increments of status and power provide motivation. Puzzled and pressed by the complexity of the paths of status in the industrial hierarchy, the fused middle class responds by working less hard and thereby losing its purpose. But it is still better off than the differentiated middle class. For this group, there is little psychic leisure; the cares of the office cannot be left behind, for relevance involves continual competition. Although the behavioral consequences are negative, there are important structural ones in the emergence of continuous interest-group conflict. The old fused middle class is increasingly split because of specialization, which emphasizes training. Part of it moves into differentiated groupings by virtue of educational and other advantages. Part of it moves downward into lower fused or differentiated sectors. Such downward mobility is likely to produce temporary radicalization expressed in terms of primordial norms. Even primitive managerial roles come to require technical skills. Any operating post develops "input voraciousness," and an enormous organizational structure is required.[13] Whereas the fused bourgeois may be a displaced person in the society he has helped to create, the differentiated individual is likely to be victimized by the situation chain. Let us examine these aspects of postindustrial society in terms of our third stratification category.

The *differentiated groups* constitute the core of the developmental bourgeoisie within the industrial sector of society. The main criteria for mobility within this sector are functional performance and education.

Among the most functionally relevant groups, there is a growing consciousness of style, manners, taste, and mode of living. The members of these groups have multiple groups affiliations based on various interests—residence, school, service club, alumni association—all of which cut across narrow occupational lines. Characteristically, such subgroup affiliations, or "miniclasses," have loose and flexible boundaries and relatively open membership. Miniclasses rank achievement on a graduated and increasingly complex continuum, whose ultimate criterion, no matter what other characteristics are taken into consideration, is functional relevance.

Each subspecialty, organizational unit, and type of work has behind it some group or corporate organization that is part of the corporate structure on which industrial output depends. The combination of miniclass and corporate structure results in very small degrees of differentiation within this stratification type. But this does not create anomic or alienated men in the Marxist sense of alienation, where work may include negative rewards, such as lack of self-esteem. In a multibonded miniclass system, given that occupation is only one of the factors determining a total status position, occupational rewards are not the sole stimulus for work. They alone do not account for the intense intellectual, social, physical, and psychic efforts frequently made by members of differentiated groups.

At each point in the multibonded hierarchy, the corporate agency works as an interest group, defining what might be called a corporate structure of group life. The corporate group, by intersecting the main points of the stratification hierarchy, helps define many of the bonds of the miniclass. If education is a key to miniclass position, corporate affiliation is a point of intersection with other bonds, including not only narrow professional associations but also clubs, neighborhood associations, old-boy associations, and so on. Hence, technical specialty, religious affiliation, social club—all depend in various ways on corporate affiliation to fix an individual's position in the multibonded hierarchy. The hierarchy defines his main interests and acts as a mechanism for further social mobility. As the corporate group becomes more of a social group, it is no longer just a work place but a social universe.

The *functional status elite* is a small group with miniclass roles that has achieved high status by its generation and application of new knowledge. This group, which we call a "theory class," is not a class at all but, rather, a small self-sustaining and slowly expanding group that has been differentiated from the rest not only by the nature of its activities, but also by its various informational languages and theories. It has its own hierarchy based on scientific and technical criteria: pure versus applied science, qualitative versus quantitative science, natural and physical versus social science. It is outside any single corporate grouping but uses many of them, particularly government agencies and universities. This group's control of information differs from administrative management's: it represents a new form of political power, already highly developed in the U.S.S.R. and the United States. The membership of functional status elites is divided on the basis of the distinction between pure and applied science. The main emphasis of the theory class is on research and creativity, the underlying assumption being that new information is better than old and innovation superior to application. Utilitarianism is not highly regarded, because that is the function of the technician rather than the scientist. Pure scientists, clustered in research institutes and universities, and, increasingly, in large industrial corporations and certain governmental agencies, are separated from others by the abstract nature of their work. Their findings become the energy for industrial development.[14]

In spite of its high degree of differentiation, the functional status elite has certain unifying features. Entry is open and is based on competition and less and less on advantages of birth. Indeed, in status elites in both the United States and the U.S.S.R., the proportion of members from immigrant stock (in the former) and the fused working class (in the latter) is quite large. As a group, the functional elite theorists are no longer nervous philistine technocrats. If anything, they are divorced from the technocrats and the rest of the population by a heightened capacity for appreciation of creativity. They show fluency in language and a sense of style. The cultural model for this elite is a mythical aristocracy (sometimes cultivated deliberately in universities). Where such roles are concentrated, they provide a pattern of social life—a desire for more grace in academia, an interest and perhaps a participation in the arts, a devotion to a certain life-style. This stylistic pattern is seen as a necessary part of professional life, especially as a contrast to professional communications, conferences, and meetings. But more than just style, the functional status elite requires the ability, as well as the propensity, to think and communicate abstractly. The models used by specialists, although they originate in a particular field, overlap epistemologically to create technical languages that not only are highly abstract but also represent a hurdle for others, part of a curriculum to be studied and examined by those who wish to enter the theory class.

The functional status elite should not be regarded merely as the top of a standardized differentiated stratification hierarchy. It may not have more social prestige than other groupings; it does not have the trappings of an administrative elite or the scale of life of an old fused aristocracy. But because of its capacity to create new theory, it is a monitor as well as a creator of new information. Increasingly, too, those of the theory class (particularly in socialist societies) are trying to find ways to make realistic opportunities available to the functionally superfluous at the bottom. The normative sanction of this group and its activities is a unique and impersonal patron-client relationship similar in some respects to the medieval lord-serf relationship. It is an open feudalism in which under the ideologies of democracy and socialism, the concept of service becomes a validating norm. In theory, at least, the patron is at the bottom and the client at the top: those who occupy roles in the theory class increasingly describe their functions as service to the public and, most particularly, that part of the public in greatest need. In the name of public service, the client, the occupant of the functional status role, claims a certain exemption from ordinary rules from his patron, the public as a whole, which pays for the client's privileges. He needs academic freedom, for example, a concept that now extends beyond universities and encompasses highly specialized agencies of government engaged in secret work (such as the RAND Corporation in the United States and, no doubt, equivalents in the U.S.S.R.).

Our emphasis on the growth of professional elites should not obscure the fact that segmental or fused groupings are still an important part of the social system in an industrial setting. Indeed, the very existence of such groups helps bring about some of the conditions that create functional status roles. The urban poor and the caste and ethnic ghettos generate experts in urban development, integration, and education. Structural changes result. Groups that in principle may be polarized are instead broken up into overlapping interest groups, each looking to experts for support. Trade unions protecting the interests of a residual fused group employ economists and other specialists, thus creating both differentiated positions and a few functional status roles that will give the unions access to the power and style of the theory class. Many members of the new functional status elite seem to be showing their concern for society by designing military hardware, weapons system, and space vehicles. But there are others, particularly in the social sciences, who are concentrating more and more on the need of marginals.[15] Such responsibility to society is necessary for the theory class if it is to justify its existence and, above all, if it is to sustain its inspiration of creativity. Whereas technical matters may separate these groups from society, the appreciation of creativity in all forms is a force that unites them. But they are more than the new patrons of the arts; they are clients with power, serving the patrons who may lack grace and knowledge but have their claim to power in numbers.

The new administrative elite are the skilled architects of complex organization and administration. They are also members of the functional status elite, but their liaison is not with populist patrons. Rather it is with other stratification groups, particularly the old industrial and professional elites (the American Medical Association, for example). Unlike these old elites, members of the new administrative elite recognize the value of the theory group, may utilize its expertise, and, indeed, are often part of it by virtue of specialized educational background (in electronics, for example). They may follow a similar style of elite. They, too, maintain close contact with universities and other research centers. What distinguishes this group from the theory class is that its members are not creators but consumers of information. They are structural innovators who can perform in any of the corporate structures of industrial society—as corporation heads, generals, government officials, and foundation or university administrators, for example. Constituting a much larger group than the theorists, they perform in more than one of these capacities during the course of their functional lifetimes, generally moving between industry and the administrative areas of public service.

Unlike the theorists of the functional status elite, they are less likely to publicly identify their interests with those of the marginals, even though they may head social welfare programs and (in nonsocialist countries) contribute time and money to philanthropic causes. They have a bureaucratic style and are committed to organization qua organization. Philosophically, they are torn between the new norms of creativity and change represented by the entire functional status elite and the old norms of the bourgeois industrialists. In terms of prestige, they are the new leaders of industrial society, knowingly dependent on the functional status elite for the information that will determine the direction of leadership and, therefore, regarding the theorists with a mixture of fear and respect.

The antithesis of the new industrial elite is a new group—the *bourgeois radicals*—that rejects the functional status groups along with all other utilitarian sectors of the social system. It, too, identifies closely with the functionally superfluous. The bourgeois radicals are bright, well educated, and often from the comfortable upper sectors of the differentiated stratification system.[16] Out of contempt for the new establishment—or a more permanent anger—they refuse to participate in society (except, perhaps, on behalf of the functionally superfluous). Quite often their anger takes the form of deliberate anti-intellectualism. Although bourgeois radicals share in the culture of the functional status groups, they will also identify with the morality of the marginals to whom they offer devotion, personal courage, and the articulation of wider meaning. They create their own subculture as well. This subculture, more than any other in industrial society, is the source of new consummatory values and the revival of older ones. Not necessarily counterelites, the angry young men often reproduce some of the conditions of intellectual radicalism of the nineteenth century, although perhaps on a much larger scale. Even arguments over spontaneity versus organization, economism versus scientific Marxism, freedom versus bureaucracy—all of which formed the substance of nineteenth- or early-twentieth-century radicalism—have been revived. In the West, this group's folk heroes include Trotsky, Mao, and Castro (the full range from Bakunin to Kautsky, from Rosa Luxembourg to Lenin, are represented). In socialist countries, the heroes are poets, writers of the past, and the members of the radical group itself who have been persecuted by the regime. Che Guevara would be the prototypical folk hero of this group.

The bourgeois radicals are caught between the new functional status and administrative elites, on one hand, and the interest and other bourgeois groups, on the other. Although they may attack the former, they are vulnerable to the latter. Characteristically, the bourgeois radicals are objects of contempt for the ordinary utilitarian sectors of society, including the residual fused bourgeoisie as a class and the multibonded bourgeoisie that makes the broad internally competitive differentiated system. Such contempt is mutual. The bourgeois radicals have a particular hatred for those associated with distribution of goods or services, whether shopkeeper, insurance agent, advertising executive, college-educated salesman, government bureaucrat, plant manager, party official, or professional educator—in fact, a large proportion of the differentiated system. They also reject their family backgrounds. The bourgeois radicals, thus alienated from the social environment that has created them, use it merely as a springboard for attack.

Because the functionally superfluous marginals present a moral predicament, the bourgeois radicals may seek to ally with them to transform the system, by creating new meaning and new functional arrangements. The administrative elite, on the other hand, will attempt to incorporate them into the system by using available knowledge created by the theory class. (Populist reactionaries either pretend they do not exist or see in them a special group to be brought into marching legions, conservation corps, or other suitable patriotic and functionally useful bodies.) Whatever the solution, it will involve the incorporation of new marginals in the differentiated middle class, increasing the demand for material rewards and thus increasing not only the consumption that is the basis of individual society but also the loss of self-respect that follows from such narrow objectives. These groups will try to avoid downward mobility with better education, in the process creating a fused middle or lower-middle class.

The members of these groups will still be different from the functionally superfluous, who lack consummatory values, except primordial ones like pariah solidarity and negative caste-ethnic identification. Whereas the multibonded groups suffer from excessive instrumentalization accompanied by the ritualization, or worse, sentimentalization, of consummatory values, the marginals suffer from an inadequacy of both.

The bourgeois radicals assume that the functionally superfluous are the group most accessible to new consummatory values. But history shows that this is not the case. Given the opportunity, they are more likely to respond to instrumental values than to consummatory ones. After they have gained some access to allocation, they are more likely to identify with the older consummatory values than with the new. That is to say, they desire embourgeoisement and are likely to respond to nationalist, fascist, and other "backward-looking" ideologies. We do not rule out a possible identification with revolutionary ideologies in the future, but for the time being, our assumption is that the functionally superfluous are most likely to opt for embourgeoisement and to avoid ideological formulas altogether.

This description of industrial society has been a bit unconventional, for it has not relied on capital goods production, the size of the industrial labor force, per capita income, or, even in general terms, self-sustained growth. As a function of all these, but transcending them in importance, we have stressed the capacity of an industrialized system to generate new information that can be translated into output in the form of industrial exports. This capacity implies an infrastructure that combines research, administration, and entrepreneurship in a different mixture from that of the usual view of class stratification.

THE NEW PLURALISM

On the basis of the foregoing observations, several general hypotheses about each of the groups that constitute industrial society may be offered.

(1) The functionally superfluous have minimum access to resources and standing outside a normative dialectic, are normatively apathetic and, therefore, difficult to organize.

(2) The segmentary caste-ethnic and residual fused groupings, particularly the old bourgeoisie whose functional roles are decreasing in significance, attach themselves to primordial normative values, reactionary values (derived from a real or mythical past), or conservative values (designed to conserve their functional significance) as a normative compensation for functional loss.

(3) The multibonded class groupings at the lower end of the scale are concerned with embourgeoisement, maximizing their functional significance, and engaging in highly instrumental bargaining for short-term gains.

(4) The bourgeois radicals, who reject functionalism and instrumentalization, occupy roles of lesser functional significance and adopt utopian progressive or other radical innovative ideologies.

(5) The administrative elite creates and recreates structures to justify the instrumental norms of the system but increasingly looks toward the theory class within the functional status elites for direction and salvation.

(6) The functional status elites represent maximum functional significance and, by virtue of the dynamic quality of the new information and knowledge they create, are continuously defining functionality. Their ideologies tend to be associated with opportunities for creativity itself.

Thus there is a conflict between residual groups that are susceptible to consummatory values and multibonded groups that stress the instrumental. Coalitions are likely between the bourgeois radicals and the functionally superfluous, and between the new technocrats and the multibonded groupings. The latter coalition would opt for a progressive, highly instrumentalized, corporatist society, whereas the former would demand a drastic reevaluation of norms relevant to equity and allocation. Other coalitions are possible, for example, between the residual-populist groupings and the functionally superfluous, and between the bourgeois radicals and the technocrats.

We have called the postindustrial stratification pyramid "emergent." It has by no means replaced the older pyramid described by Warner and others, but it is the juxtaposition of two systems, which makes possible complex coalitions. The older system involves power and prestige rankings of a fused type, rankings based on class (lower, lower middle, middle, upper middle, upper) or on descriptive characteristics (sub-proletariat, proletariat, bourgeoisie, haute bourgeoisie, aristocracy). In our theory, the lower occupants of the fused pyramid move, in a late-industrial setting, not simply into higher ranks of the same hierarchy, but into the differentiated system. It is this crossing over from one stratification system to another that is the essence of the embour-geoisement phenomenon.

Comparisons of the sort we have been making are possible in all industrial societies including socialist ones. The categories themselves are descriptive in order to enable us to determine the relative significance of the groups described, those whose power is based on aggregative populism, those whose power is based on coalitions of interests, and those whose power is based on their functional relevance. From this pattern of comparison, we can analyze the specific forms of pluralistic competition that result. This notion of pluralism in industrial societies goes well beyond the normal use of the term in representative government.

If our analysis is correct, industrial society is more likely to contain the conditions for revolution from above than from below. Revolution from above involves conflict between elites that occupy in varying degrees central and relevant roles in the society. Industrial society has two types of highly educated elites: the first type is the functional status groups, which include a theory class that creates new information and an administrative class that consumes it in order to create new structures to uphold old norms; the second type consists of bourgeois radicals, many of whom want to change the meaning of the society and break through its increasing reliance on instrumental goals. All compete for links with the functionally superfluous.

At the same time, norms associated with embourgeoisement dominate the modernizing part of industrial society. These are primordial, reactionary, and conservative and are frequently not relevant to the creative and innovative parts of the industrial society. The functionally superfluous, the fused residuals, and the downwardly mobile differentiated groups have little patience with what they accurately regard as the subversive attitudes of the intellectuals. Those for whom embourgeoisement is a recent reality are grateful to the state. They see the antiutilitarianism of the intellectuals as dangerous. The factors that allow both groups to occupy the same space are industrial society's need for structural differentiation and the separation of corporate groupings according to distributed interests. The more pyramidal the authority and the more instrumental the values, the greater the crisis of meaning at the top and the less dangerous the society at the bottom. Embourgeoisement within industrial society is thus a real substitute for tolerance and compromise.

The horizontal spread of industrial groups, as they compete, form coalitions and break apart, gives rise to what is known as "group theory," which is an assessment of the coalitions of power generated by numbers, interests, and knowledge—the three main claims to power. Industrial society also has a vertical set of linkages, however; thus it is more than a collection of the coalitions prevailing at any given time. Any individual may be a professional specialist, a member of an interest group, and a member of the community at large. The division of society into multibonded minigroups and the telescoping of all three levels of affiliation into one create a structural problem that parallels the normative problem of excessive instrumentalism. Moreover, insofar as the widest group affiliation involves the least functionality and the strongest attachment to shared consummatory values, the vertical relationship is obviously based on more than self-interest (see Figure 6.2).

What, then, can we say about the differentiated stratification pattern that occurs in industrial society? First, it creates a corporate structure of social life in which corporate interests compete. Second, it restricts populist and primordial attachments to the downwardly mobile, the functionally superfluous, or the residual fused groupings in society (like the old middle class). Third, it permits a pattern of social commitment in which the functional status groups form alliances with those at the bottom, if possible. The greater the degree of utilitarianism manifested in instrumental values based on work, the more intense the crisis at the top. The greater the degree of industrialization, the more severe the crisis of meaning. If our theory is correct, *despite the coalitional possibilities already described, there is greater pluralistic competition and more polarization in industrial society than in modernizing society.* Such are the contradictory tendencies in industrial societies: on one hand, increasing coalitional pluralism in day-to-day activities based on interests and, on the other, polarization of the antifunctional and functional. Specific normative ideologies mirror these contradictions. The least functionally relevant marginal groupings tend toward primordial norms,[17] but these groups themselves are subject to rapid change, as the industrial society exchanges one group of marginals for another.

The normative aspects of the meritocracy create two severe crises of meaning in the functional hierarchy. The functionally superfluous pose the first problem—the need for more egalitarian entry into the utilitarian sectors of industrial society. If it is correct that the functionally superfluous must be admitted to the utilitarian sectors, then they will have to develop a basis for representation. But they are unincorporated and consequently have no means of representation. One way to organize them is to revive populist and primordial affiliations; once solidarity is established, the second step is to widen access in a more generalized way, through voting, for example. A third step is to foster entry into the utilitarian hierarchy by representation of interests, usually organized around ethnic affiliations, as with Pakistani and Indian pressure groups in England and Black power associations in the United States. The problem of access to the utilitarian sectors of society is great, for conflicts between segmentary and fused groups may arise, as may the more tension-producing conflicts between the functionally superfluous and differentiated utilitarian groups. The first type of conflict is normally reflected in a fundamental social cleavage; the second is more subtle.

Interest protection is the second critical problem of the meritocracy. There is little conflict between the creation of new knowledge and its translation into use by the differentiated utilitarians. However, there is a struggle to influence policymaking. The theory class tends to be disengaged from contemporary events and thus to embody long-term social purposes. Interest groups, on the contrary, are immediately affected by changes. In a differentiated system, the overlapping role sets, the smallness of the interest groups, and the internal and external problems of competition create a highly complex pattern of cross-pressures. In other words, it is difficult to find a consistent line of activity either in pursuit of some common interest or in organizing coalitions. What is most important structurally for affecting decision making is the

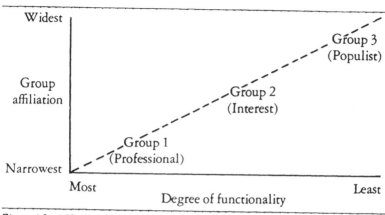

Figure 6.2 A Vertical Model of Industrial Groupings

multiplicity of relationships between interests and professions. Awareness of this multiplicity is the basis for social learning in highly industrial systems. Patterns of mutual intelligibility, accommodation, and payoff become keys to the system at the top. Results of negotiation are likely to depend in some measure on how bargaining occurs, whether accommodation of interests and professional expertise is possible, and which pattern of bargaining is employed (for example, the hard bargain to establish a norm of multiple concessions as part of the rules of the game). Moreover, the greater the proliferation of differentiated groups and functional status elites, the larger the bureaucracy needed as a mechanism of control. At the same time, individualized patterns of creativity are greatly increased by the increase in differentiated and functional status roles. A person may compare his abilities and his rewards with others and thereby have a basis for self-esteem. Self-rewarding identification depends on nonbureaucratic relationships such as friendship. Cliques are likely to form, based on mutual self-esteem and trust, reinforcing the relationships between individuals and defining outsiders and insiders. Hence, bureaucracy and personalized relationships are antagonistic social forces, but the one "breeds" the other.

Thus superimposed on the multiple coalitions and relationships between roles on the structural level (determined in very general terms by populist, interest, and professional claims to representation in decision making) are quite complicated networks of cliques and friendships, some of which may be interlocking, some of which may be polarized, and some of which may be simple.[18] The complexity of industrial society magnifies individual pressures. Multiple access implies multiple opportunities, but also multiple tensions at the behavioral level. For most of its citizens, the industrial society is no paradise, and social unrest is reflected in political action.

CHOICE AND EQUITY

In industrial society, the expansion of choice occurs at the top of the stratification system. Those near the top of the differentiated system, including the functional status elites, gain the most, but not without cost. Pressure to perform is applied earlier and earlier in the educational system, beginning at the primary level and reaching its peak at the postgraduate level. Indeed, this pressure becomes so great that the very advantages of a system based on merit—real alternatives for individuals—become almost restrictions, the absence of choice. It is not surprising that those engaged in the process become angry, exhausted, and bitter about the system.

The behavioral consequence of this situation is a loss of confidence; members of the society begin to feel that freedom of choice is an illusion. Success at the social level brings failure at the individual level, which in turn precipitates a normative crisis of meaning. The more complex the status hierarchy, the greater the number of interlocking relationships and the wider the range of structural opportunities for mobility in an increasingly egalitarian system, the more intense the behavioral predicaments created by choice. In the last analysis, how to live in a universe of choice is a question no ideology has been able to resolve. It is the special problem of meritocracies in highly industrial societies.

The greatest difficulties facing industrial societies still lie ahead, namely, when antiutilitarianism begins to spread more rapidly. The various competitive groupings in society will then be pulled in one of two directions. One pull will be toward a different kind of populist-corporate society—a kind of neofascism in which hierarchical authority and primordial values will be elevated as a mandate for rule. The other pull will be toward a secular theocratic system, in which shared but highly internalized ultimate beliefs will allow individual diversity and egalitarianism to flourish. It will be interesting to see in which direction industrial societies will go, regardless of the labels attached to the new systems.

The functionally superfluous and the bourgeois radicals share an attitude of aggravation toward the system, although the causes of their grievances differ. They both want a system in which they may participate; in this sense, the bourgeois radicals are as marginal as the functionally superfluous. Yet their vaunted identity of purpose and condition is only superficial. The bourgeois radicals may use the functionally superfluous to validate revolutionary aims, to create new norms, and to support counternorms, even though, on the whole, the functionally superfluous themselves rarely support such norms. The latter may also be radical, but not the way the bourgeois radicals want them to be. (Marx was much more aware of this problem than are today's militants.) As a consequence, the bourgeois radical is in a paradoxical position. He, too, is functionally superfluous, but he has chosen that role. He is regarded as marginal, but he has been trained by the system. How can he make himself heard in an environment where complexity is itself an obstacle and where the solutions to the problems of the marginals are largely the work of technocrats and experts?—by narrowing the gap between professionals and technocrats (the adminis-trative elite) and the more creative and generally intellectual bourgeois radicals, although it can never be closed. We are talking about cooperations, not about the two-cultures argument of C. P. Snow. How can this cooperation be brought about? First, there is a need to stress in the social and behavioral sciences the role of intellectuals as participant-observers and the ways learning and understanding occur in this type of analysis. Second, the administrative elite must involve intellectuals at the planning level. Finally, both need to perceive the obstacles to reform and organize accordingly. In terms of our model, intellectuals must combine professional claims to representation and interest claims (both expressed in terms of populist needs) in order to compete with other interest and populist groups for access to government, where they can help formulate goals for society and increase the institutional coherence of the system.

To summarize, we may say that the chief characteristic of industrial society in its upper echelons is the continuous competition for knowledge and skills that will assure mobility in a highly differentiated system. This competition is personalized in that the competitors have no sense of solidarity with a class. Rather, the chief organizational unit to which they belong, with a hierarchy composed of accessible minute increments of gain, instrumentalizes all other aspects of life. For the bulk of the middle-class population, the result is a ferocious productivity, a feverish round of activity, and, in the end, a sense of having been used up, spent, and thrown away. Meaning is doing. To stop doing is to face an abyss.[19]

This rather dramatic picture suggests a predicament that emerges to some degree in all highly industrialized systems, not simply the United States, where the tendencies described are perhaps most apparent. Less industrial societies show greater sensitivity to the aged, less ruthlessness in the differentiated sector, and more traditionalism. This is true, for example, of Great Britain and the Soviet Union. In the U.S.S.R., efforts are made by the state and party to prevent individuals from being or feeling superfluous.[20]

The competing strains of an egalitarian meritocracy have produced conditions to which public policy must respond. As fused systems of allocation give way to differentiated and functional status systems, and as consummatory values are instrumentalized, no simple answer to the basic imbalances of the variables is possible. The progressive increase of choice only intensifies the problem, as does the weakening of authority. What is required is a major attack on all four variables of the structural theory more or less simultaneously. But that is never attempted in practice, even though various types of reformers would like to stop the world and re-create it according to their own images.

Meanwhile, we remain stuck in an age of somewhat backward political ideologies, each of which purports to supply a solution. Those who want to return to a simpler day support various nationalist or fascist ideologies. Others, more or less revolutionary, support forms of communism, socialism, or liberal democracy. Each has its plan for structural reform and the revival or stimulation of consummatory values. But the problems, as we see them, reside precisely in the new hierarchies that are established alongside the old.[21]

As opportunities for choice expand with increasing knowledge and the application of that knowledge in industry, roles relevant to information and processing increase; the result is growing conflict between representatives of the various stratification groups, both between interest groups and professional elites. Such competition poses an organizational problem that affects the quality of industrial society itself. Overorganization, either through the incorporation of too many elites in decision making or the too narrow restriction of their participation, is one part of the problem. Another part is the attempt to compensate for short-term competition (a "gambler's choice" situation) by means of long-term centralized planning, because when the "hiding hand" no longer operates, as A. O. Hirschman puts it, creativity declines. This suggests that a high level of information can be generated only with a certain structural openness and normative ambiguity. Among the system types we have discussed, the reconciliation system supplies this structural condition. Not too much information and not too much control is needed, for as Hirshman says, "Creativity always comes as a surprise to us; therefore we can never count on it, and we dare not believe in it until it has happened."[22] Decision makers do not consciously begin with the intention of applying creativity to their tasks. Hence, the only way we can bring our creative resources fully into play is by misjudging the nature of the tasks, by presenting them to ourselves as more routine, simple, and undemanding of genuine creativity than they will turn out to be. The innovations that come as a surprise, bridging the narrow gaps in information, are the key to a solution of the problems of industrial society. The special skills of the knowledge-generating professional elites should provide ideal soil from which innovations can spring. Hirshman's point is extremely important. In terms of order, it means that an industrial society needs a high degree of accountability, providing a high degree of information, but not too much predictability, and a highly rationalized decision-making framework that appears to reduce all problems to a routine level. Extensive information-processing devices that are adequate both scientifically and structurally are implied. The information function involves certain other critical functions: the specification of goals, the identification of institutional conflicts and overlapping jurisdictions, and participation of various groups in the control of general social conduct. To the extent that these manifest themselves in the relationship between elites and government, they define the pattern of authority, the degree of hierarchy and accountability.

But precisely because industrial societies find it difficult to find the correct proportions, the problem of order remains unsolved. In the reconciliation system, if there is too much participation, the government will be glutted with information and become so accountable to its elites that it can hardly act independently. In a bureaucratic or mobilization system, if there is too little participation, governments may lose information (although a daring and creative honeymoon period may occur before that happens). These are continuous and insoluble problems for any government, and attempts to solve them result in many regime changes.

NOTES

1. This "technocratic alienation" is widespread among biologists, physicists, engineers, and others engaged in military research or in activities producing such consequences as air pollution, water pollution, and urban decay.

2. Problems of mass society are not characteristic of highly industrialized societies. It is in modernizing ones or in the modernizing sectors of industrial societies that there is undisguised nonparticipation. Industrial systems, on the contrary, are individualizing; they articulate alternatives for different skills, provide more opportunities for choice, and as a result intensify the burden on individuals. It is not mass man who is the problem of industrial society but increasingly personalized man who makes his claim to be treated in all his variability and complexity. This claim has the effect of enlarging the scope and number of roles of the technical status elites. Screening, evaluating, and testing in order to study how human beings achieve satisfaction in their work, their leisure, and their family relations all become relevant. The computer, symbol of wickedness, one of the culprits of the mass society hypothesis, is in that capacity a myth. Such machines, on the contrary, make it possible to take into account individual variations of increasing numbers of people.

3. If an industrial society reaches the stage when the production of goods and services continues to increase as real choices decrease, we refer to it as "overdeveloped" or "postindustrial."

4. See the useful critique of Warner's approach by Ruth R. Kornhauser, "The Warner Approach to Social Stratification," in *Class, Status, and Power*, ed. R. Bendix and S. M. Lipset (New York: Free Press, 1953). See also W. L. Warner and P. S. Lunt, *The Social Life of a Modern Community* (New Haven, CT: Yale University Press, 1941); Gerhard E. Lenski, "Status Crystallization: A Non-Vertical Dimension of Social Status," *American Sociological Review* 19 (1954), pp. 405-15; and S. M. Lipset, *The First New Nation* (New York: Basic Books, 1963), p. 125. Lipset points out that the original and gloomy emphasis by Warner on the rise of inequality in the 1930s is replaced in his later work when social mobility had increased. See W. L. Warner and J. C. Abegglen, *Occupational Mobility in American Business and Industry* (Minneapolis: University of Minnesota Press, 1953).

5. In the U.S.S.R., for example, the Soviet government has put writers and other critics in mental hospitals or forced them to do physical labor.

6. See the description of student disturbances, for example, in George Z. F. Bereday, "Student Unrest on Four Continents: Montreal, Ibadan, Warsaw, and Rangoon," in *Student Politics*, ed. S. M. Lipset (New York: Basic Books, 1967), pp. 108-13.

7. The *Economist* study from which this example is derived is analyzed by Robin Blackburn in "Inequality and Exploitation," *New Left Review*, no. 42 (March-April 1967), p. 4.

8. See Misha D. Jezernik, "Changes in the Hierarchy of Motivational Factors and Social Values in Slovenian Industry," *Journal of Social Issues* 25, no. 2 (1968).

9. Ibid., p. 109.

10. Jezernik says that

after the revolution was won and industrialization started, the country was short of professionals; people without proper professional education had to be promoted.

And secondly, when industry became nationalized, revolutionary cadres distinguished by their revolutionary zeal and political reliability were brought into managerial positions. As long as modernization did not take place and workers did not become "spoiled" by material incentives, these ineffective managers did not disturb anybody seriously. Now they are becoming the main obstacle, nearly the unsolvable problem; they do not want to quit their jobs voluntarily and they sabotage the hiring of young competent professionals who could menace their positions (Ibid., p. 110).

11. Another example of this failure is provided by the decline of Calvinism as a moral basis for business action. This is not a matter of belief versus science. The consummatory values associated with Calvinism could hardly be regarded as antiscientific, for all its fatalistic theology. Indeed, Calvinists saw in the scientific investigation of nature a "duty of love." In time, however, these very investigatory impulses became quite divorced from practice. Calvinism initially served as a specific warrant for science against religious orthodoxy. Today it is a bar to science where it is not totally remote from it. See R. Hooykaas, "Science and Reformation," in *The Protestant Ethic and Modernization*, ed. S. N. Eisenstadt (New York: Basic Books, 1968), p. 215.

12. Indeed, in the United States, where this process has gone further than elsewhere, the functionally superfluous must resort to caste or ethnic boundaries if they are to have any sense of community. Many are Black. Superfluous Whites derive status through racial violence. Kinship associations in rural areas and localized populist vigilante groups direct violence against Blacks and convert color into a caste mark. Superfluous Blacks, on the other hand, have had until recently the local church, which, in the absence of other institutions, formed a corporate focus in the ghetto. However, church participation is declining today, and a substitute is being found in political groupings whose demands are for "Black power."

13. One sees this in a modern army, where the actual combatants are a relatively small group compared with the organizational staff and personnel necessary to equip and place the soldier on the line. The same is true of virtually any other field operation or industry.

14. The social sciences show a reversal of this order of priorities. Applied natural or physical sciences, such as engineering, are quite likely to serve as the basis for theoretical models in the social sciences (as with cybernetics theories). The false starts and inadequacy of pure theories in the social sciences have limited their claims to functional significance. Social scientists have tended to elevate technique to the level of theory in order to achieve the purity that distinguishes research in the material and physical sciences. The pure social scientist is rare indeed and, where he exists, is regarded as more of a luxury than a necessity because his theories are too speculative. It is, therefore, the high-level practitioner—the social science technocrat—who is able to mobilize large resources, whether through institutes of applied studies, private foundations, or government-sponsored research. Increasingly, he is invited by industry to take consulting or even managerial roles.

15. It may be worth pointing out that the notion of putting an educational elite to work on behalf of the strategic marginals of society, that is, the industrial proletariat, was a socialist idea. The state was defined by its marginals; hence, their improvement was necessary to change in the society as a whole. It is interesting to note this early emphasis and contrast it with a later one in the U.S.S.R., in which military purposes and technology have replaced the former elite role. See the speeches on education, 1926-45 by M. I. Kalinin, *On Communist Education, Selected Speeches and Articles* (Moscow: Foreign

Languages, 1950).

16. In the U.S.S.R., this group was called the "gilded generation" and came from the families of the new administrative elite.

17. For example, in Britain today there is a tendency toward right-wing radicalism among workers, lower-middle-class groups, and the less functionally relevant that is shared with downwardly mobile upper-middle-class groups of the residual fused type, such as the old middle class. This radicalism takes the form of populist, primordial, and nationalistic consummatory values.

18. See the extremely stimulating discussion by James A. Davis, "Structural Balance, Mechanical Solidarity, and Interpersonal Relations," in *Sociological Theories in Progress*, ed. Joseph Berger, Morris Zelditch, and Bo Anderson (Boston: Houghton Mifflin, 1966), p. 88.

19. Within these groups, there is an intense fear of aging. (Indeed, the retired are viewed as somehow embarrassing, shameful, and often grotesque.) Intense activity and rejection of its consequences by the new generation compounds the fear of death, for one can no longer look to the young for earthly immortality.

20. The problems are only a little different in advanced socialist countries. There, creative intellectuals are the marginals and are regarded as dangers to the utilitarian foundations of socialism. The crisis of meaning, similar but not the same, is localized, at the moment, in a small group of writers, a larger group of students, and some creative artists looking for some exemption—the extension of academic freedom, in the widest sense—from an otherwise bureaucratized universe.

21. Such a double hierarchy exists in all contemporary industrial societies, although it is more significant in nonsocialist industrial societies than in socialist ones. But even in the latter, the older hierarchy persists, more openly at the bottom, to be sure, because socialism favors the working class, at least in theory, and more subtly at the top. To some extent these residual upper-class and middle-class groups, which retain and cultivate an outmoded style of life, have mingled with the functional status elites to emerge briefly when the political situation allows, as it did during the Polish, Hungarian, and Czechoslovakian crises.

22. A. O. Hirschman, *The Principles of the Hiding Hand*, Reprint no. 130 (Washington, DC: Brookings Institution, 1967), p. 13.

PART II

AGAINST THE STATE

7

SANRIZUKA
A Case of Violent Protest
in a Multiparty State

This leads us to a consideration of the disordering side of development, and violence in particular. The mediation and prevention of violence is a primary task of any state. In democracies, the causes of such disorder are commonly regarded as pathologies the most serious of which either reveal some kind of injustice or result from the malfunctioning of representative institutions. Knowing how to deal with the more serious pathologies is difficult in part because it is very difficult to link protest and violence directly to injustice or institutional unresponsiveness. (There is no "justice quotient" the variation of which will predict the outbreak of violence.) Nor is it possible to gauge when political temperatures will rise to a point where violent protest seems likely to break out. One reason for the lack of indicators is the weakness of current explanatory theories. Highly generalized structural ones lead to overkill conclusions. Those concerned with individual psychological variables are mostly devoid of interpretative understanding. They treat circumstance and situation as residuals. It is precisely on these residuals that the present study focuses.

The concern is with a particular form of citizen protest that I will call extrainstitutional, that is, which expresses itself outside of normal linkage channels. In the case I will examine, the issues are by no means fleeting. Indeed, the movement has lasted over a period of 25 years. Its causes and effects and the role violence has played in it need to be analyzed over time. Its durability is all the more surprising because it occurred in Japan, one of the most successful examples of a democratic reconciliation system.

Analytical materials will be drawn rather arbitrarily from two different sources. One, political economy, emphasizes how violence can result from marginalization, in this case of small farmers driven into the labor force by deliberate governmental design. The other, deriving from structuralism, indicates how this experience of violence can be translated into special languages, symbolism, speech acts, and semiotics. The two very different ingredients come together in the events occurring at an old imperial crossroads in rural Chiba, which is also the present site of the new Narita International Airport.

Confrontation between farmers and police at this site escalated over time. As it did so, it led to increasingly generalized and polarized views about a number of socially and politically important questions. Some pertained to the negative social consequences of Japan's economic policies. Others were about Japan's role as an international power. So powerful was the symbolism evoked by such confrontation that very diverse protest coalitions were effectively united. For some in the opposition, the construction of the airport led to a rejection of the democratic polity, posing challenges to the authority of the state itself.[1]

Although the facts are straightforward enough, the story is complex. Perhaps the best place to begin is not at the beginning but at the crossroads itself and at a mass rally held in Sanrizuka Park on March 28, 1982, by farmers of the *Hantai Domei*, the Sanrizuka-Shibayama Opposition League Against the New Tokyo International Airport, their militant allies, and supporting groups. Clad in face masks, helmets, and "combat" dress, surrounded by antiriot police in full regalia, and under police observation from circling helicopters, the leaders read the following statement to the assembled crowd:

> The whole world faces now a grave crisis of imminent war—nuclear war; the human being is now threatened with holocaust and total annihilation. An urgent demand for peace expressed in anti-war, anti-nuclear protest is becoming more and more common, not only among the Japanese people but also among people all over the world.
>
> We, members of the Opposition League and those who are rallying around it, have been fighting for 17 years against the construction of Sanrizuka military airport under the banner of "Stop war! Fight for peace!" in diametrical, violent confrontation with the state power.
>
> Now that antiwar, anti-nuclear struggle is gaining momentum anew, we feel it our duty, as ones [sic] fighting in Sanrizuka—a fortress of people's struggle of the whole of Japan—to fill responsible positions in this struggle.[2]

In the audience were representatives of a variety of citizen groups as well as students, trade unionists, members of the Chiba branch of the locomotive union, and, of course, followers of sects manning fortresses in the area. Waving huge banners and massed flags imprinted with slogans attacking the airport, imperialism, and militarism, the leader proclaimed the most peaceful intents. Sanrizuka Park, the staging area, is itself of some significance. It is the last remnant of an old imperial estate whose lands once composed a good deal of the terrain on which the present airport is constructed. While the rally was going on, planes were taking off and landing every few minutes from the one runway the government had been able to build, although passengers remained totally oblivious to what was happening just a few thousand yards away. Even though the two crossroads, the airport and Sanrizuka, are cheek by jowl, those who use the first neither know—nor would they much care—most of them, what happens at the second. It is the second, Sanrizuka itself and its environs, where people care very much about the first, either for or against. The more they care, the more serious the protest. The more serious the protest, the greater the tendency to violence. The more violence, the more polarization between the movement and the state, and the more passionate their ideological differences.

The protest itself began as a simple conflict of interests between the farmers, in the area of Chiba Prefecture designated for the construction of the New Tokyo International Airport, and the government. The first site selected in 1965 was Tomisato, some 66 kilometers from Tokyo. The original decision aroused such spontaneous reaction that the site was changed to Sanrizuka, a few kilometers away, a more thinly populated area where imperial land was available. Again there was protest. This time the government refused to give way. Violent confrontations occurred. In 1967, the movement, which until then consisted of farmers, was joined by New Left sects and became increasingly radicalized.

As confrontation became more bitter, violence escalated, as did mutual estrangement between those protesting against and those favoring government policy. As other issues became joined to the original protest, principles became more important than interests. A variety of groups from all over Japan came to regard existing laws as repressive, representative institutions as unresponsive, and political leaders and senior civil servants unaccountable at best and coercive at worst. Lack of an effective political opposition also contributed to the sense of frustration. The Communist Party, which initially supported the farmers, tried to use them for its own purposes. The Socialists were largely ineffective in a system controlled and dominated by the Liberal-Democratic Party.[3] Given the circumstances, lack of consultation, ineffective due process, inadequate power of local governments, and an ineffective opposition in Parliament, the statement read at the rally becomes less surprising. As violent protest continued, this movement, like many others, came to demand a place in history, and in heroic moral terms. The more it did so, the more it was able to establish a common front with other groups representing many different expressions of public grievance. What makes this movement particularly special is not the magnitude of its claims, but the place and role it came to occupy in the protest politics of Japan.

1. THE SANRIZUKA MOVEMENT

This small place with its few inhabitants came to be taken seriously as a surrogate for the most abstract and pressing moral concerns. So Sanrizuka, a rural pocket of Chiba Prefecture, could become a "fortress of people's struggle" whose leaders would claim "responsible positions in this struggle." Eventually, the Sanrizuka movement accumulated such a variety of principles that it seemed to represent a fault line for all forms of citizen protest, something volcanic, a shifting terrain where all other cleavages joined to form a concrete disjunctive community in a "mobilization space." As it gained momentum, the movement converted considerable numbers of citizens into partisans on one side or the other and created a wider circle of public opinion willing to suspend judgments instead of automatically supporting the government position. People became less passive, more interested and alert. On the fringes they were passionate.[4]

The movement was composed of three components. The first and original group consisted of farmers and their households, divided into those living in the environs of Sanrizuka itself, in neighboring hamlets and villages, where the main agricultural product is vegetables, and those in nearby Shibayama, where the main product is rice. The Sanrizuka area came under the general administration of Narita City, Shibayama under the general administration of Shibayama Town. The farmers' movement, or Hantai Domei, had representatives in both the Narita City Assembly (including the Secretary-General of the movement) and as well in the Shibayama Town Council. Both supported the movement and both reversed their support under pressure from the Chiba Prefecture government, which shares responsibility with the airport authority and the ministry of transportation for acquiring land and keeping the peace under the Liberal Democratic Party (LDP) government.

Although the first stage of the airport had been built, protest continued over construction of the second. On the original site, where the airport is today, all villages, farms, woods, and so on have, of course, disappeared and the original inhabitants dispersed. Families inside the second stage site have dwindled to 8. The main farmers' support remains Shibayama, where the inhabitants are concerned with problems of land use, ecology, irrigation, and other factors affected by so large an undertaking as the airport. Together, the Sanrizuka-Shibayama Hantai Domei consists of about 120 households of which a dwindling number continue to be active in the struggle with the authorities.

The second component of the Sanrizuka movement consists of radical militant sects living in fortresses and solidarity huts on land made available by farmers, or on airport land on which construction has not yet begun. Some of the members are cadres living more or less permanently in these huts and fortresses. Others come part-time from universities and jobs to help the farmers protest, and to work for them in the fields. Some have married into farm families. Some have been fighting for as long as 20 years alongside the farmers.

A third component consists of supporting groups belonging to sects with larger networks. Some of these sects are very powerful, such as *Chukaku-ha* which originally, like many others, split off from the Japan Communist Party, and came to prominence during the student struggles in 1960 led by the student organization *Zengakuren*. These supporting networks not only provide funds for the movement and supporters, but help rally support in trade unions such as *Chibadoro*, the Chiba branch of the locomotive union on which supplies of fuel to the airport depend.[5]

Until recently, control of the movement was with the farmers. However, as the number of farmers has declined (and as the mood in Japan shifts to the right), farmers have split into two groups. The sects that originally came to the area to support the farmers and confront government while their own main bases remained outside find that as their outside support erodes, their stake in Sanrizuka increases. They have no other place to go.

The loose organization of the Hantai Domei has been both a strength and a weakness. The death by cancer of an exceptional president in 1979 left something of a vacuum at the top. The tough old farmer who replaced him as Acting President was subsequently forced to resign under pressure from some of the sects that charged him with collaborating with the airport authorities. Several other key members of the Hantai Domei had to resign as well. For a time, the movement was dominated by the secretary-general, who ran it from his headquarters in a kimono shop. But as he came to favor Chukaku-ha over Fourth International and other sects, he became less effective as a liaison person between farmers, sects, and supporting groups. Eventually, the farmers split into two Hantai Domei groups, one favoring coalition with Socialist sects including the Fourth International, and the other favoring Chukaku-ha and its allies.

The power of the movement always depended heavily on personalities. It survives mainly because of its strength in tiny village and hamlet organizations. In such bodies, support comes from women, elders, youth, and other groups. A few key figures, survivors in every sense of the word, keep the struggle alive. It takes only a small number of dedicated people to mobilize outside support. In this activity, the sects are crucial.

So small, fragile, and divided an organizational structure gives no hint of what this movement has been able to do nor the extent to which a stalemate continues at the airport. Even though the first round of violent confrontation came to an end in May 1978 when the airport opened for business, delays, overruns, security, and the like have resulted in astronomical costs. The airport, which was supposed to open in 1970, remains only partly constructed. It continues to be controversial for a number of reasons, not all of them having to do with farmers or sects. Businessmen and other travelers, too, complain that the airport is too far from Tokyo. It takes too long to get there and back. There are traffic delays. It is inconvenient. It also remains vulnerable to attack by militants. Indeed, the government's plans to complete both a fuel pipeline and a *Shinkansen* or bullet train have been thwarted by confrontations and sabotage.

Militants and farmers have maps showing every conduit of the airport, and all the facilities, rooms, control points, and so on. In the last outbreak of major violence, they entered through the sewer system and hid there overnight. The next morning they went to the top of the control tower, smashed equipment worth millions of dollars, and hoisted a red banner out the window, delaying the opening by several months.

Indeed, from 1967 until the airport opened in 1978, the movement was widely seen as a metaphor for struggle, the airport serving as a surrogate for the "one-party" state, a state that, in turn, served as a symbol of imperialism and militarism, and a potential instrument of nuclear holocaust, an issue that is particularly important in Japan. Immediate events of violence on the site served as reminders of these and other issues of wider significance. Previous loyalties to the state came to an abrupt end when old people invaded the hall during ceremonies celebrating the handing over of the imperial estates at Sanrizuka to the government airport authorities. A fight against government teams of surveyors invested the terrain itself with a kind of independence, Sanrizuka becoming a world partly outside the jurisdiction of the state. Watchtowers and fortresses were built by farmers and militants on lands the government wished to acquire for the airport, and attacks against them by government police came to represent the defense of the "revolution." Taking over the airport control tower just before the airport opened in March 1978 showed that the defenders could take over the commanding heights of power. Each of these events came to be seen as a logic of history in common with the logic of revolutionary movements elsewhere, as I will try to show.

The movement became a mixture of action and story in which the protagonist represented an enduring alliance of small farmers (all grandfathers and ex-soldiers who fought in the World War II) and militants from New Left sects of postwar Japan. Their movement, lasting for a whole generation, raises broad questions about the limits of party politics in the absence of an effective opposition and the substitution of factional politics of the LDP in its place. It also suggests how concern over some of the more negative aspects of modern industrial life manifests itself politically. Even in a successful society such as Japan, progress has its victims. What this case suggests is some of the costs as well as the benefits of economic transformation. It is the other side of the corporate Japan, "Japan as number one," as Ezra Vogel puts it.[6] For if Japan today is a monument to discipline, intelligence, and hard work, and its political leaders have served as shrewd guides to effective policy, as always there is another side to the story.

II. THE ISSUES

The airport, not yet complete but functioning, stands athwart the old crossroads at Sanrizuka, where the emperor once owned large estates, experimental farms, and a horse ranch dating back before Tokugawa times. The landscape, sufficiently beautiful to have earned the reputation of being the Barbizon of Japan, was a place of much local pride and affectionate nurture over many generations. The transformation of it (and the farms and villages adjacent to it) into a runway and terminals converted the terrain itself into a metaphorical landscape. The government decision to put an airport there transformed the entire area into metaphors of organicism, fertility, nature. It also retrieved another "history"—or better, a "memory"— which, underlying all this charm, summoned a bitter legacy of struggles between peasant and lord, tenant and landlord. As "history," both have their place in this movement.

Traditions aside, there is wide agreement within the movement that the airport irrevocably destroys certain values essential to life itself. Hence, the original question of self-interest was the farmers' defense of their land, their private property, their patrimony. As conflict continued, self-interest became the most trivial part of the movement, which saw itself as an alternative politics, setting itself against the general drift of society. It represented a minority view, of course. All the more reason that as a protest army it marched up the hill of principle so quickly. And once confrontations occurred, and violence (in which a few were killed, thousands wounded, and more thousands arrested), it became virtually impossible for the government to convince people to pack those principles up and march right down again to the practical world of bargaining and negotiation.

And not only for reasons of confrontation and alternative views of life. There were specific and directly significant political issues involved. We have already mentioned several—the dominance of the LDP, the weakness of the legitimate opposition, the lack of effective due process, the inadequacy of local government, the absence of appropriate consultative mechanisms and procedures outside of elite circles. It is a result of this movement and others like it that many political changes have occurred. Local governments have learned better how to protect local interests. National government has had to take responsibility for the negative effects of economic growth, which, in the name of progress, resulted in pollution and environmental disaster. Today the worst effects of both are being mitigated. It took movements of this kind and extrainstitutional protest to force the government to act.[7]

Nevertheless, these are changes in practice more than organization or principle. The government still has no institutionalized way to deal with movements of this kind, especially at a local level. In Japan, perhaps more than in other democracies, it is very difficult for the government to deal with them without confrontations. Lack of effective institutional development at the bottom is also made worse by the lack of effective opposition parties at the top. Both circumstances contribute to extra-institutional protest as a strategy of opposition. The government's chief weapons remain secret negotiations and private manipulation against both of which movements like this one take every possible precaution— from mutual surveillance to self-criticism. They treat as traitors those who would favor negotiation or compromise. They react immediately against those who suggest temperate solutions. Indeed, this movement has been reluctant to back away from the largest principles to accommodate the most practical needs of the farmers themselves, a practice which in the end will prove to be its undoing.

In the end, the farmers of the Hantai Domei will be forced to give up lands needed to finish the airport. Nor can they ignore financial compensation from the government and offers of alternative lands that the government promises to provide. After all, farmers have responsibilities to their own households as well as to those in the movement. It is for this reason that the movement has tried to involve whole families, including wives and children, in active protest. For the group just outside the airport area, irrigation and noise pollution are the crucial issues. Offers by the government to support new irrigation schemes have already so reduced the number of Hantai Domei farmers that all know the government will win. If they want to preserve their way of life, they will need government help in order to do it.

But this movement has been much more than a farmers' movement, although farmers were at the core of it. It has served as a lightning rod for protest movements all over Japan: antinuclear, environmental, peace, those protesting discrimination against Koreans in Japan, or against a pariah caste like the *Burakamin*. Through its links with the 17 supporting New Left sects, the movement also fights against the presence of American forces and nuclear ships and facilities. Together, farmers and sects maintain some 33 fortresses and solidarity huts scattered about the airport. They continue to confront the fences and watchtowers of the airport authorities, sometime nose to nose, eyeball to eyeball.

III. THE VIEW FROM ABOVE

From the government perspective, the issue is completely different. The airport was a part of a more important decision reached by the

Japanese Cabinet in 1960 that emphasized industrial over rural development in a program popularly dubbed "income doubling." Its principal objects were to reduce the size of those sectors of the economy that were relatively inefficient, and where income was lagging behind more productive sectors, by diverting the labor force into needed and better-paying occupations. Regarded by the government as a forward-looking program of general economic and social improvement, it also marked Japan's coming of age as an industrial power, and a way of putting firmly behind her the legacy of defeat in the war, and the long years of poverty and reconstruction that were its aftermath. With this changed policy, the new airport was decided upon in part to handle the increased commerce projected. It also was to be a symbol of the new role Japan would play in the world.[8]

Not until 1965 was a site decided upon. The problems involved in site selection and the decision and politics of their implementation tell us a good deal about the workings of Japanese political life, both parliamentary and bureaucratic. The selection took a long time for reasons of party politics and because of factional patronage struggles within the ruling LDP, and also for technical reasons. With only 15% of land area of Japan arable, virtually every proposed site for so large an undertaking simply had to be controversial. Even if assessments of relative costs and benefits were limited to technical matters, the political consequences could not help but stimulate hard bargaining and dirty politicking within the governing LDP. So complex were the issues in these terms that those in charge forgot those not directly involved in making the decisions. They ignored the local people themselves.

Nor did the government believe that opposition would endure. Despite the political embarrassment caused by confrontation, officials had plenty of reasons for self-congratulation. Under the guidance of the LDP, the government had gone from success to success, and not only in economic but social terms. LDP politicians had a sense of their own sureness, expertise, and, through factions and party bosses, a degree of openness to public need that enabled them to mediate problems rather than legislate solutions. From their perspective, the problem of the airport was a technical rather than a political one, despite the opposition from below. The airport was the biggest single project ever undertaken by the Japanese government, and those responsible were more concerned with its complex organizational, jurisdictional, and decisional aspects. Hence, while officials could be sympathetic to the farmers' plight, they believed the airport to be a self-evident public good. Modern industrial Japan needed an additional facility to serve metropolitan Tokyo and the industrial-petrochemical complex that much of Chiba Prefecture had become. The government was perfectly willing to negotiate terms with farmers, but not compromise on the airport itself. When militants appeared on the scene, such negotiations became almost impossible. For the government, the militants were the cause of the difficulties. They were the ultimate subversives.

At the first site chosen, Tomisato, farmers protested so violently that the government gave it up and secretly moved the new site to Sanrizuka. The latter was a more thinly populated area. Much of the land already belonged to the Imperial Household. The government assumed that the opposition would be less strong and effective. It considered the site change a tribute to its own flexibility because, after all, officials had responded to public outcries at Tomisato.

There was, to be sure, a good deal to this view, although it was not the way it appeared to threatened farmers for whom the lack of consultation was outrageous—an act of aggression against them and their way of life. But clearly there was principle on the government side as well. In line with its industrialization policy, it wanted to drive small farmers off the land and into the industrial labor force in order to raise incomes, something the government regarded as a self-evident benefit to all. However, both militants and farmers alike interpreted this as an example of how state-capitalism negates democracy, generates a surplus by means of primitive accumulation, creates an industrial reserve army, and generates a class struggle between capitalists and farmers. Hence, what was a confrontation over competing interests from the perspective of the government became a class struggle from the standpoint of the movement.

The latter also saw the state as a bureaucratic capitalist agent of both United States and Japanese imperialism with the new airport being built mainly to serve U.S. needs in Vietnam. As the struggle with the government evolved, the movement became more and more heroic, epic, and remarkable both in its own eyes and to a widening circle of admiring supporters. It gathered such strength, momentum, and outside support that almost a million people over the years came to this place to protest. It was a tocsin for the "AMPO" generation, fighting against Japanese remilitarization and changes in the U.S.-Japan Treaty. Within this increasingly radical alliance, the broadest principles were married to the most immediate concerns in a rhetoric reflecting and appropriate to the escalating violence of the confrontation with government.

IV. SANRIZUKA AS A "MOBILIZATION SPACE"

A key factor was indeed violence. The combined opposition sought to isolate the airport physically by means of the fortresses constructed around it at key points. Mobilizations served not only to focus on specific issues but were occasions in which surveyors, architects, builders, engineers, indeed, the airport workers themselves, were transformed from instruments of construction to destruction, their activities despoiling the land, the patrimony, the sacred soil itself. Displaced grave sites became violations of ancestral property. Wounds and deaths were final expressions of desecration. The airport authority, which had the central responsibility for building and running the airport, became not only an instrument of an insensitive bureaucracy of which one might approve or disapprove, but an agency of government serving as a comprador and partner of the U.S.-Japan alliance for remilitarization. So a moral architecture was created within this crossroads, this confrontational space, which intensified as the bulldozers cleared the land of its trees, houses, farms, and people. The combined opposition fought back with Molotov cocktails, sticks. Old women sprayed the police with night soil, and chained themselves to trees. Bunkers were built underground. Watchtowers were built toward the sky.

Violence was endowed with legitimacy, and legitimacy with violence. The incidents were not isolated from other protests in Japan and they need to be seen in the context of a retrievable legacy that goes back a long way before this movement.[9] Prototypes can be found in early turn-of-the-century conflicts brought about when Meiji governments sought rapid industrialization and fostered militarism.[10] Some farmers came from a tradition, which, antibourgeois, was imbued with the spirit of the "warrior-peasant" and had more in common, at least originally, with the tradition of the radical right, with its nostalgia for the rural hamlet and its hostility to Meiji industrialization and urban embourgeoisement. Others were members of the Japan Socialist Party or the Japan Communist Party. This dual tradition, the one associated with the class struggle, the left, and the other the unity of the rural community, the right, has been combined today in an endogenous radicalism that is essentially nondoctrinaire but highly militant. It constitutes a specific ideology constructed out of the events in which farmers and militants have themselves participated, what we will call a *mytho-logics.*

Here then is one secret of why this movement became important despite its small size. It retrieved an inheritance that was originally divided between left and right, yet that stemmed from some of the same original causes, and combined them around a common set of problems, a political economic problem represented by Japan's successful pursuit of an innovative capitalism that has allowed her to surpass the U.S.S.R. in economic power and to become the world's second industrial force. It retrieved, too, a tradition in which those who become marginalized in the process became the concrete manifestation of all those others in society penalized in one way or another by development. So the ideology drew upon an ensemble of grievances, few of which could be rectified by prevailing means of legitimate party, interest, and factional politics.

In this case, too, there is even more hidden under the surface, including a radical version of Protestant Christianity in which religious pietism revealed itself not in textual exegesis but living out as a practice the precepts of disciplined Christian corporatism within which a unique degree of individualism was allowed, an alternative to the primacy of group affiliation so characteristic of Japanese social life. (In this there was a specifically Tolstoyan strand.) Christianity also retrieved earlier links with the left. From the pre-World War I period to the beginnings of the Japan Communist Party, it was common for students to become Socialists after an initial involvement with Christian precept under circumstances of specific protest and mobilization, not so different from this case.[11].

There is then a complex radical inheritance. Some groups trace their origins to Marxist study groups, which, attracting people to the study of texts, made some of them into virtual monks, provided them with "safe" houses, and divided them by sects in which doctrine became all important. Most of the sects involved in the Sanrizuka movement derive from breakaway movements, mainly from the Japan Communist Party from 1956 on.[12] Japan's was the first New Left, and its rise and successes on university campuses, and its own historic 1968, when it took over the main tower of the University of Tokyo, was noted throughout the world.

The consciousness of such multiple retrievals by participants was a very significant aspect of the struggle itself. Just as every year the storming of the control towel is commemorated by a mass rally serving as an occasion to enunciate principles of antistate action, so the control tower event was itself an explicit reminder of an internal struggle in which a key tower had been destroyed by the riot police in Sanrizuka, which, in turn, was a reminder of the storming of the tower at Tokyo University itself. The iconography is explicit. The symbolism is understood by all. Each event overlaps with others to constitute a structure behind a narrative, a structure that can itself refer to the logic of arguments against the state. Retrievals then lead to projections in the form of a mytho-logics.

These symbolic displays were hardly lost on the authorities. They, too, understood what was going on. They were deeply disturbed by the link between the farmers and militants. Government regarded the alliance between farmers and militants as unholy. While farmers might have a just cause, because their livelihoods were at stake, militants did not. When the latter encouraged the farmers to build fortresses and underground bunkers, this was outright rebellion. To oppose the airport on the grounds of ideological principle was to oppose the legitimacy of the state and to challenge the authority of the government itself.

In a sense, the government was right. But the question it could not answer was how militants were able to radicalize farmers so successfully. Even more curious was how those on the fringe of society could generate such widescale support. How did it happen that old women, subservient in many ways to their men, became the most radical in their actions? Why did old people, who could be expected to regard matters from the sidelines, prepare to commit mass suicide on the grounds of the imperial estate as a protest against construction of the airport there? Why, after the farmers initiated the first violence, did they elect a president who was an artist, a militant Christian, and something of a local intellectual. If such a fellow saw himself as a Christ standing in the field (*Standing in the Field* was the title of one of his books) and invoking Christian precept, he was just a crank from a government perspective. Tomura may in his own mind have represented a logic of revolution that he claimed was inspired by the example of Christ's martyrdom, but it was very hard for the government to take him seriously.[13] For that mistake, they paid dearly. For it was Tomura who, after being beaten by the riot police, brought in the militant sects and made them into his disciples.

Above all, what the government could not understand was that under the surface of the events themselves, other principles were being enacted than those made explicit in confrontation—the continuity of the society, the unity of opposites involved when farmers and militants joined forces, a sense of immortality resulting from that unity, a rejuvenation when youth and aged came together that made violence celebratory. When farmers revived the hamlet with its more egalitarian tradition, and organized the Hantai Domei around women, elders, youth, and other corps, they captured the imagination of many because this seemed so essentially Japanese. Even the fortresses built by militants had as their prototypes the sect houses and original study groups of early radical days. In the struggles that followed, the farmers saw the fortresses as World War II bunkers against the enemy while the militants regarded them as the equivalent of underground peasant fortifications in Vietnam.

These then are some of the ingredients of a conflict that gave an ideological dynamism to a movement that was very different from its ostensible issues and causes. Moreover, the episodes of violent confrontation were understood in precisely this complex way by a much larger audience, so much so that the little crossroads of Sanrizuka became a "mobilization space."

A *mobilization space* is a particular terrain in which groups converge to confront an "outside" force. Each contributes its own issues and grievances to the whole and thus escalates the principles on which confrontation is based. In this case, the terrain was the imperial crossroads. It served to retrieve old grievances. Within it, new projections were projected. Each confrontational event added particularly to the ideology, enabling the movement to generate its own mythology out of the events, its heroes and martyrs, speaking to a wider audience and translating the sequence of experiences into a narrative that struck the sensibilities of people other than those directly involved. The narrative illustrated a logic of what was wrong. The events were epic, the stuff of which myths are made. Because I want to suggest some reasons that this happened, and use this case to draw some more general conclusions relating extrainstitutional protest to ideology, let me clarify certain key assumptions.

Ideologies become effective when they enable events to symbolize "deep structures." Their narration as "history" retrieves. Their representation as text projects. With interpretation, action becomes necessity, necessity becomes morality, and morality becomes logical—that is normative. Required are "transformations," changes of meaning; in this case: from a "terrain" or place to a surrogate for a field of forces, from an ecology of functional relations to a moral architecture, from leadership to messianism, from interests to principles, from principles to necessity.[14] Let me discuss some of these a bit further.

From Place to Surrogate

Sanrizuka was not a place where traditional life had been preserved as if in a museum. The farmers living there and in the hamlets and villages around the crossroads were not peasants but small-scale agribusinessmen, concerned with the market, investment, mechanization of farming techniques, government agricultural policy, and the like. They were voters involved in rural cooperatives and active participants in the polity. Not a few were bosses and local officials in the Japan Socialist Party and the LDP. The days when they were a small, semi-independent yeomanry with some being tenants and others landlords disappeared rapidly after 1947 reforms that gave everyone land. Moreover, changes in farming had been associated with the imperial estate ever since Meiji times. Sanrizuka was then not a pocket of traditionalism fighting progress. It had been and was a place where shrewd farmers innovated and had become highly efficient. They were not poor and they were good farmers.[15]

Hence, the selection of the site for an airport did not pose traditionalism against modernity, or peasant revolt against the state, but one kind of modernism against another: commercial agricultural as a way of life against the internationalization of industrial activity. Each side, farmers and government, then, represented two sides of the modernity coin. The one side was agribusiness. The other side was industrialization. The latter would create irrevocable alterations in the actual conditions of social life, as had already occurred in Chiba Prefecture—pollution, ecological change, and so on—and dislocate and displace the population, pushing farmers into the industrial labor force. The farmers then came to represent "society," the state, bureaucratic capitalism. The airport became the surrogate for the state. The Sanrizuka crossroads was the surrogate for society. Hence, the confrontations by farmers were designed to create a no-man's-land around the airport, erecting fortresses, and so on to isolate the state from society until it could become more responsive to society's needs as they defined them. The field of forces explicitly engaged by this included anti-

Vietnam, antipollution, environmental, and a variety of citizen protest groups the most important of which were associated with the Hiroshima peace movement on the one hand and the Minamata movement on the other.[16]

From Functional Ecology to Moral Architecture

By *ecology*, what is meant is the understanding of a space in terms of its functional relationships, land and water, irrigation and crops, the social ecology that follows from it, farmers, merchants, and so on, to the political ecology of interests that generate political participation. Perhaps the best exposition of the politics of an ecological terrain is the work of Stein Rokkan and his associates showing how institutional politics work as a reflection of "ecologies" in this ramified sense of the term. *Ecological politics* is essentially bargaining politics within well-defined institutional frames.[17] Translate the terrain into a moral architecture and it is precisely the bargaining aspect that drops out in favor of a mobilization aspect using or prone to use extrainstitutional means. This translation occurred in Sanrizuka when the airport was seen to be an excrescence on the actual land itself, changing the agribusinessman into the protagonist of a way of life that was self-legitimizing.

Here retrieval becomes important. The imperial estate itself was a place where artists used to come from all over Japan, and visitors who in spring would witness the cherry trees in bloom. The landscape itself, especially around Sanrizuka and in Shibayama, was charming and miniaturized, with small meandering roads, ribbonlike lanes leading out to meadows or rice paddies. Not that the entire landscape was bucolic; far from it. There were the beginnings of urban sprawl, and a network of fast transportation. But the Sanrizuka crossroads still led out to hamlets and villages, some very old, some dating from Meiji times, some populated by "pioneers," ex-soldiers who had built up their farms from scrub land. The social ecology constituted a network of "mediations," funerals and weddings, three-generation families, in which modernity facilitated rather than threatened social life.

The airport violated this space, this way of life. The nature of its transport was seen as the ultimate aggression. In this battle of the two crossroads, hamlets and villages, solidarity huts and fortresses, towers and underground bunkers came to represent a moral architecture, the hamlets and villages representing a superior moral existence based on nurture and cultivation in contrast to the careless ruthlessness of the runways and buildings of an airport and the industrialization, pollution, ecological disaster they represented. The solidarity huts and fortresses were the defense points against all this. The bunkers burrowed into the land as a sacred soil, the defenders going underground while the towers claimed the sky, the rain, the weather, against not only airplanes but against the monopoly of the sky held by the American armed forces that controlled the air lanes. The battle between the Sanrizuka crossroads and the airport was thus a battle between civility and ruthlessness, peace and war. Farmers in their headbands, women in their baggy pants and straw hats, militants in their helmets peopled those constructions and arrayed themselves against the glass, steel, and concrete of the airport itself. It is in this explicit physical sense that Sanrizuka constructed a moral architecture, all the more compelling because the airport was ringed with double-linked chain fences, topped with barbed wire and electrified, a dry moat between, and guard towers constructed with electronic surveillance equipment while nearby were barracks for thousands of riot police, all to be attacked by staves, spears, sticks, stones, Molotov cocktails, excrement, and other instruments of a "people's war."

From Leadership to Messianism

A moral architecture is a function of a special language. The language cannot be entirely written. Nor can it be exclusively articulated in public places. Both are important, text and articulation, but neither are sufficient. What is needed is a language able to convert retrievalism into projection, and use events to illustrate a logic, a logic to endow the events with symbolic power. An agent is required, one who seems to speak not on his own but simply as a vessel, a container for what everyone understands and shares but cannot voice, not a leader but a mythic spokesman. In this movement, it was Issaku Tomura, the insider-outsider, the Christian whose little church became the moral center of the movement, the Christ who stood in the fields, and by his austere personal conduct, his compassion, and his reserve seemed to be the essential Japanese. His grandfather had come to Sanrizuka to build new kinds of farm equipment for the experimental farming being undertaken there. He himself knew all the farmers because he sold them farm equipment from his shop in Sanrizuka. But he was also an outsider who had been opposed to World War II, who made modern sculptures out of old equipment parts, and who stood aloof from local-interest politics. Indeed, it was this latter factor that made him the only candidate to lead the farmers movement. Given all the other diversions and factionalism that divided them, his capacity to be one of them while being above them made him a unique figure.

It was Tomura who turned the events themselves into a language of violence. When the riot police brought in bulldozers to clear the land, remove villages, and do the necessary survey and construction work, Tomura turned this into an invasion of the cosmological space of the "authentic" Japan. He saw it as governmental contempt for the people, a lack of respect, and more, for he insisted that parliamentary government did not and could not represent the people's interest. It was not only the failure of due process, of effective local government, and other aspects of democracy that he found wanting, but, for him, capitalism and parliamentary government were ultimately contradictory. It was this view that enabled him to embrace radical militants whose behavior would have otherwise offended him for he was in his outrage a deeply conservative man, like the farmers themselves.

Language and moral architecture were molded by Tomura's simple but persuasive biblical rhetoric into a set of slogans that could be hung from towers and worn on headbands. The militants built a huge tower called a Farmer's Broadcasting Tower, which was to enable messages to be shouted to all the participants, and to the four quarters of the cosmological, almost Confucian, space that constituted its natural heaven, and to the world of journalists, photographers, and, above all, television cameramen who came rushing to the site when the tower was attacked by water cannon, bulldozers, cranes, and so on. In this way, the instruments of construction were converted into weapons of destruction at the hands of a government composed of riot police and bureaucrats against farmers whose weapons were their farm implements, and who sang folk songs, and grieved over their lands.[18]

It was Tomura then who was more than a leader. He was a messiah who described the fall, and promised grace through resistance, devotion to the cause, and moral discipline. By bringing in the militants, he thought he could not only provide reinforcement for farmers and outside support as well, but through their concern for the future, find a solution, a new way of life.

From Interests to Principles

In the end, however, no matter how shrewdly articulated, symbolism and its political expression as myth and logic, or its embroidery as retrieval and projection, can only have a transitory effect if it does not translate into some kind of stable picture of the world as it is and the world as it ought to be. For Tomura, and for the Hantai Domei and its militant allies, no hard and fast ideology could be acceptable. There were too many differences between them for that, and as well in a movement so small, too many personalities. Required were principles broad enough to be considered as unifying moral aims, and capable of inspiring lofty convictions on one hand, but that also provided for experiments, alternative routes to a final solution. For farmers and their children, this meant seeking ways to live principles in new modes of farming. Hence, the movement spawned a variety of concrete experiments, organic farming, a small collective group called the "One-Pack Movement," and several others.[19] Most of these were efforts to reduce the vulnerability of the individual farmer and to make farming attractive to a next generation. They sought not only new and different modes of personal living through joint or collective enterprise, but also a principled alternative to commercialization and capitalism.

There was good reason for trying to enunciate "practical" as well as abstract principles. To convert abstraction into real life is to drive out precisely those pressures to convert principles into interests, and to bargain, a goal that was the main hope and strategy of the movement. The government never saw the matter as one of principle, but only of interest, and watched with bewilderment as the principles piled up, one on top of the other, in a crescendo of antagonism against the LDP and its policy. But it assumed that, in the end, interest would win over principle, given patience, craft, and manipulation. In turn, the government failed to recognize sufficiently that it, too, had principles, of a public-interest kind. Neither was it prepared to convert opposition into a basis for reforms at the local government level, and for the provision of more effective due process, procedures, not to speak of other institutional arrangements and safeguards for private citizens that we associate with virtually every functioning democratic system. It was the bureaucrats who refused to see this, more than the politicians, some of whom were caught in the middle, like the governor of Chiba Prefecture. Hence, the more the Sanrizuka movement spoke in the name of principle and the more public sympathy was aroused both by the confrontations and issues themselves, the more the government tried to convert principle into interest. It succeeded in buying out a large number of farmers. But it made itself appear corrupt and corrupting in the eyes of many. When the weak articulate principle against the strong and a David takes on a Goliath, the political consequences are rarely those intended.

From Principle to Necessity

Indeed, it was precisely because of the government's success with so many of the farmers that those who remained in opposition came to represent an embattled moral force, the inner Japanese, whose wishes should have been "mediated" by government rather than "corrupted." Farmers and militants were able to touch on a wider sense of public discomfort over precisely the larger issues that had been troubling many Japanese before the movement actually began, concerns over what kind of society the new Japan should properly become. Surveys taken at the time this movement began, conducted by the office of the prime minister, indicated troubled responses to the question of Japan's future role in the world, and as a world power. Today Japan is more confident of its place. In the mid-1960s, the questions of government, the relationship to the United States, the problem of militarism, were complex and troubling. No one can calculate the consequences of nuclear holocaust like the Japanese. Memories were shorter than today. Despite friendship and admiration for the United States, and a frenetic adaptation of many American things to fit local ways, there was much that troubled the Japanese about Americanization, not least of which was the Vietnam war itself.

The movement offered a logic to this ambiguity. In the pursuit of industrialization, a way of life was to be shut down. Small farmers were to be driven into an industrial reserve army. The class struggle that was occurring in Vietnam and had occurred in China was not recapitulating itself among the small farmers. Primitive accumulation was the precondition of bureaucratic finance capitalism. Polarization, visible in confrontation, constituted the visible aspect of this class struggle. Socialism would begin in the rural sectors and spread to the urban centers, where fighting had already begun in the universities. The alliance between militants and farmers would win over the workers, especially the teachers and the railway workers who had been radicalized by the Japan Communist Party but would break away from it because of its conservatism. What these principles articulated then was not the necessity *for* revolution, of favoring it, but the necessity *of* revolution, of doing it—a necessity with parallels to the great revolutions of the past, most particularly the Russian, Chinese, and Cuban. All began small. All were in accordance with history. Principle revealed necessity. Theory was action. Action was theory. So went the logic of necessity.

We should probably end our discussion here. It was apparent that despite the success of the movement in preventing the airport from being completed, necessity was wrong, principles were faulty, the messianism was overblown, the moral architecture hollow, and the terrain in the end was just a terrain. Today there is squabbling within the movement. Tomura is dead. Most of his successors have been expelled. The farmers are deserting the movement. The sects fight on because they have no other place to go. The public is no longer concerned.

But this would perhaps miss the different ways in which this movement and others like it are important. I now want to show how and why this movement—one more in a history of protest movements that cannot win on their own terms—like the others, will leave more than a memory or a trace. Such movements are events that reinforce a language of protest, one able to provide authenticity to protest and a continuing ground for extrainstitutional activity and the legitimization of violence. Because of this capacity, it has had permanent effects on Japanese politics. It also suggests some of the general problems movements of this sort raise in the way we think about the state and most particularly the democratic state.

V. SANRIZUKA AS A "SEMIOTIC" SPACE

Precisely because it was a mobilization space, Sanrizuka was also a "semiotic" space.[20] Events were "read" like an epic narrative, a tale that seemed to come down from the old times that it, of course, retrieved, and also as a logic of projection, a theory, for confrontation was a necessity. So the Sanrizuka struggle itself forms an underlying layer for other future events. My assumption is that despite the triviality of the circumstances bounded by the terrain of the two crossroads, they became part of a more fundamental and ongoing debate about the character, design, and moral purpose of modern society itself, posing the problem of the limits of democracy and, indeed, the limits of the state. Representing enduring and perennial themes: the last becoming first, society against the state, the weak becoming strong, interest being converted to principle, it reinforces a radical logic with a set of informing acts.[21] By defining a larger cosmological space, underground to a sacred soil, aboveground to the sky itself, and, within the space, a moral terrain, it shows how a real architecture and a moral one confirm each other.

It represents a battle that continues at the center of "developmentalism" itself for the process no longer seems as benign as it once did. As the social overhead costs of industrialization increase rather than decline, even this small struggle contains the larger question of what development means for the state. It raises questions, too, about how development itself changes society. For the farmers resisted becoming marginals, functionally superfluous people whose existence becomes an embarrassment, a problem only now becoming significant in other parts of the labor force as technology changes.

Finally, it suggests that underlying the logic of necessity is a logic of exchange that offers the basis of an exchange of meaning. By seeking necessity in the event, the airport becomes not simply a surrogate for a state, but a metonymy for a theory of the state. Opposition to it is not simply protest but revolution. In the end, as already indicated, the momentum of "revolution," even when it fails, can be perpetually reinvoked in succeeding protests, with previous events an inheritance embodied in a language that passes for rationality itself.

The way this can happen is illustrated by this struggle. Each of the main episodes became punctuation marks in a text and a narrative, a story read by the public with considerable attention and an instruction that some at least took seriously. The narrative of events is composed of specific violent occasions: the outer rim land survey, the transfer of the imperial estate, the first and second expropriation struggles, the control tower takeover. Each constituted battles in a war against the state, complete with accounts of violence as well as rituals of sacrifice. There is principle here as well, and, within narrative and text, instructions deriving from and defined by each episode. The first, the outer rim land survey, was widely understood as a metaphor of rape and a metonymy of state capitalism. The second, the transfer of the imperial estate, was both a metaphor of betrayal and a metonymy for primitive accumulation. The first and second land expropriations were seen as metaphors of violence and death and metonymies of marginalization and polarization. The final violent episode, the control tower takeover, was a metaphor of transcendence, a capturing of the commanding heights and a metonymy for revolution, the revolution this movement hoped to accomplish. In turn, the episodes constituted a history, a narrative of the struggle and a test representing a radical theory, violation of local and private space, illegitimate conveyance, polarization, the creation of an industrial reserve army, and the legitimization of the struggle. Such a theory is designed to convince and persuade. More, it becomes a logic of necessity, impelling action. So a semiotic space is filled and ideology becomes a form of "instruction."

What is the instruction? The rape of the land, the ending of farmers' obligations to the state, the violation of the sacred body of society itself, all require that selfless resistance that will prevent the state, as a ruthless superlandlord and instrument of imperialism, from having its way. Yeomen must fight to prevent their conversion into marginals even more debased than tenants in the old days. In this way, each episode forms with the others as a structure of explanation and a theory of the antistate as Figure 7.1 suggests.

At its outer limit, the conversion of each episode into metaphorical and metonymical "deep structures" suggests a universal dynamic appropriate to revolutionary movements elsewhere. In more specific terms, we see first a unity of opposites between farmers and militants, opposite in age and occupation and unified by an almost familial and ideological embrace. There is second the set of contradictions that sets revolutionary episodes in motion—Japaneseness versus Americanization, marginals versus state capitalism, society versus the state, and, of course, the stage for all these, Sanrizuka versus the airport. Finally, there is the search for that mass support that will lead to a disjunction in which the parliamentary state will give way to citizen participation and collective enterprise.

VI. SOME CONSEQUENCES OF THE MOVEMENT IN JAPAN

A mobilization space doesn't always become semiotic. When it does, it creates its own power, a mytho-logics, which, when it works, can have a persuasiveness that defies number. It generates commitment. It

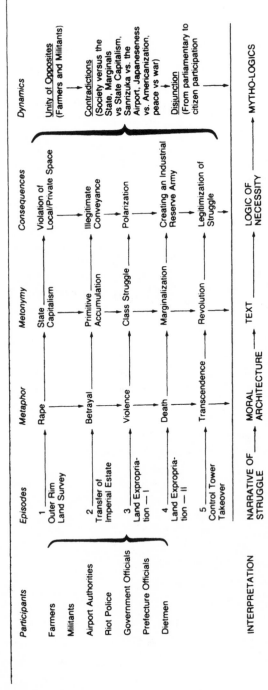

Participants	Episodes	Metaphor	Metonymy	Consequences	Dynamics
Farmers	1 Outer Rim Land Survey	Rape	State Capitalism	Violation of Local/Private Space	Unity of Opposites (Farmers and Militants)
Militants					
Airport Authorities	2 Transfer of Imperial Estate	Betrayal	Primitive Accumulation	Illegitimate Conveyance	Contradictions (Society versus the State, Marginals vs State Capitalism, Sanrizuka vs. the Airport, Japaneseness vs. Americanization, peace vs war)
Riot Police	3 Land Expropriation — I	Violence	Class Struggle	Polarization	
Government Officials	4 Land Expropriation — II	Death	Marginalization	Creating an Industrial Reserve Army	
Prefecture Officials	5 Control Tower Takeover	Transcendence	Revolution	Legitimization of Struggle	Disjunction (From parliamentary to citizen participation)
Dietmen					

INTERPRETATION NARRATIVE OF STRUGGLE → MORAL ARCHITECTURE → TEXT → LOGIC OF NECESSITY → MYTHO-LOGICS

This diagram, derived in part from the work of Roland Barthes, Claude Lévi-Strauss, Edmund Leach, Paul Ricoeur, and Pierre Bourdieu, describes episodes of violence as they are interpreted by the participants themselves. The meanings given as metaphors and metonymies were derived from interviews and written descriptions of events provided by those deeply involved in the movement. Together they form a narrative of moral outrage and a radical text. They constitute both the moral force and logical integrity of the movement and make convincing, at least to followers, the idea that such a small group of participants can win such a big victory. The ingredients of the ideology represent what Lévi-Strauss has called a mytho-logics. Evidence is provided by the actual episodes. A complete and total system, the mytho-logics serves as an interior discipline of language and an ordering of signs. By the same token, what orders within is disordering without. It captures certain critical ambiguities of modern life in Japan, ambiguities which are widely felt but rarely articulated, the shock value of the incidents attracting outside clienteles.

Figure 7.1 Sanrizuka and the Narita Airport: Two Crossroads and a Terrain as a Semiotic Space

motivates action. The question is, however, to what purpose. I now want to suggest that even if the consequences of this movement in Japan have been few in terms of institutional changes, it has stimulated considerable political learning. Both government and private citizens' groups have learned a good deal from the Sanrizuka struggle. People have become much more willing to fight against what appears to them as government arbitrariness. They have been encouraged to join forces with other opposition groups and appeal to public opinion in ways perhaps lacking in Japan in the past. In effect, a moving equilibrium of opposition coalitions has been possible, despite the single-party dominance of the LDP and the relative impotence of the opposition parties. Indeed, the latter depend for survival on their ability to mediate various forms of extrainstitutional protest, making compromise more palatable. Indeed, one might argue that, in Japan, institutional opposition derives some of its functions from extrainstitutional activity rather than by making such activity superfluous, its more conventional and traditional role.

In turn, government itself has learned how to be more shrewd, to anticipate political problems, and to avoid conflicts of this kind by taking necessary preliminary steps, most specifically by widening the scope of consultations, and blurring a little the boundaries of bureaucratic jurisdictions. Moreover, local authorities are becoming more adept at bargaining with the national government. So is the private sector. As all sides have learned to bargain more efficiently, they prevent the translation of interests into principles, the creation of a mobilization and semiotic space, and the formation of a mytho-logics in which ordinary solutions become virtually unacceptable.

Moreover, in other circumstances, like the Osaka International Airport case, the government has allowed consultation to take place while maintaining that the dignity of all those involved be preserved. For if we can pick out one factor most immediately consequential in converting Sanrizuka into a mobilization space, it was that the government deeply offended the farmers' dignity. It ignored their wishes in the decisional process. It ignored their efforts to protest by constitutional means. It attacked them when they refused to give up.

Indeed, it was the ultimate indignity of the farmers' position that gave the movement its original moral force and rallied public opinion and sympathy. Even those who disapproved of the tactics of confrontation and violence saw government as reprehensible and came to understand why, from a farmer's standpoint, ordinary bargaining and mediation rules and the conventional processes of party and interest-group politics were the cause of the problem rather than the solution. Government efforts to co-opt leaders of the movement, or to compromise them on the matter of compensation, were taken not as illustrations of government flexibility but of duplicity, moral laxity. Hence, farmers established themselves as the "party of principle" against a government defined as a "party of expediency" and, by so doing, appealed to a broad spectrum of liberal and socialist sympathizers.

As for militancy, the point of no return was crossed after Mr. Tomura, the president of the Hantai Domei, was badly beaten by the riot police. After that, it was the state itself that became the target. The new agenda for the movement became after that not merely an amendment of the decision to build the airport at Sanrizuka but a rupture in the relations of power; not an extension of political coverage but an alteration in the rules of politics. In such circumstances, grievances convert to ideology, issues that are plural become singular, clienteles intersect and link up as networks, and individual "speech acts" become systems of actions.

Above all, then, the government today tries to avoid just that kind of activity that will generate militancy. Since the control tower takeover, it has refrained from provocative acts. It has not proceeded with dispatch to the next phase of the construction. It has avoided confrontation.

In terms of the actual issue itself, the construction of the airport, each side has won something and lost something. Today the airport is in use despite its truncated quality. More than 30,000,000 passengers have used it since it opened in 1978. Fighting continues over the second phase, although the tactics have changed and it is the government that now eschews violence even though it seems determined to press on and complete the construction. Moreover, there are now doubts that the airport will ever be completed as envisaged. Indeed, it may be becoming partially obsolete. Government has won in the sense that it has a functioning airport at Sanrizuka. But the cost has been very great and the victory partial.

Farmers and militants have also won a partial victory. The government has been forced to accede to the principle that small farmers should not be obliterated by state policy. Militants have found in Sanrizuka a semipermanent staging area, an arena of action, a stage for confrontations, which some believe will continue to "reveal" the fundamental contradictions of state capitalism in Japan. Rightly or wrongly, they have successfully endowed the issues with a more fundamental significance, a matter of the state versus a sector of society whose embedded symbolic value in Japan is part of the tradition of "Japaneseness." They have attached the universality of their ideologies to the particularities of a society in continuous change, and transformed a conflict of rural versus industrial interests into a problem of marginality, functional superfluousness, and the social overhead costs of development itself.

So, in Japan, the Sanrizuka movement came to represent the most generalized expressions of all postwar extrainstitutional protest, including the anti-Vietnam war movement, the peace movement, the antinuclear movement, and so on. Around this struggle and within the confines of its mobilization space, all the problems of capitalism and bureaucratic power have been articulated, and then made into something more, a semiotics of protest going well beyond its concrete substance. So much so that for some, the Sanrizuka movement is the defining case of citizen protest in Japan. For others, it was less important, simply one among many protest movements and a minor tune played in a major key. Both assessments have merit. There is a sense in which its importance has been less in terms of the impact it has had on the larger drift of Japanese politics and society than how it reflects the ambiguities of the drift itself.

VII. SOME LARGER IMPLICATIONS

So much for the implications of the movement in Japan itself. What about the wider problem, the problem of the state when confronted with extrainstitutional protest? What this movement suggests is that as developmental change generates increasingly high social overhead costs, more and more interests are offended, and more and more people are adversely affected. The problem is not, nor can it be, opposition itself. Any exercise of power is bound to generate some opposition. No one at the top, even those who appear most impervious to demands made from the bottom, would argue that, in today's world, sovereignty itself can offer the privileges of sole jurisdictions. Even centralized power is diluted by the actual forces and geometrics of organized political groups. Some pluralism and accountability always exist.

The problem is that, even in Japan, whose economic success is second to none, the fit between growing political resources and public needs is becoming unstuck. The dilution of centralized authority through regularized forms of accountability, what we mean by "institutionalized" politics, the elaboration of which in terms of regular instruments of popular political participation is the special virtue of democracy, does not enable a sure and identifiable public interest to prevail. This means that democracy itself is in growing trouble. For only in a democracy does the legitimate exercise of power depend on participation—a participation that, moreover, not only accepts the principle of opposition but makes it the dynamic factor within a state in which citizen rights are broadly as well as specifically defined and applications of coercion limited. Such opposition is constitutionally provided for along with appropriate channels and instruments for its expression. In contrast, extrainstitutional opposition, or protests that take place outside such channels and by other means, are disturbing, irresponsible, dangerous, and aberrant, a kind of pathology.

Such a view is necessary, especially in a democratic state. Any system that, in the last analysis, depends on accommodation and mutual deference must maintain a clear boundary between legality and illegality, proper and improper behavior, and the respect for authority itself. Yet it should not be entirely forgotten that virtually all the mechanisms and instruments of politics and the ways and means and scope of representation and participation, all of which appear to make extrainstitutional protest redundant, themselves originated with one or other aspects of such activity. What we call democracy then is a result of extrainstitutional protests that produced institutional modifications. Electoral reform, expansion of the franchise, the right to organize in trade unions, the basic protection of individual liberties—all have experienced as part of their specific history and evolution some degree of extrainstitutional origins and force. The democratization of access to power, the widening of political participation, indeed, the evolution of democracy itself is bound up with such activities. Accomplishment should not blind us to the continuing need for such kinds of opposition, at least to the degree that these lead to corrective modifications within the principles of democracy itself.

Equally, we ought not to be blinded to what has changed. The increasing articulation of opposition issues, in principle, can lead to the formation of an oppositional space, extrainstitutional in character, part mobilization, part semiotic, in which institutional adaptation and government response make things worse instead of better. We may be reaching a point where governments have already accepted responsibilities and obligations beyond their means of effective discharge. If so, it will be increasingly difficult for governments to make the necessary amendments in policy and adaptations in institutional structure to render necessary changes politically acceptable. As this becomes so, movements of this kind pose the question of the limits of the state itself.

What this suggests is in part the need for renewed speculation on classic themes, the problem of system and jurisdiction, accountability and responsiveness, and perhaps a renewed concern with alternatives to sovereignty and power other than those currently available. We say "movements of this kind" to describe those that press fundamental principles in a way that cannot be ignored and whose political acts can have wide repercussions of the sort described (i.e., when groups organize around the belief that they cannot effectively utilize prevailing and organized structures of political participation in order to affect government policy).

For another part, we need to utilize new concepts for the analysis of ideologies, more structuralist perhaps, more phenomenological as well, to understand the dynamics of behavior, language, and interpretation that these movements generate. Analysis like Pierre Bourdieu's *Outline of a Theory of Practice* in the first instance or Paul Ricoeur's *The Symbolism of Evil* are perhaps too rarely read by those willing and able to go to the field to study such matters firsthand.[22] Indeed, for the examination of such issues, the heavy weapons of modern survey and computer analysis may play us false, for what they show us as empirical reality may be further away from certain truths than looking at the moon through the wrong end of a telescope.

While this is not the place to argue such issues, clearly what I have tried to suggest is this. The older and more obvious solutions to the problems of extrainstitutional protest, namely, to widen the circle, expand the system, and include inside more effectively those who are currently left out, are more and more difficult to employ. More, mobilization movements that construct a semiotic space are very difficult to absorb. If our analysis is correct, and governments are in increasing difficulty over how best to deal with responsibilities already incurred, then further increases in such responsibilities are likely to be counterproductive, adding more layers of institutional indigestion and adding to the bureaucracy and to government by committees so that they will be less accountable rather than more, and less efficient in catering to public demands. The danger is that institutional accommodation of a kind bound up with the evolution of democracy itself may not produce an opposite effect. No ready solutions are at hand.

Governments try to deal with the problems as best they can, vacillating between giving in and holding firm, hoping by these means to locate those strategic points at issue where mediation can occur without threats to the basic structure of politics. But such circumstances are increasingly frustrating on all sides, with each pointing the finger of recrimination at the other, a condition under which events provide the circumstances for confrontation, violence, and the formation of those mobilization spaces that have semiotic impact and consequence.

If these assumptions are correct, offended groups will have few options if they already lack power, so that the only real alternative to passivity and compliance is force or the threat of force. But, as soon as violations of legal and institutional limits of politics are advocated by a movement, no matter how small it is or insignificant, and a signal goes out to those in authority—an alert, events can easily take on these wider semiotic proportions. There is a quickening of concern all around. Beyond a certain point, such circumstances in a democratic state invite not simply extrainstitutional protest but the extreme version of it that involves terrorism, the semiotic of death and transfiguration, a phenomenon that captures the greatest publicity and involves the smallest and most extreme groups. As long as the public is repelled by their activities and clienteles remain limited, terror remains the semiotics without the mobilization. But terrorism also tries to reverse the order and go past a semiotic space defined as a symbolism of violence and convert citizens into a network of counterelites, mobilized out of the ensemble of those increasingly alienated from prevailing institutional politics. The aim is the conversion of such counterelites into counterclienteles, the two forming that revolutionary mobilization that is the specter haunting all democratic governments.

Movements like the one in Sanrizuka stand between terrorism, which is proscribed, and more ordinary citizen protest. Raising issues that are not easily negotiated, such movements reject the ordinary processes of political bargaining and accommodation. To the extent that they touch on fundamental issues of principle, they must be taken seriously enough to enable political learning to occur on all sides, and to stimulate a review of issues in terms larger than immediate instrumentalities. Such movements renew interest in old themes. How to respond to extrainstitutional protest, how to separate legitimate grievance from illegitimate, how to sense deeper structural concerns and how to decide what it is necessary to defend. If extrainstitutional protest is part of the natural inheritance of democracy itself, today its extreme alternative—terrorism—prejudices that inheritance. If between protest and terror there is a huge gap, it will repay us all—scholars and politicians—to listen, learn, and try to accommodate to those groups far away from the commanding heights of politics and society, and concern ourselves especially with those becoming marginalized and estranged. The spokesmen for the Sanrizuka movement who proclaimed at their rally that "the whole world faces now a grave crisis" could have added to their list of potential catastrophes the democratic state itself. For in the end, like everything else, it is just a representation, just an idea—one of the better ones.

NOTES

1. David E. Apter and Nagayo Sawa, *Against the State* (Cambridge: Harvard University Press, 1984). This study was made possible by funds from the Japan Foundation and the Center for International Studies, Yale University. The research represents a collaborative effort with Nagayo Sawa, co-author of the book from which part of this material is taken.

2. David E. Apter, *Fight* (Tokyo: Mobilization for Sanrizuka and Doro-Chiba, 1982).

3. Allen B. Cole, George O. Totton, and Cecil H. Uyehara, eds., *Socialist Parties in Post-War Japan* (New Haven: Yale University Press, 1966).

4. David E. Apter, "Notes on the Underground: Left Violence in the National State" in *The State*, ed. Stephen R. Graubard (New York: Norton, 1979).

5. Chukaku-ha, together with its ally, Chibadoro, has been responsible for continuing acts of sabotage, not only of the airport but of other facilities such as the Japan National Railways. Robert A. Scalapino, *The Japanese Communist Movement* (Berkeley: University of California Press, 1967).

6. Ezra Vogel, *Japan as Number One* (Cambridge: Harvard University Press 1979).

7. Kazuko Tsurumi, "Aspects of Endogenous Development in Modern Japan," in *Part III, Man, Nature and Technology: A Case of Minamata* (Tokyo: Institute of International Relations, Sophia University, 1979).

8. William W. Lockwood, *The Economic Development of Japan* (Princeton, NJ: Princeton University Press, 1968). Also, Anne Androuais, "Le processus de restructuration de l'economie japonaise," in *Japon, Le Consensus: Mythe et Realites*, ed. Bouisson and Faure (Paris: Economica, 1984), pp. 395-428.

9. Thomas C. Smith, *The Agrarian Origins of Modern Japan* (Stanford, CA: Stanford University Press, 1959).

10. E. Herbert Norman, *Soldier and Peasant in Japan* (Vancouver: University of British Columbia, 1965); and Roger Bowen, *Rebellion and Democracy in Meiji Japan* (Berkeley: University of California Press, 1980).

11. Richard J. Smethurst, *A Social Basis for Prewar Japanese Militarism* (Berkeley: University of California Press, 1974). Also Henry DeWitt Smith, II, *Japan's First Student Radicals* (Cambridge, MA: Harvard University Press, 1972).

12. Robert A. Scalapino and Junnosuke Masumi, *Parties and Politics in Contemporary Japan* (Berkeley: University of California Press, 1962); and Scalapino, *Japanese Communist Movement.*

13. Issaku Tomura, "Ten Years of Struggle: Sanrizuka and Its Links with Asia," *AMPO: Japan-Asia Quarterly Review* 7, no. 4 (October-December 1975), pp. 39-44.

14. Paul Ricoeur, *The Symbolism of Evil* (Boston: Beacon Press, 1967).

15. Ronald P. Dore, *Shinohata: Portrait of a Japanese Village* (New York: Pantheon Books, 1978).

16. Robert J. Smith, *Kurusu: The Price of Progress in a Japanese Village* (Stanford, CA: Stanford University Press, 1978).

17. Stein Rokkan, *Citizens, Elections, Parties* (Oslo: Universitetsforlaget, 1970).

18. J. L. Austin, *How to Do Things with Words* (Oxford: Oxford University Press, 1962).

19. Apter and Sawa, *Against the State*, pp. 191-192.

20. Umberto Eco, *A Theory of Semiotics* (Bloomington: University of Indiana Press, 1979).

21. See chapter 10 of this volume.

22. Pierre Bourdieu, *Outline of a Theory of Practice* (Cambridge: Cambridge University Press, 1977).

8

THINKING ABOUT VIOLENCE

The murder of General Rene Audran in front of his home just outside of Paris on January 25, 1985, followed almost immediately by the assassination of Ernst Zimmerman in Germany, signaled a new phase in the evolution of terrorism. The theater of war is Europe. The context is American imperialism. The targets are the individuals and facilities associated with NATO and the Council of Europe. The specific issue was cruise missiles. The larger object is to polarize the struggle between Europe and the United States. A unified guerrilla communist front for Western Europe has been set up. Its core is an alliance between the German Red Army Faction and the French Action Directe in association with the Belgian Fighting Command Cell, the Italian Red Brigades, and several more shadowy groups. Although such coalitions are not new, this one represents more than a tactical shift.

Until now, confrontation was between homegrown terrorist groups and their governments. "Internationalization" mainly referred to links between certain movements in Europe and those of the Third World: Latin America and the Middle East. For example, certain PLO factions served as links between a Japanese group, the so-called Arab Red Army (Arab Sekigun) and the RAF (Baader-Meinhof). The identification with anticolonialism and imperialism remains intact, but it is diminishing. The Japanese Arab Sekigun has dispersed (some of its erstwhile leaders live in Paris) and the surviving member of the three-man team that committed the Lod massacre in 1972, and who is still in prison in Israel, has "applied" to the Israeli authorities to become Jewish.

A number of obvious reasons account for the change in venue to Europe. Recent events in the Middle East have made the PLO look like a sideshow. The "primordialization" of the conflict has led to bitter rivalries between Muslim extremists. In such a context, radical terrorists are also suspect. Radical terrorism and religious xenophobia do not set well with one another as a good many Iranian Mujaheen would attest.

Refocusing on Europe and stepping up the pace of violence against NATO and other institutions gives terrorism a sharper focus. It appeals to that not-inconsiderable part of society increasingly discontented with the lack of progress toward peace made by the antinuclear and environmental movements. The deployment of cruise missiles invites terrorist targeting. Moreover, such "international" issues can be directly linked to more domestic ones—the growth of unemployment, a decline in trade unionism, the marginalization of industrial labor—giving radical intellectuals a sense of urgency and beleaguerment and enlarging potential clienteles. Indeed, the purpose of the present rash of attacks is to make manifestly clear that every European state that continues to accept American hegemony through NATO has lost its sovereignty and its legitimacy.

The sudden increase in the number of violent episodes comes at a time when it was believed that terrorism was losing ground. Police infiltration, the fact that a number of terrorists were now willing to talk, the rather spectacular accomplishments of the police in capturing, jailing, and killing important terrorist leaders, made it seem as if terrorism was on the run. More and more people were learning to adjust to violence, almost as one accepts the weather or natural catastrophes, as just another damn thing to live with, one more in a succession of life's bad jokes.

The present stage of terrorism in Europe requires rethinking. It is dangerous to lump together different kinds and causes of terrorism. Nor is it useful to ascribe it to a few mad extremists, a view to which many professional observers are prone. On the other hand, to focus on social causes does not mean that solutions will be forthcoming. A good many remedial measures are politically unacceptable.

Hence, if gains have been made in our understanding of terrorism, finding out about it is one thing, knowing what to do is another. A great deal of specific information has been accumulated on movements and individuals. World directories have been compiled. We can look up names of organizations and their leaders as if in a telephone book. Detailed biographical information is available. It is known how terrorists are recruited and trained, the code names of leaders of the clandestine international underground (like Carlos the Jackal), how linkage was accomplished, using the Palestinian connection to establish contact between such diverse bands as the Japanese United Red Army,

Italy's Red Brigade, and Germany's Red Army Faction (Baader-Meinhof).

Such information is deposited in worldwide archives, collected by government secret services, psychologists, lawyers, jurists, university professors, and police officers. Collected also by professional students of terrorism in their "cells," in research centers like the Rand Corporation (where computer printouts spew out information in the gnomish language of relative deprivation, rising expectations, or the J curve of the authoritarian personality), these archives contain data banks, surveys, classifications, terrorist profiles, case histories—not to speak of information on police techniques, legislative strategies, instructions on the use and protection of informants. Today they constitute a unique corpus that includes such investigative techniques as the use of fiber optics for surveillance during a siege, linguistic analysis of threat credibility, as well as new methods of tracing, screening, and detecting weapons.

Techniques of cost-benefit analysis are applied to crisis management, the evaluation of options (patience versus military intervention, talking versus shooting). The exchange of such materials is made available through informational *internets*, international conferences, scholarly journals, and confidential and secret reports. Tested in terror games, and sold or otherwise made available for the benefit of captains of industry, diplomats, oil company executives, journalists, bankers, army officers, and politicians, it is no wonder that studying violence has become a modern growth industry.

Increasing violence has also been accompanied by an explosion of theories with fancy names: conceptual modeling, bargaining and indemnity frameworks, communications models, deterrence and negotiation techniques, organizational analysis, "futuristics," role-playing, gaming, not to speak of public opinion surveys to correlate public support for a government with probabilities of violence against it. As countermeasures have been internationalized, the exchange of information across national jurisdictions has increased. New instruments for regional cooperation have been established. The Club of Berne was set up in 1971, the Trevi Group in 1976, followed by the Club of Vienna. More recently, a French-West German Operational Group has been established to take countermeasures against the RAF-Action Directe command, all within the general framework of the Council of Europe Convention on the Suppression of Terrorism. (One notes the "sporting" quality of these names, as if they were hunters' associations.)

Despite these accomplishments, the professionalization of anti-terrorism brings its own dangers. Some people, closer to the firing line, tend toward a police sergeant's view of the human race, regarding everyone as a potential terrorist. Others prefer a more psychological view, regarding terrorism as a result of individual pathologies, a view that has proved singularly successful in extracting very large sums from government for research. Because terrorists set themselves up as lord high executioners of their fellow citizens, prosecutors and judges of who shall live or die, it is not surprising that one wants to treat them as mad, as mad as any self-styled Napoleon in an insane asylum. Explanations vary. One may attribute terrorism to negative family experiences, individual lack of self-esteem, shattering rebuffs from members of the opposite sex, fears of emasculation, and so on. Whatever the preferred explanation, the common theme is violence as a form of personal compensation, a settling of scores against society and authority.

To those in authority, such explanations are preferable to sociological or political ones. It is inconvenient to consider terrorism as an indictment of society, or even a consequence of political mistakes. In any case, more radical views of the matter that place the blame on capitalism or the bourgeoisie are just as guilty of terrible over-simplification as any bomb thrower. Worse, sociological explanations tend to provide a cover for terrorism, giving it legitimacy.

Whatever the views of the professionals, they work closely with government while building up their own institutional structures. These range from research facilities to special forces, complete with newly designed weaponry and other equipment. Some are like terrorists themselves, enjoying the staged and theatrical quality of their encounters. To be exclusively preoccupied with terrorism produces its own dangers, the most obvious of which is to exaggerate its dangers. Worse, professionals become a political interest group, anxious to impress on government the need for secrecy and exemptions from public and legislative scrutiny. Some advocate the suppression of civil rights for terrorists. In most countries, they are intimately connected to powerful agencies of government. Some may, in collaboration with their military and police counterparts, sponsor right-wing terrorism as a means of combating its left-wing versions. Inviting coercive solutions, they tempt the state to engage in terrorism from above. They make populist appeals for greater vigilance, weakening the civil institutions they claim to protect. "Irangate" is one of the more visible consequences.

I. VIOLENCE AND
THE INTELLECTUALS

Radical intellectuals are the main enemy of the professionals. Regarding terrorism as a social pathology, they absolve individuals from blame. Some see terrorism as the essential "cure," acting as the mediaries between the underground and the straight world. Including professors, lawyers, doctors, and writers (i.e., the radicalized wing of the middle class), they express what people less fortunate than themselves "should" feel. They seek to penetrate the ordinary commonsense world of reality with a deeper reality obscured by it. By elevating principles over political institutions, they bring the latter into contempt. Moreover, if caught red-handed in terrorist acts or implicated in such activities, they claim the protection of freedom of expression and use the very safeguards of the state they want to undermine. Their antecedents go back to Babeuf, for example, or Buonarroti. But there is no lack of contemporary prototypes. Just before and after 1968, the cult hero was Sartre, who brilliantly defined in his own actions the way that mind might transcend responsibility. Others include Genet, Fanon, Foucault, Boudrillard, Lacan. Today's radical intellectuals include a few more directly engaged, like Tony Negri.

All see violence as an "overcoming project," necessary in order to lift the dead weight of convention, the dead hand of bureaucratic power, and the deadly boredom of bourgeois life. Their followers, intoxicated with 1968 and all that, consider the underground life as the dialectical opposite of the oppressive state. Violence is the means to liberation.

Society represents the reproduction of all forms of capital, including mental capital (knowledge) and symbolic capital (political power) in the individual. Each person evolves as a reflection of the state that negates his true self. Everyone has a repressed mirror image (Lacan). Most have a secret love affair with this repressed self to which the terrorist appears as Anti-hero.

Of course, the terrorist is only the most recent in a chain of redeeming Anti-heroes. Sartre's candidates were the thief and the homosexual. Foucault's was the madman. Their liberation will be our own, because they are the negative doubles of our social selves. Thus Sartre writes in his introduction to Genet's *The Thief's Journal*, "the thief and his double are alike sacred ... behind the first-degree myths—The Thief, Murderer, the Beggar, the Homosexual—we discover the reflective myths: the Poet, the Saint, the Double, Art".

In the last few years, the Anti-heroes include both the terrorist and the pornographer. They have a good deal in common. Both manipulate desire, appealing to death and lust. They transform citizens from passive spectators into voyeurs and co-conspirators. The pornographer tempts the senses with forbidden desire. The terrorist thrills us with death, his violent acts engaging an audience by manipulation of the media, press, newspapers, books, films, television. The terrorist knows very well that violence is autoerotic.

The intellectuals do not make violence respectable so much as they make society contemptible. Rage is a cure. So much so that one can favor violence without being concerned with the consequences, if the Anti-hero will lead to the Anti-class, universalizing the overcoming project. In Algeria, Black rage was unleashed against White colonialism. Capitalist colonialism is transformed into revolutionary socialism. Similarly in Vietnam, or anywhere else that terrorism will turn the world upside down, PLO, IRA, and so on. What radical intellectuals do is give terrorism on the left the force of history—terrorism as agency.

II. TERROR ON THE LEFT

For all that, radical intellectuals make the left, the "real" left, uncomfortable. Some, like the neo-Leninists of the Red Brigades, regard their views as so much post-Sartrean rubbish, an invitation to irresponsibility, anarchism. What the radical intellectuals do is provide a sympathetic discourse within a larger intellectual community, important perhaps in creating clienteles for terrorists, but of not much use to terrorists themselves.

Moreover, one cannot trust such intellectuals. Most of them are only a step away from opportunism, personalism, and arrogance. For neo-Leninists, one is not, in any case, much interested in form-smashing but in the formation of guerrilla and revolutionary movements. Required above all is a correct theory. This will not only guide the movement and identify its class base, but indicate when polarization sets the stage for transformational confrontations. How does one know when such a base exists? It is when the classes that create the most value and the largest shares in a society receive the least shares and the smallest reward, and their condition is perpetuated by an ideology that fetishizes commodity production. Violence is the means of exploding this false consciousness and, by ending it, bringing down the hegemony of the bourgeoisie and the state that pretends to stand above class interest.

That much agreed, the extreme left disagrees about virtually everything else. For some, the revolutionary class remains the proletariat, even when the proletariat seems noticeably uninterested in revolution. For others, a peasantry constitutes the natural clientele of the radical terrorist, as shown by Cuba or China. Some groups, like the Montoneros and the FAR in Argentina, have tried to combine a rural revolution with urban guerrilla warfare. Whatever their views, those on the extreme left are far away from classical Marxism. For example, they regard with indifference the debate over terror engaged in by Kautsky, Lenin, Trotsky, and Luxemburg—whatever their preferred redeeming class. Neo-Leninists, Maoists, and a radicalized version of Trotskyism increasingly join forces not only against NATO and the United States but also against bureaucratic communism, the U.S.S.R., and the post-Stalinist legacy.

For a Maoist band like Sendero Luminoso, terror is necessary to mobilize the peasantry and paralyze the state. The first step toward revolution is the actual cell. The primary organ of the movement acts as surrogate for revolutionary texts. Leninism and Maoism provide tracts that are studied. Repeated like prayers, they create social discipline. The cell personifies the idea. The parallel is with Catholic social discipline. So too with the Red Brigades and the Montoneros.

The more "theory" and discipline count, the more the left is likely to be divided over questions of orthodoxy, strategy, and tactics. In Japan, splitting into sects was carried perhaps further than anywhere else. For example, in 1963 the Revolutionary Communist League (itself a breakaway from the Communist Party) split into two sects, Kakumaru-ha and Chukaku-ha. Declaring war on each other, Chukaku-ha's leader was killed by Kakumaru-ha. Many Kakumaru-ha members have been killed by Chukaku-ha. Similarly within in the Japanese Red army. One breakaway group holed up in the mountains and killed several of its own members (including a pregnant woman) because their "self-criticism" was considered insincere.

In general, the Neo-Leninists have contempt for personalism and reject the flamboyance and sexuality of more anarcho-syndicalist and anarcho-communist sects that emphasize violence first and theory later (a position taken by those following such ancestral anarchists as Proudhon, Blanqui, and Bakunin).

Today's extreme left includes former "situationists" like Action Directe which oppose Stalinism, as well as official communist parties. Their clientele is the displaced, the dispossessed, and the marginalized. If terror is socially induced, so they put society on trial. Trials are an essential part of the struggle. When the state puts terrorists in the dock, it puts itself there too. It too can be judged by a public opinion that the defendants try to mobilize. Hence, the courtroom becomes their tribunal. But one does not rely on state trials. Terrorists put their own captives on trial as surrogates for the state. They play with the state when they play with their captives. To treat the one with contempt is to bring the other into contempt, the Aldo Moro case being perhaps the most celebrated and shocking example.

III. TERROR ON THE RIGHT

Although the intellectual justification for terrorism is associated with the left, in some respects it is better represented by the right. For the right regards violence, terror—even war—as intrinsically liberating and creative. The right no less than the left has a particular hatred for bourgeois society. Purification by death, transfiguration by violence, both are needed to produce an elite whose will is a precondition for order once the state is demongrelized, racially purified, becoming what it should be: an organic community. It is a view that appeals to the romantic, the phallocratic. All guns, youth, and fertility, it is the very opposite of businesslike dullness and the commercial corruption of bourgeois life.

Egalitarianism means mediocrity. Hierarchy means ritual. Ritual invokes memory, mystery, motion, explosion, and both vulnerability and vitalism, an exquisite combination. Almost any violence will do. Guns, whips, chains, dogs, bombs, uniforms, boots, are among its more erotic symbols. The more naked the violence the more fully clothed the state.

The extreme right addresses itself to the same displaced, dispossessed, and marginalized people as the left, but moves them toward the center of their society on the basis of primordial ties, an original authenticity. The uniqueness of the people is asserted against those who violate the patrimony and are the cause of the present debased condition. The right seeks those final solutions that will eliminate pariahs, corruptors, the violators of the purity and authenticity of society. Social discipline and hierarchy, guaranteed by the state, will prevent the return of the pariahs.

Terrorism has its own raison d'être. It is *la strage,* the massacre. But the right like the left is also very divided—particularly between fascists, neofascists, Nazis, and the like. Pre-World War II fascism consisted of hoodlums engaging communist bands in a "street dialectic." Becoming uniformed and paramilitary, recruiting among "lumpens" as well as the middle class, they formed an equality of privilege among those sharing the right racial, religious, and ethnic patrimony. In a world of purity and danger, the strong have dominion over the weak. Honor and ideals, Christianity and virtue, race and blood will come together. The ancestral memory is the Crusades.

After the war, such doctrines went underground. The right prospered only where it could establish connections to extremist military and police officers, and high-ranking government officials. Some movements sought to connect aristocratic remnants, nostalgic for an ordered hierarchic society with social "dregs," criminals, perverts, and other "lumpens" as did the "momios" (mummies) of Patria y Liberatad in Chile. Others engaged in a dialectic of violence with left terrorist groups like the Montoneros and the ERP in Argentina during the "civil war" (1973-1976).

The third and most recent stage is "terrorism noir." It favors neither taking over the state nor pushing the government to the right. Opposed equally to the United States and the U.S.S.R., the ideal is not the executioner but the exterminator: cold, lucid, faithful to his friends, eliminating his enemies professionally like human cockroaches. The task is above all hygienic. Represented by movements like Terza Posizione and Armed Revolutionary Nuclei (NAR) and leaders like Franco Freda, the aim is to force citizens in a democracy to monitor their lives, to live behind locked doors, to insulate themselves electronically or with guns.

Under such circumstances, even if the state wins—putting down this movement or that—it loses. A dreary and limping democracy is easy to finish off. As one of the leaders of the group responsible for the Bologna station massacre put it, "Le terrorisme, qu'il opère sans discrimination ou vise des objectifs précis, a aussi l'avantage d'impliquer directement la population. Neutre à l'origine, elle sera ensuite portée à nous craindre et à nous admirer, méprisant, part contrecoup, l'État pour son incapacité à la defendre. . . . Par des actions spécifiques et répétées, non nécessairement revendiquees de notre part, il sera possible aussi d'augmenter jusqu'à la limité de l'insoutenable cette tension dans le tissue social du pays."[1]

IV. PRIMORDIAL TERRORISM

Although it may intertwine with the other two forms, primordial terrorism is at once the least intellectual and the most compelling of all. It is the most important single cause of terrorism today. It generates the greatest amount of sympathy. It produces the most extreme forms of fanaticism. When marginalization, displacement, and dispossession are defined in ethnic, religious, linguistic, or other terms, the desire for liberation is at once to found a new society, to redeem an ancient one, and to commit a revolutionary transformation. Increasingly, primordialism includes radical and right ideological strands. The more multiple these are, the greater the sources of legitimacy, and the greater the likelihood of support from various clienteles—as with separatist movements like the IRA and the ETA (Euskadi ta Askatasuna, or Freedom for the Basque Homeland).

Primordial affiliations are mutually reinforcing. Ethnicity, language, and religion are particularly so. Language may also be a way of reviving primordialism. For example, ancient Hebrew was revived in order to become the living national language of Israel. Similarly with the IRA and Gaelic. Combine such affiliations with longstanding social grievances, and not only is the result likely to be explosive, but primordialism will give depth to nationalism and the latter will make primordialism directly political. The Tamil movement in Sri Lanka, Hindu-Muslim conflict in India, Kurkish nationalism in Iran and elsewhere in the Middle East, Shiite and Sunni conflict (not to speak of competing Zionisms, Israeli and Arab) constitute some of its various manifestations. Primordialism represents what might be called the modern version of Plato's "noble lie." It rests on the idea that there is some inviolate and original moral and social identity unique to each people, a claim to immortality as a nation and a state.

The more primordial a terrorist movement, the more fundamentalist, and the more difficult to deal with. Compromise is like miscegenation. Separatism is ritualized. Individual acts of daring not only create individual heroes but recall previous ones. Primordial terrorism is retrievalism through violence.

The longer such movements go on, the more the history of violence becomes part of a cultural inheritance, and the more an obligation for the living. Hence, the militancy of the young PLO cadres whose sense of loss and suffering may indeed be greater than that of their elders. One thinks too of teenage Iranian militants marching off to martyrdom in Iraq carrying their own coffins. Death by violence not only redeems the patrimony, it is the legacy of the young.

Such revivalism is remarkable if one recalls that both liberals and Marxists alike assumed that primordialism would erode as economic development occurred. Quite the opposite has happened. If primordialism has declined among some, there has been an equal and opposite reaction, passionate in its defense. Indeed, never has there been so much approval of primordial claims as legitimacy. And never has the world been witness to so many armed fanatics.

Perhaps the worst effects of fanatic primordial terrorism can be found in Lebanon today. There, Shiite and Sunni Muslims, Druse, Catholic Maronites, Christian phalangists, each with its own terrorist wing, have literally dismembered the society, destroyed the state, and undermined its economic infrastructure. There is no room for moderation. Nabih Berri, the moderate leader of a Shiite underclass in full rebellion, tries to keep control of the Amal (Hope) militia but he is under increasing attack from the ranking Shiite leader Sheik Mohammed Mahdi Shamseddin. Killing, kidnapping, torture, random violence have all become more widespread, spurred on by the extreme fanatics of Hezbollah (Party of God) and Islamic Holy War.

The Shiites in Lebanon are perhaps the most prone to terrorism. They are also the most extreme example of multiple marginality. The most dispossessed and poor, they oppose other religious and social factions, most of all the Christian Phalangist Party of President Amin Gemeyal. Their hero is the Ayatollah Khomeini. At the head of the enemies' list as devils incarnate are Israel and the United States. Using extreme terrorist means, they are making a transition from being a pariah to a chosen people, from the margin to the center, from the dispossessed to the repossessed.

Most primordial terrorism aims at independence, autonomy, a state of one's own. It also aims at purification within the ritual boundaries of primordial affiliation. So it was with the Sikhs at the Golden Temple. So it is with the Iranian revolution under the Ayatollah Khomeini. Some seek redemption in a "return from exile" as with Jewish Zionism on one hand and Arab Zionism on the other, and the founding of a new state on an old nation. Some extremists draw their inspiration from movements that fall short of terrorism but can help to support it. One example is that of the Jewish terrorists who want to liberate holy places and shrines from the infidel and stake their claim to lands because there—according to tradition—their "nation" was "born," a view sponsored by the Gush Emunim who seek to annex the West Bank. (Judea and Samaria representing the "cradle of Judaism.") Whatever its particular form, primordialism is always a revolution of the saints.

V. SOME COMMENTS
WITHOUT CONCLUSIONS

Just as there is no single cause of terrorism, so there can be no single cure. What this brief excursion into different aspects of terrorism suggests is that if terrorists are terrible oversimplifiers, those who must respond to them must not be. The solutions cannot help being complex. One danger is from the professionals, particularly because of their preoccupation with techniques, both those used by terrorists and those necessary to neutralize them. The narrow view obscures the larger picture. Moreover, the institutionalization of antiterrorism is dangerous because it has its own dynamic, posing threats to democratic principles in the name of protecting them.

For a good many intellectuals on the left, the preoccupation with the negative side of society and the pathologies—while it has stimulated some of the best thinking we have, and the shrewdest theories about how to put things right—has few solutions for today's complexities. To replace theories with liberating violence is doubly irresponsible. It makes action a substitute for principled thought. It violates the very basis of intellectual life itself.

As for the different expressions of terrorism, left, right, and primordial, each is quite different. But all are nourished by the same grievances: marginalization, dispossession, displacement. Terrorism is always aimed at repossession—of the self and the society—by those whose alternatives are in short supply. The left projects outcomes that it claims accord with history. The right emphasizes will, especially the will of the elite and the exceptional figure. Primordialism is a claim to a lost patrimony. Whatever their expressions, none can exist without larger clienteles who provide support groups and public sympathy. While the state must take measures to protect society from terrorism, in the main it is toward the elimination of these clienteles that government policy ought to be directed.

The redirection of public support is only possible where a government is able to listen, to observe, and to understand. Such public sensibilities are difficult enough to realize in the rough and tumble of ordinary politics. They are far more difficult to observe when government is being attacked and the state is the target of abuse. To read violence as a social text, and act accordingly, is the best line of defense a democratic society has, given a little luck and some political intelligence.

NOTE

1. Quoted from *Le Monde*, 1 January 1985.

9

NOTES ON THE UNDERGROUND
Left Violence and the National State[1]

Terrorism is just one more thing the state may have to contend with. But it will pass, and the state will live on. Yet, there is a difference between crisis as such and terrorism, for terrorism aims not only to overthrow the state as it is, but to convert ordinary problems into something larger. Terrorists seek to demonstrate that the ordinary business of coping, the capacity of government to conduct the business of the day, is done so at the expense of some large, disadvantaged section of society—a class, an ethnic group, a religious body. By doing so, terrorism has as its aim the accomplishment of some practical end by extraordinary means. It is not an interest group gone wild. Rather, it seeks to raise matters of principle so fundamental that they will discredit the moral basis of the state as constituted. To do that, ordinary crises need to be converted from wearisome tribulations into convergent contradictions in which the state is rendered impotent. If this occurs, or better, such a convergence of predicaments can be made into what we will call a "disjunctive moment," terrorism will increase, spread, and get of hand, and even the most strongly armed state, if it loses its legitimacy, will fail. (Iran is a case in point.)

Normalcy must be transformed into heightened danger. The more visible the police guards, strong points, checkpoints, watchtowers, and armored cars, the better. They are signs of the weakness of the state rather than its strength, testimonials to the success of terrorists.

Terrorists, of course, differ in purpose, object, and tactics, but they share a common aim—to make the state morally bankrupt and to generate a disjunctive moment. After that the picture blurs. Some terrorists seek to abolish the state, such as modern anarchists or anarcho-syndicalists. Others want to reconstitute it, to make it into an instrument of revolution from above, like modern neo-Leninists who favor government by the dictatorship of the proletariat (and emphasize the former term over the latter). Still others seek to create new ethnically or linguistically based territorial units carved out of old ones.

Whatever their purposes, the common target of terrorism is the legitimacy of the state as given, its moral credibility. Hence, the means, no matter how repugnant, represent judgments. Their outrageousness is a measure of moral seriousness. The more outrageous they are, the more they paralyze public activity, forcing suspension of the public's judgment, atrophying normal support, and turning citizens into bystanders rather than participants. The first act in the social drama of terrorism is a psychological battle of the good against the evil, the oldest human story of all. But the second act is to create a disjunctive moment in which crises seem to converge. It is the second stage that terrorism rarely accomplishes.

However, if there are chronic difficulties that the state as we know it cannot resolve, if disjunctive moments are more likely than we believed possible, if, indeed, the state is no longer able to cope as well as in the past, we may be facing a new condition, one in which it is not terrorism that produces a crisis in the state, but rather the crisis of the state that produces terrorism. That possibility must be confronted. But before doing so, let us examine terrorism itself, and particularly terrorism on the left.

TERRORISM AND ITS EXPLANATIONS

Perhaps no topic has been subjected to as many ad hoc explanations as terrorism. Certain facts are well known. The incidence of violent acts against the state has been escalating steadily since 1968, although unevenly, in bursts, and in different forms. Hijacking is out of favor; murder is in.[2] Killing selected individual targets or maiming (society maims, therefore maim the maimers) have become more favored tactics.

There is also a consensus, indeed it is almost dogma, that, especially in Germany and Japan, terrorists tend to come from middle-class families. A high proportion are the sons and daughters of professionals, teachers, and other respected representatives of the bourgeoisie. Women are prominent among them. In Italy, militant terrorists include in their ranks the educated children of working-class Southerners who moved north to work in industry (educational reforms having made it possible for almost anyone who completes secondary school to go on to university). In general, modern terrorists have intellectual interests, are employed in jobs that are bureaucratic, and when they live underground, it is on monies gathered by a variety of means, from bank robbery to ransom.[3]

A few more commonplace characteristics of specifically Left terrorism generally: elite terrorists from better educated and intellectually sophisticated families tend to stand apart from, and distrust the inconsistancy of, their radical militant peers, especially at universities; at the same time they use the universities as their main recruiting ground. The most violent terrorists in Germany and Japan are among the "best" products of the democratic state but hate its meritocratic aspects with an abiding passion. Liberal scholars, who considered democracy as the solution, not the cause, of such behavior, find terrorism of this sort so revolting that they prefer to put it down to individual causes and personal pathologies. There is the great desire to normalize violence by making terrorism plausible, the rational explaining the real.

In general, most of us believe that terrorism breaks out in rashes or erupts like boils on the body politic; while there are many reasons for each outbreak and many explanations, most make sense but none are crucial. The few general characteristics that can be described do not stand up well under close inspection, such as the notion that violence is a function of rising expectations. It may, in fact, also be a function of declining expectations. But so far there has been little discussion of how the meaning of terrorism changes with circumstances, or of the effects of different types: for example, *primordial*—racial, ethnic, linguistic, or religious movements; or *radical*—Marxist, anarchist, and other Left extremist movements or their equivalents on the Right.

Even less examined is what one can speak of as a "dialectic" of terrorism, especially of the Left-Right variety. For example, in Argentina, Brazil, and elsewhere in Latin America, and in Italy as well, left-wing and right-wing terrorism have literally fed off each other, and in the first two instances, terrorists have been divided between antistate versus pro-state forces, the right wing being in part sponsored by the police. Left terrorists also try to create a military dialectic by transforming terrorism into civil war and provoking the government into using military forces, a situation that not only dignifies the struggle but gives terrorists the status of soldiers. Finally, such a dialectic recaptures symbolically all previous "just" wars on behalf of the oppressed, making heroes of terrorists, justifying their acts, and ensuring that they will become the text of history rather than merely a footnote to it.

These are only a few of the considerations appropriate to an understanding of the phenomenon. Here, however, I want to make a more selective argument, namely that terrorism and the state are reciprocals of each other. The state is the target of terrorists. Terrorism defines the limits of the state. This suggests that those defending the state are normal citizens while those seeking to destroy it are not. But what is surprising is the extent to which those on each side are "normal." Indeed, if terrorism is in some part an aberration, it is one to which many quite ordinary people are prone. (One of the more remarkable findings of interviews with terrorists is how normal they seem to be, at least to outward appearances.)

What makes a difference is, first, the particular events that embroil individuals in terrorism, and second, once involvement has occurred, the discipline, the militancy, indeed, the life of the cell that nurtures terrorism by creating a singular network. Then, the terrorist discovers how to transform ordinariness into an "event" in one explosive moment. He lives on sudden action—the "coiled snake syndrome."

This leaves open the question of when terrorism is effective apart from the short-lived publicity. (The public can adjust to terrorism as just another form of "natural" catastrophe.) What is required is a "disjunctive moment," a multiple crisis in society that reveals to a significant segment of the population that the society can delegitimize the state, with violent acts exposing the government as a losing proposition—its control, its grip, and its rationality all withering away.

Jürgen Habermas describes the components of such a disjunctive moment as a composite set of crisis tendencies as follows:

Crisis Tendencies	Proposed Explanations
Economic	(a) The state apparatus acts as unconscious naturelike executive organ of the law of value
	(b) The state apparatus acts as planning agent of united "monopoly capital"
Rationality	(c) Destruction of administrative rationality occurs through opposed interests of individual capitalists

	(d)	The production (necessary for continued existence) of structures foreign to the system
Legitimation	(e)	Systematic limits
	(f)	Unintended sides effects (politicization) of administrative interventions in the cultural tradition
Motivation	(g)	Erosion of traditions important for continued existence
	(h)	Overloading through universalistic value-systems ("new" needs)[4]

When these conditions are present, terrorism can be effective. It is not necessary to agree specifically with Habermas's formulation. The point is that, if terrorist acts can combine these crises into a single disjunctive moment, government can only fail. Fortunately, such moments are rare, and few terrorist movements have the leadership and organization to produce such crises. Indeed, where the crisis potential is high, as in Italy, the state is preserved not because of its power, but because of the weakness of terrorism as a political method.

ORIGINS AND LEADERS

If leaders of terrorist movements are as diverse a lot as political rulers, pious, foolish, and presumptuous, the issues they fasten on are deadly serious. What distinguishes terrorists is their special ability to identify crisis issues and to use them against the state.

The most interesting trace their pedigree to the French Revolution, particularly its Left, late-Jacobin phase; their putative ancestor Rousseau had numerous followers in France and elsewhere, especially those who upgraded the romantic spirit and made it into a solidaristic bond, like Fichte with his *Bund der freien Manner*.[5]

Farther back we find the Anabaptists, led by the redoubtable Thomas Muntzer and his teacher Niklas Storch, whose millenarian visions were embodied in the League of the Elect that was to bring the New Jerusalem.[6] The antecedents of terrorism even include social banditry, the Mafia, and mob action, with leaders striking heroic poses, Robin

Hood adventurers who favored the poor for personal gain.[7] All these used violence instrumentally. But in terrorism, violence is a modern Archimedes lever, not only enabling a small group to effect vast changes in government, but the terrorism of means becomes intrinsic to the terrorism of ends. The millennium, redemption, and the New Jerusalem become essential parts of an unfulfilled mission of historical necessity.

To understand this more fully, it will be helpful to consider the lives of the prototypes of Left terrorism, Filippo Michele Buonarroti (1761-1837), the "first professional revolutionist," as Elizabeth Eisenstein calls him, and Francois-Noel Babeuf (1760-1797), the first radical victim of the Thermidor. Babeuf was the premier communist. He differed from his fellow Jacobins over the issue of property. He regarded the abolition of private property as essential to the abolition of classes that divided people into the exploited and the exploiting. He formed a radical society that included Buonarroti among its members, the *Club de Pantheon,* whose purpose was open agitation. It had a journal, the *Tribun de Peuple.* The society was driven underground by the government in 1798, and a secret directorate was established that included Babeuf, Buonarroti, Sylvain Marechal, Felix Le Peletier, and A. A. Darthe. Its aim was to rally the people of Paris to bring about the overthrow of the established government. Babeuf, leader of the peasantry, became an organizer of the *sansculottes.*[8]

Babeuf not only founded Jacobin communism, he claimed it as the only proper legacy of the revolution of 1793.[9] (As such, it endures as a form of romantic realism, retrieved, or rather resurrected, as in the Commune of 1848, 1870, or even the October Revolution.) By challenging the state's claim to a monopoly of violence, he gave violence itself a revolutionary meaning. "When a nation takes the path of revolution it does so because the . . . masses realize that their situation is intolerable, they feel impelled to change it, and they are drawn into motion for that end."[10] His slogan, "The aim of the society is the welfare of its members," became an inspiration for Lenin.

> Every step in the development of the revolution rouses the masses and attracts them with uncontrollable force precisely to the side of the revolutionary programme as the only programme that consistently and logically expresses their *real, vital interests* . . . the destructive force of the revolution is to a considerable extent dependent on how . . . deep [was] the contradiction between the antediluvian "superstructure" and the living forces of the present epoch.[11]

Here we begin to see the relevance of Habermas's crises. For Babeuf, when the "superstructures" of the French state became not only obsolete but oppressive, terror became its equal and opposite force. Then, no matter how weak and halting in the first instance, terror was decisive. Thus terrorism came to have meaning as history and as revolution, one that finally smashes the bourgeoisie. This still remains the hallmark of Left terrorism, indeed, the militant Left generally. As Lenin added, one cannot ally with the bourgeoisie; to ally with it will produce "an abortion, a half-baked mongrel revolution." Of course, Leninism is not simply Babeuvism upgraded. "We shall . . . have, if we live to see a real victory of the revolution, new methods of action, corresponding to the character and aims of the working-class party that is striving for a complete socialist revolution."[12] But there is a sense in which for neo-Leninists, like the Red Brigades, the real ancestor is Babeuf.

If Babeuf is the original communist terrorist, Buonarroti is the prototypical anarchist. He regarded the French Revolution as a new beginning, a disjunctive moment, a new phase in human history, with terror a kind of essential human energy, a force for the good. He was a patrician of a distinguished family, skilled in mathematics; an urbane and talented literary scholar; and a musician, a role he used to disguise a career punctuated by "arrests, expulsions, deportations and imprisonments."[13] For him, the underground life consisted of lodges, circles, and codes, a life of permanent danger. There he organized cells and was a follower of the *Illuminati*, a radical freemasonry, and the *Sublimes Maitres Parfaits* (whose supreme command was called the Grand Firmament). His closest friends were the Babeuvists. The French Committee of Public Safety was his model of the state.

Buonarroti represented the revolutionary in romantic guise; his bravado was often carried to the point of foolhardiness, and he was no doubt a bit mad. He had a mania for rules, statutes, ciphers, and certificates, and thought "that in order to form an efficient and permanent political association, men needed to be tied to each other by signs, by mysteries that flatter their sense of self-importance" (p. 53). Nor is this different today, for the terrorist cell has its own "legalism," rituals, and texts.

Buonarroti's own text was an unoriginal combination of the writings of Rousseau and Robespierre. It specified the enemies and manipulated friends, and created a myth out of Babeuf's conspiracy. He venerated Jacobins for causing

the Constitution of 1793 to be replaced (until the peace) by a form of authority which preserved to those who had commenced the great work, the power of completing it and substituted at once, for the hazards of an open war against the intestine foes of liberty, prompt and legal means of reducing them to impotence. This form was called the *revolutionary Government* and had for its object complete redemption, had not subsequent events destroyed all (p. 71).

He thus legitimized violence and made hortatory visions into a romantic accomplishment. The revolutionary government changed the vast population, once the sport of voluptuousness, cupidity, levity, and presumption, from hedonists to zealots content with "demanding for their all, bread, steel, equality" (p. 70).

For the first time, terror forced people to be free, a necessary purge to save them from themselves. The public could not be expected to govern until it was free of all corruptions of the old regime. So Buonarroti exploited the idea of being linked to a select and secret company that "set in motion the Great Revolution, and bequeathed to surviving colleagues the task of bringing it to its ultimate conclusion" (p. 44).

He saw the significance of the cell as the revolutionary nucleus. Whatever its impact at the time, the *Sublimes Maitres Parfaits* was an institution which set a pattern for the future, especially in the strict authority which characterized its relations with similar societies outside its auspices, in the techniques of infiltration and creation of "fronts," and in its cosmopolitan composition. Like the secret societies formed later by Blanqui and Bakunin, it might be described as the private army of the professional revolutionist who created it, who wielded it, and whose life span set a term to its existence. As a product of romantic individualism, it set a vogue that would pass with the Romantic generation itself, but traces of Buonarroti's fine Italian hand would remain in the tactics adopted by the more impersonal conspiratorial organizations that followed (p. 49).

THE CELL AS
REVOLUTIONARY NUCLEUS

Modern terrorists retrieve Babeuf and Buonarroti both as leaders or organizers when they act out in their own lives equivalent metaphors of an underground and violent struggle. Both countenanced terror as the way to freedom, and bequeathed to Left revolutionaries their legacy of legitimate violence. Both believed in the cell as a unique organism, an autonomous life-giving, life-sustaining unit whose violence punishes those living aboveground in their crimes.

In opposition to the cell is the society. Against the revolution is the state. Against the conspiratorial movement is the aboveground cell of the prison and the classroom, both opposite to the clandestine life, both weights of the institutional apparatus applied to the limbs and minds of a citizenry captive and without rights. The life of the revolutionary thus depends on the death of society. Revolutionary punishment is reserved for the crime of the state. The purpose of violent and clandestine acts is to separate society from state and to redeem the former by destroying the latter.

While life "below" is very different from that "above," not much is known about it. Do recruits have feelings of impotence or intellectual inadequacy for which violence compensates (as Stalin is supposed to have felt when he went underground as a party terrorist, compared to Trotsky, who went abroad)?[14] Does a high degree of personal guilt, transmuted into passionate hatred, distinguish such people? Do they act out early social betrayal after previous attempts to "act" fail? Do some make a fetish of violence and its instruments?[15] Are violent acts proof of authenticity? Does the willingness to engage in outrageous attack serve as a ritual transposition of previous shames? Do terrorists engage in competition with one another to take on the most visible dangers and risks? These questions have particular relevance to the xenophobic life of the cell when it has achieved total affiliation.

Moreover, with total affiliation comes the paradox of complete devotion and extreme wariness. Available evidence shows that even in the most disciplined cells there is much wavering between loyalty and suspicion. Everyone is potentially unreliable; thus members are continually tested for proof of loyalty or renewal as new initiatives inspire more terror-prone activities, which in turn reinforce or renew commitment. Although leaders operate within intensely personal networks of relationships, they are haunted by the possibility of informers and agents provocateurs. Meanings become peculiarly joined. Political acts of devotion reappear as shared sexuality. Self-accusation and vindications add to the internal torture. The occasional outrageous crime is both a demonstration of purity and commitment and a necessary catharsis. There is also a curiously abstract quality to such personalism that has long-range effects on the personality.

These and other factors are common to Left terrorism in particular. Connections between intimacy and discipline are crucial in each group. Freedom of action requires intimacy, obligation to a leader. But the leader is metonymic for the doctrine. If the cell is to be sufficiently tough to survive under any and all conditions, the individual must be entirely controlled. And the cell is everything. A biological metaphor that not only extends outward to society, it operates inwardly as well. Males and females not only manipulate weapons, but each other. The cell is subject to the same pressures and tensions that all biorelationships generate.

One can extend the metaphor. The cell is produced in a "culture" that provides virtually no initial warmth, moisture, or protection. It grows in dark places underground, shielded from the sun. Yet no matter how vulnerable and primitive a form of life, it must become the foundation of renewal. This simplest form of existence, capable of infinite growth and permutation, requires intimacy without a corrosive dependency. The cell is as independent as its members, for once they have been controlled by abstract personalism, the cell itself is as free as its members are collectively to act, depending on the quality of its leadership.

Finally, the power of abstract personalism is that of infinite regeneration. Thus this most primitive form of existence, cell *life*, becomes important, not as any particular cell, but as life itself. And if any member is destroyed, it does not matter much. Another will take his or her place.

The cell is the metaphor of the minimal life, the microunit of "deconstruction." Its aim is to reduce to impotence all remedial solutions and all *democratic* responses. Its tactics are to force liberals and communists to reveal their detente, to expose their common repressiveness.[16] From this standpoint, it matters little whether the enemy is the social welfare state or a state-capitalist bureaucracy.[17] The terrorist cell as a nucleus for the new society lives on the anticipation of the death of society.

The symbolism is cell versus superstructure. It is not individuals, who might indeed be quite likable fellows, who are destroyed, but roles— father, king, philosopher, scientist—all those who are part of an institutionalized network that controls, dominates, organizes, and mediates.

Destroying those who represent death in order to liberate life brings us face to face with chaos, the original condition of primitive myth. Transcending it is the necessary starting point for a new order, a new sequence of creation and redemption. Terrorism in its widest sense not only aims to destroy the state, but the place the state occupies as a rational center of modern life as well. Hence, terrorists can attach themselves to virtually any cause, giving voice to any nonsense, plausible or implausible, if it helps to contrast the wordlessness of violent death—which itself becomes a "language"—with the wordiness of a despised legalism. And the cell rejects the failures of previous revolutions; it carries no failures in its genes—only potentiality—despite its pedigree, and repudiates weariness of the kind that beset the radicals of 1968. Such terrorism also universalizes class war as war. (The Japanese Red Army proclaimed this when it announced the third world war had begun.) Hence, too, the cell as army or brigade. It uses such military labels to emphasize *class* war against a generalized middle class, and to radicalize the young to prevent their joining its ranks or becoming part of a technocratic elite. Most Left terrorists seek to mobilize workers and "marginals"—the unemployed and the unemployable—against the social welfare state to bring down liberal-democracy with all its attendant evils, like the "culture of commodities," the "embourgeoisement" of the poor, the co-optation of radicals. But for hierarchy and hegemony to disappear there is need for extreme confrontation and the cooperation of terrorist forces—PLO, the Japanese Red army, Baader-Meinhof. Such radical and primordial combinations use appropriate tactics to randomize the structure of the most highly organized industrial states, and relies on a moral, universalizing, "expropriated" class (the marginals, the functionally superfluous, the proletariat) and a radical intelligentsia (teachers, lawyers, psychiatrists, and others) to intervene between society and the radical underground, the cell creating its own clientele and its diaspora.

TYPES OF TERRORISM

Having speculated about its diverse origins and some of the characteristics of its cellular life, I want now to distinguish between different kinds of terrorism, emphasizing not only their differences, but also what they have in common. It should also be clear that by terrorism I mean the use of illegal violence to gain political ends.[18] Violent tactics alone do not define terrorism. These have always been available, and in one form or another have been used throughout history. Terrorism begins with acts of violence designed to "violate" the legal basis of the state and to injure permanently the instruments on which it depends for order. Left terrorism is against the democratic state, root and branch, and not in favor of rectifying its errors. It has no specific target save the bourgeois state itself. Its definable aims are general—to promote fear, to demoralize, and to randomize social life—but its means are specific—attacking selective targets, real and symbolic. Its purpose is to discredit the state in the eyes of a large sector of society, to cause people to lose faith in the efficacy of democratic solutions, and to become so frightened, they will be a pushover for a militant takeover.

By restricting terrorism to violent acts directed against the state, we not only identify it as a specific phenomenon, but also emphasize the acts of individuals or small groups as opposed to the mass mobilization of cadres or armies, as in a revolutionary war. This definition also implies that acts of terrorism are in some way a retaliation for some presumed violation to a pariah class or other wronged or exploited population. Terrorism thus by its very existence serves as its own explanation for what is wrong with the state, a self-evident morality that legitimizes violence.

This also distinguishes between terrorism and the use of terror by the state. The state can be only metaphorically terrorist, although the terror it uses may be real enough. In modern society, even where the state itself is hated, it is widely accepted that implicit in the very definition of "state" is its legitimate monopoly of violence. This explains why terrorism against the democratic state is so explicitly against it *as a state*, for it can be said only for a democratic state that the use of its coercive power is a truly legitimate way to exercise force. Hence, acts of violence against the democratic state must discredit the state while validating violence. And violence must be restricted in form: it does not include looting or mob action that break out during blackouts or in race riots, because these not only lack specificity but also political ends.

Ends, then, are important. (Robbery, assault, and other violent acts, or random murders are more characteristic of right-wing than left-wing terrorism.) To deserve punishment, the victim must in some recognized way represent a hegemonic class or an organ of state power. Distinctions must be made between the goals and tactics of the kidnappers of Hans Martin Schleyer or the executioners of Aldo Moro, on one hand, and fascist bands like *Ordine Nuovo, Avenguardia Mazionale*, and other such extreme right-wing groups, on the other.[19]

But there is a second kind of terrorism that may not be directed against the state per se, what we can call primordial terrorism, that is based on ethnicity, religion, race, language, or nationality—a kind associated with nationalism, independent states, revolutions, or civil wars—including terrorism that seeks to break up the domination of a large state over a particular religious, ethnic, linguistic, or racial minority. Among these are Basque, IRA, PLO, and other primordial terrorist organizations whose successes have brought on virtual civil war.[20]

Radical terrorism can easily join with primordial terrorism, so much so that it may be difficult to separate one from the other. Nor can a clear line be drawn between Left or Right primordial or radical terrorism. For a time it was not at all clear whether the Italian Red Brigades were fascist or Leninist (especially where radical Left extremists were anti-Semitic in the classic sense of the term and took pains to ally themselves with the PLO). In turn, primordialism can be Left and Right at the same time. Arafat, for example, despite his "moderate" position among the Palestinians, is a primordial terrorist seeking a national state. He virtually venerates violent means in terms redolent of fascism while supporting Left programs in the name of Arab socialism. Such affinities make possible many alliances and frangible coalitions that defy ordinary detection or control.

A Typology of Terrorism

	Predominantly Left	Predominantly Right
Primordial terrorism	Fanonism	IRA
	Basque nationalism	Kurdish nationalism
Radical terrorism	Japanese Red Army Red Brigades Baader-Meinhof	Neo-Nazism Neo-fascism Third World equivalents like the Chilean FNPL *(Frente Nacionalista Patria* *y Libertad)*

Of the various types of terrorism, Fanonism was perhaps the most explicit about the need for violence as a creative and cathartic transformation (that is, the act of violence itself is the emotional transformation). The purpose of violence is to create a revolutionary consciousness to enable the damned and the wretched by the same acts to become the redeemers of themselves and their colonial masters.[21] Other movements of a primordial kind may employ specific radical goals, such as the Popular Front for the Liberation of Palestine (in contrast to *Al Fatah*).

Under the general heading of Left forms of radical terrorism are the various Leninist, anarchist, and anarcho-syndicalist groups, including those that have roots in Cheism, Maoism, and Left Trotskyism.[22]

Finally, under the general heading of right-wing radical terrorism are neo-Nazism and neofascism and their counterparts in Argentina, Spain, and Italy, where they attack the state *and* the Left, as, for example, the bombing of Communist headquarters by *Anno Zero, Fenice,* and *Avanguardia Nazionale.*[23]

For all groups, the use of terror is both instrumental and consummatory. Instrumental terror is used tactically against carefully selected targets; consummatory violence is an end in itself, an expression of fundamental commitment, a form of discipline where outrageous action is counterposed to the outrageousness of the state. Each act is a metaphorical opposite of the other, with terrorists and police engaged in a ballet of action and counteraction, a ritual killing on both sides.

TERROR ON THE LEFT

A special characteristic of Left terrorism is that it requires a theory: the closer terrorism is to Marxism, the more theory becomes crucial; the more one moves away from Marxism toward anarchism, the more the act speaks for itself. Thus there is a spectrum of Left radical terrorism with neo-Leninism at one pole and anarcho-syndicalism at the other. (The Italian Red Brigades represent the neo-Leninist; the various "autonomia" groups, the more anarchist.) The more neo-Leninist the group, the more important the text, and the greater the tendency to split or break up over dogma. In contrast, the more anarchic groups are more personalistic. Leadership, money, and love affairs all play more important roles.

For neo-Leninists, discipline is crucial. As individuals, they reject the world in order to rise above it. Their conduct should be exemplary, their lives inspiring a new standard of revolutionary conduct. A disciplined radical consciousness is essential to extend proletarian class war. But the proletariat remains the universalizing class. (For anarchists, the lumpens occupy the place of honor.) The purpose of a Marxist theory is to show when terror can and cannot be used: if it cannot serve the interests of the working class, it cannot universalize its gains; it should not be used indiscriminately; and its final acts must be politically self-liquidating. The particular arguments take off from the debates of Kautsky, Lenin,

Trotsky, and Luxemburg, all of whom linked terrorism to the state under capitalism.

Kautsky ruled out terrorism in all forms as antithetical to both socialism and democracy.[24] Lenin maintained that Kautsky, by using a classic liberal definition of democracy and in its nineteenth century individualistic form, had "deliberately" misinterpreted the distinctions Marx had made between the state and forms of society and argued for state terror, but not for terrorism as such. It is permissible, indeed necessary, for the dictatorship of the proletariat to engage in violence against the hegemonic power of the bourgeoisie in a society in which the laws of governments are instruments of that power. Parliamentary democracy or bourgeois democracy only serves the interests of the bourgeoisie.[25] However, violence against the exploiter is a precondition of the successful revolutionary transition to socialism. In theory, there is appropriate terror and inappropriate terror. Trotsky believed that "terror can be very efficient against a reactionary class which does not want to leave the scene of operations," but he reserves its use until after a successful revolution.[26]

The original debates centered on whether the revolutionary state *should* apply terror. Neo-Leninists today argue that, if the world of the clandestine cell is the mirror image of the aboveground cell, it is, in effect, an underground government, an incipient revolutionary dictatorship of the proletariat; thus violence is appropriate before the revolution has been realized. Terrorism applies, then, before and after the revolution. This is Curcio's answer to the Communist party and to Euro-Communism. Terror alone, and of the most directed kind, will enable the revolutionary neo-Leninist party to go aboveground.[27] This expanded use of terror is an amendment to classic Leninist theory, one in accord with history, an instrument to be used as a substitute for revolution itself.[28] And if it should prove to be the case that the revolutionary dictatorship of the proletariat is rejected by Communist parties, they become part of the state and thus legitimate objects of neo-Leninist violence.

Left terrorism employs a theory that suits its purposes and justifies the necessity for acts by persons against persons, supremely situational acts that violate the essential space, the privacy, and the "property" that mark the individual off from his neighbor. Each act serves as a lesson, an instruction, and thus every nuance must be exploited. Hence, the exceptional importance attached to a captive's voice heard pleading or the public distribution of his photograph, taken as in a police photo. The "prisoner of war" must look broken, his eyes showing fear and vulnerability, his expression passive and defeated, his hair disheveled. But it should also show the face as guilty and villainous, so that the captive is no longer perceived as a real person but merely an impotent representative of his class. All his other characteristics must disappear, and the record made to show he is guilty of crimes, regardless of his virtues, private or public. The prisoner as "filler of the role" is killer of the dream of the bourgeoisie. Hence, too, the impersonality of his murder, the body dumped out of a car or left in a hotel room or a gutter, whatever represents the ultimate gesture of contempt.

But contempt alone is dangerous, "Rightist"—what is required is a durable ethic embodied in a class ally. A good theory provides both, and provides as well a basis for connections—to a proletariat, to primordial movements like the PLO. (The Palestinians, displaced from their land, are the new pariahs, the new marginals of the world, the objects of a new racism, of religious discrimination. In their redemption lies the mutual acceptance of all by all.)

By applying theory to violence in this way, the most rationalistic and primordial affiliations can be combined. Behind the theory is drama and myth. Terrorist acts enable individuals to figure in events like legendary heroes. Metaphors penetrate the "theory," giving it symbolic density. The job of the leader is to wound the social body, to make it "bleed," to interrupt all those preferred reciprocities of role and class that compose the interstices of power—technical, political, and bureaucratic. Each event—kidnapping an individual, murdering a child, capturing a jet plane loaded with "successful" tourists ("oppressors" condemned to death by the price of a ticket)—is carried out alone or with one or two others, using a relatively primitive technology of grenades, pistols, or rifles against heavily armed gendarmes and tanks); using, in effect, their own bodies, their youth and vitality, to confront the great sagging, tired bulk, the bureaucratic weight of organized society. Monteneros, Red Brigades, Red Army factions, armed Proletarian Nuclei, the Baader-Meinhof—whatever their names, each implies militant collective action. Each offers a theory plus itself as the unit of social restructuring (such as the Italian Worker's Autonomy) or the agent of permanent revolution (such as the Italian *Lotta Continua*). All oppose Euro-Communism as too bourgeois, the U.S.S.R. as too state-capitalist, and bureaucratic and social democracy as corrupt and exploitative. All have elements of fascism in the "vitalism." [29]

THE DISJUNCTIVE MOMENT

If any or all of these different kinds of terrorism are to be regarded as significant, it cannot be because terrorism, owing to its appeal to those profoundly opposed to the status quo, creates more terrorism, although this may be important. In the final analysis, it is the state that creates the conditions for its own downfall; terrorism can only be an efficient cause. Learning to live with terrorism will make it as ordinary as crime or poverty or undisposed garbage. Analysis of terrorism is its own form of social restorative. Sufficiently studied, nothing is shocking. Indeed, examining terrorism has become a growth industry. Psychologists, police chiefs, specialists on violence and deviant behavior, counter-intelligence professionals—all are busy helping to repair the damage and restore "rationality" by determining causes. When terrorism becomes commonplace, it can be accepted. Accommodating to terrorism is certainly one solution.

But such solutions do not always work. A historical parallel might be useful. Compare the "revolutions" of 1848 and 1968. Both failed. The failure of the first stimulated anarchist and other terrorists movements in Europe, particularly in Russia. The failure of 1968 left a small but powerful residue of intensely passionate political doctrinaires and exalted revolutionaries.

In Tsarist Russia, where there was no possibility of liberal political reform, the most totalistic solutions seemed plausible. A sophisticated elite, unable to mobilize a backward peasant society, and subject to the most rigorous terror, turned to romantic populism and the extreme response. Acts of violence were interpreted as proof of personal strength, of purity of emotions, and of inner liberation from political fear. One remained a Hegelian, albeit a tormented one, to preserve transcendence as the only possible solution. One knew what to be against with all one's might, not only the despotic state, or the depraved state of society, but weak-kneed liberals,

especially those who begin revolutions and then try to extinguish their consequences, who at the same time undermine the older order and cling to it, light the fuse and try to stop the explosion, who are frightened by the emergence of that mythical creature, their "unfortunate brother, cheated of his inheritance," the worker, the proletarian who demands his rights, who does not realize that while he has nothing to lose, the intellectual may lose everything.[30]

Transpose to 1968. Replace the despotic state with the corrupt bourgeoisie, the peasantry with the lower middle class. Add a new Hegelianism, revive Gramsci, Lukacs, and an overdetermined Althusser. Once again the enemy is the despised liberals and their democracy. Nor are orthodox socialists or communists immune, for they, like liberals, have betrayed the workers. One is against the social welfare state or the totalitarian Stalinist. It is all the same. And just as the liberals in Russia betrayed the working class by fleeing abroad, erstwhile militants of 1968 voted with their feet into the ranks of the bourgeoisie, the administrative service, or the Communist party. Like old soldiers reveling in chic nostalgia, they live off radical capital, the "coupon-clippers" of the Left. Terrorists, looking back in anger on the generation of 1968, see it as all self-indulgence and no self-discipline. Its revolutionary "production" consisted of nothing but theater and text, books attacking books, pamphlets attacking pamphlets, a battle that only mystifies as its revolutionary rhetoric exhausts. Radical terrorism is the hard core Left after the meltdown of a protorevolutionary generation.

But such parallels do not really work. More structured explanations of terrorism, more linked to development and its discontents, are required. Indeed, we live in a world that promises more and delivers less all the time. And if ours no longer is an age of development, a decline in belief in it prejudices normal solutions. Add to this the doubt that science in the service of mankind will live up to its promise. Accept that poor states will continue to be plundered by rich ones; that the prospects for man will worsen rather than improve, that the golden age of man's intelligence is gone, turning our patrimony into a wasteland; and that perversity rules through a privileged caste, reducing most of the world's population to a condition of marginality—and we confront the disjunctive moment, the specter of superfluous man, an insight so Gothic as to make terror seem like a natural outcome.

Indeed, if "curvilinear growth," with its booms and busts, is associated with crisis and the modern state, this, then, is the general predicament to address. If under these economic conditions the state appears powerless to prevent a new class struggle between the functionally superfluous (the unemployed and unemployable) and the functionally significant (those whose skills are essential to the economy); and if functional polarization and expanding marginality—overwhelming numbers on the dole—increase the social overhead costs of society while productivity declines, one can expect, in due course, new opportunities for modern versions of Babeuf and Buonarroti. How easy it is to revive the radical Jacobin tradition is the basic lesson of the 1960s. What may save us is the gap between the disjunctive moment, in which all crises are blended into one grand overdetermined condition, and how well terrorism has prospered; for to seize the moment, terrorism requires an appropriately cosmocratic leadership, an effectively organized cell structure, the support of a more general radical elite, and a significant degree of identification with a class, either proletariat or marginal. If all are in place, terrorism will have a chance in precisely those liberal and democratic states that fail to cope with the negative consequences of curvilinear growth, the inequities that result from it, and the deepening of public uncertainty to the point where primal chaos looms large as the common personal predicament. Then the primitive solution, the mythic one, becomes plausible as a substitute for more realistic solutions. Then terrorism can grind bureaucratic institutional facilities to a halt, invade the psychic space of individuals, explode the natural meeting grounds of people, and ensure that the conventional mediating institutions work at cross-purposes.

The success of terrorism thus needs to be measured by the impotence of government, but also in the degree that people withdraw from society, retreat from civility, and avoid public space, to live instead with alarm systems, dogs, and guns, all instruments of a society where every man is for himself, the hermetic society, a society without trust or obligation—a condition under which cell life prospers. Under such circumstances, too, a wider clientele makes itself available to terrorists. Those more sympathetic to violence place themselves in the service of moral or redemptive ends, and liberal solutions and democratic means become so discredited, they appear as part of the problem, not the solution. The whole distance between 1848 and 1968, and between the French Revolution and the Russian, is the idea that the pluralist state cannot transcend its developmental predicaments, and in the act of trying, will only make matters worse.

TERRORISM AND THE STATE

This brings us to the relationship between terrorism and the state itself. Braudel, in his massive work on the Mediterranean, showed how, at the moment of their apotheosis at the end of the sixteenth century, the city-states of Europe—Venice, Genoa, Ragusa, and Florence—had already passed their prime. For a brief moment, the Spanish Empire replaced them as an instrument of world commerce, trade, and political power. But the latter, unable to extricate itself from an oppressive mercantilism and an excessive political centralization, became vulnerable to the twin forces of capitalism and the territorial state that replaced both the city-state and the mercantilist empire.[31]

Today we question whether the nation-state is not similarly endangered. Increasingly fragile, overextended, and unable to handle the major problems and predicaments of curvilinear growth, the fundamental question is whether old forms of political jurisdictions are becoming outmoded and new responses to functional needs required. Although it seems unwise and premature to prophesy the death of the nation-state or to suggest that it is likely to wither away now or in the near future, it is an open question whether it can endure intact in the face of chronic difficulties. If violence remains endemic, some new forms, new jurisdictions, indeed, new solutions will be necessary. These are matters we have barely begun to confront.

Moreover, we are theoretically and politically unprepared for the uncertainties and contradictions of modern social life. The alliance between growth and government that has prevailed within a context of nationalism, the connection between territoriality and democracy, and the notion of government as a system of public rationalities and choices can no longer be taken for granted. In this sense, development generates not only economic crises, but the crisis of rationality and legitimation suggested by Habermas as well. If these lead, in addition, to a crisis of motivation, the decline of the nation-state and terrorism may easily become mutually precipitating. Only a small number of violent people are necessary for terrorism to become effective. Not surprising, it is in Italy—where the effects of curvilinearity are already visible, and government falters—that terrorism is having its greatest success, so much so that even bands of 25 or 50 terrorists, if they are sufficiently determined and shrewd, can give the impression that society is falling apart.[32] When curvilinear growth helps stimulate terrorism, terrorism itself creates additional terrorism and the support of an outside clientele, a body of sympathizers who share the aims and purposes, if not the method, of the terrorists. Add a diaspora, an external population more "terrorist than the terrorists," as in the case of the Provisional IRA or the PLO or the FALN, and a given terrorist movement can depend not only on its own internal activities, but on the support of groups abroad as well, a worldwide collaboration, a clandestine "pluralism," an underground of coalitions that can share any occasion and use one another's facilities and good offices.

If, on the other hand, governments can prevent functional polarization and a decline in productivity, and the social overhead can be paid for by the general population without too much sacrifice, opportunities for terrorism will remain episodic and irregular.

This suggests that if we are to avoid disjunctive moments and overdetermined crises, neither the liberal social welfare state nor its Marxist alternative will do. Each is a better critique of the other than a solution. It may be that we need to think in terms of multiple jurisdictions and to reconsider whole constructions of territory and new concepts of governing them.

> Freedom, wherever it existed as a tangible reality, has always been spatially limited. This is especially clear for the greatest and most elementary of all negative liberties, the freedom of movement; the borders of national territory or the walls of the city-state comprehended and protected a space in which men could move freely. [33]

It was the job of the liberal territorial state to add more positive liberties, and for this purpose, it enlarged its territories and jurisdictions. It may be that the lesson of both development and terrorism is that such jurisdictions and the forms that go with them now need more substantial modification than we think. And if we resist the kind of projective consideration these require and cling to more modest solutions, it might be useful to recall Marx's comment that

> the more powerful a state and hence the more political a nation, the less inclined it is to explain the general principle governing social ills and to seek out their causes by looking at the principle of the state, i.e., at the actual organization of society of which the state is the active, self-conscious and official expression. Political understanding is just political understanding because its thought does not transcend the limits of politics. The sharper and livelier it is the more incapable is it of comprehending social problems. [34]

The large question posed by terrorism is whether the state as we know it is becoming obsolete.

NOTES

1. The research on which this chapter was based was made possible through a grant from the Concilium on International and Area Studies at Yale University.

2. For example, the Japanese Red Army has apparently rejected hijacking as a tactic. A Japanese Red Army terrorist wrote in an open letter to his mother from Beirut in 1978 (published in a radical but ephemeral journal) that, after the Dacca incident, his faction had decided such tactics were wrong. Too many innocent people were endangered, taking away from the seriousness of the Red Army's purpose, that is, to show that terrorism was a necessary response to the "official" terrorism of the state.

3. Michael Baumann, "The Mind of a German Terrorist," *Encounter* 61, no. 3 (April 1978).

4. Jürgen Habermas, *Legitimation Crisis* (Boston: Beacon, 1975), p. 50.

5. Peter C. Ludz, "Ideology, Intellectuals and Organization: The Question of Their Interrelation in Early 19th Century Society," *Social Research* 44, no. 2(Summer 1977), pp. 260-307.

6. Norman Cohn, *The Pursuit of the Millennium* (New York: Harper, 1961).

7. E. J. Hobsbawm, *Primitive Rebels* (Manchester: Manchester University Press, 1959). See also Anton Blok, *The Mafia of a Sicilian Village 1860-1960* (New York: Harper, 1975).

8. John Anthony Scott, *The Defense of Graccbus Babeuf* (Amherst: University of Massachusetts Press, 1967), p. 7. The sansculottes were "men who possess, as it were, no means of livelihood other than the work of their hands." See also Robert Legrand, *Babeuf et ses compagnons de route* (Paris: Société des Etudes Robesieristes, 1981).

9. J. L. Talmon, *The Origins of Totalitarian Democracy* (London: Seeker and Warburg, 1955).

10. Ibid., p. 44.

11. V. I. Lenin, *Two Tactics of Social-Democracy in the Democratic Revolution* (New York: International Publishers, 1935), p. 47, emphasis added. This pamphlet was written in July 1905, after the split with the Mensheviks.

12. Ibid., p. 48.

13. Elizabeth L. Eisenstein, *The First Professional Revolutionist: Filippe Michele Buonarroti (1761-1837)* (Cambridge, MA: Harvard University Press, 1959), p. 19. All subsequent quotations in this section are from Eisenstein.

14. Robert C. Tucker, *Stalin as Revolutionary* (New York: Norton, 1973), pp. 91-143.

15. Baumann, "The Mind of a German Terrorist": "Baader was a weapons maniac and later had almost a sexual relationship with pistols" (p. 82).

16. From an interview with Renato Curcioi's lawyer, 16 February 1978, Turin, Italy.

17. In the French election of March 1978, the extreme Left lumped centerist Raymond Burke, Jacques Chirac of neo-Gaullist right, Francois Mitterand of the Socialists, and Georges Marchais of the Communists all together, calling them "the gang of four." *New York Times,* 17 March 1978.

18. See Walter Laqueur, *Terrorism* (Boston: Little, Brown, 1977).

19. In the case of Moro, the "main aim was to eliminate the central figure of the system of mediation on which the delicate balance of Italian politics, including the shaky accords negotiated between Christian Democrats and Communists, depended. They intended to bring the hostage to trial as the symbol of their concept of an 'objective enemy,' and of themselves as agents duly appointed by history and invested with powers of life and death." Albert Ronchey, "Guns and Gray Matter: Terrorism in Italy," *Foreign Affairs* 57, no. 4 (Spring 1979), p. 826.

20. Conor Cruise O'Brien, *Herod, Reflections on Political Violence* (London: Hutchinson, 1978), pp. 57-81.

21. G. C. Grohs, "Frantz Fanon and the African Revolution," *Journal of Modern African Studies* 6, no. 4 (December 1968), pp. 543-56.

22. Daniel and Gabriel Cohn-Bendit, *Obsolete Communism, the Left Wing Alternative* (New York: McGraw-Hill, 1968).

23. Ronchey, "Guns and Gray Matter," p. 928.

24. Karl Kautsky, *The Dictatorship of the Proletariat* (Ann Arbor; University of Michigan Press, 1964), p. 4.

25. V. I. Lenin, *The Proletarian Revolution and the Renegade Kautsky* (Moscow: Foreign Languages, 1952), p. 48. "There can be no real actual equality until all possibility of the exploitation of one class by another has been totally destroyed."

26. Leon Trotsky, *Terrorism and Communism* (Ann Arbor: University of Michigan Press, 1961), pp. 58-59.

27. Ibid., p. 179.

28. A sophisticated attack against this view was made by Rosa Luxemburg. See *The Russian Revolution and Leninism or Marxism?* (Ann Arbor: University of Michigan Press, 1970), pp. 90-108.

29. G. P. Maximoff, *Bakunin* (New York: Free Press, 1953); Sam Dolgoff, *Bakunin on Anarchy* (New York: Knopf, 1973); and D. E. Apter, "The New Anarchism and the Old," in *Anarchism Today*, ed. D. E. Apter and James Joll (New York: Doubleday-Anchor Press, 1973).

30. Isaiah Berlin, "Herzen and Bakunin on Liberty," in *Russian Thinkers* (New York: Viking Press, 1978), p. 99.

31. Fernand Braudel, *The Mediterraneans* (New York: Harper & Row, 1972).

32. A January 17, 1978, Italian Communist Party (PCO) survey put the number of underground guerrillas at 700 to 800 and the extremists living on the fringe of legality—and often armed—at about 10,000. According to an autobiographical account by the member of the Prima Linea faction published in the Italian weekly *Panorama*, the "combatants" number about 3000, or about the same as the number of Italian partisans who were active between September 1943 and March 1944. See Ronchey, "Guns and Gray Matter," p. 924. This says nothing of the large numbers of student and ex-student sympathizers and a wide circle of intellectuals, some of whom might be deeply involved on a sporadic or temporary basis, such as Professor Antonio Negri, a professor of political science at Padua University, or some of the sociology professors at Trento University who were teachers of Curcio and other Red Brigade leaders.

33. Hannah Arendt, *On Revolution* (New York: Viking, 1963), p. 279.

34. Karl Marx, "Critical Notes on the King of Prussia and Social Reform," in *Early Writings* (New York: Random House, 1975), pp. 412-13.

10

THE NEW MYTHO-LOGICS AND THE SPECTER OF SUPERFLUOUS MAN

It seems to be a lesson of history that the commonplace may be understood as a reduction of the exceptional, but that the exceptional can not be understood by amplifying the commonplace. Both logically and causally the exceptional is crucial, because it introduces (however strange that may sound) the more comprehensive category.

Edgar Windt
Pagan Mysteries in the Renaissance

There is, of course, myth as we really know it: a recounted tale beyond living memory in which the whimsical, the magical, and the fantastic remain persuasive. Antique myths are easier to recognize than contemporary ones. The distancing of time and the ritualization of recounting allow them to keep their shape and make for a certain definiteness. Old myths stand up remarkably well.

Modern myths are part of ideology and often the hidden part. Modern ideologies consist of various mixtures of myth and theory, which, over time, have a tendency to be transformed into each other. Myth becomes theory; theory myth. Theory provides a logic for the resolving of certain political problems and their projective transcendence. Myth does the same by means of "overcomings" that defy ordinary logic. Political myth is a tale of overcomings embodied in the history and culture of a particular state. Political theory is a logic of power, rulers and ruled, for which a particular state is the surrogate.

The combination, *mytho-logics* synthesized as doctrine and represented by the state, forms out of disjunctive moments. Such moments represent one way exceptional meaning is created out of events, and exceptional political events out of meaning. Each represents a double break. One from a previous political economy. Another from a previous episteme.[1] So considered, every state is a history of its own becoming, a sequence of events, a narrative consisting of metaphors—noble lies. Each state is also a text, a set of metonymies for a logic of which it is a surrogate—noble truths. It is in the intertwining of noble lies and truths that the state takes on exceptional power. It is in disjunctive moments that old mytho-logics are destroyed and new one created.

Such moments are rare and can be typically represented by three basic but overlapping situations: the founding of new states, revolutionary transformations, and theocratic redemptions.[2] How myth combines with theory to form a new mytho-logics is a first concern in this discussion. How contradictions of modern development generate disjunction is a second.

I. THE PROBLEMATIQUE

The problems we want to analyze are as follows: (1) to locate and identify modern myth in the context of developmental theory (the mystical kernel in the rationalistic shell), (2) to examine how modern mytho-logics form out of particular experiences in order to (3) link these experiences to structural changes induced by developmental innovation in modern industrial societies (changes not anticipated or mediated within the context of the conventional developmental theories themselves).

We will consider the state as the chief venue for political mythologics, particularly as each represents, stands in for, or serves as a surrogate for, a particular developmental theory. The most important theories contain projective teleologies for which the state is the chosen instrument, that is, the liberal state vis-à-vis liberal theory, the Marxist state vis-à-vis Marxist theories. Each surrogate state creates a corpus, amendments, exegesis, the elaboration of which is built up in a structure of exceptional texts complete with specialists who interpret them.

The text also realizes as theory a myth of its own becoming. This characteristically includes the events or struggles that enabled a state to become a surrogate. Each surrogate state treats its theory as truth, a statement of reality. The result is the reinforcement of the mythic by the theoretical, and in reinforcement of the theoretical by the mythic. Two boundaries are created. One is against internal and doctrinal opposition. The other is against other states' surrogates for antagonistic theories. So considered, the actual terrain becomes sacred, physical boundaries inviolate, and the state immortal. To the extent that universality is claimed, a state can both establish and play by its own rules, an exceptionalism that in the modern world can easily lead to a balance of terror.

With terror and morality representing the outer limits of the state, mytho-logics is the defining order within them. Text is structure, events are narrative. The state provides the dramatic frame. Citizens are spectators. It is bit like Barthes's description of a wrestling match. The wrestlers are in full view of the audience. Unequal in power, what they act out in their trials and tests of strength are morality plays of good versus evil. As well, in the actual movements of the match (straining bodies, bulging muscles, sweat, grunts, the thuds of the slammed torso, the grimace over the twisted leg) physical responses are created among the spectators. They sit in the dark while the wrestlers are drenched in white light. Their attention is riveted on the actors. Their darkness is both private and public, private in their feelings, public in their reactions. So terror and morality are scaled down and rendered as spectacle.[3]

With the state as the stage, everything is scaled up. (So too the spectator may become the victim.) This is what prevents normal politics from becoming utterly boring. Drama and ritual are essential. But they need to follow a script. Moreover, as with other spectacles, they require audience complicity, a certain neutralization. This is so even with the most important choices a society can make, the changing of the guard, the circulation of elites. Here we find political drama at its most expressive. Take, for example, elections. What we witness are periodic and highly ritualized spectacles of combat that reenact and celebrate both the myths and theories of the state and enable an exchange of power without an exchange of meaning.

Like with a wrestling match (or a ballet), randomness is abhorred, but uncertainty is essential. One watches to see how each contender will perform and what strategy will win. Each political trial, each campaign, each selection of a leader is an event in a history true to its script. And each script embodies the memory of its previous metaphors in retrieving, echoing past trials, episodes, and personalities. But as well each is a moment of invention, redefining and projecting some moral teleology within the larger frame.[4]

These, the smaller punctuation marks of ordinary politics, celebrate and prevent disjunctive moments. The changing of the guard, the play of party politics and personalities, the shifting of alliances and support, these are among the uncertainties that give life to politics and for the most part reinforce rather than erode. But there are circumstances when the shape of time changes. Uncertainty gains on resolution. Larger events beyond control begin to impinge. Violence, external threats, the danger of chaos and randomness, breakdown, these are the conditions under which normal politics is transformed.

Then the audience may join in, the political stage becomes an arena for contending and polarized forces. When struggle becomes the order of the day, we confront the larger punctuation marks of history, disjunctions, the moments when a new mytho-logics forms, and the illusion of the fresh start, renewal. These are moments when interpretation and reinterpretation constitute the ultimate political acts, the last instance when the way to change the world is to reinterpret it.

Which brings us back to the analysis of myth. As part of an interpretive system, it is equivalent in structure to theory (although different in form and content) and in the last analysis intrinsic to the language of the state.[5] As for the state itself, the question is under what circumstances do normal politics and a mytho-logics of continuity lend themselves to antimyths and antitheories, that is, to the conditions where disjunctions open up opportunities for new and drastically different interpretive propensities.

Put into social terms, disjunctions occur under the following circumstances: when social polarization leads to conflict rather than mediation, government policy exacerbates rather than ameliorates, and differences over the script lead to random violence, extrainstitutional protest, terrorism, and ultimately revolution. Polarization in this sense involves states versus antistates in concrete struggles the object of which is to create or prevent a disjunctive moment.

Having said this, we can now address a central political problem. These pathologies are growing in most modern industrial democracies. They are increasingly difficult to mediate and contain. There are reversals occurring for which we have no good texts. For example, the liberal corpus is based on a notion of an expanding and generalized middle class, a party of stability and civility at the political center of society, a productive and functional class providing the means for a mediating social policy within the context of the welfare or social democratic state. It gives the lie to Marxist theories of polarization, and stands as an example of how they are wrong, mythic, and dangerous. Polarization may occur in developing countries, especially those of Africa and Latin America where development has been the occasion for polarization between elites and marginals, urban and rural, leading to conditions of instability, citizen protest, terrorism, military coups, guerrilla warfare, revolution. But these are the natural result of innovation and development the negative effects of which include dispossession, displacement, marginalization, both in rural and urban areas. If violence and unrest are the indicators of where the state leaves off, the phenomenon is temporary. One must hold the line and prevent Marxist alternatives to come to power.

But what if precisely the effects of innovation and development are to create polarization and, with it, dispossession, displacement, and marginalization within the liberal and democratic industrial state? What if polarization occurs within a generalized middle, producing tendencies toward a social bifurcation that begin to change how we interpret and assess our own predicaments? What if theory becomes mythic, and myth theoretical? What if political leaders, insisting on original positions as a kind of purity, reinvoke the past, its sufferings and accomplishments, and treat them as obligatory commitments? And if the results are more violence, extrainstitutional protest, terrorism—do not terror and morality define each other?

II. POLITICAL MYTHS

If so, these are the occasions for myths, old and new. In normal politics, they not only perform political functions but there is sheer pleasure in having them as well. They vary in intensity and consequence from society to society, place to place, and time to time. Each state is in part a uniquely mythic entity, a retrievable mythic inheritance, the power of which Plato called its noble lie. It constitutes a lexical code.

But let confrontation challenge that code then watch out for the consequences so triggered. For insofar as political myths are in a sense political deep structures consisting of tales of the fabulous, narratives of past overcoming (and as such obligations), confrontation can lead to polarization. Then, in a context of events and living experiences, political myths can as easily take an antistate as a pro-state form, leading to a dialectic of violence in which myth is involved in the establishment and disestablishment of authority, the acceptance or rejection of the social contract. Behind every constitution there is a specific narrative of a mythic struggle testifying to the authenticity of the text as a grand design. So too, violence and death are testimonials of their transformation into the oppressive. The dialectic in modern states is as follows: myth goes hand in hand with theory, narrative with text, the "magical" with the "scientific." So the state is caught between authority and violence-prone antistate movements.[6]

III. SEARCH FOR A METHOD

We turn now to the question of how to study political myth itself. We have already indicated that antique versions are easier to examine than contemporary ones. Moreover, scholarly interest in them goes back a long way. Codified in various versions, inscribed by travelers, writers with a taste for the exotic, or anthropologists, myths have been subjects of more or less exhaustive analysis. They have been compared according to their structure, for the stories they tell, and also for their omissions, their silences. They can be seen as venues for randomness or regarded as systems of ordering relationships. We can make use of a good deal of the work done on antique myths for the analysis of modern mytho-logics. We can accept the fact that myth and theory are two sides of the same ordering process revealing—if one likes—the common and deep structures of mind itself. But myth and theory are not the same thing. And their combination can be terrifying.[7]

Contributors to the study of myth include such diverse figures as Evans-Pritchard, Turner, Douglas, Leach, and a host of others. More referential, however, for our purposes are Lévi-Strauss, Barthes, Althusser, Foucault, Ricoeur, and Bourdieu. Each offers an instruction if not a precise method for the study of myth. Lévi-Strauss, for example, provides an originating and negative pole for ordering social relationships in the incest taboo out of which principles of social and ideational reciprocities and exchanges evolve, each refracting the other according to a structure of binaries, a parallel to linguistics. Barthes offers the treatment of myth as semiotic field, a language or discourse. Althusser suggests the principle of the overdetermined or disjunctive moment, a fusion of base and superstructure. Foucault suggests how the principle of marginality leads to inversion and reveals institutional and representational repression. Ricoeur suggests the idea of moral overcoming, a metaphorical distancing from a negative pole; whereas Bourdieu suggests the connections between mental and physical space as terrain and jurisdiction.

All these contribute useful ingredients for the study of political mytho-logics in which to construct a framework for examining mythologics in modern industrial states. None of the above theories were designed for this purpose. All can be made useful because they enable us to take a next step that goes perhaps from Kant to Cassirer to all those others who considered myth as a kind of primitive reason, capable of being refurbished, but fundamentally primordial, antirationalistic, and certainly dangerous.[8] Myths can certainly have these effects, but we consider them as more complex, intrinsic to the interpretative process, and as interpretation performative as well.[9]

Hence, we will need to pay attention to a framework for a theory, rather than a theory itself, a prolegomena perhaps, and attempt to combine some of the contributions of the above authors so that they can apply to political situations, and most particularly those in which structural contradictions of development lead to social conflict or what some call contestation. Such a framework must also suggest how it is that theory can establish conditions for myth and myth for theory. The contradiction we consider most crucial in the specific analysis that follows we will call functional polarization. The emphasis is close to Marx, a method of contradiction, and not to functionalism, a method of equilibrium. The process originally described by Marx is here borrowed, renamed, and treated differently in terms of its dynamics.[10] Functional polarization represents a social tendency opposite to that emphasized in liberal theory, that is, the generalization of the middle sectors as a result of development. That is, we want to show that the developmental tendencies that produced a generalized middle, crucial to liberal notions of balance, mediation, and democracy, have begun to change to produce what might be called a polarization tendency. Not a class struggle, it nevertheless produces random violence, extrainstitutional protest, and, at the extreme, terrorism. It involves dispossession, displacement, and marginalization. These are some of the conditions under which modern myths are produced, myths for and against the state. Our concern is with the latter, and above all with what we will call the "specter" of superfluous man.

The terrain for the consideration of such matters is the state. We consider the state as a membership unit, that is, a concrete entity. But it is also a mental construct. As the latter, each state embodies a retrievable mythic inheritance, the memory of its remarkable and logic defying previous episodes of overcoming that serve as a sediment deposited on the present, a layering, and an endowment. Containing nostalgia, the recollection of previous sacrifice helps define present obligation. In turn, theory is embedded in the representation of the state, projective, logical, and teleological. It defines a negative pole and provides a method and an instruction for transcending it. Liberalism and Marxism in various versions and mixtures are examples of such theoretical systems. Each offers a complete corpus, a language, and a method of closure, as well as an interpretative frame for the analysis of events. Both have the capacity to produce myths, especially in the context of their surrogate states, just as such myths of the state help create the space for them as theories. This is why we said earlier that, in the context of the state, mytho-logics constitutes both an interpretative field and a system of obligation.

Indeed, obligation works only when myth and theory reinforce each other and together offer explanations of what is in order to demonstrate what ought to be. This is not to suggest some easy functional connection or automatic relationship between a political economy of needs and a set of mythological "interests."

If not, this leaves us with the question of how mytho-logics works as an interpretive field. Unfortunately, definitive answers are not forthcoming. However, the writers indicated above can offer a few guidelines. As an interpretive field, mytho-logics consists of narratives and texts, retrievals and projections, metaphors and metonymies. With these as the main components of mythic and theoretical languages, we can perhaps explore the role of the ideational in the context of contradictions and disjunctions with which the state must deal. Doing so will highlight some of the possible connections between a political economy base, the state as an arena for confrontation, and what Jameson and others have called the "explosion of the superstructures."[11]

An interpretive field is consolidated during disjunctive moments, that is, how the polis (or the state) was founded, how it was transformed, and how redeemed (from the faults and lapses of its members). Each has a fairly representative structure. In all, there is a successful demonstration of special powers: the intercession of the divine, the intervention of a magisterial figure, the architectonic vision of a cosmocrat.

Historical events give particularity to these configurations. For each state, there is a kind of chaos overcome by a new order, the physical world may be overcome by the human. Feast replaces famine, abundance poverty, light darkness, and, of course, good triumphs over evil. Each disjunctive occasion then represents overcoming and transcendence, that is, from a lower to a higher condition, from a worse to a better. Here theory blends with myth to locate, identify, and particularize.

To do this, theory must be transformed into myth and myth into theory linguistically. That is, the logical and textual mode is translated into the narrative, and the narrative translated into the textual. But conditions require a special cadre—priests, diviners, interpreters, exigetes. Normally, too, one central voice or figure transcends the others, a chosen figure, a vehicle capable of speaking for others, or translating. In some communities, such a figure may be worshipped as half man and half god, offering the possibility of creation, immortality, redemption.[12]

He may be an Odysseus figure who, exiled, deprived of his patrimony, stripped of honor, becomes one of the fallen mighty. So the deposed father or the king suffers a negative inversion—a wanderer, disguised, despised, and dispossessed, but who in a second and positive inversion will triumph. Gaining a unique wisdom from his trials, he overcomes impossible obstacles. He perseveres no matter how much suffering is involved. Eventually, fate is won over through the knowledge so won with difficulty. In the return there is a struggle, the patrimony is reclaimed. Peace, justice, and stability follow.

Of course, not even an Odysseus does all this on his own. He needs loyal followers who also are purified by suffering. Persecution at the hands of the authorities or usurpers turn them into an elect, perhaps a holy band, certainly disciples. They have special insight. They see the future as it is intended to work.

Such narratives occur when theory becomes myth. Whether we deal with an Odysseus or some universalized or secular version of Anabaptism, variations on these themes are embedded in the history of a state. Disjunctions, past or future, provide the specific context for reinterpretation.

Myths of foundings, transformations, and redemptions, whether represented in recognizable myths or embedded in accounts of developmental states, correspond to Plato's noble lie, they establish the conditions for affiliation, loyalty, identity, and logical necessity. Such myths of disjunction are the foundation points for all states. They constitute originating events. They define negative and positive poles. They represent points of structural departure for reciprocities and exchanges, most particularly the relations between rulers and ruled.

But more, these mythic disjunctions provide ingredients for a mythic language, including signs, codes, traces, multiple signifiers, metaphors, and metonymies.

But how and in what ways does a mytho-logics actually form? A good deal of present analysis has employed linguistic and semiotic models, both in the social sciences and in literary analysis. There is the use of syntagmatic chains and metonymies, narratives and metaphors. Some articulate the internal structure of myth and emphasize the connections between addressee and addresser. Others regard myth as a kind of semiotic mobilization, language, or discourse, what Barthes has called a "logothetic."[13] Whatever the preferred terms, their political effect is to come down on one side or the other of a disjunctive moment, either as a distance from a negative pole, or to achieve a positive one, defining what is to be overcome in the first instance and realizing it in full in the second.

To analyze them, we will use the ingredients of the discussion so far. Put together as a framework, the outline looks as follows:

Disjunctive Moments
(foundings, transformations, and redemptions)

Participants	Episodes	Metaphor	Metonymy	Consequences
	1			
	2			
	3			
INTERPRETATION	NARRATIVE OF STRUGGLE	MORAL ARCHITECTURE	LOGIC OF NECESSITY	MYTHOLOGIC

The emphasis is ahistorical. But to explain how myth is formed out of events, one needs to put sequence into a frame of history, to combine the syntagmatic with the paradigmatic, contiguity and similarity, especially in the history that people experience in contemporary events. For the study of contemporary myth, one must stand Lévi-Strauss on his head.

IV. POLITICAL DISJUNCTIONS

The framework outlined above begins with contenders and events and leads to an interpretive field, a mytho-logics the elements of which form out of experience, with their own narrative and logic, the necessity of which makes them "exceptional" in Windt's sense of the term. What makes for the exceptional is the disjunctive moment. Representing a double overcoming, there is a break in the discourse arising out of new interpretations of a more general contradiction, and a program of overcoming or going from the negative pole to the teleological intention. When this double overcoming obtains, we can say that a mytho-logics is radical whatever its specific content, that is, radical in terms of the state.

Spectators, citizens, participants, are forced to take sides, to line up on one side or another (neutrality is itself a position), according to some social fault line. Events of confrontation take on metaphorical and metonymical significance. Sequence is then interpretation. Narrative and text combine, reinforcing each other.

Familiar examples include nationalist movements in which militants successfully mobilize against colonial governments. The "disjunction" is the handing over of power. The mythic side will ordinarily include metaphors of birth, sexuality, a release of new energy, a surge of vitalism. The old is not only to be swept away. The new, which realizes the programmatic ideals of remarkable leaders who articulate in texts the logical and projective principles to be achieved, defines the transcending project as a sequence of metonymies, some accomplished, others representing the unfinished task.

After the struggle and the triumph (the unique endeavors of a population succeeding to their unity), there is the celebration, rebirth, a new beginning. There is the sacred moment, the handing over or seizure of power, the lighting of a flame to celebrate immortality, and the impregnation of the political body by the sexed and immortal figure of the founder, the phallocratic impulse realized.

Similarly with revolutions. The great ones are embedded in historical consciousness. Their surrogate states are examples of the laws of developmental processes working their way toward the more just society. Their leaders are cosmocrats whose transforming deeds are testimonial to the superiority of their ideas. They leave behind a body of texts to be reinterpreted as both votive and instructional activities. The leaders' remains tend to be embalmed in crypts.[14]

With transformational disjunctions, it is the last who become first. The marginals inherit the patrimony. The text is transformed. The text may be a political economy. It may be theocratic. In the language of the seventeenth-century, biblical texts became revolutionary; a liturgical translation occurred in which the same mythic stories that served the forces of order now worked to undermine them. So history is expressed as a kind of mystical moral power, the power of the oppressed, the marginalized, an antihistory. There is "linguistic killing", denunciation. Individuals who personify the state may be signaled out for abuse. Grievance coalitions are formed. They articulate inequities. Moral outrage retrieves previous episodes, reviving them in the concreteness of confrontation or violence. The logic and universality of the events appear as political texts, tracts, and other documents. One thinks in this regard of the French revolution as protypical, complete with its polarizing internal struggle between liberals and Jacobins, and all the symbolic appurtenances of revolution, from heads on pikes to Jacobin caps, rituals and incantations, secular religious goals and the committees on public safety, a world truly turned upside down.[15]

Redemptions are becoming more familiar today, especially in the form of religious revivalism. But they have, of course, a long and fascinating semiotic history going back to the individualization of the collectivity in the human body itself. One can connect present-day redemptions to early Christian episodes in which anchorites used their bodies to symbolize lapses and corruptions from purity. Their own bodies became the visual negative poles, standing for stain, shame, and supplication in contrast to the purity of the body of Christ. Physical filth represented defilement, the corruption of the flesh.[16] Self-immolation, flagellation, mortification, provide the ways back to salvation, defining the distance to redemption.

Rejection, penance, and congregation result from such mythic retrieval and religious projection. The power of worship is the power of the performative. Retrievals are particularized in holy fragments, bones, pieces of hair. Projections in the poring over the text to seek its hidden meanings.

The collective version of such redemptive occasions would include such examples as the Iranian revolution. It uses Shiite mytho-logics to locate in the golden age of Islam an age of presumed unity and social puritanism and an appropriate political teleology. The redemption will occur through the power of the elect of god, the Ayatollahs and mullahs through whom truth speaks to power. They are god's chosen instruments. They will purify and privilege the dispossessed. They destroy heretics, pariahs, and polluters of inferior faiths (like the Bahai, or more secularized militants). Moral rearmament is the goal. To go backward is to go forward. To go forward is to restore the patrimony from the evildoers, the pariahs, and the backsliders—all those of little faith or the wrong one. It is mytho-logics as exorcism.

Disjunctions then are both endings and beginning points and, as such, mythical and theoretical occasions. Each founding, transforming, or redeeming event embodies an original and projective design, the blueprint, for a political and collective overcoming by means of institutionalized and collective power. Each produces inversions and new reciprocities. Some are very well known, the purity of the thief, the last becoming first, the wisdom of the mad, the innocence of the wrongdoer.[17]

In recent times, it has been the failure of foundings, the weaknesses of new states to redeem their promissory notes, and, as well, the bureaucratization and authoritarianism of so many revolutions that have contributed to religious revivalism. If one side of the coin is the restoration of man's purity, sense of responsibility, and austerity, the other side is rituals of violence—linguistic killing leading to the real thing.

This brief excursion into disjunctions suggests the moments in which the mythic side of mytho-logics transforms experiences into a sequence, and sequence into a metaphorical history, that has little to do with historian's history. In the present context, congealing history as myth particularizes the state. It makes noble lies possible.

On the theoretical side, a developmental text enables the state to represent a logic of necessity. It is above all a claim to universality. The claim is hegemonic.

V. THE NEGATIVE POLE

This brings us back to the main problématique and the central question. What if, as a result of developmental changes, the modern state can no longer serve as the framework for the accomplishment of commonly accepted ends? What happens if, in the effort to promote more equity, justice, and material benefits, contradictions set in that have an opposite effect? What happens if, in a state in which development rationale and theories of development provide both the logic and the text on which the relations of rulers and ruled are based, it no longer can square the circle between theory and practice? What will happen to a state that, in trying to become more responsive to the welfare of its citizens, confronts declining resources? We have already suggested the answer, the elevation of myth within the framework of theory and the context of the surrogate state. It is in highly industrialized societies that this tendency is now beginning to occur.[18] That is the argument we now want to pursue.

Evidence is various. One indication is the extent to which extra-institutional protest and violence attack prevailing or conventional theories and create, out of events, their own mytho-logics; one that establishes a negative pole, defining a fault, that the state cannot or will not transcend or mediate. In social life, such a negative pole normally consists of three factors: dispossession (i.e., removal of a class of individuals from a patrimony), displacement (i.e., a loss in functional significance), and marginalization, the specter of superfluous man. In turn, the latter can be defined as those who remove more from the social product than they contribute to it. Polarization in this sense is between the functionally significant as defined by their contributions to developmental innovation including both design and technique, and the functionally superfluous whose contributions to the social product are negative (i.e., a tax on the rest of society.)

But there is a political side to the analysis. Isn't the emphasis on polarization similar to that described by Marx even if the variables leading to it and the classes representing it are different? Does this elevate the structure of the Marxian argument over the liberal one even while changing his special theses? The answer is yes and no. It is yes in the sense that one seeks for systemic contradictions. But it is no in the sense that the argument would include socialist societies as well as capitalist, and is pitched at the level of the state. And it is no in the sense that with today's social forces the struggle between proletarians and bourgeoisie is itself the mythic element in Marxism.

What are some of the implications of the present formulation? We have already suggested several. Liberal assumptions about the social consequences of growth do not work well enough. The generalized middle as an omnibus class is slowly being pulled in opposite directions, downward toward the negative pole, where life shows greater randomness and uncertainty, and upward to the more predictable circumstances of the functionally significant. The language at the bottom is more metaphorical, and at the top more metonymical. At the bottom it is situational. At the top it is abstract. A mytho-logics forms when those at the bottom conclude an alliance, "linguistic" and coalitional, with those at the top; between "situationists" and "abstractionists," creating a common language, one that embodies inversionary texts of the last—becoming first-variety, the negation of the negative pole, repossession.

Second, occasions for such a mytho-logics are increasingly found in specific events of confrontation between states and antistates, events that form a record, an account, a history of lived experiences in which conflict endows a specific locale with meaning. The site for such conflict becomes a mobilization space. As events occur, it becomes as well a semiotic space, symbolizing struggle between both sides, the forces of order confronting the forces of disorder, and, typically, the marginalized and their allies against the state. The former thus challenge authority, and, in seeking to overcome it, offer alternative solutions. Then the discourse is performative. It is storied, instructive, self-referential, self-isolating, articulating (creating its own signs), eudaemonistic, showing transcendence, the way to a higher order.[19]

We now want to use these ingredients along with narrative and text, metaphor and metonymy, myth and theory, marginalization, repossession and the overcoming project, in three examples. One was a theoretical project of breathtaking proportions, a script-myth there for the reinterpretation, but never realized in a surrogate state. It is Plato's *Republic*. Another, occurring at the beginning of the industrial revolution in England, and that, although it failed, has left a trace, a permanent mark in the form of an authentic radicalism that is embedded in contemporary radical politics. The other is taken from the most successful industrial society today, Japan, and retrieves a history of past grievances in a context of present confrontational events.

VI. THREE DISJUNCTIONS THAT FAILED

In all three, the state is a dramatic frame. All define citizens as spectators. Each attempts to transform them into participants. They focused attention, the one as text seeing objectivization, the others as objective situations seeking to realize their texts. All three are mythic as well. Plato's object is to build up the state and establish the proper conditions, mythic and theoretical, for its immortality. The others want to tear it down as it is constituted, overcome it, and transform it into something else. The first stands for the state as the chosen instrument of the functionally significant. The other stands for the marginalized, the dispossessed, the functionally superfluous. The first is magisterial. The other two develop new codes, indexes, linguistic traces, overtones, tropes that link the spectators to the contenders. Sensitized by combat, the discourse turns strident, a kind of screaming, symbolic obliteration, linguistic killing.

In the last two, we have concrete events. They occur in a "mobilization space." As confrontations occur, it also becomes a "semiotic space." In turn, this is "realized" when a moral architecture is translated into a physical one, of fortresses, huts, defensive perimeters, and other evidences of violent combat.

We turn now to the three examples. One is Plato's great classic model of mytho-logics. It failed to realize itself in a surrogate state. The second occurs at the beginning of modern or developmental history. The last is contemporary. Where the first is concerned with the power of a functional elite, the other two are concerned with displacement, marginalization, and the loss of power we call *functional polarization*.

First Plato. What he shows us is a mytho-logics as an act of deliberation, a creation. What is missing is a narrative of struggle. But the rest is there, moral architecture, logic of necessity, mytho-logics. It is the first example of its kind. Indeed, Plato is the first mytho-logician. As he tells a story, he weaves a spell. He includes the fabulous. But it is a "cold" story. There are no hot events.

The starting point is how individuals can be made conscious of the benefits of a particular kind of state, the reasons for being loyal to it, and ambitious for its prosperity. The noble lie is the instrumental precondition for the state as surrogate for a theory. The theory in turn has as its main object a rationale for a functional and hierarchical relationship between rulers and ruled. Those at the top are privileged by their ability and knowledge. These enable them to comprehend the language of forms, that is, a totalizing rationality that comprehends a unified theory of justice, the only condition under which the social contribution and performance of each class can be made to work for the general welfare.

But Plato does far more than establish conditions for the general welfare. He provides a dialectical epistemology. It is used as a method of discourse. Embedding its logic in a story, his myth in a text, truth emerges as power. To emphasize this kind of truth, he includes in the same text an easily recognizable myth, the "myth of Er." It stands in complete contrast to the logic. It is composed of magic, numerology, heavenly whorls, and salvational reward. It is not designed to convince a reader of the main text. It is designed to heighten the purity and clarity of the logical argument. Politics is one solution or the other. Yet Plato puts them together to remind us that rulers will need to rely on myth to convince and awe those lesser folk incapable of comprehending political philosophy and, therefore, accepting the privileged rule of the philosopher-kings, the functionally significant. Plato provides an instrumental theory of myth, within the framework of a double discourse.

If the text is a dialectical representation of a hierarchy of forms as a hierarchy of powers, the combination is a singularly transcending vision. On one hand, the proper polis is established, with boundaries and an inferred set of rules guaranteeing appropriate performance from each class according to its work. On the other hand, there is a revelatory mysticism, the final and redemptive refuge for dead souls.

The aim, a universal and timeless order, is entirely transcendental, a solution to the problem of decay (the decay of good political institutions when human behavior becomes perverse parallels the decay of the living body, hence, the redemption of the soul). Here too is the hero as Ur philosopher-king, the Socrates, the phenomenological "I," part legend and part history, part god and part man, the prototypical cosmocrat. So everything is in place: cosmocratic figure, political context (the state), intentionality (what to be against, what to be for), a dialectical logic (projection), a totalized goal (justice), mythic retrieval (narrative). All this in a text as delicious as it is beguiling, to be reinterpreted down through the ages. But as drama, discourse, language, it goes far beyond any functional or instrumental theory of the state.[20]

Plato's theory never occurred in objectified form. If it had, he would have created the first state properly surrogate for a theory. There were plenty of surrogate states in his day. But they were theocracies, surrogates for religions. (Indeed, it would have been difficult to find any other kind of state.) Today the most powerful states are surrogates for developmental theories, with all the totalizing, teleological, and, one might add, transcending implications that that implies.

Plato serves as a referent, not a pedigree. He provides a model for the knowing mind as authority. He is the original architect of a conscious mytho-logics. Since his time there have been many others. So indeed with developmental mytho-logics. The creation of texts designates, instructs, and provides intentionality. Liberalism, its texts, its surrogate states, its cosmocratic figures, is one example. Marxism and its equivalent ensemble is another. Both in the framework of a theory far more elaborated and formalized than Plato's create the language of mytho-logics.

Indeed, the common thread between his model and more modern concerns is the presentation of fault in a world of becoming, that is, institutionalized fault and human becoming. To find the appropriate institutional framework of politics is the Holy Grail of mytho-logics, a kind of "going," to use the term of Ricoeur, from man's perdition to his salvation.[21]

We turn now to the other two examples: seventeenth-century England and contemporary Japan. We only have space to describe them very impressionistically. The emphasis in the first instance is on marginalization. In the second, although marginalization is a central factor, we want to elaborate the way in which a mytho-logics is formed out of violent confrontational episodes. We will then turn our attention to contemporary polarization, marginalization, and the indicators we use for contradiction, random violence, extrainstitutional protest, and terrorism. The general context is "deindustrialization."[22]

Our first example is drawn from Christopher Hill's account of the Levellers, Diggers, Brownians, Ranters, and Fifth Monarchy men. We choose this case in part because it established an authentic radical tradition, a tradition that is periodically retrieved in a country where there remains a great deal of unfinished social business under conditions of apparently irreversible economic decline (despite, and some would say because of, massive changes brought about by a social democratic state). England, the country of the first industrialization, is now the example of the first deindustrialization.

The story is reasonably well-known. It is of people dispossessed, forced to become wanderers, hiding in forests, fens, and wastes. Hill describes how they become a pariah population abhorred by the rest of society and, as a consequence, marauding, violent. They took the land and dug in it, growing things in marginal land to show how it could become fertile. Creative and organic in symbolic impulse, they sent shock waves through society. Formed into resistance movements, they established armies. They proclaimed equality as the only viable justice. They defined private property as evil because it violated the canons of such justice. In short, they defined the social distance between themselves at the margin and those at the center in terms of an inversion, the closer to the center and thus to political and ecclesiastical power, the more corrupt. The necessary transformation was to exchange periphery and center, the last becoming first, the world turning upside down.[23] They used biblical text and language to project the logic of equality. They revived a golden English past, retrieving the tradition of an ancient and democratic England, but in a mythical context, as one of the lost tribes of Israel, pure, before being polluted by the Norman conquest. They looked ahead to a rural communism, the abolition of private property. The pamphlets and texts written by the Levellers and Diggers expropriated biblical language and with it the resonance of its liturgy as a logic of necessity. The previous orthodoxy became the violating heresy. Biblical myths became theoretical precepts, providing the logic of a new moral order. The texts not only provide the necessary translation but serve to define and exalt a membership. The tract "To Your Tents Oh Israel" is a call to arms for a new elect, its episcopacy. Through struggle, and the totalism of the disjunctive moment, the redeeming rabble would gain the seeing eye, and, grasping the totality of the social condition, seize power from the defenders of church and state. Each event became a specific metaphor in a narrative of events associated with struggle. And, equally, each event became a metonymy for a social, natural, and moral physics.

In the actual event, church and state won out. But the redeeming rabble nevertheless left its residue. Seeking the disjunctive moment, it claimed too much. The result was a revolution that failed, a revolution against private property and the state as the authority for it. What won was another revolution, for private property and the authority for it. But the first has left its trace, not least as it is embedded in the symbolism and ideology of those in contemporary England who, today's marginals, have become angry, truculent, and embittered as the deindustrialization process continues.

We turn now to another failed case, a particular movement in Japan. In this case too there is marginalization of a yeomanry, the sense of vanished security, self-respect, and the memory of a previous age of mutual respect within feudal obligation, a reciprocity of moral as well as economic order, and offering a symbolically dense inheritance.

There is no doubt about Japan as an economic success story. But our story is about what might be called the other side of Japan as number one. Although Japan has made a unique transition to a condition of high industrialization without suffering many of the difficulties of industrial societies such as England, nevertheless there have been social costs. Because the story already has been dealt with in depth, we will be very brief.[24] The Sanrizuka-Shibayama Hantai Domei or Anti-Airport League consisted of farmers fighting against the government and protesting the establishment of the New Tokyo International Airport in Japan. The movement has been going on for more than 25 years, during which time the airport has become the symbol of the state. The farmers, the enragées, have in effect been marginalized by government policy where once they were originally at the very center of their society. Joined by the representatives of 17 radical militant sects, the two groups have formed an alliance of the dispossessed. The farmers are old, veterans of World War II. The militants are young, many of them veterans, however, of the years of New Left confrontation, which began in the late 1950s.

Conflict began in 1965 when the Japanese government decided to construct the New Tokyo International Airport 66 kilometers from Tokyo. Farmers in the area protested and the site was moved to the Sanrizuka area, without consulting the farmers. The farmers, protesting unsuccessfully, tried to prevent the surveying of the land and construction of the airport. The latter was identified as a military airport and, in the context of the Vietnam war, this was taken seriously by groups protesting remilitarization, the revision of the U.S.-Japan treaty, the presence of American forces, the antinuclear movement, and a host of others. The airport came to represent capitalism and imperialism. The farmers, all engaged in small-scale agriculture, retrieved the past in terms of previous serf and peasant conflicts (the tradition of the warrior-peasant), landlord and tenant conflicts, and began challenging the state itself.

The militants, recalling a radical tradition that included earlier conflicts with industry and government and previous alliances with farmers going back to the origins of the radical movement itself around the turn of the century, saw their role as one of resistance to imperialism, bureaucracy, and the oppressive state. They built fortresses around the airport, isolating it and beleaguering it. Over the years, a series of pitched battles were fought between airport authorities and the Hantai Domei and its allies. Over the years, thousands of participants came from all over Japan. For the militants it was a mobilization space, a rallying point for a revolution that never came. For the farmers it was a digging in against marginalization, the marginalization of a way of life, as much as their own particular patrimonies.

The fighting, the violence, the interpretation of these within the context of a movement, created out of past experiences and present ones (and the sense of grievance as well), an effective and militant ideology that has helped keep the movement alive even though it can no longer hope to win. Each of the main battles became a metaphor and a metonymy. For example, when the first government surveyors entered the site, they were resisted violently, especially by the farm women who saw in it a form of rape. For militants it was a metonymy for state capitalism. A second event was the transfer of land owned by the imperial household to the airport authority, land so beautiful it was called the Barbizon of Japan. For farmers it was a betrayal, for militants an example of primitive accumulation. When the land was occupied by force, the ensuing battle was regarded as state violence against society by the farmers and as a class struggle by the militants. A second invasion meant death for the farmers and marginalization for the militants. Finally, in a last confrontation when militants destroyed the control tower of the airport, delaying its opening, this represented for the farmers a transcendence of the movement, and revolution for the militants.

The sequence of events constituted a narrative of the struggle. The sequence of metaphors constituted a moral architecture. The sequence of metonymies constituted a text. The consequences of episodes, metaphors, and metonymies were a retrieving and projecting mytho-logics, layered in terms of the following: the violation of local and private space, illegitimate conveyance, polarization, creation of an industrial reserve army, and the legitimization of violent struggle, a logic of necessity inside the mytho-logics, its performative side (see Figure 7.1 in Chapter 7).

VII. DEINDUSTRIALIZATION AND THE SPECTER OF SUPERFLUOUS MAN

The examples described above failed. But the first remains as the model mytho-logical statement. The others are small events—indeed, minor bits of antihistory. Yet, despite their relative insignificance, in their time they sent shock waves throughout their societies. Examples of what happens "developmentally" at the base, their importance for our purposes, is twofold. First, they represent a kind of "sedimentation." Each has left a historical trace. Each retrieved and was itself retrievable, footnotes that can become part of a text.

The latter two are examples of dispossession and displacement leading to marginalization—marginalization that led to polarization. The same phenomenon on a much more elaborate scale is what produces revolution.

In the case of England, the events described were the points of departure for an authentic and retrievable radical tradition. Moreover, just as these events took place in the first phase of English industrialization, so today equivalents can be found as England becomes the first case of deindustrialization and the wheel begins to turn full circle. Today the English manufacturing sector declines, and marginalization has occurred. Violence and confrontation have broken out. The radical inheritance is being retrieved. The mythic aspects of class conflict and historical episodes have begun to re-form. As conflict escalates against the state, the metonymies are those of class struggle.[25]

At the base is the lowest rate of productivity of any major industrial power. Along with declining productivity and the displacement of the manufacturing sector from labor- to capital-intensive forms of industry goes increasing unemployment, and increasing social overhead costs. The only way out is greater technological innovation, which is essential if productivity is to be increased. But the consequence is further displacement of manufacturing employment. Job creation cannot keep pace with displacement.[26] Transcending that is the theoretical "project."

A variety of scholars are now concerned with such matters. They share the following concerns: that rising social overhead costs cannot be mediated on a political level, that efforts to do so by innovation will lead to marginalization, and that marginalization will lead to polarization—society versus the state. These are conditions for disjunctive moments, random violence, extrainstitutional protests, terrorism, revolution.

One reason for their concern is that what was once the English disease is now much generalized. Most modern industrial states have run head on into what some writers have called the fiscal crisis of the modern state. It may lead to retrenchment, financial austerity, and what the French call modernization, laying off redundant workers in an effort to solve the fiscal crisis. Or, the state may intervene more directly in the productive process through a variety of devices including remilitarization, as in the United States. But either way, the state is in trouble. The more it intervenes in the productive process and takes responsibility for it, the more vulnerable it becomes for its failures. These are conditions under which mytho-logics prospers.[27]

The problem is enlarged if what begins as growing unemployment becomes converted to real marginality. Marginalization, as the term has been used so far, is a condition resulting from prolonged functional superfluousness. Marginals are people who not only do not contribute to the social product, they consume more than they produce. The more marginal, the more roleless, that is, they are deprived of virtually all the roles of which functioning society is composed. At the extreme, they are random actors. They constitute identifiable subcultures. Considered by the rest of the population as pariahs, morally and even perhaps biologically distinctive, they appear to be stained in some fundamental manner, perhaps defective in intelligence and certainly lacking in moral character. Their greatest crime is to be self-reproducing. They remain more or less permanently on the perimeters of society, the negative moral pole, a social disgrace.

Marginals are notoriously hard to organize. They define the limits of social obligation by the rest of society. They show where the state leaves off. On occasion, under the right conditions, they may define those limits in ways that can undermine society itself. Hence, the state tends to react vigorously against them and mobilize prevailing discrimination if it can, treating them as a tax on the rest of society.

When the unemployed become unemployable, and a pariah subculture emerges, we have the ingredients of a structural maladjustment for which solutions seem less and less likely within the resources of even the most powerful domestic economies. Nor is an expansion of manufactures likely to resolve the problem. If manufactures increase but employment continues to decline, marginalization will not be mediated.

To recapitulate, modernization as the term is being used today is a function of innovation, but innovation can lead to deindustrialization. In turn, if deindustrialization produces endemic marginalization, then the state is set for violence, the search for disjunctive moments, for a world turned upside down.

Pictures of the world in which immigrants set off to conquer new worlds, or came down from the highlands into the cities, or off the farms to seek urban employments, education, new opportunities for their young, are no longer accurate. The idea of the city itself as a place of civility, a center for the arts, of neighborhoods, does not extend to marginals. In turn, marginals make life in the city precarious for all. For the latter, especially those born into ghetto environments, the universe is one of high risk and vulnerability. People become gamblers not workers. The force of immediacy is overwhelming, and at a very early age. Sheer survival is a zero-sum game with death, with each person for his or her own self. Violence of all kinds is a more or less everyday occurrence, a commonplace. This may caricature many urban environments. But in the United States, in parts of France, in England (in immigrant communities or the poverty rows of Liverpool, the Clyde or

Glasgow), in New York and Chicago, what one sees is an enduring condition of functional superfluousness and with it the specter of superfluous man.

The liberal and social democratic response has been various, but mostly it has been to emphasize the need to retrain and educate, modernize, and innovate, hoping to expand opportunities. Increased social benefits to the marginalized plus investment, a kind of revisionist Keynesianism will presumably bring about necessary increases in productivity to stimulate growth and reemployment.

It is precisely this logic that is insufficiently realized in reality. Indeed, as the logic fails to work, the theories of industrial development, and the vast superstructure of knowledge, the corpus, the texts, the science of it, become increasingly mythic. One turns increasingly to medicine men in the form of political leaders, second-rate actors, iron ladies—preachers of the virtues of austerity who, however, make it more respectable to ignore the problem.

As for the problems themselves, there is no doubt that the absorption of marginals is a vastly underrated project. Moreover, if in trying to do something about it overhead costs continue to rise faster than increases in productivity, while the problem itself shows no signs of being alleviated, one runs the political risk of the increasingly alienated middle, itself vulnerable to downward as well as upward mobility. While innovation leads to new opportunities for a technologically sophisticated and educated functional elite, the latter is increasingly meritocratic and competitive. For those in the middle who fail to utilize the institutional instruments the state provides for self-improvement, downward mobility becomes a very real likelihood. As for most of the functionally superfluous, they are likely to reject precisely those facilities that might enable them to rise out of their condition, indeed, to destroy them, for they know in advance that the risk of failure is very high. They represent, for the rest of society, the negative pole, a blight on the society, pariahs, recognizable by self-perpetuating stigmata, ghettoized.

Indeed, there is a question here of the more general character. One might ask whether or not the conditions we think of as exclusive to marginality are not spreading. For many young people, including those not at all in a marginal condition, what was once a relatively predictable world has begun to dissolve. The relationship between knowledge and plan, work and achievement, investment and reward is becoming increasingly randomized in the event. Many people now suffer from some of the high risk, high uncertainty conditions of marginalism, without necessarily being in a marginal condition or confronting extreme violence. In contrast, those entering the ranks of the functional elites are among the best and the brightest. It is for them that policy and social system work best. For the designers, the rationality of the state makes the most sense. They are the principal beneficiaries of modernization. And if deindustrialization occurs, these are the people government turns to to rectify the situation.

This suggests that the class and social structure is changing in ways we do not fully understand. We think of classes as obsolete in the nineteenth-century sense of the term. Indeed, many would replace it with role, or network, or more simply a pluralism of group competition. Class implies cleavage when multiple affiliation is the rule. This may be true at one level while at another the polarization we describe occurs.

One truth does not necessarily drive out another. If, as this analysis suggests, modernization within a context of industrialization will lead to more marginalization and polarization tendencies, then the theories we have based on linear or unilinear progressions, and the connections between developmental logic and moral teleology, will no longer hold. The more the state tries to mediate contradictions developmentally, the more complex the problem becomes. The state also becomes more responsible for failure. A state of inadequate solutions is vulnerable indeed.

It is here that the mythic factor comes in. The state is more and more likely to cling tenaciously to its beliefs, its myths, and its theories. The more vulnerable from within, the more truculent abroad. The more the theory doesn't hold, the more imperial its claim. It depends more and more on its mythic retrievals. It converts myth into theory and theory into myth—the myth of the state. And it is myths of the state that require confrontational enemies, holy wars between the surrogates, between good and evil empires, led by stupid and foolish old men.

From a radical perspective, this is the starting point for revolutionary activity. Such polarization, if it continues, will reveal fundamental contradictions in the modern industrial state, especially the state that pretends to transcend class by entering directly into the productive process.[28] Moreover, this suggests that a conventional socialism is as obsolete in its solutions as a conventional liberalism. It is a more general problem and not at all limited to capitalist states.

No wonder that a good deal of modern radicalism fits into no convenient categories. The radical project can be left or right. It follows its own logic: to convert the disorganized into the organized. The extreme project is to convert the random violence of marginals into the moral justification for terrorism. The latter carries the logic to its extreme. Terrorism of this kind is a theory looking for a myth.[29] The mythic potentiality is in violence itself—and the disjunctive moments it produces.

More frequent is extrainstitutional protest of the kind described above. Violence occurs but its purpose is to mobilize rather than offend the public. It seeks to build coalitions and attract clienteles. To the degree that it is successful, the government must respond. If it does not (or more important if it cannot), then the conditions for more massive confrontations, more generalized violence, are in place, and, as well, the possibilities for disjunctive moments increase. So far nothing like this has happened in any Western industrial society. Perhaps the memories of fascism are a factor. Most people back away from disjunctive moments. They distrust its mytho-logics, fear randomness, disorder, and the erosion of authority. But especially among young people, the attractiveness of the antistate is there, under the surface. One should not dismiss the lessons of May 1968 (and its counterparts elsewhere) as some passing madness.[30]

But it is certainly true to say that for most people, marginals will not redeem the world—at least not as long as they remain beyond the pale. Indeed, the very notion of marginality is perceived in most societies as a matter of choice. Marginals are those who prefer to take away from society more than they contribute to the general wealth and prosperity. Hence, the need to seal them off in their ghettos, and within the self-perpetuating confines of their subcultures. Indeed, their moral claims seem to count for less, as time goes on, rather than more.

All this may be true in the short run. But if our analysis is correct and marginality leads to growing polarization, the problem will be seen as collective rather than individual, rooted in necessity rather than choice, and a new logic will follow. If those currently at the center of their societies become vulnerable, so the occasions for violence will increase.

All those failed disjunctive moments are potentially retrievable. They can provide an authentic inheritance for the antistate. Old myth and new theory, a new mytho-logics built around the specter of superfluous man—that is the possibility that needs to be confronted.

The question is whether or not a new mytho-logics will develop, and if it does, whether or not it will lead to a double polarization, at the base between the functionally superfluous and the functionally significant, and at the level of superstructure, between a mytho-logics of the antistate versus the superstate, the magical transcending force of myth taking over where more ordinary theories fail.

In turn, this question contains a larger one. It suggests that the state itself will be a less and less suitable framework for the resolution of the problems described. If not, is there a replacement? Are there more practical arrangements possible in which sovereignty erodes, new functional arrangements and jurisdictions become more possible, and the states become more like political parties? There are straws in the wind, no more. Certainly nothing like this is in sight. Indeed, we do not even have an appropriate language for considering such prospects. We confront instead the prospect of more retrieval and projection, more metaphor and metonymy, more political stridency and linguistic killing both within and without the state.

What then is the "new mytho-logics"? It is the total rationalistic inheritance of developmental theory, the liberal and Marxist epistemes embodied as doctrines in modern surrogate states. Not that either is wrong or right, but neither is right enough to provide programmatic guides to deal effectively with the developmental tendencies described above. They are beyond ordinary amendment and need to be replaced with epistemes more appropriate to today's conditions. To the extent that we bind ourselves to them in the face of growing evidence, they become mythic.

Moreover, the myths of the state—out of which all those unique ingredients come together to form a patrimony (accomplishment, obligation, and a political culture)—increasingly require a theory, one that will realize the past in new and different kinds of terrains, jurisdictions, and affiliations. So it is that theory creates myth and myths creates theory. Despite all the analysis of myth (or ideology for that matter), not much attention has been paid to these matters. Few efforts have been made to examine the state in these terms, to raise questions about sacred terrain, a mobilization space, a venue for the dramatistic (i.e., as something more than a boundary around needs and wants, distributions, costs and benefits). The state as surrogate for a theory is increasingly surrogate for new myths.

The three examples we used perhaps contain instructions. Plato's was a warning against what might be called the "things fall apart" syndrome, mytho-logics for the state. The English and Japanese cases represented what can be called the "world turned upside down" syndrome, a mytho-logics against the state.

In terms of our discussion, each poses certain questions: Can multiple affiliations transcend the state and erode noble lies? Will sovereignty be diluted? Will regional and other commitments be allowed to increase at the expense of coventional national interests? Are there better ways to organize innovation, ways that reduce marginality rather than enlarge it. Indeed, can marginals be made productive? Can we rid ourselves of the specter of superfluous man, and not only within modern industrial states but, equally important, in modernizing ones where the problems are overwhelming?

To all these questions, good answers are lacking. We suggest them as an agenda for political analysis. Of course, one thing should be very clear. One will never eliminate mytho-logics. Nor would one want to. The question is whether it can be made to serve good works.

The need to reconsider the state in terms of its mythological propensities becomes compelling if one accepts the view that the democratic state, particularly, will not—under general conditions of structural decline—be able to deal with its own contradictions. It will, instead, create its own mythic objects out of a perverse logic of necessity. We see it already in the war between the good and the evil empires that is accompanied by linguistic and symbolic screaming, and that is capable of destroying us all. The implication then of the new mytho-logics and the specter of superfluous man should be clear enough. Either we do away with the state as we have known it, or it does away with us.

NOTES

1. The term *episteme* refers to the grounds of knowledge on which a theory is based. See Michel Foucault, *The Order of the Things* (New York: Pantheon, 1970). See also the discussion in Hubert L. Dreyfus and Paul Rabinow, *Michel Foucault, Beyond Structuralism and Hermeneutics* (Chicago: University of Chicago Press, 1983), p. 18.

2. The concept of the disjunctive moment corresponds to the Marxian idea of a transformational break. Many others have used similar terms to describe somewhat the same phenomenon, *conjunction* (Braudel), *overdetermination* (Althusser), and so on.

Marx himself provides many superb examples of the disjunctive moment as both mythic and theoretical especially in his political writing as in the following example:

Bonaparte throws the entire bourgeois economy into confusion, lays hands on everything that seemed inviolable to the Revolution of 1848, makes some tolerant of revolutions, others desirous of revolution, and produces actual anarchy in the name of order, while at the same time he divests the whole state machine of its halo, profanes it, and makes it at once loathsome and ridiculous. The cult of the Holy Coat at Threves he duplicated at Paris in the cult of the Napoleonic mantle. But if the imperial mantle finally falls on the shoulders of Louis Bonaparte, the iron statue of Napoleon will crash from the top of the Vendome column.

See Karl Marx, *The Eighteenth Brumaire of Louis Bonaparte* (New York: International Publishers, n.d.), p. 120. See also David Harvey, "Monument and Myth," *Annals of the Association of American Geographers* 69, no. 3 (September 1978), pp. 362-81.

3. See Roland Barthes, *Mythologies* (New York: Hill and Wang, 1983), pp. 15-25. See also Clifford Geertz, *Negara* (Princeton, NJ: Princeton University Press, 1980), pp. 135-36.

4. See Paul Ricoeur, *The Symbolism of Evil* (Boston: Beacon, 1969); see also Roger Callois, *Man and the Sacred* (New York: Free Press, 1959).

5. Political theory begins with the fictional (like Rousseau's sublime state of nature, or the social contract) in order to create a methodological point of departure for a theory. The text so created claims to interpret historical facts, but these are instead metaphors of fiction, as Paul de Man suggested. See Robert Moynihan, "Interview with Paul de Man," *Yale Review* 73, no. 4 (Summer 1984); Claude Lévi-Strauss, "The Structural Study of Myth," *Journal of American Folklore* 68 (1955), pp. 428-44.

6. "According to Socrates, a noble lie is the only way to insure that the men who love the truth will exist and rule in a society. The noble lie was intended to make both warriors and artisans love the city, to assure that the ruled would be obedient to the rulers and, particularly, to prevent the rulers from abusing their charge." See Allan Bloom, *The Republic of Plato* (New York: Basic Books, 1968), p. 369. See also Claude Lévi-Strauss, *Structural Anthropology* (New York: Basic Books, 1963), pp. 182-83.

7. As well a text can be used both to create a new text out of historical events and at the same time to destroy a previous one, not least by ridicule as Marx did with Louis Napoleon in *The Eighteenth Brumaire.*

To my mind no work is as brilliant and as compelling in the exactness with which circumstances . . . are shown to have made the nephew possible, not as an innovator, but as a farcical repetition of the great uncle. What Marx attacks are the atextual theses that history is made up of free events and that history is guided by superior individuals. By inserting Louis Bonaparte in a whole intricate system of repetitions, by which first Hegel, then the ancient Romans, the 1789 revolutionaries, Napoleon I, the bourgeois interpreters, and finally the fiascos of 1848-1851 are all seen in a pseudo-analogical order of descending worth, increasing derivativeness, and deceptively harmless masquerading, Marx effectively textualizes the random appearance of a new Caesar.

See Edward W. Said, *The World, the Text, and the Critic* (Cambridge, MA: Harvard University Press, 1983), p. 45. See also Clifford Geertz, *The Interpretation of Cultures* (New York: Basic Books, 1973), p. 357; see also his "Slide Show, Evans-Pritchard's African Transparencies," *Raritan Review,* Fall 1983, pp. 62-80.

8. See Ernst Cassirer, *The Philosophy of Symbolic Forms* (New Haven, CT: Yale University Press, 1955); see also his *Myth of the State* (New Haven, CT: Yale University Press, 1965).

9. See J. L. Austin, *How to Do Things with Words* (Oxford: Oxford University Press, 1955).

10. See D. E. Apter, *Choice and the Politics of Allocation* (New Haven, CT: Yale University Press, 1971).

11. See Fredric Jameson, *The Prison-House of Language* (Princeton, NJ: Princeton University Press, 1972); see also James Clifford, "On Ethnographic Authority," *Representations* 1, no. 2 (Spring 1983), pp. 118-46. In addition, see George E. Marcus and Dick Cushman, "Ethnographies as Texts," *Annual Review of Anthropology* 11 (1982), pp. 25-69.

12. See Mircea Eliade, *Myth and Reality* (New York: Harper & Row, 1963).

13. See Barthes, *Sade/Fourier/Loyola* (New York: Hill and Wang, 1976).

14. See Jacques Derrida, "Fors," *Georgia Review* 31, no. 1 (Spring 1977), pp. 64-116.

15. See Crane Brinton, *The Jacobins* (New York: Russell and Russell, 1961).

16. See W.E.H. Lecky, *History of European Morals* (New York: D. Appleton, 1895), Vol. 2, pp. 139-61.

17. See Michel Foucault, *The History of Sexuality* (New York: Pantheon, 1978).

18. See Lester C. Thurow, *The Zero-Sum Society* (New York: Penguin, 1981); see also Mancur Olson, *The Rise and Decline of Nations* (New Haven, CT: Yale University Press, 1982).

19. See Roland Barthes, *Mythologies*.

20. See Sheldon S. Wolin, *Politics and Vision* (Boston: Little, Brown, 1960), p. 36.

21. Ricoeur, *The Symbolism of Evil*, p. 163.

22. See Frank Blackaby, ed., *De-Industrialization* (London: Heinemann, 1978).

23. See Christopher Hill, *The World Turned Upside Down* (London: Penguin, 1975).

24. See Chapter 7 of this book, and D. E. Apter and Nagayo Sawa, *Against the State* (Cambridge, MA: Harvard University Press, 1984).

25. See Leo Panitch, *Social Democracy and Industrial Militancy* (Cambridge, MA: Cambridge University Press, 1976).

26. See Blackaby, *De-Industrialization*, p. 16.

27. See James O'Connor, *The Fiscal Crisis of the State* (New York: St. Martins Press, 1973).

28. See Jürgen Habermas, "Neo-Conservatism in the U.S. and West Germany," *Telos*, no. 56 (Summer 1983), pp. 75-89. See also, Pierre Birnbaum, *La Logique de L'etat* (Paris: Fayard, 1982).

29. See David Moss, "The Kidnapping and Murder of Aldo Moro," *European Journal of Sociology* 22, no. 2 (1981).

30. See Mattei Dogan, "How Civil War Was Avoided in France," *International Political Science Review* 5, no. 3 (1984), pp. 245-77.

About the Author

David E. Apter, Ph.D., Princeton University, 1954, Henry J. Heinz II Professor of Comparative Political and Social Development, Yale University, has served as a member of the Governing Council, American Academy of Arts and Sciences and as a consultant to the American Council on Foreign Relations. He was a Visiting Lecturer, St. Anthony's College, Oxford University, and a member of the Institute of Advanced Study, Princeton, New Jersey. He has been a Visiting Fellow at All Souls College, Oxford, a Fellow of the Center for Advanced Studies in the Behavioral Sciences, Halevy Professor of Political Science, Foundation Nationale des Sciences Politiques, Paris, France, and will be Wayneflete Visiting Fellow at Magdalen College, Oxford University in spring 1988. He has had grants from the Fulbright, Guggenheim, Ford, Rockefeller, and Carnegie foundations, and from the Social Science Research Council. He is a former director of the Institute of International Studies, University of California at Berkeley and executive secretary for the Committee on the Comparative Study of New Nations, University of Chicago.

His publications include *Ghana in Transition; The Political Kingdom in Uganda; The Politics of Modernization; Comparative Politics* (with Harry Eckstein); *Ideology and Discontent: Some Conceptual Approaches to the Study of Modernization; Choice and the Politics of Allocation* (winner of the Woodrow Wilson Award of the American Political Science Association); *Contemporary Analytical Theory* (with Charles Andrain); *Anarchism Today* (with James Joll); *Political Change; Estudio de la modernizacion; The Multinational Corporation and Development* (with Louis Goodman); *Introduction to Political*

Analysis; and *Against the State* (with Nagayo Sawa). His research and teaching interests are in the politics of development, comparative theory, and case studies of violent protest in different regions of the world. His most recent work deals with the Yan'an period in China.

NOTES

NOTES

Printed in the United States
98554LV00002B/277/A

9 780803 929722